CHURCH AND REAL

Peter Heath graduated in history at ___ ___ ___,
London. After national service he returned to pursue
research on the late medieval–early Reformation church, a
subject on which he has published a number of books and
articles. Best known for his book *English Parish Clergy on
the Eve of the Reformation*, he has also written on the
medieval diocese of Lichfield as well as on the medieval
fishing industry. He is currently on the staff of the
University of Hull.

FONTANA HISTORY OF ENGLAND

Edited by G. R. Elton
Regius Professor of Modern History at the
University of Cambridge

The aim of the series is to reinterpret familiar and unfamiliar aspects of English history. There will be a pair of volumes on each chronological period (except the first) which will throw new light on the age in question by discussing it in relation to contrasting themes.

ALREADY PUBLISHED

Malcolm Todd, *Roman Britain 55 BC–AD 400*
M. T. Clanchy, *England and its Rulers 1066–1272*
H. E. Hallam, *Rural England 1066–1348*
Peter Heath, *Church and Realm 1272–1461*
Anthony Tuck, *Crown and Nobility 1272–1461*
Claire Cross, *Church and People 1450–1660*
D. M. Loades, *Politics and the Nation 1450–1660*
J. R. Jones, *Britain and the World 1649–1815*
Maxine Berg, *The Age of Manufactures 1700–1820*
Michael Bentley, *Politics Without Democracy 1815–1914*

Peter Heath

CHURCH AND REALM
1272–1461

Conflict and collaboration
in an age of crises

Fontana Press

First published in 1988 by Fontana Paperbacks
8 Grafton Street, London W1X 3LA

Copyright © Peter Heath 1988

Set in Linotron Imprint

Printed and bound in Great Britain
by William Collins Sons & Co. Ltd, Glasgow

Contents

Acknowledgements		11
Introduction		13

1   EDWARD I (1272–1307): PRINCIPLES AND
       PRECEDENTS   21

Pecham, Pluralism and Prohibitions	23
Legislation and the Church	34
Winchelsey, Taxation and Crisis	42
The Origins of Convocation	50
The Last Decade	52
Parliament and the Church	54
Edward and the Papacy	57
Prospects	61

2   EDWARD II (1307–27): PRECEDENTS EXPLOITED   65

Gaveston and the Ordainers	66
The Despensers	70
Deposition 1322–7	73
Scottish Warfare	80
Taxation and the Establishment of Convocation	85
Anglo–Papal Relations	89
Bishops and Bishoprics	92
The Suppression of the Templars	96
The King's Clerical Servants	98
Lost Opportunities	101

3   EDWARD III (1327–77): WAR AND THE CHURCH   103

War	104
Prayer, Preaching and Propaganda	107

The Clergy in Arms   110
The Seizure of Alien Priories   112
War Finance   113
War and the Stratford Crisis   118
War Diplomacy and Anglo–Papal Relations   123
Patronage: Royal and Papal   124
Papal Provisions   125
Praemunire   132
Pluralism, Provisors and Fiefdom   133
Clerical Grievances and Redress   135
The Episcopate   138
John of Gaunt and the Clergy   142
Sovereignty   143

4   PLAGUE AND DISRUPTION   149

5   LEARNING AND LITERACY   157

6   WYCLIF AND LOLLARDY   167
The Prophet and His Message   167
Transmission   175
The Receivers   180
Diffusion and Survival   182
Political Dimensions   185
Defensive Measures   186

7   RICHARD II (1377–99): THE CLERGY UNDER
     ATTACK   189
Poll Taxes   190
The Peasants Revolt   192
Despenser's Crusade   195
Convocation and Clerical Subsidies, 1383–9   197
Opposition and the King's Revenge, 1381–99   201
State Trials and Tyranny   205
Jurisdiction   209
Provisions and *Praemunire* Again   213
The Bishops   218
King and Church   220

8   HENRY IV (1399–1413): THE CLERGY AND
    USURPATION   223
    Archbishop Arundel and the Change of Dynasty   224
    Opposition and the Clergy   232
    Crown Oppression   244
        (i) Financial Demands from the King   244
        (ii) Royal Writs and Menaces   247
    Crown Defence   251
        (i) Measures against Lollardy   251
        (ii) Church Lands Saved   256
    Schismatic Popes and the Usurper King   260

9   HENRY V (1413–22): DEFENDER OF THE FAITH   269
    The Warrior King   270
    The Devout King   273
    Heresy Repulsed   274
    War Efforts   279
        (i) Prayer and Propaganda   279
        (ii) Money and Men   281
    Church Liberties   285
    King's Bishops   289
    Papal Relations   293

10   HENRY VI (1422–61): ADVANCE AND RETREAT   297
    The Era of Bishop Beaufort, 1422–47   298
        (i) Politics   298
        (ii) Finance   302
        (iii) Papacy   305
    Lollardy   308
    Church and Government   312
        (i) Clergy Supplanted   312
        (ii) Clergy Promoted: Clerical Diplomats   317
        (iii) Clergy Promoted: Episcopal JPs   320
    Church and Lack of Government   321
        (i) Bastard Feudalism   321
        (ii) Benefit of Clergy   328
        (iii) Excommunication   330
        (iv) Arbitration   332

Decline and Fall   333
   (i) The Suffolk Crisis, 1447–50   333
   (ii) Changing Bishops   335
   (iii) Church Liberties   337
   (iv) The Last Act   339

Conclusions   347

Glossary   359
Abbreviations   371
References   373
Select Bibliography   397
Index   417

Acknowledgements

I am especially grateful to the General Editor for his invitation to write this volume and for his adamantine patience, timely encouragement and helpful criticism subsequently. Equally long suffering and helpful have been my publishers at the Fontana Press. My debt to fellow scholars is enormous and quite inadequately attested by the bald references in the notes and bibliography: it is easy enough to indicate their numbers, names and titles, quite impossible in a text of this kind to do justice to the quality and richness of their work. I offer my thanks particularly, though, to John Palmer who read and commented on the whole book, to Richard Davies and Robert Dunning for their help and advice, and to Drs Virginia Davis, Roger Highfield, Charles Kightly and Philip Saunders for permission to cite from their unpublished theses. I also wish to draw attention to the generosity of many American scholars who have made their theses so readily available on this side of the Atlantic through xeroxed editions. To the University of Hull, my academic home over many years, I am obliged for two terms of study-leave; and I gratefully acknowledge the unfailingly helpful staff and the splendid resources of the Brynmor Jones Library, aptly named after its keenest sponsor and benignly presided over for so long by Philip Larkin. Finally, I record the crucial and incalculable support which I have received from my wife throughout the long preparation of this book.

The cover picture, reproduced here by kind permission of The British Library, is from a contemporary manuscript of Creton's eyewitness account of Richard II's deposition (Harley Ms. 1319). Henry of Lancaster in the tall fur hat is nearest the throne and with him on the right of the picture are the lords temporal; on the left among the spiritual peers sits Archbishop Arundel, bareheaded and in a blue robe; in the foreground are Henry's noble supporters, the earls of Westmorland and Northumberland. In all, sixteen illustrations, of which this is the last, adorn the manuscript; the unknown artist clearly attempts individual portraiture of some of the recurring figures, and others are identified in the text.

Introduction

The church in late medieval England has not been the subject of an extended and detailed survey since the publication of A. H. Thompson's *English Clergy and their Organization in the Later Middle Ages* and W. A. Pantin's *The English Church in the Fourteenth Century*, respectively in 1947 and 1955. Neither of these sought to be comprehensive and both, in their different ways, were pioneering studies: the one especially exploiting bishops' registers to expose the administrative machinery of the English church over some 150 years; the other focusing upon the social context of the church and the didactic and pastoral concerns of the clergy. Since them only J. C. Dickinson's *The Later Middle Ages* (1979) has offered a general synthesis. His volume, however, spans the period from the Conquest to the Reformation so that, of necessity, it scarcely has room to do justice to all the research which has followed after – and often from – the works of Thompson and Pantin. A synthesis, however, has been made urgent by the sheer volume of recent scholarship which has radically revised previously received interpretation and immensely extended earlier knowledge. The text notes and bibliography which follow here are signposts to a hinterland of accumulated research and writing, some of it still in unpublished theses and papers, much of it in specialist journals.

The arguments for a study such as this rest not simply upon absent syntheses and neglected learning but no less upon the needs of current generations for a fresh view of the past. The secularization of recent society, the impact of sociology – at least by its direction and emphasis if not by its example – and the dissolving traditions of our mental world all render ecclesiastical history less immediately appealing and less obviously important than once it was. This is particularly so when the church is viewed largely as a self-contained and self-justifying institution. Such an approach continues the pervasive habit of marginalizing, and failing to measure, the church's national political role. Inescapably Thompson was too busy with the fundamental task of exposing how the church organized itself to attend to its external role. Pantin, who sought 'to explain the relation of the church to the contemporary society in which it was embedded', was primarily interested in the novel question then of how the crown and society affected the church rather than in the church's national importance. J. R. L. Highfield's notable Oxford thesis (of 1952) – on church and crown relations under Edward III – although it paid some attention to the church's political impact, was likewise church-centred, yet it anticipated and set the pattern for some later approaches. In the wake of Thompson, Pantin and Highfield, modern scholars – on both sides of the Atlantic – have opened up vistas seldom suspected or rarely admitted previously. Following their lead and drawing upon their findings and my own researches, the present book is a study of the interrelationship of the church with the political community of the realm.

Neither church nor crown was an island cut off from developments in the community at large – developments which were both substantial and dramatic in the period under review here. This was the age which witnessed the Hundred Years War, the Black Death, the Peasants Revolt, the advent of Wyclif and the lollards, the spread of schools and growth of lay literacy, the emergence of the graduate civil servant, the rise of the profession of common lawyers, the arrival of parliament, the evolution of bastard feudalism, and the deposition of kings. A church bent on reform and engulfed in the world could hardly be unaffected by these happenings. A church which counted as its members all the people of the realm (from the king down to the lowliest peasant), which served the crown by its clergy and its censures and even by its prayers and processions, which possessed its own jurisdictional and administrative structures and had its own elaborate heritage of law and ethics – such a church could not fail to affect profoundly the encompassing society and its politics. The church, moreover, was an international body with the pope as its earthly head; his influence, too, left its mark on English affairs even while sojourning at Avignon (1305–78), or during the Great Schism (1378–1418), or when shadowed by the conciliar movement in the fifteenth century.

Here, therefore, the church is studied as a constituent of English history, and, in order to emphasize this point, the arrangement is largely by reigns. One can be too pedantic about the dates of kings, of course, but little attempt is made here to depart from the framework which those dates provide, if only because in medieval government the age, character and condition of a king set a peculiar, if complex, pattern for his reign and posed distinctive opportunities and problems for the church. Amidst the ineluctable and impersonal forces of nature and society which frame and shape church and crown relations, individual personalities – of kings as well as of bishops, clergy and laymen – are not to be discounted.

What might be called the 'ecology' of church and realm was obviously not something new in the thirteenth century, but it intensified then as both organisms became more sophisticated. Magna Carta is a useful witness here.[1] The clergy were deeply involved in its adoption and defence: the 1215 preface records that it was compiled with the advice of bishops and that it was for the honour of God, the salvation of souls, the exaltation of the church and the reform of the realm. Its very first chapter affirms the rights and liberties of the church, even if in terms so general and capacious as to beg rather than settle questions; chapter 14 prescribes the summoning of prelates, along with earls and barons, to advise on the levy of feudal contributions or aids; and many of the other sixty-three clauses bore upon the clergy no less than the laity. In an effort to elude the alliance of archbishop and barons in which this document had its origin, and in order to avert opportunist threats from France, King John had in 1213 surrendered his kingdom to the pope and received it back as a feudal fief; in witness of this he had sworn fealty to Innocent III and committed himself and his successors to paying popes an annual tribute of 1000 marks. Innocent responded by condemning John's enemies and in 1215 annulled Magna Carta as 'an agreement which is not only shameful and demeaning but also illegal and unjust', since it was obtained under duress. In 1216, however, when Henry III, a minor and therefore a papal ward, became king, Innocent's own legate approved a revised version. During Henry's reign papal legates and agents came to England and played a more active and effective part in the nation's politics than they were ever to do again. The clergy were taxed by the pope; bishops were provided and translated by him; the crown was expensively embroiled in papal adventures in Germany and Sicily; and when the barons rebelled in the 1260s, the legate Cardinal Ottobuono acted as mediator. Meanwhile, Magna Carta (together with its accompanying Charter of the Forest) was several times revised and re-issued with papal and prelatical support. For the rest of the century and beyond, it was invoked by clergy and laity alike against the king, but well before 1300 much of it was rendered irrelevant or inadequate by the intervening changes in government and society.

Magna Carta laid down a norm for the king's treatment of his barons and clergy; it marked out some boundaries to royal prerogative and power.[2] Yet where it was not too general or vague to be effective, it was occasionally so precise as to become anachronistic. Society and the demands on and of government changed rapidly during the thirteenth century: hence the crown's deliberate – as well as inadvertent – evasion of Magna Carta, counterpointed by the barons' uncomprehending insistence on observance. The increasing expense of warfare and of government in a period of inflation and population growth far exceeded the traditional dues envisaged in that document, and by the end of the century no king in Europe could live on customary resources alone. Under Edward I levies of taxation, customs duties and prises became a recurring burden on the realm; some of the mechanics and some of the theory to justify taxation derived from earlier church practices. Prolonged war and effective taxation added to royal bureaucracy and the dependence of the crown on clerical servants. At the same time, an expanding population which gathered in towns, multiplied new markets and fairs, and encroached on marginal lands (clearing forests and exploiting wastes) created problems of boundaries and entitlements which required administrative or judicial solutions. Even in the twelfth century the crown had sought ways to attract more business to its courts; the thirteenth century witnessed an extension of inducements – in Magna Carta itself – not only by new writs and better procedures but also by the gradual rationalization of the king's court, the *Curia Regis*, into separate benches (King's Bench, Common Pleas) which paid ever more attention to the convenience of suitors. The conflicts which arose from the changes in society led to violence as well as litigation and stimulated the organization of criminal justice. The more society and conditions changed, however, the greater the need for general solutions, or law-making, to resolve contradictions, clarify ambiguities, and redress grievances: legislation was as much a consequence as a cause of litigation. During all these changes and until the end of the thirteenth century the king's judges were ecclesiastics who left their mark, as we shall see, both on individual judgements and on statutes. The common law – the king's law and the subjects' – was in no small degree the creation of the clergy.

During that same century the church shared in the prevailing prosperity and buoyancy. Monastic foundation and endowment, though no longer so frenetic as in the twelfth century, had not yet abated entirely. Some three hundred religious houses were added in the period from 1216 to 1350 (most before 1300), but only the regular canons (around one hundred) and the new orders of friars (approaching two hundred) shared significantly in this. By 1300 English religious houses – over nine hundred – had almost reached their maximum number. They were commonly alleged to possess a third of the land of the realm – an impression which is easily understood simply by noting, for example, how the estates of Westminster Abbey stretched across the Midlands, and how great Cistercian houses like Fountains shared in the international trade in wool.[3] The friars, who arrived from 1221 onwards, challenged stolidity by their radicalism and intellectualism, by their preaching and by their active and vitalizing presence in the universities. Oxford and Cambridge, with few colleges as yet, were ecclesiastical institutions, subject to episcopal surveillance; they provided vocational training for preachers, theologians and lawyers (civil and canon). Not till the next century did graduates come to dominate the administration of church and kingdom.

The parochial structure of England was virtually complete in the thirteenth century. Some nine thousand parish churches with their chapels of ease served the people of England. The endowments varied enormously and the patronage was valued, in proportion, for social and political as well as for economic and dynastic reasons. Patrons, ranging from the king down to minor gentry, included bishops, abbeys, colleges and corporations. As a consequence the parish clergy were no homogeneous group but as diverse as were their benefices and patrons, a fact which was to embarrass a number of archbishops.

In one sense the national church did not exist, for England was divided into two ecclesiastical provinces, Canterbury and York, which contained unevenly between them seventeen English dioceses, only three of which were in the northern province. The clergy of the two provinces met separately, and the archbishop of either ventured into the other with some circumspection, for chronic disputes over precedence and cross-carrying continued until the middle years of Edward III. To confuse notions of a national church, before 1300 the four Welsh sees had been added to Canterbury province and not a few English bishops began their episcopal careers at Llandaff or St Davids or Bangor or St Asaph's; some men never progressed beyond those poor, blighted sees. Nominally bishops were elected freely by their cathedral chapters (of monks in the monastic cathedrals, secular canons in the rest); by canon law and by a concession of King John they should only have been appointed so. In practice, however, the king who conferred upon them their considerable estates (or temporalities), for which they swore fealty, exerted no small influence; he could coerce chapters by withholding the temporalities and bishops by seizing them, although in neither instance was victory guaranteed to him. Increasingly the papacy – claiming sovereignty over the clergy – was intervening directly in episcopal (and indeed in other) appointments, sometimes to defeat, sometimes to abet the king, but in both cases superseding local election by the chapter. Bishops were no more simple ecclesiastical appointees than were many parish clergy and cathedral canons.

All of this must be set against the background of thirteenth-century reform. The challenge of the Albigensian heresy in southern Europe had led Dominic to found his Order of Preachers and Pope Innocent III to convene in 1215 the Fourth Lateran Council. The seventy-one decrees of this assembly were a clarion call to, and a blueprint for, the defence of orthodoxy: doctrine was defined, the clergy prepared, heresy condemned, and in a final crescendo of fervour the Jews were oppressed and taxes for a crusade imposed.[4] Orthodoxy required annual confession, for which an educated clergy was a prerequisite; grammar masters in each cathedral and a theology teacher in each metropolitan church were accordingly prescribed. To preserve the integrity of the clergy's status, they were barred from secular callings and from all involvement in capital sentences – a difficult ban when such sentences were commonplace and when judges and their clerks were usually in orders. More awkwardly for the crown, the Council invalidated any ecclesiastical appointment marred by the abuse of the lay power. At a great many other points, too, the Fourth Lateran decrees threatened the interests or customary practices of kings and laymen, but underlying all these items was a passion for reform in order to repulse or expunge heresy. Reform, however, depended upon a degree of clerical independence and authority which could prove embarrassing for the king. It took some while for these measures to be implemented in local churches through synodal and diocesan promulgation, interpretation and adaption, but when Edward I ascended the throne the English church was fully apprised of them and had adopted many of their prescriptions. The tensions implicit in all this were to be amply realized in his reign.

1

Edward I (1272–1307)
Principles and Precedents

When he succeeded to the English throne in 1272 Edward I was already in his thirties and a man of wide experience. A renowned (albeit not a very successful) crusader who had been on three expeditions, he had met and been entertained by the ablest monarchs in Europe. He had fought and intrigued successfully against the rebel barons of his father's reign and at the end of it he had acted as viceroy until he took off on crusade again in 1270. Even apart from his experience, his descent admirably equipped him for kingship: son of the impetuous, vacillating and prodigal Henry III he may have been, but he showed more affinity with his grandfather and great-grandfather, King John and Henry II. Vigorous appraisal of a problem and tenacious pursuit of its solution characterized Edward's whole life. His energetic intelligence was evident in the servants whom he employed, in the policies which he countenanced or sponsored, and in the skill which he displayed and the pains which he took in order to get his own way. Vigour and tenacity, however, were softened by a talent for propaganda and persuasion. No shrewder opportunist had sat on the English throne, but his opportunism was harnessed to some guiding principles. Edward was ruthless where he needed to be; although his resolution sometimes involved treachery, this was a means to an end and never simply a wanton habit.

Edward's idealism emerges from his statutes and their preambles. These have something of the character and purpose of propaganda about them and they therefore need cautious exegesis, but they at least manifest the king's view of his subjects' expectations and in doing so reveal the model to which he felt he should conform. They certainly express viewpoints which find echoes among his contemporaries and they are not out of key with

21

what we know of his character and of his piety, which was
manifested in his crusading enthusiasm, the expulsion of the Jews,
the Eleanor crosses, the foundation of Vale Royal abbey and his
almsgiving.[1] In 1275 the first statute of Westminster spoke of
Edward's concern to improve the lot of both the church and the
realm generally: the statute was issued

> Because our lord the king had great zeal and desire to
> redress the state of the realm in such things as required
> amendment for the common profit of Holy Church and
> of the realm; and because the state of Holy Church had
> been evil kept and the prelates and religious persons of
> the land grieved many ways, and the people otherwise
> entreated than they ought to be, and the peace less kept,
> and the laws less used, and the offenders less punished
> than they ought to be.[2]

In 1284 the statute of Wales declares that 'all those which are
subject unto our power should be governed with due order, to the
honour and praise of God and of Holy Church, and the
advancement of justice'.[3] Towards the end of his reign, in the
ordinance of the forest of 1306, the king speaks of being confronted
'with the inspection of human weakness' and the wide burdens that
fell upon him, he being 'inwardly tormented with divers compunc-
tions, tossed about by the waves of divers thoughts', and being
'frequently troubled, passing sleepless nights, . . . hesitating in
our inmost soul upon what ought to be done, what to be held, or
what to be presented'; 'about this chiefly is our mind busied
without intermission, that we may prepare the pleasantness of ease
and quiet for our subjects dwelling in our realm, in whose quiet we
have some rest, and in their tranquillity we are inwardly cherished
with odours of satisfaction and the flowers of hoped-for peace.'[4]

   In church affairs Edward followed a traditional line with a
vigour and resourcefulness dictated by his legal and martial
preoccupations, not by any concern to alter the balance of
church–state relations. His piety was conventional, shot through
with assumptions of lordship and patronage, and was never

allowed to interfere with political necessity and daily government. The clergy were his servants and subjects; they had no separate identity from his realm: they were part – distinctive and important, certainly, but integral and subordinate, too – of his realm, neither more nor less. Edward's treatment of the clergy during his reign was no different from his dealings with his lay subjects. Yet it was just here that friction and innovation entered, for since the eleventh century church theorists – theologians and particularly canon lawyers – and successive popes had been claiming for the clergy immunities and privileges quite distinct from lay expectations. When these claims conflicted with Edward's needs, he challenged them with a resolution and skilfulness that recalled Henry II. Edward pushed forward the bounds of secular authority usually in reaction to some clerical move or in defence of the needs and customs of royal government; but as much as by the king this boundary was advanced by his subjects, whether suing for their individual rights and interests through the king's courts or acting as royal justices, and not a few of these aggressive subjects were in fact clergy themselves.

Pecham, Pluralism and Prohibitions

In 1272 the see of Canterbury was vacant and the pope provided the Dominican prior-provincial, Robert Kilwardby, an academic theologian, after setting aside both the chapter's choice of its prior and the king's favourite, Robert Burnell. One of the new archbishop's first public duties was the coronation of Edward and his queen in August 1274. For the most part Kilwardby lavished his attention on his clerical subjects, conducting visitations of suffragans' dioceses and holding frequent clerical synods. On the king's behalf in 1276 he urged Llewellyn, Lord of Snowdonia, to acknowledge Edward as his feudal lord, and in February 1277 he excommunicated Llewellyn for refusing an offer of mediation. Otherwise his pontificate has little political significance. In 1278 Pope Nicholas III, dissatisfied with Kilwardby's attempts to resist secular encroachment and to implement the decisions of the recent Council of Lyons (1274), promoted him to be cardinal bishop of

Porto and Sta. Pagina, a move which at that time necessitated his resignation from Canterbury.

The pope again provided to the see, this time choosing the former prior-provincial of the English Franciscans, John Pecham. For some years now Pecham had been lecturing in Rome where he was noted for his austerity, his learning and his authoritarianism. The mainspring of his actions as archbishop he spelled out in a letter to the king in 1281: all Christian rulers derived their authority from, and were subordinate to, ecclesiastical law, to which kings, by virtue of their great dignity, were bound in a degree exceeding that of any other layman. The earthly commonwealth being a reflection of the divine, secular power was therefore subordinate to spiritual. Disobedience to the laws of the church was equivalent to heresy.[5] The primacy of the church and the defence of clerical privileges were viewed by Pecham as the self-evident basis of a sound secular government and a healthy society. The newly arrived archbishop quickly manifested his reforming zeal by convening a provincial council at Reading in 1279 at which he proceeded to publish the decrees of the Council of Lyons against pluralism and non-residence, and to condemn royal encroachments on the church's liberties. Both these acts brought him into conflict with the king and with some of his own clergy.

Thirteenth-century reformers expended much energy and ingenuity trying to ensure that parishes were properly served and that the souls of parishioners were not exposed to perdition by the negligence and greed of pluralist incumbents. Some steps against pluralism were taken at the Fourth Lateran Council in 1215, but an altogether more far-reaching measure was promulgated at the Council of Lyons in 1274. This distinguished between benefices which involved the cure of souls and those which did not (which were, in the Latin term, sinecures), although these last were not necessarily without responsibilities and duties. In the former category, to which the cure of souls pertained, were the parish livings of rector and perpetual vicar, the cathedral and collegiate offices of dean, chancellor, precentor and treasurer, and the diocesan office of archdeacon. Among the sinecures were chiefly the remaining canonries in cathedrals and colleges. The decree of 1274 henceforth banned the holding of two or more cures of souls simultaneously except where a papal licence to do so had been obtained. It further entailed the immediate resignation – on pain of excommunication – of all but the last cure of souls which had been obtained by the unlicensed pluralist; the licensed pluralist was allowed to keep whichever two he chose.[6] Both categories could keep any number of sinecures with their permitted number of cures. For the cures of souls which they retained, they were required to provide an adequate deputy to serve the parish or parishes.

When Pecham introduced this measure at the Council of Reading he at once aimed a major threat, unintentionally but inescapably, at the king's government. Suddenly an army of civil servants were to surrender substantial proportions of their remuneration and were forced to seek, at no little expense, dispensations from – and at the discretion of – the pope, not a prospect which they would welcome. Nor was it an appealing thought to the king that while his own bureaucrats and servants were being thus harried, the pope's men were assured of dispensations enough, and that since the resigned livings were vacated by papal decree, and therefore in effect at the Curia, they were to be filled by papal provision, not by the previous or usual patron. Still less pleasing to him must have been the prospect that if his clerks ignored the order to jettison their excess cures of souls, they would suffer excommunication with all its attendant disabilities and interruption of his service. Neither the servants nor the king were amused by Pecham's decree; nor indeed were some bishops who had themselves risen to the episcopate on a mounting tide of benefices with and without cure of souls, and who were even now rewarding their own diocesan officers with a plurality of cures. From all three directions Pecham met hostility, which was further aggravated by his imperious exercise of his metropolitical rights over the sees of his suffragans.

In defence of church liberties Pecham also decreed at Reading that Magna Carta was to be posted in every cathedral and collegiate church in the land and expounded in every parish church each Sunday; violators, particularly those who resorted to writs of prohibition, or seized or wasted church property, or neglected to arrest unreconciled offenders when required to do so, were to be excommunicated. Writs of prohibition, of which there were many forms, suspended a cause before an ecclesiastical judge and removed it to a hearing in the king's courts. Although the procedures for obtaining and defending such writs often worked to the advantage of the church courts, prohibitions nevertheless constituted a serious threat to ecclesiastical jurisdiction. These writs were not new and by Edward's reign the church had long been fighting against their use in such matters as tithes and debts, testaments and matrimony. No ecclesiastical courts – not even those of a papal judge delegate – and very few causes were safe from writs of prohibition. It was no comfort to the church that many of the king's judges were themselves clerics, for in Edward's reign they clearly gave their first loyalty to the king who was employing them; they seem seldom to have challenged his interests. Nor was it much consolation to the church that the extension of prohibitions was less the result of deliberate crown policy (though the king certainly assisted by the provision of new writs) than of popular demand among suitors, often clergy litigating against clergy. The principles and advances thus established on behalf of individual litigants and at their prompting redounded to the benefit of the king, not least when his own servants were suing other clergy and patrons for possession of benefices to which the king had presented them; in particular the livings affected by the new pluralism laws would be likely subjects of such writs. The king's patronage as well as his jurisdiction were advanced and defended by prohibitions. No wonder Edward, in order to protect suitors from ecclesiastical censures or reprisals, made available a new form of the writ which was issued 'on behalf of many' – *ex relatu plurium* – in which he substituted himself for the unnamed petitioner or petitioners; this form of the writ enjoyed wider popularity after the Council of Reading.

The condemnation by Pecham of those seizing and wasting church property was particularly aimed at the king's exploitation of the temporal lands of vacant bishoprics. On the death of a bishop, while his spiritual jurisdiction and income were administered by the dean, or prior, and chapter of the cathedral church, the temporalities of the see – as with any tenant-in-chief during a minority – reverted to the crown for the duration of the vacancy;

they were usually farmed or leased out to the profit of the crown and of the farmers who were naturally inclined to extract as much as they could from the windfall.[7] On occasions the fruits of such temporalities were earmarked for particular royal projects or expenditure, such as the building of the Welsh castles, and the temptation was for the king to define 'temporalities' ever more widely as his burdens increased. During Edward's reign vacant sees added some £60,000 to royal income.

If those whom the church excommunicated by name were still unreconciled after forty days, the church in England, as in western Europe generally, could call on the secular arm to assist.[8] The bishop signified to chancery the names of such offenders and chancery issued a writ *de excommunicato capiendo* ordering the sheriff to arrest and detain them until they had submitted to, and were absolved by, the church. This procedure acknowledged not only the interdependence of church and realm but also the weakness of excommunication as a sanction unless it were backed by secular coercion. It was vitally important for the church, therefore, that sheriffs and other recipients should implement the writs *de excommunicato capiendo*. Difficulty arose when Pecham in attempting to enforce reforming measures required sheriffs and others to act against the king's own servants and clerks, but it should be remembered that, overwhelmingly, cooperation characterized this procedure in Edward's reign.

Pecham's decrees at Reading, therefore, struck from several different directions at vital areas of crown government: its patronage, jurisdiction, servants and administration and finance. Little wonder, then, that Edward reacted fiercely and swiftly. At the parliament which met in November 1279 Pecham was forced to withdraw not only the order to display and expound Magna Carta but also the excommunication against royal officers who ignored writs of caption or seized or wasted temporalities and against any of the suitors of illegitimate prohibitions. This reversal was brought about both by Edward's own pressure and by the hostility which Pecham encountered from some of his suffragans and from royal clerks. Although in 1281 Pecham revived the excommunication of such offenders, the king, trusting to his writs and courts, felt able to ignore this. Edward's protection of his servants from excommunication – tenants-in-chief had been exempted since the twelfth century – applied not only to those servants who were permanently in his employment, but even to those on *ad hoc* commissions. In 1281 Edward informed the bishop of Chichester that

> our clerks, while they are on our business, ought not to be compelled to take necessary orders [holy orders, that is] or to make personal residence in their benefices, or in any other way to be molested and disturbed.[9]

This, in fact, referred to the sequestration of a clerk's benefice by the bishop rather than to excommunication, but its principle was all-embracing and even included the servants of royal servants. In 1291 Archbishop Romeyn of York was to be imprisoned and fined 4000 marks for excommunicating the bailiffs of Bishop Bek of Durham while the bishop was abroad on the king's service.[10]

All this had a debilitating effect upon ecclesiastical morale and discipline, for not only were the king's servants who enforced his claims upon church property and privileges thus protected, but they were also exempted from necessary reforms: as late as 1303, precisely on the question of pluralism, the bishop of Worcester and his advisers declined to take action against the multiple pluralist, Ralph Hengham, because he was a royal judge and a member of the king's council.[11]

If Pecham had harboured any idea of renewing the struggle when his second provincial council met at Lambeth in 1281, it was forestalled by a royal writ of prohibition of the general kind which simply barred some action. Addressed to the archbishop and all the prelates assembled at Lambeth, it commanded them, on their oaths of fealty, to do all that they could for the defence and conservation of the king's rights and of his realm; it then continued:

> On pain of loss of temporalities which you hold from us, we strongly inhibit you in the council now called at Lambeth from presuming to attempt anything to our

prejudice, or that of our realm, or against us or our rights which our predecessors, kings of England, enjoyed by ancient and approved custom, or to assent to any such move.[12]

The reference to 'ancient and approved custom' might have tempted ingenious demur by the bishops, but Edward left them in no doubt where their best interest lay: 'know for certain that if you so act, we shall forcefully seize your baronies.' The extensive and notable reform measures which issued from Lambeth carefully avoided the perilous jurisdictional boundaries crossed at Reading.

Thereafter Pecham and the king worked together in relative harmony, avoiding further crises, not only because the king had decisively cowed or suborned the clergy but also because of the archbishop's paternalist view of his role and Edward's astute sops to his ideals. Implicit in Pecham's letter of 1281 which outlined his hierocratic principles was the paternalist view that the church's task was to affirm and support the king to meet his divinely imposed responsibilities to the Christian commonweal, the realm.[13] In line with this, the archbishop gave his willing support to direct royal taxation of the clergy in order to defray the costs of the conquest of Wales; he was also aware that such a conquest would enable him to establish control over the wayward Welsh church and bring it into line with the rest of post-Lateran Christendom. Pecham was equally ready in 1290 to raise taxes for a king who had followed up his crusader's vow with the expulsion of the Jews. Already their numbers had been so diminished by persecution and by unfavourable trading terms in Henry III's reign that the tallage which they paid annually to the king was less under Edward I than he might gain by seizing their estates and inducing a clerical subsidy by their expulsion.[14] Nevertheless, the move of 1290 was not quite as cynical as all this may suggest. Edward himself had increased the disabilities of the Jewish community in 1275 with the statute of Jewry. He was, too, a keen crusader and he had witnessed Christian measures against the Jews on the continent. Furthermore, in the later 1280s English society in London, and prelates such as Archbishop Pecham in particular, had been scandalized by the apostasy to the Jews of an eminent Dominican preacher who was now openly proselytizing for them among Christians. On this occasion as on others Edward persuaded the church to do his bidding by an action which commanded wide support, legal precedents, and political emotions. The Jews would probably have been expelled very soon anyway, and it is the timing, rather than the nature, of the action which was determined by Edward's need for a subsidy from the clergy.

In 1286 and 1290, moreover, Pecham had no doubt been further reassured by the two statutes of *Circumspecte agatis* and Consultation, which respectively defined some boundaries of jurisdiction and allowed ecclesiastical courts to proceed where writs of prohibition had been inappropriately obtained.[15] The one act, as we shall see below, curbed some over-exuberant royal justices; the other ensured that plaintiffs in the courts Christian could challenge the writ of prohibition before the king's chief justice or the chancellor.

Meanwhile, the collaboration of the secular arm in bringing excommunicates to heel not only continued but apparently gathered pace. Altogether between 1250 and 1435 over sixteen thousand excommunicates were notified to chancery, and of these almost three thousand occur in the decade 1275–84 and another two thousand in the remaining years of the century.[16] Some of these figures resulted from litigants pressing the church into action, but as a record of defiance, and presumably as just a fraction of total excommunications in those years, they are unquestionably revealing. Moreover, from 1279 and with the active encouragement of Archbishop Pecham and his successor, Winchelsey, crown aid was invoked against clergy who were excommunicated for failing to pay clerical taxes. As yet the numbers were modest, but late in the fourteenth century they became, in F. D. Logan's words, 'a torrent'. Ironically, excommunication was devalued as much by royal assistance as by royal defiance.

The secular arm could only be enlisted in specific cases against named and duly warned individuals; it could offer no aid against those categories of offenders pronounced, in various general and local sentences, as excommunicate *ipso facto*. In 1279 Pecham had ordered the general cursing of a wide range of malefactors against the church; this was to be pronounced four times a year in each parish church with solemn ritual.[17] Yet since the offenders were not individually named and were as much prospective as retrospective, the impact of the general sentence was more educational than coercive. In the next century it came to include offences not only against the church but also against society and the realm at large.

Most of the antagonism between the archbishop and the king in 1279–81 had centred on those personnel indispensable then to effective royal government, the king's clerks. In the later thirteenth century – partly as an indirect result of legislation, partly the urgent consequence of war – the number of royal clerks multiplied and the king's need of ecclesiastical patronage grew accordingly. The eligibility of the clergy for royal service was, of course, based on their long-established Latin literacy, but it was enhanced by the fact that, unlike noble and laymen, they had no dynasties to create or support; they were paid with ecclesiastical benefices which could be held in plurality and served by hired deputies. Altogether, Edward I presented on average twenty-six candidates a year to church livings, more in the years after 1290.[18] As they progressed in the king's confidence and service, their benefices became more numerous and more lucrative.

The king's needs, however, were challenged by the popes' own obligations to reward their growing army of servants. In 1265 the papacy had reserved to itself the right to provide candidates to a wide variety of livings in the gift of ecclesiastical patrons and to bishoprics vacated at Rome. The pluralism decrees of 1279 further complicated and threatened the king's patronage. Edward protected his resources and extended them in various ways.

Firstly, he certainly thwarted some papal provisions by taking vigorous action against any bishop involved in the process. Thus when in 1304 Archbishop Corbridge of York admitted to a canonry a papal providee instead of a royal presentee, he was summoned for contempt and was told by the king's judges that as the pope's acts were not subject to the English courts, no one should prosecute anything at Rome or elsewhere to the detriment of crown rights and royal dignity. For his contempt in abetting such an action his temporalities were distrained until he did prefer the royal clerk – such a humiliation that it was said to have occasioned his death.[19]

Secondly, with the aid of prohibitions and compliant judges, Edward extended the definition of lay fee. Since Henry II's time the advowson, or right of presentation to a benefice, had been construed as though it were a piece of landed property justiciable in the king's courts, not the church's. This was so in respect of rectories but not of vicarages. However, in 1285 chapter 5 of the second statute of Westminster declared that advowsons of *all* benefices fell under the king's jurisdiction, a claim repeated in 1300. Included in episcopal temporalities were not only the advowsons which he possessed in his own right by virtue of the endowments of his bishopric but also those which it fell to him to exercise by default of the usual patron and the appointments to the cathedral chapter, two categories of patronage which he exercised by virtue of his spiritual authority over the diocese, not because of any land which he held. Judicial decisions gradually shifted vicarages from the second category to the first; before the end of Edward's reign, royal judges had deemed more than a score of advowsons of perpetual vicarages to be lay fee. Moreover, capitular appointments were now construed as belonging to the bishop's barony and therefore within the king's regalian right.[20]

Unsatisfied with this development, Edward even began to claim his *sede vacante* rights retrospectively: thus a benefice which was empty when a new bishop was appointed and was subsequently filled in the normal way by him, was sometimes claimed by Edward to be unlawfully filled, the patronage belonging by regalian right to the crown, even though the king had not exercised this during the vacancy of the see. Should the bishop or his candidate protest, the king's nominee would soon obtain an appropriate writ from chancery whereby the issue could be decided in the king's court by the king's judges.

Benefices, however, were not the only church assets which the king exploited for his clerks. By Edward's reign it was usual for the monarch to extract from a newly elected bishop or abbot a pension of about 3 or 5 marks for a royal servant until such time as the prelate could promote him to a suitable living. As yet this seems not to have been a frequent occurrence and the request was successfully rebuffed by some abbots of religious houses which did not own the king as patron, but a door had been opened which subsequent monarchs were to push far wider.[21]

In addition to pensions, Edward I and his successors increasingly requested religious houses to provide corrodies for laymen retiring from royal service. A corrody was board and lodging which normally such houses sold to applicants; the precise terms varied, often specifying the accommodation as well of servants and horses, and going into details of food and firewood. The king, however, did not pay for them, not least because he was saving by this means the need to provide the beneficiary with a pension from the exchequer. Only occasionally under Edward I and his successor were these corrodians clerks; for the most part they comprised king's messengers, serjeants, ushers, cooks, laundresses, keepers of hounds, and the sick and injured. Between 1292 and 1307 the Close Rolls, which by no means preserve a full record, contain 150 requests made by the king for corrodies. Such approaches, of course, were ordinarily difficult to resist, for a house never knew when royal gratitude might be of value to it in some application of its own or in some lawsuit; a number of larger houses, like Bury St Edmunds in 1303, even found themselves accommodating more than one royal corrodian; furthermore, the recipients of these requests ranged far outside the hundred or so houses of which the king was patron. Although later in the fourteenth century some limits were placed upon the vulnerable houses, those outside royal patronage which had once yielded to pressure had forfeited their immunity. Once again Edward had set precedents and opened opportunities for extensive royal exploitation subsequently.

During his reign Edward made nearly a thousand presentations to church livings, as many as sixty-nine in one year alone in 1304–5. This takes no account of the same man being the subject of multiple presentations nor of those clerks who prospered by indirect royal patronage, pressure on newly elected prelates or on other vulnerable patrons. What is clear, however, is that the numbers of royal clerks who identified their interests with the

crown's and defied Pecham – and later Winchelsey – were
formidable and growing.

Legislation and the Church

The first half of Edward's reign was characterized by legislation on
a scale unprecedented in England.[22] The great statutes of
Westminster I and II of 1275 and 1285, with respectively fifty-one
and fifty chapters, some of them long, most of them technical,
covered a wide variety of matters, civil and criminal, personal and
real, procedural and substantive. The statute of Gloucester in
1278 with its fifteen chapters mainly concerned with land law; of
Acton Burnell in 1283 resolving some aspects of credit; of Wales in
1284 extending to the newly conquered territory the advantages of
English common law; the statute of Merchants in 1285 drastically
revising the statute of Acton Burnell; the statute of Winchester in
1285 which was concerned to protect society from robbery and
violence; the statutes of *Quo Warranto* and *Quia Emptores* in 1290
which respectively clarified a resented enquiry and terminated
subinfeudation: all these constitute a staggering corpus of law-
making in a matter of fifteen years.

This impressive series of statutes may owe something to the
influence of Justinian's *Code* and *Digest*, which was the core of
Roman law and the foundation of the training of civil lawyers; yet
while Roman law was part of the atmosphere breathed by nearly all
lawyers in the thirteenth century, and at least one outstanding civil
lawyer, Vacarius, was familiar to Englishmen, the statutes on
the whole betray little impress of Justinian, concerned as they were
largely with the clarification of traditional indigenous and feudal
problems. It is not unlikely that in his crusading travels and
meetings Edward garnered ideas and experience from the Roman
world of the Mediterranean and sought to emulate that great
legislator, his father-in-law, Alfonso X. Not less probable,
however, is the influence of the church, and this at several
different levels. In the first place, throughout the century popes
were adding to the corpus of canon law by collections of their own
decisions and of conciliar decrees. Edward had gone on crusade

with the future pope Gregory X, convener of the Council of Lyons. Later contemporaries of Edward, namely Boniface VIII and Clement V (who was Edward's own subject), emphasized the tradition of papal legislation in this period by their further additions to the body of canon law. But it was not only the head of Christendom whose example would remind Edward of the prestige attached to making and coordinating laws. Following upon the decrees of the Fourth Lateran Council in 1215, a whole succession of English bishops had been publishing this legislation and adding to it their own diocesan statutes; Pecham himself in 1281 drew upon the legislation of two archbishops – Langton (1222) and Boniface (1261) – and two papal legates – Otto (1237) and Ottobuono (1268).[23]

A bridge between the legislating church and the law-making king might be found in the role of the clergy who until *c.*1290 still dominated the royal judiciary, although by no means were all these men canon lawyers. By far the most famous of these clerical judges is Henry Bracton: he died in 1268 as chancellor of Exeter cathedral, but he had served in the meanwhile as a justice in eyre, a judge on assize, and from 1248 to 1257 on the King's Bench and on the king's council; his fame rests on the fact that not only was he the foremost jurist of his age and possessed of an extensive and precise knowledge of Roman law but he was also credited with the authorship of *The Laws and Customs of England* which became – in the words of Dorothy Stenton – 'the Bible of the coming legal generation'. Among this generation was Ralph Hengham to whom are attributed not only two short legal treatises but also the initiative for much of Edward's legislation. After serving on various eyres and assizes, he became chief justice of the King's Bench in 1274 and remained so until 1290; in the last ten years of the reign he was chief justice of the Common Bench. That, however, was only half his story: in the course of his career he held so many ecclesiastical offices as to provoke a constant outcry – prebends in Hereford and London, the chancellorship at Exeter, the archdeaconry of Worcester, and in the course of 1294 no fewer than fourteen churches! His heyday and influence were paramount before 1290, just when royal legislation was most copious. If his departure from the King's Bench coincides with the virtual cessation of statute-making, it also marks the change from a judiciary which was largely clerical to one which was increasingly and predominantly lay. Before 1290 two successive chief justices of the King's Bench were clerics, but the next two – from 1290 to 1307 – were laymen; out of the fifteen judges of that court during Edward's reign, eight were laymen, most of them in the later years. Ironically this transformation was in no small degree the consequence of the increasing technicality of the law to which the clerical judges themselves had so fertilely contributed by their advice, judgements and writings; it had now become necessary to recruit judges from those who had served their apprenticeship pleading in the courts and had perhaps sought instruction from the law lectures and books which were then being provided.[24] One possible conclusion from all this is that Edward's legislative impulse was as likely a product of his contact with indigenous clergy as with contemporary popes and kings.

Of all Edward's legislation, three pieces particularly affected the church: the statutes *De Viris Religiosis*, or Mortmain as it is commonly called, *Circumspecte Agatis*, and Westminster II, chapter 41. The first of these survives only in the form of a writ sent out by Edward I on 14 November 1279, informing his judges that henceforward no religious or other person should receive any land in perpetuity, on pain of seizure by the chief lord, or, if he should neglect to do so, then by the king himself. The justices were ordered to have this statute read before them in their courts and henceforth it was to be firmly kept and obeyed.[25]

At first sight, the statute looks like a piece of blatant, novel and radical anticlericalism, but on closer inspection another view emerges. Within its brief text is contained a world of mystery. It claims to have been made 'on the advice of prelates' as well as of 'earls, barons and other faithful subjects of our realm who are of our council', that is to say in the parliament which was then sitting. More significantly, it counterpoised the acquisition of land by the church – 'whereby the services which are due from such fees [i.e. freehold] and which were provided from the beginning for the defence of the realm are unjustifiably withdrawn and chief lords in respect of them lose their escheats' – with the good of the realm, for which the present ban is imposed. 'Mortmain', or dead hand, refers to the fact that the church was an undying institution so that any land which it held in fee (or freehold) was never vacated by the death of its owner or came into the possession of a minor or an heiress; thus it would never revert (or escheat) to the chief lord for the duration of the vacancy or minority, so depriving him of the valuable rights of wardship and marriage appertaining to feudal tenure.[26] Yet the statute did not in practice provide the absolute ban which it seemed to promise, nor did it deprive the church of acquisitions. Within months royal licences were being issued for the alienation of property to the church despite the statute. The subsequent chronology of the licences, as well as the varying charges for them, reveal that the king was granting them for political and financial ends, to make friends and raise cash, particularly from the late 1290s when he desperately needed both. Although it was the king, not the chief lord of the fee, who issued the licences, he seems to have done so from the start – and certainly after 1292 – only with the assent of the chief lords. Indeed, politically he could not ignore their wishes and interests. From the 1220s chief lords had been able to license alienations by their tenants to the church, as the king was doing in respect of lands alienated by his tenants-in-chief. The novel effect of Mortmain was thus to extend the king's supervision to alienations by his mesne tenants and, at least after 1299, to raise money from this. He had acquired in effect a veto over all grants or sales of land to the church, but it was against his political and financial interests to enforce this ban.

The endowment of religious houses and other institutions, though greatly reduced until the end of the century, was thereafter far from contained by this statute and cannot be measured simply by the licences enrolled in chancery, since various devices were employed to circumvent the law. Demands for licences grew steadily during the fourteenth century, but endowment of the religious orders never regained its earlier level, and alienations were increasingly directed to the establishment of chantries and secular institutions; by mid-century almost as many licences were for the secular as for the religious churches, but this has more to do with declining enthusiasm for the vastly endowed monastic orders and the growing popular appeal of the mendicants who lived from alms, and not from farming extensive estates. By 1279 one may speak of monastic foundations in England – nearly a thousand of them – as having reached saturation point. There must have been a tacit appreciation among many potential benefactors at the end of the thirteenth century that there were already too many religious houses: whereas over seven hundred new houses had been founded in the twelfth and thirteenth centuries, just over sixty followed in the next century and most of those were friaries. Already by the time of Mortmain, however, the problem was less about *donations* of land *to* the religious houses than the *purchase* of land *by* them, but this too was curtailed more by monastic poverty than by statute; in fact the king not long after this had to ban houses of which he was patron from selling their endowments.

If Mortmain did not protect feudal lords by ending the transfer of property to the church, what then was its aim and why was it passed? Its timing and its fitful application might suggest that it was the king's answer to the decrees of the archbishop's reforming council of Reading. Yet Pecham had already retreated before Mortmain was promulgated and in that very parliament; moreover, as we have seen, he was to resume his attack on royal writs after it. Nevertheless, it did add to royal pressure upon the archbishop and further reminded him of the realities of royal power: in 1285 he petitioned for the relaxation of the statute, especially in respect of grants to parish churches, but Edward reserved his right to licence – to confer or withhold favour. If Mortmain was occasioned by Pecham's actions, its choice as a weapon would testify to Edward's political skill and shrewdness, for it dealt more importantly with a long-standing problem to feudal lords and it would therefore command influential lay support – and perhaps even ecclesiastical, too, insofar as bishops and abbots were themselves landed magnates and feudal lords. Again, it seemed to complete earlier laws on the matter dating back to Magna Carta in its 1217 version. More than this, there were well-known precedents abroad – in the cities of Lombardy and in France, for example – and there existed already such a restriction in some English boroughs. That is to say, Edward's action had social, feudal and legal justification. Where he exceeded expectation and all precedents was in making the ban total, but this clearly was just the element which was negotiable and it had the effect of extending the king's patronage of both church and laity.

Despite the opportunities for patronage and profit which resulted from the statute, what we need to note here is the existence of an explicit legal restriction on endowments for the church, a limitation which found its way on to the statute books and into the consciousness, therefore, of lawyers and members of parliament for the rest of the Middle Ages. Those who were now beginning to pay lay subsidies might think about that wealth and this statute, particularly about its words contrasting the defence of the realm with the endowment of the church – words which were to be echoed by Wyclif in the 1370s and in a royal grant as late as the 1440s.

The second statute specifically affecting the church was about jurisdictional boundaries. In the thirteenth century, itinerant royal justices were sent out from time to time with a list of enquiries to put to local communities. They tried the resulting complaints as the King's Bench would have done, but they dealt with private suits as well as with crime. In 1285 in Norfolk they offended the church not only by sitting in church courts and gathering evidence there for indictments of the clergy but also by hearing cases of violence and defamation against the clergy and matrimonial and testamentary suits, all of which were traditionally matters for church courts.[27] Among other offences committed by these royal justices was the denunciation of bishops for employing, on the visitations of their dioceses, the sworn evidence of groups of parishioners; the practice of the sworn inquest, so these justices maintained, was solely the prerogative of the king. As there was little justification for the lengths to which these itinerant justices went, when a vigorous protest was made to the king he promptly issued a writ ordering them to refrain from hearing testamentary, matrimonial and moral causes; these matters were confirmed to fall exclusively within the competence of the church courts. The use of prohibitions was either barred or restricted in certain cases – in those concerned with less than a quarter of the tithes of a parish, and with violence against the clergy, for example. This writ, issued in 1286 from Paris, where the king then was, began with the words 'Act circumspectly' – or in Latin, *Circumspecte agatis*. In the next century it came to be held as a statute and was regarded as a *locus classicus* defining at least one boundary between clerical and lay jurisdictions.

Nevertheless, *Circumspecte agatis* deserves attention because of the circumstances which brought it about as much as for the harmony which it established in some controversial areas of justice. It signifies the widening activity of the king's judges in the localities of England and it witnesses to the relish and vigour with which the king's authority was implemented over rival jurisdictions. It also represents a maladroit and unintelligent extension of the twelfth-century practice of enlarging crown jurisdiction at the expense of private and local law courts by the offer of procedures unavailable in them. That the king yielded to the resulting complaints of the clergy as far as he did might be explained by his preoccupations in Paris when he could hardly afford serious embarrassment at home; yet it seems more likely that he recognized the powerful tradition by which the matters in conflict were long deemed to have belonged rightfully to the church. His response underlines how much more royalist than the king were some of his judges and how the dividing line between church and crown jurisdiction was under more pressure from the king's subjects and agents than from the king himself or from any royal policy. Yet there remained room for further definition of boundaries in matrimonial, moral and testamentary suits, and the very specific terms of the writ left, by implication, other areas open to royal poaching later.

Another noteworthy aspect of *Circumspecte agatis* is that it reminds us that legislation at that time was by no means limited to parliamentary acts, but could result from decisions of the king and his councillors, expressed in general writs to his justices and sheriffs. Some years were to pass before statutes could only be made in parliament.

In part the attempt by the Norfolk justices to appropriate canon law matters to the king's competence was all of a piece with other measures which the king and his judges were taking to suppress rival jursidictions and to reduce all justice within the realm to the crown. Certainly this was the purpose of the protracted and much resented *Quo warranto* enquiry into private franchises and liberties, an enquiry which extended from 1274 until 1294 when baronial opposition finally forced its abandonment.[28] Little was recovered for the crown by these proceedings, but recognition was gained that all secular jurisdiction was exercised on behalf of the crown by explicit or inferred royal licence. Private and local jurisdiction was also shrunk by the reorganization of the royal courts to provide a more convenient service to litigants and prosecutors, who would rather get justice in the king's court than risk appeal from lesser courts. Not merely the presence and procedures of the crown courts, but also the availability of writs, helped to swell the business of the king's judges.

In some respects a much more significant piece of legislation than either Mortmain or *Circumspecte agatis* was chapter 41 of the second statute of Westminster in 1285.[29] This provides that if any religious houses alienate tenements given to them by the king or other founders, those tenements shall be recoverable by the donor or his heirs, the buyer losing both the tenement and the purchase price. Similarly, tenements given for maintaining a chantry or lights in some church or chapel, or given for some other alms, if they were alienated, were also to be recoverable by the donor or his heirs. Even more striking is the provision that if such a tenement is not alienated, but the alms for which it was originally given are neglected over a period of two years, then the property shall again be recoverable at law by the donor or his heirs. The implicit argument is almost a feudal recognition that such land is given conditionally and that where the obligation is broken the gift shall revert, on action, to the donor, founder or patron. Where the king is patron, he can seize the lands at will; where his subjects are patrons, they can sue for a writ ordering reversion. As yet, so far as religious houses were concerned, it was the alienation of the gift, not the failure to fulfil the condition, that prompted recovery by the donor. More radically in the case of chantries, lights and other alms, not only alienation, but simple and protracted failure to meet the conditions rendered the gift liable to recovery by the donor. This provision was, as the chapter itself states, analogous to the provision in chapter 21 of the same statute, that when the recipient of land devised for rent failed over two years to pay the rent or to fulfil the conditions required by the lord, that land should be recoverable by the lord. Nor is the provision of chapter 41 far removed in spirit and intention from the statute of Gloucester of 1278, which went some way towards enlarging the traditional right of a lord to distrain *chattels* of a tenant who failed to render his dues into a right to recover the *property* involved. And indeed, in the very first chapter of the 1285 statute of Westminster, the chapter 'On conditional gifts' (*De donis conditionalibus*), the intention had evidently been to protect the wishes of the original donor of the land with respect to its future possession and use.

Chapter 41, therefore, was no expression of suspicion, dissatisfaction or hostility on the part of anticlericals, but a modest and guarded application to church property of principles then being applied to lay property. Ironically, a well-known papal decretal of the early thirteenth century enabled a donor to recover land from a church when the conditions of the grant were unmet over two years.[30] Nevertheless, chapter 41 embodied in statutory form a principle which was to be resoundingly extended and proclaimed a century later by Wyclif: that church property might be recovered where the purpose of the original benefaction was neglected. No perceptible direct line connects Edward's law with Wyclif's radicalism, but what can be asserted is that in this matter – as in so many others – Wyclif was not breaking new ground but appealing to ideas already long current in certain circles.

Winchelsey, Taxation and Crisis

On Pecham's death in December 1292 the Canterbury chapter unanimously elected Robert Winchelsey in February 1293, probably with the king's good will, but because the papacy was then vacant the archbishop-elect was not consecrated until September 1294 and only arrived in England in January 1295. He was unlike his two predecessors in not being a mendicant, or a religious at all, and in having had some experience of diocesan administration for some years in the 1280s when he was a diligent and preaching archdeacon of Essex. He resembled them in having studied theology at Oxford and Paris; and like them he was devout, modest, ascetic, energetic, and a zealous upholder of papal authority. He, too, conceived his task to involve the protection not only of the church but also of the realm, which was, after all, both a papal fief and the kingdom of a crusader. No less hierocratic than Pecham, Winchelsey eagerly supported the king with clerical taxes when the realm was in danger and when papal decree or canon law did not prevent it; in 1295 and late in 1297 he evinced an almost unseemly – and not widely shared – enthusiasm to assist the king with clerical subsidies, but much of his tenure is remembered rather for his resistance to the crown's efforts to tax the clergy.

War dominated the 1290s. There had been military expeditions to establish English authority in Wales in 1277 and to maintain it there in 1282–3 and again in 1287, and these were costly enough in their way, but they paled in comparison with the activity and demands of the 1290s. In 1293, as relations with France deteriorated, plans for a full-scale campaign via Gascony and Flanders came to dominate internal politics during the ensuing years. No sooner was Edward embroiled with the French than the Welsh seized the opportunity in 1294–5 to recover their independence. Edward's cup of troubles was yet to overflow: Scottish resistance to his dynastic claims burst into open warfare from 1295 to 1298 and smouldered and crackled until the end of the reign. In the years 1294–8, therefore, Edward faced the prospect of warfare on four fronts: Gascony, Flanders, Wales and Scotland. It was in trying to forge the necessary alliances and to equip the essential forces that Edward then came into conflict with the laity and the clergy at home.[31]

Whereas in a normal year the king's usual revenue barely met his obligations, in years of hostility expenditure outran income at an alarming rate. Forced to exploit his extraordinary sources of money and support, Edward had need of very costly bridging loans from Italian bankers to fill the gap between spending the revenue and actually collecting it. Yet still his outgoings, swollen by servicing the loans, were not covered in their entirety.

By the late thirteenth century armies had very largely to be paid for, the feudal element being both small and hedged about with inconvenient restrictions on how long and where the cavalry might serve. Armies also had to be fed, chiefly by purveyances (or prises), that is to say by confiscating local crops and produce on the understanding that they would then or subsequently be paid for at a fair price, though often they were not. In addition, the castles which Edward built in Wales were as awesome in their costs as they were to behold. Some idea of the strain to which the realm was submitted by these wars will become evident from a few sample years.

The king's need has been calculated by M. Prestwich: between 1294 and 1297, to fight in Gascony and Flanders and to pay bribes to such allies as the king of Germany and archbishop of Cologne, some £615,000 was required. The Welsh revolt of 1294 and the Scottish campaign in 1296 and subsequently absorbed another £140,000, bringing the total for those years to around £750,000. The earlier Welsh campaigns of 1277 and 1282–3 had cost a sum approaching £150,000, while the building of the castles had added another £80,000 to this throughout the reign. Scottish campaigns between 1301 and 1304 used up a further sum of around £177,000. Throughout the reign, therefore, extraordinary war expenses added over £1,120,000 to the king's usual expenditure. If we bear in mind that even the normal expenses of government by this time exceeded the normal income of the crown, we shall appreciate why Edward I sought to extract from his subjects more than any previous king had attempted. To some extent he was at first exonerated from confronting them with this reality by grants of papal crusading tenths, sexennial ones levied on the clergy only, authorized in 1274 and 1291, and yielding about £20,000 annually. However, this was so clearly inadequate in the 1290s that Edward was forced to resort to his subjects, lay and clerical, for direct taxation on a national scale. In 1294–7, it has been calculated, the laity and clergy together yielded £280,000 in direct taxes to the king. Over the whole reign the figure was £800,000, far short of the extraordinary needs totalled above.

The laity contributed about £500,000 in subsidies throughout the reign, almost a third of this figure within the space of four years. In November 1294 a tenth was demanded of them in the shires, a sixth in the boroughs; in December 1295 an eleventh and a seventh were sought; a year later, in December 1296, a twelfth and an eighth; in July 1297 an eighth and a fifth, although this grant was not in fact raised. To be taxed in four successive years was without precedent, yet this was not the only burden which fell upon the king's lay subjects. In January 1296 the king attempted to array all £40 freeholders appropriately equipped, while in November of the same year he distrained all £30 freeholders for knighthood. In the period May–July 1297 overseas service in Flanders (while the king was off to lead a force in Gascony) was demanded of all £20 freeholders, to whom no promise of payment was made.

Clerical taxes levied by the king throughout his reign totalled some £300,000 of which, again, almost a third was raised in the four years 1294–7. The clergy, however, had already contributed handsomely to royal coffers before the crisis of the 1290s. The 1275 lay subsidy of a fifteenth fell also upon their temporalities. In 1279–80 Canterbury province granted a fifteenth for three years, and York province a tenth for two years, towards the Welsh campaign and the truce with France, for both of which Archbishop Pecham showed enthusiasm. Faced by the Welsh emergency of 1283, Canterbury province granted a triennial twentieth, and York in 1286 possibly a thirtieth, although they did so reluctantly because they were still paying off arrears of the subsidy of 1279–80. In 1290, however, having just expelled the Jews, Edward elicited a ready grant of a tenth from both provinces. Yet beyond all these sums levied directly from the clergy by the king, there were papal taxes raised by the pope to the benefit, intentionally or eventually, of the king.

In 1272–3 the English clergy were yielding to the papacy a crusading tenth on behalf of Edward and his brother, Edmund of Lancaster, arrears from which were still outstanding in 1276. Meanwhile, in 1274 at the Council of Lyons, Gregory X imposed on the English clergy, for the next six years, a tenth based on a new assessment. These funds, probably amounting in all to something just over £100,000, were accumulated for Edward's eventual

resumption of the crusade, but from them meanwhile he drew at
intervals according to his need: for example, in 1283 he temporarily seized £40,000 of the sexennial tenth. In 1291 another
sexennial tenth was imposed. When the crisis broke out in 1294
considerable arrears had accumulated on all these clerical levies:
from the lay subsidies of 1275 and 1290 on their temporalities;
from the direct clerical subsidies of 1279–80 and 1290; and from
papal tenths granted both in 1274 and especially in 1291. But the
screw was soon to be turned yet tighter. First of all, clerical
taxation in the 1290s was to be based on the new and higher
valuation of their livings made for the purpose initially of papal
taxation in 1291; this assessment replaced that of 1276 which had
itself supplanted the valor of 1254. Secondly, livings exempted
on account of poverty were successively reduced in number: in
Canterbury province all livings under 10 marks were exempt in
1294, next year only those under 6 marks, and in 1297 those under
5 marks. Thirdly, direct royal taxes were levied more frequently
than ever before, often overlapping with papal dues, and sometimes occurring twice a year and at unprecedented rates, not just
a fifth instead of a tenth, but in 1294 a half! No wonder the collapse
and death of the dean of St Paul's is attributed in some chronicles
to his learning of this last demand. In these very years not a few of
the lesser clergy were contributing as well to purveyances and local
commissions of array, and suffering with the whole community
the repercussions of wool customs. In 1294 when the king
demanded a half of their incomes from the clergy, a half based
upon the revised valuation of 1291, Canterbury was vacant, and
York and Durham were occupied by royal servants. Permission
was soon granted, therefore, by the higher clergy, but their lesser
brethren and subjects were only coerced by the visit of royal
knights uttering threats of outlawry to their provincial assemblies.
Late in 1295 with more than three quarters of the moiety already
collected, and with its arrears added to those of previous years, the
clergy were asked for yet another subsidy. The newly elected
archbishop, Winchelsey, while sympathetic to the clergy, took a
paternalistic view of the realm, which he saw threatened on three
fronts, and urged his clergy to make a grant to the king.
Nevertheless, the king had to send his justices to the clergy's

deliberations and threatened to take the names of opposers, and it took all Winchelsey's good will and best arts to elicit from them a grant of one tenth for the current year and another, should it be necessary, in the following year. Only just over half of this had been collected when in November 1296 Edward approached the clergy for yet more help: on this occasion Winchelsey took a very different line.

During 1296 Boniface VIII issued the bull *Clericis Laicos*, banning all royal taxes from the clergy without prior papal consent and threatening collectors and payers of such taxes with excommunication which only the pope could lift.[32] Winchelsey learnt of this bull in December 1296 and published it in the assembly of January 1297, called to consider the royal demand made in November on which they had deferred a decision. Thereupon Edward sent Hugh le Despenser, knight, and John de Berwyk, clerk, to order the clergy on behalf of the king and his loyal subjects to 'provide such a subsidy by which the land may be defended, lest the king, earls and barons ordain and dispose of your ecclesiastical goods at their will'.[33] This threat was very soon implemented. In February the clergy were outlawed; although Winchelsey's response was to excommunicate the violators of *Clericis Laicos*, Edward had already seen a way past this. Sheriffs were ordered to seize and sell the goods, chattels and moveables of all clergy with benefices worth more than 3 marks (£2) who had not bought pardon of their outlawry by Easter; such confiscated goods were to be kept until further instructions from the king. Many clergy, especially the royal servants among them, began to buy pardons as early as February, and in York province, which was more immediately threatened with Scottish invasion, the vast majority of the clergy had soon done so. Although Winchelsey stood firm, his clergy were persuaded – and he allowed them to follow their consciences – to buy their pardons, which, of course, could be construed as no grant of tax, even though its rate of one fifth of the value of their benefices was exactly that of the tax which they had refused. Among their reasons for submitting was a fear that outlawry would lead to the destruction of the church; in February the king was already threatening to make the outlawry permanent, and in March even the archbishop had his horses seized by royal officers while he was *en route* from Maidstone to London.

However, in May Winchelsey learned of a papal concession to the king of France admitting the king's right to tax clergy without papal licence for defence of the realm in an emergency. In July 1297 Winchelsey had news of a still more recent document, issued in February, conceding the whole principle of taxation of the clergy by the French king. For his part, Edward sensed that the ice was cracking and since he desperately needed money, preferably without political complications – his lay subjects were restive now – he restored the archbishop's lands and offered the primate and several magnates what they were by then demanding – confirmation of Magna Carta, the Charter of the Forest and some additional articles. What the clergy particularly wanted confirmed was the freedom of the church, notably from the kind of arbitrary seizure of its property and goods so recently experienced; but all subjects were eager to curb the malpractices which accompanied (in these years and for long afterwards) the collection of prises or purveyances as well as the uncustomary burdens by which Edward tried to augment his revenue. While the prospect of reconciliation between the king and the archbishop grew, it did so because on the one hand the papal ruling on royal taxation of the clergy had been relaxed, while on the other the king's relations with his leading magnates were now rapidly deteriorating as he sought to raise and pay for an expeditionary force to Flanders. Winchelsey, as paternalistic as ever, embraced the role of mediator. Yet although archbishop and king were reconciled in July 1297, difficulties were soon resurgent. The fines by which the clergy had bought their pardons for outlawry had yielded more than double the proceeds of the tenth collected in 1296, but Edward was still desperate to find even more money so that he could launch a continental campaign, and he put a new demand to Winchelsey. The problem for the archbishop was that while the king could now expect the clergy to offer subsidies for the defence of the realm, a campaign in Flanders and Gascony did not seem to be defensive of the realm, nor could the French claims to homage for Gascony be immediately construed as imperilling the kingdom. For the clergy to grant such a request as Edward was now making would undoubtedly require, in the archbishop's mind, papal assent, and so he told the king. Edward responded by barring any such appeal to the pope, by issuing a proclamation calculated to cajole the clergy and enlist the support of the laity, and by imposing a tax on the clergy:

> he has for the aforesaid common good and defence of the realm ordained that as clerks ought not to defend themselves by force of arms, the third part of the present year's temporalities of prelates and clerks and all persons of holy church, religious and other is to be seized.[34]

He urged that the tax should be collected without undue violence ('moderately'). No one showed himself more resourceful in circumnavigating clerical consciences and objections or more resolute in extracting from them his needs; even force – used tactfully – was employed to ease conscience as well as to produce cash. One man, of course, Winchelsey, was proof against such cajolery, but his proposed excommunication of those who violated the rights of the church and collected the levy was barred by a writ of prohibition. By the end of August Winchelsey resolved to save his church and the kingdom by allying with the laity who were now on the edge of rebellion.

Back in February 1297 the barons had objected to a summons to serve away from the king. By July they were objecting to overseas service at all. Later that month an ambiguous assembly in the king's chamber granted a subsidy of one eighth and a fifth and a wool prise of 8000 sacks in return for a royal promise to confirm the charters. In August the earls Bigod and Bohun protested at the exchequer against the grant of an eighth, which was already being collected. Declaring it a dangerous precedent, they sought letters patent assuring them that it would not be so used and letters of indemnity for not following the king overseas on campaign. Five days later Edward I appointed his son regent and set off for Flanders. Early in the next month the regent began the process of reconciliation, granting the magnates their letters patent and agreeing in a parliament (which met after the Scottish victory at Stirling Bridge) to renew and confirm the charters, which was done in October following. To these charters were now added the concessions, mostly concerning prises, which had been granted during the summer and autumn. The confirmed charters and additions were then published and guaranteed by the church. The texts of the charters were to be kept, and published twice a year, in cathedral churches throughout the land, and on those occasions all violators were to be pronounced excommunicate.

Mollified in the autumn of 1297 by these gestures on behalf of the king, entrusted with the custody of the charters and their additions, and convinced by the recent Scottish success that England was in peril on that frontier at least, Winchelsey enthusiastically encouraged the clergy to grant the king a tenth. Reluctant tithe-payers were threatened with excommunication and sequestration, and *pour encourager les autres* Winchelsey himself advanced 300 horses and a loan of £8000 to the king. The lower clergy were to pay at the reduced rate of the 1254 valuation, but, far more significantly, the tax was to be collected, supervised and delivered to the king by the clergy themselves – a procedure thereafter tenaciously preserved by Winchelsey and his successors. It was to be delivered to the king by March 1298; however, once the Scottish threat had abated, the archbishop refused in June 1298 to hand over the balance of the grant. Clerical taxation by the king was allowable only when and so long as the realm was endangered, a condition which the clergy were to judge. Clerical subventions to Edward I did not end here, but in future they were to issue from papal taxation.

The Origins of Convocation

Winchelsey's pre-eminent objective had been to ensure that clerical taxation by the crown – conceded in principle at the Third Lateran Council in 1179 – was subject to clerical consent and was collected and managed by the clergy, a necessary corollary to their freedom of consent. Coupled with the question of consent was the procedure by which, and the body from which, it was to be obtained.

The Fourth Lateran Council in 1215 had prescribed regular provincial assemblies for the clergy. In England in 1226 it had been made clear to the king that he could not tax the clergy diocese by diocese; such an attempt in that year had been frustrated by the request of the Salisbury cathedral chapter for consultation with the clergy of other sees; the proctors of the cathedral and collegiate clergy subsequently attended a provincial council armed with instructions from their 'constituents'. Almost thirty years later, in January 1254, when Henry III tried to tax the clergy through the prelates at a parliament or great council, he was reminded that the assent of representatives of all the clergy was necessary. At the ensuing parliament in April 1254 clerical proctors armed with plenary powers did attend and offered a grant but on a condition which the king found unacceptable: that he should remedy their grievances. This was the first time clerical representatives had attended a parliament. After proctors of the lower clergy had objected in 1269 to being committed to a grant simply by the assent of the bishops, a council of prelates in the next year agreed on their own behalf to a subsidy of one twentieth for the king, but only extended it to the rest of the clergy after approval by diocesan synods. In 1279 the purely clerical assemblies of both provinces made a grant to the king towards the cost of the Welsh wars, but again only after there had been discussion in diocesan assemblies. Provincial assemblies met thereafter always with clerical proctors present when a subsidy to the king was at issue and sometimes when it was not. In 1283, on the failure of the king to coerce both clergy and lay representatives at York and Northampton, subsequent provincial clerical gatherings convened at London in 1283 and at York in 1286, attended by proctors of the lower clergy with full powers to treat and consent, and duly made grants; the proctors acted as agents of diocesan synods which had already discussed the grants. Although Edward attempted in September 1294 to tax the clergy at a national assembly of both clergy and laity, the clergy's decision was postponed to their own provincial assemblies early in the new year. This must have been the result partly of the astonishing scale of the royal demand and partly of the absence of any prior diocesan discussion. In 1295 Edward taxed them in a parliament attended by clerical proctors, though there were difficulties. In November 1296 Winchelsey succeeded in postponing a decision to a provincial assembly, at which, however, he invoked *Clericis Laicos* to thwart royal pressure, albeit in vain. Later in the year, for defence against the Scots, convocation granted a tenth, but in 1298 it refused a possible second instalment on the ground that the Scottish threat had passed.

A provincial assembly of the clergy, to which proctors came in greater numbers than to parliament and which *all* abbots and priors were entitled to attend, was increasingly the body through which the clergy were taxed; gradually the name of convocation, which had been applied haphazardly from the early twelfth century to a variety of ecclesiastical gatherings, was reserved for this assembly. But precisely because Edward I could not take their consent for granted and in his later years preferred to tap the clergy's wealth instead by mandatory papal levies, the survival and role of an independent clerical body for the gathering of taxation remained uncertain at his death.

The Last Decade

As Denton has shown, Winchelsey had used *Clericis Laicos* tactically to keep the king at bay while evading the full implications of that bull – that the pope alone could give consent; Edward spent the last years of his reign dexterously reversing this and nullifying the commitments which appeared to have been extracted from him by the Confirmation of the Charters in 1297. He had done this by various means: avoiding direct taxation as much as he could; resorting to prerogative levies; borrowing as heavily as he dared; and finally relying upon the pope to tax the clergy for the benefit of the crown. In 1301 Boniface VIII ordered a tenth to be levied for three years; in 1305 Clement V imposed a septennial tenth upon the clergy. Not only did the papacy by these grants assist the king in his evasion of his 1297 commitments, but in 1305 Clement V even absolved him from his oaths to observe the Confirmation. The following year, on the king's initiative, Clement V summoned Winchelsey to Rome and suspended him.

All this must have raised in the laity ambivalent feelings. On the one hand papal taxation was preserving them from Edward's attentions, except for customary feudal dues and prerogative levies; it is safe to assume that the laity were adapting readily to the notion of leaving the tax burden, or as much of it as they could, to the clergy. On the other hand, the popes were financing and abetting Edward's evasion of his commitments to the nation in 1297–8 and 1301, and this may lie behind the statute of Carlisle which in 1307 restricted the movement of cash from English religious houses to their mother houses on the continent and particularly affected the Cistercians.[35] The matter had been raised in a petition to the parliament of 1305, but was only confirmed now, presumably because, the papal see then being vacant, Edward was waiting to employ the statute as a lever on the new pope. Such was Maitland's theory, probably encouraged by the subsequent citation of the statute in later antipapal legislation; but the statute of Carlisle makes little sense as a measure against a pope as obliging as Clement V, nor did the statute itself directly affect the papacy at all. Rather is it more closely related to the problem of alien priories.

In 1295 Edward had confiscated for war purposes the *apport* (or fixed due) which religious houses and estates in England dependent on mother houses abroad, particularly in Normandy, paid annually to those mother houses. Cistercian abbeys fell to some extent outside this category. In September 1295 custody of alien priories had been seized by the king and they were only restored on payment of fines. This measure was repeated in 1297 and fines were paid during the next four years.[36] The statute of Carlisle is best set in this context. The Cistercian houses, meanwhile, had continued to face increasing burdens of royal taxation in all its forms and unabated demands for *apports* from Citeaux, itself subject to papal and French royal taxes. Both the laity and the English Cistercians themselves – who raised no objections to the statute – were doubtless eager to eliminate the *apport*, whether it went to finance indirectly either the pope or the king of France. The statute of Carlisle effectively did this and as well it barred English and foreign religious from carrying money out of the realm. But perhaps the precise reasons for its origin and the timing of its confirmation are not so important; of greater significance is that it became a key precedent during the ensuing century for those who wished to restrict the outflow of money from the English church to the church universal and in particular to the Roman Curia; its appeal to the interests of patrons whose intentions were thwarted or impaired by impositions on the houses so that 'infinite loss and disinheritance are like to ensue to the founders of the said houses and their heirs' was to reappear in the later statute of Provisors. The seizure of the priories themselves was to be repeated in the course of the century on a much more extended scale and with immense consequences for royal patronage and ideas of lay proprietorship.

Parliament and the Church

From 1275, with the exception of a certain number of years, usually two parliaments met annually, even three in 1278; altogether fifty assembled during the thirty-five years of the reign.[37] 'Parliament', however, was a flexible term which was then applied to a variety of bodies called to assist the king in government. As yet the list of lords who were individually summoned to attend had not hardened, so that lay peers (as they came later to be called) fluctuated from around fifty to a hundred, and alongside the twenty-one bishops a varying number of abbots and priors – sometimes as many as seventy, occasionally more, often fewer – were invited to attend. In addition, the eleven cathedral deans and sixty archdeacons were summoned as a rule. When we turn to the representative element in parliament, the commons, a similar uncertainty obtains. In Edward's reign clerical proctors were called to several, but by no means to all, his parliaments: like the lay representatives, they were absent from at least a dozen assemblies convened between 1295 and 1307. The clerical representatives were a formidable number – forty-two diocesan proctors (two from each diocese) and twenty-three cathedral proctors (including Bath as well as Wells, and Coventry as well as Lichfield) – and with the rest of the clergy they constituted something over a third of the whole parliament. Of the 650 members in the parliament of 1305, 240 were prelates and clerical proctors, 200 were burgess representatives, and 177 were lay barons and knights of the shire; 33 – many of them clerics –

were royal councillors and ministers.[38] Even without the clerical proctors, the clergy's influence in and on parliament was considerable. The bishops and abbots among the lords often outnumbered the lay peers; in addition, the king's chief officers and councillors who sat in parliament *ex officio* included the chancellor, the treasurer and several of the king's clerical judges. Furthermore, the chancery clerks or council clerks who kept the records and serviced parliament were also clerics. In view of the scale and seniority of the clergy's membership of parliament, it seems unwise to dismiss the possibility of their influence upon its procedures and business.

Although taxation was a common reason for convening representative members, it was by no means the only reason for doing so; nor was it, in proportion to the time spent on it, the principal or most demanding business of parliament. Until 1290 the king taxed his subjects on only two occasions, one of those, in 1283, through the agency of separate assemblies for his northern subjects (clerical and lay) at York and for his southern subjects at Northampton, neither a parliament even by the loosest definition. Representatives were summoned to assent to taxes on a number of occasions, as in the 1290s, but they were also called when no tax was being demanded – in 1300, 1302, 1305 and 1307, for example. In these years, by relying upon papal grants, Edward had largely escaped the need to seek subsidies from parliament.

An important part of parliament's business concerned affairs of state: decisions about royal marriages, war and trade were of this kind. Yet even more of parliament's time was occupied dispensing justice in response to petitions from the king's subjects on all manner of grievances. These petitions, addressed to the king or to the king and his council, fill the largest part of the surviving parliamentary rolls. Mostly they were for acts of right and grace, for example the granting of overdue wages or expenses, but a significant minority concerned complaints against royal and other officers. In fact, petitions – which are scarcely known before 1272 – quickly became so numerous that by 1280 most were being redirected to the appropriate departments of royal government (the exchequer and the chancery above all) and only the remainder were dealt with by the king. By 1305 royal clerks were acting as receivers of petitions and sorting them out among auditors or triers, crown ministers and lawyers, who were usually clerics. Parliament was a vast clearing house for the grievances of the king's subjects, not just in England but also in Ireland and Scotland, and in Gascony and the Channel Islands. Some of the complaints, of course, reflected political strains which called for general solution by legislation.

Helen Cam once suggested that parliamentary petitions may have sprung from the already practised art of the clergy in drafting lists of *gravamina*, or grievances, which at intervals since 1237 they had submitted to the king for redress; but G. O. Sayles traces the origin more directly to the legal procedure of bills of complaint submitted to the king's itinerant justices, and certainly the character of the early parliamentary petitions seems to bear this out: clerical *gravamina* were corporate complaints directed against general practices rather than particular people and they lacked the specific quality which individual parliamentary petitions naturally displayed. Petitions from communities, or common petitions, were few in Edward's reign, and though they may have derived something from the example of clerical grievances, they could hardly have failed to have developed from private petitions. Nevertheless, in view of the substantial presence of the clergy in parliament, it requires no special pleading to suppose that the example of clerical *gravamina* exerted some formative influence upon the growth, if not upon the origin, of parliamentary petitions.

In a sense the development of such petitions is of far greater interest to the ecclesiastical historian in respect of its consequences rather than its origins; for what this system entailed was public cognizance, and a public memory, of grievances; when these complaints were directed at the church, parliament inevitably served to institutionalize and to unify countless discontents, and thus to provide kings and others with ideas, excuses and encouragement for actions against the church which might otherwise have remained unrealized. The statute of Carlisle, discussed above, and the measures taken under Edward III against papal provisions well illustrate this point.

Public opinion and attitudes were formed, influenced, hardened and diffused not merely by the fact of their repetition and record in parliament but also through the growing experience of parliamentary representatives. As they were more frequently summoned, so numbers of them came to be more frequently re-elected and brought increasing continuity from one assembly to the next. Popular political memory was accumulating, albeit very slowly. In 1302, for example, the shire knights were almost equally divided between new members and former representatives who had been re-elected.[39] Although the new burgesses then exceeded the re-elected ones, by the first parliament of Edward II's reign, at Michaelmas 1307, the reverse was true. This developing experience was at that time still a precarious feature: in the last twelve years of Edward I, after all, several parliaments met without any shire or borough representatives being summoned. Yet for the growth of the later strident and vigorous anticlericalism, the self-consciousness of the laity was a prerequisite, and on a national scale it is by no means certain that this lay identity would have come about so forcefully or so quickly had parliament not been ready to hand as a vehicle in which to rally hostility and an instrument by which to further it.

Edward and the Papacy

Nowhere does Edward's political skill emerge more clearly than in his relations with the papacy. To some extent he was lucky: at the beginning of his reign he encountered a pope, Gregory X, whom he had already met in England in the 1260s and on crusade in 1272–4; at the end of his reign Edward had to deal with a pope, Clement V, who had been his subject and his servant in Bordeaux; in the interval between these two popes there were ten others, but nine of these together occupied the papal throne for barely fifteen years, five of them for less than a year each, two for four years apiece, one for nearly three, and one for two only. The longest pontificate was that of Boniface VIII, from 1294 to 1303, and it was undoubtedly the most difficult one for the English king. This was due not merely to its length, but also to the character and personality of Boniface; yet even here Edward was in luck.

Boniface made claims which were so large and so tactless as to produce enemies like dragon's teeth, and the French king's own ambitions eventually drove Boniface into Edward's camp. Finally, Edward held one genuine trump card which he persistently and most profitably exploited: his crusading vow. The intention and the vow itself were no cynical charade, for Edward had already been on crusade and shared the piety and the military enthusiasm which impelled so many to the Holy Land. That he never did go there again may be explained by his increasing problems at home, yet successive popes continued to hope in vain.

Almost certainly if we had the full text of Edward's coronation oath, we should find that, like his predecessors back to the early twelfth century and his successors to the end of the Middle Ages, he promised to protect the liberties of the church, which, after all, was also the substance of the first clause of Magna Carta.[40] All that we know for certain about his coronation oath is that he promised to preserve the laws of the realm unimpaired and to do nothing touching the dignity of the crown without first obtaining the consent of his prelates and chief magnates. This was a clause which he frequently invoked against the papacy. Thus in 1296 he consulted his council of magnates who advised him that a certain papal provision would prejudice the crown; and in 1299 he contested the pope's claim to sovereignty over Scotland as a threat to the dignity of his crown. It has to be said that he also invoked this oath against his barons when it suited him to do so, as in 1301: it served against the laity no less than against the clergy.

A particular irritant in Anglo–papal relations was England's temporal subservience to the pope. Since 1213 when King John tactically surrendered the kingdom to Pope Innocent III and received it back as a fief held of the papacy, the English crown had owed the pope an annual tribute of a thousand marks (£666 6s 8d). It was not paid for the years 1268–72, and the king's envoys to the Council of Lyons in 1274 registered a protest against the feudal bond. The following year Edward warded off the papal demand for payment by invoking his obligation – in matters affecting the crown – to consult his parliament, the meeting of which on this occasion was unavoidably delayed. Thereafter the tribute was only paid to grease the wheels of Anglo–papal diplomacy, but even these sporadic payments ceased from 1289.[41] The popes were prepared to be tolerant in this matter, in the hope that Edward would eventually get launched again on crusade, a hope stimulated by his taking the cross in 1287 when he vowed to depart in June 1293 and by the fall of Acre in 1291.

Edward gave successive popes few grounds for complaint with regard to episcopal appointments. He acquiesced in the papal preferment of Kilwardby and Pecham to Canterbury instead of his own candidate, chancellor and friend, Robert Burnell; he tried again to intrude Burnell into Canterbury in 1278 and into Winchester in 1280, on each occasion yielding to the pope. Towards the end of his life Edward attempted to get Winchelsey deprived of Canterbury, but he had to settle for his suspension. Otherwise the reign is distinctive for the want of evidence of royal pressure and of protracted vacancies. Nevertheless, most of his senior officers – including Burnell – were rewarded with bishoprics, usually in the secular sees where election was by a chapter infiltrated by royal clerks. Where the pope provided candidates to bishoprics, Edward was quick to scotch any papal claims to confer the temporalities by the same act of provision. In 1272 Kilwardby, in 1399 Salmon of Norwich, and in 1303 Gainsborough of Worcester were all required to take an oath to receive their lands at the king's pleasure and not by papal grant, an oath which was thereafter usual whenever a bishop obtained his see by provision. Thus the king preserved a vital control over his episcopate.[42]

It was in the promotion of canons and prebendaries that Edward most tenaciously defended his patronage claims against papal interference. Thus when Archbishop Corbridge preferred to obey the pope in a matter of patronage, he was told by the king's judges that he was wrong to do so because the pope's acts were not subject to the English courts, and that no one should prosecute anything at Rome or elsewhere contrary to crown rights and royal dignity.[43]

A combination of clerical opposition and papal objections thwarted his attempts to tax the clergy directly, but to the king Winchelsey constituted a far greater problem than the pope who, susceptible to more and wider pressures, gradually modified his objections to Edward's aims and granted him a papal tenth in 1301.

A few years later Clement V, formerly archbishop of Bordeaux, granted Edward further papal tenths, and thus relieved him of the need to tax the clergy directly or even to seek subsidies from his difficult lay subjects. That was not the only service rendered by Clement to Edward: he exonerated the king from his oath to the barons concerning the Confirmation of the Charters in 1297 and annulled the clauses in the Articles on the Charters in 1300 which prescribed twice-yearly excommunication of all violators of Magna Carta and of the Forest Charter. Clement's final assistance to Edward came in 1306 when, resisting the king's call to deprive or translate Winchelsey, he suspended the primate and summoned him to exile in the Curia.

From all of this Edward gained immediate advantages, though they were not of long-term benefit to the English monarchy; they were decidedly disadvantageous to the papacy. The papal ban on royal taxation of the clergy provoked ephemeral and unspecific objections from the laity, aimed more at the archbishop than the pope. But the concession of the papal taxes of the clergy to the king was all too clearly to release the king from baronial pressure when his oath to the barons was cancelled and the obdurate archbishop recalled. The summons of Winchelsey to Rome only served to redirect baronial irritation away from him to the pope. And there were other embarrassments for the pope.

In 1299 Boniface VIII ordered Edward to abandon war in Scotland since that kingdom was a papal fief, and he invited Edward to send proctors to Rome to establish his right to the Scottish crown. Dubious though Edward's claims in Scotland may have been, they were more soundly based than the claims to overlordship made by Boniface. Exploiting Boniface's injudicious move, Edward sought to rekindle popular support for his Scottish campaign by a debate in parliament on his and the papal claims, in the course of which he employed no little historical research to justify his own rights, to refute the pope's, and to persuade the public of all this.[44] A great deal of fervent and unfavourable publicity was heaped upon the papacy as a result of this issue. Papal abandonment subsequently merely confirmed Englishmen in their righteous indignation, and when Boniface and Clement V began to assist Edward in eluding his earlier commitments to the barons, the English reputation of the papacy sank lower still. Nor was it much higher among the clergy who found themselves not only heavily taxed without the discretionary right of refusal which they enjoyed in respect of royal taxes, but also threatened with excommunication and ecclesiastical penalties for non-compliance. They were being taxed to abet the king and to nullify his concessions which were as valuable to them as to the laity. Not only did this latter-day alliance of king and pope alienate much sympathy, lay and clerical, from the papacy, but it doubtless served also to drive further wedges between the clergy and the laity within England.

Edward's dealings with the papacy reflect his approach to the English church itself – at once forceful, resolute, adroit and supple. He preserved against threats from all quarters his claims to patronage in order to support a rapidly growing number of servants, whose loyalty he protected and encouraged with writs of prohibition and seizures of episcopal temporalities. The widening definition (and appropriation) of temporalities – the incoming tide, as it were – swept away some papal as well as episcopal claims. He barred papal providees as readily as he warned a provincial council off royal interests; yet he acquiesced in the papal choice of primates and presided over three remarkable decades of church–crown cooperation in the arrest of excommunicates. Conflicts did not exclude collaboration, and the church in England, as well as the papacy, contributed significantly to the fortunes of crown and realm: money vital for the wars; manpower crucial for administration; experience nourishing royal legislation and parliamentary development. Yet both collaboration and conflict usually worked to the detriment of the church, so that at the end of Edward's reign clerical morale and independence were seriously impaired and dangerous fissures were becoming apparent between the clergy and laity, and between Englishmen and the papacy. Ironically, the papacy must bear some responsibility for these developments.

Prospects

The crisis of 1297 with the church had highlighted one very clear lesson for kings in the future: not to let the see of Canterbury go by default.

Secondly it had demonstrated that the clergy were well nigh powerless against royal tax demands: if they would not make a grant, the king could outlaw them and raise the money by fines, or he could simply seize their temporalities. The archbishop could delay and immensely complicate matters, but his appeal to Rome in August 1297 had been barred, his excommunication of violators was countered by a writ of prohibition, his resolution was isolated by the alarmist fears of some clergy and the divided loyalties of others, especially those who were the king's servants; above all, Boniface VIII's temporizing in France suggested that no archbishop henceforth could rely on papal support. The pope, it was shown, was impotent to defend the clergy against royal demands: Boniface himself had sold the pass by his concessions of principle to Philip the Fair; moreover, popes henceforward had too much need of diplomatic and financial support to impose interdicts and risk schism. Far from protecting the English clergy from royal demands, Boniface VIII and Clement V added their authority to royal exactions and incidentally took on the odium as well.

No king would welcome the tensions and conflict with his clergy on the level and scale of 1297, least of all when relations with the laity were also strained and external tension threatened; yet precisely in those circumstances Edward had demonstrated the power of the crown to enforce its will.

Moreover, useful as the clergy's and particularly Winchelsey's aid was to the magnates in the summer of 1297, the laity had been encouraged to think that the clergy, especially because they did not fight, should bear a significant share of the financial costs of defence. They had even witnessed the confiscation of the clergy's goods and chattels to defray the nation's expenses: a potent lesson for the future.

The events of 1297 marked a new era in crown and church and in clergy–laity relations, one in which the endowments and incomes of the clergy were increasingly raided by the king and coveted by the laity to meet, above all, the soaring costs of warfare and diplomacy. It marked a notable advance for the crown which far surpassed the temporary and prevaricating concessions represented by the Confirmation of the Charters and the Articles upon the Charters. By the scale and regularity of taxation, both of the laity and of the clergy, and through the growth of machinery which it necessitated, a new dimension was added to clergy–laity relations.

It is all the more significant that while Anglo–papal relations at the formal level were not imperilled, the attitudes of Englishmen were more vulnerable to alienation as successive popes underwrote an unpopular king or unpopular crown policies. Increasingly and unintentionally, the papacy assumed the odium of tax gatherer on behalf of the king.

As taxation became a common feature of government and society, tax payers looked with new eyes at each other and at the tax leviers and granters. The notion that clerical wealth was at the disposal of the realm when need arose was echoed and supported by some other developments of the reign: the practice whereby donations of land to the church first required royal licence (and at a price); the growing, though still limited, legal procedure and principle whereby endowments whose purposes were neglected by the receiving clergy could be recovered by the donor; the practice of founders and patrons 'resuming' possession of the lands of religious houses embarrassed by debts (not least debts resulting from taxation) until they could again operate effectively; the seizure of alien priories; and lastly, the widening definition of temporalities at the expense of spiritualities. Not always through royal initiative, and certainly not by a deliberate policy, Edward I's reign witnessed some major developments much to the long-term disadvantage of the English church. Some serious steps had been taken towards that outburst of anticlericalism and, in particular, antipapalism which marked the later fourteenth century: suspicions had been raised about the church's landed wealth and envy of it had been fanned; resentment against the papacy – by the clergy as well as by the laity – was growing; above all parliament was providing an assembly where hostility could be orchestrated, diffused and preserved. What an irony that a king renowned for his piety, who prefaced some of his legislation by alluding to his duty to defend the church, and who sought a quick end to his wars in order to pursue the crusade, should preside over these changes!

2

Edward II (1307–27)
Precedents Exploited

It might be thought that in a reign which saw bitter struggles between king and nobles the church, if astutely led, could gain some significant concessions in exchange for support carefully distributed. A king who sought to defy his magnates and preserve his favourites, who was threatened from Scotland and France, who was distrusted and despised by his French wife, would surely need all the support he could get from his clergy and from the pope in order to survive; and for this, one might expect him to pay dearly by concessions. Edward II was such a king and yet this did not happen. The church actually lost yet more ground under Edward II than it had done under his father. With regard to taxation, jurisdiction, provisions, patronage and vacancies, even where the church suffered no new encroachments, it certainly recovered nothing which it had already lost. Diplomatically the Avignon popes gave more to Edward than they gained from him, and by their intervention, first to save his favourites and then to bring about peace with Scotland and with France, the terms of which were not relished by the people, the papacy went further towards gaining that ill-reputation which dogged it in fourteenth-century England. Edward II was a tough king, resolved to do as he wished regardless either of convention or of baronial pressure. If he reluctantly yielded on several occasions to such pressure, he much more quickly, and quite as often, violated his word afterwards; in this he was but his father's son. Three times he recalled his favourite, Piers Gaveston, from an exile imposed on him first by Edward I and then by the barons; the Ordinances, to which the king was sworn in 1311 and again in 1317, he treated with contempt; the expulsion of the Despensers, father and son, was reversed almost before it was enforced. On each of these occasions Edward found crucial support from the pope or from some of the bishops.

Gaveston and the Ordainers

Throughout his reign Edward's rule was marred and imperilled by his inordinate affection for, and reckless promotion of, men more tactless even than he was. Piers Gaveston had been exiled from the household of Edward when he was Prince of Wales, but was quickly recalled after the prince's accession in 1307. Before long Gaveston was given the hitherto exclusively royal title of earl of Cornwall, an affront to the established councillors and nobility which he did nothing to palliate by his swaggering arrogance, especially at Edward's coronation in which he played a leading role; just as outrageous were the lands and revenues which went with titles, office and power. Opposition to the king's favourite was so soon mobilized that by May 1308 Edward was compelled to banish Gaveston from the realm.

Meanwhile, against the pope's better judgement, Edward had recalled from the papal Curia another exile, Winchelsey. The archbishop came back under papal orders to avoid giving offence to the king. Now sixty years old, failing in health, and without papal backing, Winchelsey was unlikely to present the new king with the problems which he offered to the old one, but he did not hesitate to support the barons against Gaveston. He issued a decree, which was to be read in all churches, excommunicating Gaveston if he failed to leave the kingdom by the set date (25 June 1308) or afterwards tried to return; all those who assisted the favourite in either offence were encompassed in the sentence.[1] Winchelsey's action, explicitly 'for the tranquillity of the realm', reflects his abiding interventionist view of his responsibilities and won him friends, if not much influence, among the baronage.

Notwithstanding this, in 1309, protected by a papal bull which annulled the sentence of banishment and excommunication,[2] Gaveston returned to England. Clement V had been brought to this action not only by his own need of royal collaboration in his moves against the Templars but also by careful preparation on the king's part. In June 1308 Edward had accompanied a letter to the pope on Gaveston's behalf with the grant of the castle of Blanquefort to the pope's nephew; later that year, at the pope's request, the king released some prisoners, among whom was Walter Langton, bishop of Lichfield, who had offended the barons by his corruption and extortion at the exchequer and the king by earlier siding with Edward I against Gaveston. In January 1309 the king bought jewels as a gift for the pope.

Disconcerted by Clement's bull, Winchelsey at first sought advice from his fellow bishops: Simon of Ghent, bishop of Salisbury, equivocated; Henry Woodlock of Winchester, after consulting his advisers, concluded that the bull was genuine and had to be obeyed.[3] It was after Winchelsey had accepted the bull as genuine that Gaveston returned. An attempt to cajole lay opposition was made by the issue of the 'Articles of Stamford' in July 1309, but they were little more than a reissue of the Articles on the Charters, *Articuli super Cartas*, of 1300.

Whatever steps the king took, however, Gaveston's actions and presence, as well as the king's indulgence of him, quickly revived baronial opposition: in 1310 the twice-exiled Gaveston was appointed keeper of the realm during Edward's absence in Scotland. Not surprisingly Edward was soon facing increasing demands to accept a number of reforming ordinances along with a commission to implement them; predictably Gaveston's exile was the key stipulation. Only in the autumn of 1310, after various desperate manoeuvres, did Edward finally accept the Ordinances and the so-called Ordainers. Among the twenty-one Ordainers, there were eight earls, six barons and seven bishops; naturally Winchelsey was one of the seven. At an early stage the archbishop and ten of his suffragans had signed a declaration that they intended no prejudice to the king by their support for the reforms, and the Ordainers themselves swore to work for the benefit of church, king and people. Yet what brought Edward to heel – temporarily at least – was a baronial threat that they might have to find another king if he would not keep his coronation oath, which in their minds meant observing the Ordinances. In September 1311 the bishop of Salisbury, acting for the sick archbishop, published the Ordinances in St Paul's churchyard in the presence of several bishops and leading barons. A fortnight later Edward sealed the text and issued it to all sheriffs.

The influence of the bishops, and of the church generally, on the content of the Ordinances was negligible. The prelates were concerned, as explicit statements show, primarily to defend the church's liberties. The church figured in this document only in the same general terms as it figured in Magna Carta; there was one reference to prohibitions, but begging still the question of what were temporalities and what were not. This in itself bears witness to the limits of clerical influence. Although Winchelsey was a leading figure in political opposition to the crown in 1297 and in 1310–11, his influence on the two occasions differed, for whereas in 1297 both clergy and laity shared a common grievance over taxation, this was not so in 1310–11. The laity had little interest in protecting church liberties and franchises, and the clergy were mainly set in motion by the archbishop's concern for the harmony of the realm.

The archiepiscopal and clerical contribution to these reforms was very largely limited to issuing further decrees of excommunication against Gaveston, if he returned from this third exile, and against violators of the Ordinances. While this gave support to baronial and lay measures, it did not guarantee their success. The king withdrew with his household and the major departments of state to York where he revoked the Ordinances and recalled Gaveston in January 1312. In response to these actions, while convocation debated the necessity to uphold the Ordinances, the archbishop summoned a meeting in March of bishops and magnates to denounce Gaveston and to defend the realm; excommunication was published on all offenders and on Gaveston. In June 1312, however, he was captured at Scarborough and soon afterwards was murdered while in the earl of Warwick's safe-custody: thus, no longer an embarrassment to the king, Gaveston by the circumstances of his death divided the nobles.

In the summer of 1312 papal emissaries arrived in London to make peace between the king and his barons but their overtures were quickly rejected by the barons who, as one chronicler put it, 'had no notion of letters, but were skilled in military affairs and the use of arms' and were quite unwilling 'to discuss their own deeds or business of the realm with any foreigner or alien'.[4] In fact, when peace was briefly restored it was as a result of the divisions and recriminations among the baronage after Gaveston's murder. Only the earl of Lancaster among the nobility and Winchelsey among the prelates were committed to the Ordinances; others seemed to regard them as a measure, or cover for measures, against Gaveston; Winchelsey, however, died in 1313, leaving Lancaster alone to pursue his ambitions in the name of the Ordinances.

In this whole affair the clergy – even Winchelsey – had been unable to keep the favourite at bay, and had exercised negligible influence upon the formulation and implementation of the governmental reforms. The pope had been more effective, conniving with the king to thwart the opposition, lay and clerical, though vainly attempting in 1312 to reconcile the antagonists. Clement V aimed to pacify the realm and threw his weight – as a monarch – behind the monarch. Winchelsey was no doubt distrusted as a meddler, too quick to denounce the king and align with the barons against him. The injustice of this view only reflects the deficient understanding which a pope could have of internal English politics. When he sent ambassadors here, they got no sympathetic hearing from the barons; the king, however, was a master of the timely gesture.

The minor importance of the church in the early opposition to Edward II is evident enough from the forty-two Ordinances in 1311, of which only two specifically concerned the church. The Ordainers, despite having a third of their number drawn from the bishops, treated church interests perfunctorily. On the one hand, the barons were confident that few clergy would rally to the support of Edward II. On the other hand, for all his ferocity in matters of principle, the archbishop was an aged and a sick man who had suffered too many humiliations and had offended too many of his fellow prelates in the 1290s and since to command strong support from them; he was still unsure of papal backing for his measures, and indeed found them countermanded by Clement. All this is not to say that the clergy lacked grievances generally against the king, but that they were neither of the kind to excite lay sympathy nor even sufficiently widespread or fundamental to unite the clergy themselves. As for the pope, his prime concern was to promote peace in the realm, an aim which he judged best served by siding with the king.

The Despensers

After the murder of Gaveston the baronial opposition disintegrated and Edward was able to prepare for a campaign against the Scots, but when this ended in the humiliating defeat of his forces at Bannockburn in June 1314 the earl of Lancaster again united the hopes of the disillusioned baronage. His dominance was all the greater after the death of the earl of Warwick in August 1315, and at the Lincoln parliament in January 1316 he was recognized as head of the council. By April, however, his disagreements with the king led to his retirement from the government and to a state of almost civil war between them. Much of the next two years was passed in efforts to avert just such a development, and in these efforts the clergy played a positive role. They were aided by the vulnerability of Lancaster's support; baronial suspicions of his ambitions and jealousy of his wealth and power were compounded by the king's astute distribution of patronage: the lines of confrontation were never clear or secure for either party. Until recently historians have believed that between the opposing parties there emerged around 1317 a so-called Middle Party, which had its beginning in a mission to Avignon in that year. In his biography of the earl of Pembroke, however, Dr Phillips has effectively disproved this notion and shown the baronial conciliators to have been royal supporters, rather than independents. If there was a middle party at all, it was more plausibly composed of bishops than of barons. In August 1317 seven bishops were represented on the king's mission to Lancaster, and a few months later ten bishops from the southern province attended a council meeting to resolve the political dispute; one outcome of this was that in January 1318 the bishop of Norwich negotiated with Lancaster. In February a provincial council of the Canterbury clergy met to discuss affairs of church and realm to such good effect that further meetings of magnates with Lancaster resulted. And by April 1318 a group of bishops which included Canterbury,

Norwich, Chichester, Winchester, Llandaff and Hereford reached an accord with Lancaster about his attendance at future parliaments. His distrust of the king was such that he had recently refused to attend or to do so without a large and menacing retinue; now he agreed to be present and to keep the peace, while the bishops guaranteed his safety. The prelates continued to act as mediators throughout the summer months, assuring Lancaster of safety from the threats of the king's latest favourites. The outcome of their efforts was the treaty of Leake in August 1318 which provided for a meeting of Lancaster and the king. These favourable developments, however, were aborted by two events: the king's adoption of the young Hugh Despenser as his newest favourite, and the disastrous campaign to Scotland in 1319. Despenser, made chamberlain of the king's household in the autumn of 1318, was son of an old servant of the king who was also called Hugh, but the young man was greedy and tactless on a scale which surpassed Gaveston and alarmed and alienated particularly the lords of the Welsh Marches (where he laid claim to extensive lands) and drove them into uneasy alliance with Lancaster. The army which set out to recover Berwick from the Scots in July 1319 was some 14,000 strong, but it ended with a humiliating retreat and flight into England; undoubtedly the Scottish outflanking movement which penetrated deep into England was the major contributor to this disaster, but acrimony between Lancaster and Edward may have helped bring it about and was certainly magnified by it, so that afterwards the relations of the two men rapidly deteriorated just at the time when Despenser the younger was antagonizing other magnates as well. In 1321, despite attempts by several bishops to reach a settlement with the Marcher lords, open civil war broke out and Edward was forced to acquiesce in the parliamentary exile of both Despensers, father and son. Twelve articles were laid against them, including charges that they had intruded evil and false counsellors about the king (men such as Master Robert Baldock, keeper of the privy seal) and that they extorted fines from newly elected prelates before admitting them to be presented to the king.[5]

As happened a decade before, the king quickly set about securing the return of his exiles. Despite the banishment,

Despenser the younger was still in close touch with the king and may even have devised the tactics by which his return was contrived. By December 1321 the king was touring the country – ostensibly 'to restore order' – while Lancaster and the Marchers were demanding the abandonment of favourites by the king. In September, Archbishop Reynolds, 'considering the tumult in the realm', had summoned a convocation to meet in London in December.[6] The council was soon addressed and – in effect – directed by the king's messengers. Hugh Despenser the younger had already petitioned the king on the grounds that the charges against him were erroneous and his condemnation illegal, particularly because so few prelates were present in the parliament which gave judgement.[7] Edward sent certain earls, barons and other councillors to put before convocation the charges against the Despensers and to enjoin the clergy on their fealty to advise him whether the banishment did violate his coronation oath. After 'most diligent discussion' convocation concluded that the process against the Despensers was erroneous, sinful (*sic!*) and revocable; on the king's orders these conclusions were solemnly published as quickly as possible in each church in the land, together with an indulgence of forty days for those praying for the health of the king and the peace of the realm.[8] It mattered not that only five bishops were present at the assembly; the rest were ordered to send their opinion to the king. Of these, two – Cobham and Stapledon – were strongly of the opinion that although the king could quash parliament's judgement on the Despensers, annulment by parliament would be much more secure.[9] The verdict of convocation was read to an assembly of the earls who duly concurred, though whether out of respect for the clerical judgement or from expediency is uncertain. Afterwards, similarly approached by the king, judges and others of his council also agreed. The Despensers were formally pardoned in the York parliament of May 1322 which met after the king had routed the Marcher lords and defeated and executed Lancaster at Boroughbridge. In that same parliament those of the Ordinances of 1311 which most offended the king were repealed, no champion of them surviving the earl of Lancaster. In June a papal bull releasing from their oaths those who had sworn to destroy the Despensers was published – in Latin, French and

English – in cathedrals, churches and other public places throughout the land, on Sundays, feasts and other days.[10]

The role of the clergy in all this should not be regarded too cynically. Not all bishops were employed by the king and some of them had acquired their sees in the face of royal opposition; they cannot be dismissed as king's men. Even those who were royal servants, like Archbishop Reynolds himself, by their efforts in the preceding months and years to reconcile king and barons had demonstrated their concern with the peace of the community, which may explain also why they thought it prudent to prefer the Despensers – able royal servants that they were – to the unpredictable and scarcely less disruptive earl of Lancaster. They probably had in mind, too, the concern of the pope – demonstrated in his letters and by his emissaries – to restore peace to the realm so that the king might proceed on crusade. Whatever doubts there may be about Edward's commitment to crusade, none can be entertained of John XXII's, for he did all that he could to bring England to a state of peace and Edward to the point of departure.

Deposition 1322–7

The defeat of Lancaster and the Marchers did not produce stability and peace. Edward's extravagant revenge on his erstwhile enemies – the so-called Contrariants – was hardly calculated to reconcile them and was too excessive to repress them. Many were imprisoned and most suffered huge fines or the seizure of their lands; the king's friends often exploited the vulnerability of the Contrariants in order to plunder and pillage with virtual immunity to their own profit. The example was set by the Despensers, especially the younger, who flourished in the king's continued favour and looked to their own profit while they extended his. By 1326 there were few men more hated than the Despensers and few more feared than the king. Edward took no constructive pains to build support for his rule but was content to make it financially sound, in itself a notable achievement yet one secured at an exorbitant political cost.[11] His precarious position was compounded by his difficulties with Scotland and France, and his reign ended with his deposition.

In 1323 Andrew Harclay, earl of Carlisle, who was of critical importance for the defence of the northern border of the realm, was executed on suspicion of treason. Without his aid, Edward was bound to negotiate for peace with Scotland; but the best he could do was to conclude a thirteen-year truce in 1323. It is a measure of Edward's desperation that by its terms he surrendered any claims which Englishmen had upon Scottish lands and thus alienated further support among his magnates.

That same year the new king of France, Charles IV, pressed his claims of overlordship in Gascony to the point of open hostilities. So great by now was Edward's paranoia that in 1324 he seized the lands of his queen, Isabella, and dispersed her servants to safe-custody in various religious houses, lest they be employed to aid her brother, the king of France. These moves were hardly calculated to win her loyalty, already strained by Edward's favourites. Her alienation was of particular significance because she was soon after enlisted to mediate between her husband and her brother. This role, first suggested by the pope in July 1324, came about because Edward refused to send his son to do homage to Charles for Gascony, but relied instead on Isabella to secure more acceptable terms. She left for Paris in March 1325 and by June Edward was compelled to acquiesce in terms which still required his homage. Not daring to leave his kingdom in its current state, in September 1325 and probably on the suggestion of Bishop Stratford of Winchester, who was then negotiating in Paris, he very reluctantly despatched the Prince of Wales to act for him.

Although the king thus gained temporary peace in Gascony, he had conceded the principle of homage and, far more dangerously, had lost control of his wife and son, both of whom were now in France. Isabella ignored his order to return to England and stayed on in Paris with the prince and in the company of Roger Mortimer of Wigmore. Mortimer was a Marcher lord and a Contrariant who had been imprisoned in the Tower and threatened with death; he escaped to Paris in 1323 where he became the centre of a group of exiles and fugitives. The alliance of the queen and the custody of her son was sealed when Mortimer and Isabella became lovers.

The last quarter of 1325 and the first three quarters of 1326 were rife with rumour, alarm, threatening manoeuvres and unavailing diplomacy. In January 1326 Isabella wrote to Bishop Stratford, now back in England, indicating that she would not return until both Despensers had been banished from court. In May papal backing was given to her conditions for return; two legates brought letters urging the younger Despenser to assist the reconciliation of the king and queen, virtually a request for him to abandon the court, but they got no further than Dover where the king interviewed them and threatened them with death if they dared to publish the pope's letters. In September, open hostilities having been resumed in Gascony, Isabella, Mortimer and the prince, accompanied by a small force of Hainault and German troops, crossed from Dordrecht to East Anglia and were soon joined by dissident magnates and prelates. Among the latter were Burghersh, bishop of Lincoln, Orleton of Hereford, Hotham of Ely, and Bicknor, the primate of Dublin. It was Orleton who put Isabella's case persuasively to the magnates gathered round her and Mortimer.

From Orwell Isabella and her forces reached London on 6 October, but by then the king was fleeing westwards to Wales, through Gloucester and Chepstow to Neath; pursuing him, Isabella's forces reached Bristol, where on 26 October the Prince of Wales was proclaimed the keeper of the realm. Among those present on this occasion were not only the four bishops who had joined the queen in Suffolk after her landing but also Stratford of Winchester and Ayermine of Norwich. On 16 November Edward was captured and four days later Orleton, with the earl of Leicester, took away the great seal. The Despensers, also captured in the west country, were brutally executed after summary trials. About that time the Tower of London fell to the rebel citizens and Bishop Stapledon of Exeter, whom Edward had left in charge of the city, was lynched: he was dragged from his horse to the great cross in Cheapside, stripped of his armour and beheaded with a bread-knife. The immediate impact of this event was to dissuade other prelates from publicly defending the king. Archbishop Reynolds, who had excommunicated the invaders on their arrival in England, now fled from London on horses appropriated – so it is said – from the bishop of Rochester who had to make his way to safety on foot.

The following weeks were passed in scheming, debate, riot and propaganda. Isabella had sought the removal of the Despensers, which had been achieved, yet Edward's whole reign had shown how resilient he was in these circumstances, and recent years had demonstrated the extent of his power and the ferocity of his vengeance. Favourites, reform commissions and ordinances had come and gone with no sign of improvement either in the king's government or in public order; indeed, the realm was now in a state of virtual brigandage. It is hardly surprising, therefore, that deposition should be mooted again – it had been talked of in the Gaveston crisis. There seems little doubt that Mortimer, who now commanded the queen's affections and her actions, was the principal advocate and agent. Such a move, however, was into uncharted waters fraught with dangers and complexities.

What purported to be a parliament, called in the name of the Prince of Wales as keeper of the realm, and presided over by Isabella and Mortimer on the prince's behalf, met in January 1327, having been postponed nearly a month while some doubts and difficulties were resolved.[12] After its opening Archbishop Melton of York demanded that the king should be brought before parliament; Bishops Stratford and Orleton were thereupon sent to Kenilworth, where the king was imprisoned, to request his attendance but they came back to report with some zest his offensive words of refusal. Meanwhile, the city of London saw various manoeuvres to promote Edward's deposition: assemblies at the Guildhall included one which resolved to depose him in favour of his son, a decision reported to parliament and supported by a sermon from Orleton on the text 'Where there is no true ruler, the people will be destroyed'. At one of these city assemblies Mortimer delivered an address which is thought to have been aimed primarily at Edward's episcopal supporters – Melton, Reynolds, Hethe and others – who were cowed into swearing before the massed Londoners (whose violence had already been demonstrated against Stapledon) to uphold the queen's cause and the liberties of London: thirteen bishops, some notable abbots and two dozen other clergy took the oath that day. Afterwards representatives of all the estates of the realm, led by Sir William Trussell and including four bishops, four friars and three other religious, went to Kenilworth to secure the king's abdication – as an alternative to the disinheritance of his dynasty. Orleton once again seems to have taken a leading part, delivering a harsh and bitter address to the king. Edward reportedly surrendered and abdicated, whereupon the estates renounced their homage to him and then returned to inform parliament. Bishop Stratford, preaching on the text 'My head is sick', announced the decision to depose the king nevertheless and asked for the assent of the commons. Archbishop Reynolds, taking as his theme 'The voice of the people is the voice of God', confirmed the approval of the commons and – in the view of some – thus completed the process of deposition. Edward's reign ended on 20 January 1327. Prince Edward was acknowledged as the new king, and Isabella and Mortimer as his regents. Thus the first deposition of a king since the Conquest was consummated.

In the progress to this climax bishops – particularly Stratford and Orleton – had been prominent: seeking his abdication, reporting his defiance, bullying him into acquiescence, and inducing parliament to consent to deposition lest doubts about his abdication remain. At an early stage four bishops had joined the queen in Suffolk; six had later witnessed the proclamation of Prince Edward as keeper of the realm; towards the end, more than a dozen prelates had been coerced by the London mob into support for the queen's party. Among these last was Archbishop Reynolds who had at first excommunicated the invaders by pressing into service a ten-year-old denunciation against the Scots! His capitulation has been condemned by some comfortable historians, unthreatened by a London mob and remote from Stapledon's horrifying end. On 16 January a provincial council of the southern clergy met at St Paul's and added further impetus and justification to deposition by presenting thirteen of their own complaints or grievances against the king, though none of these concerned an offence peculiar to his reign. At every stage, therefore, members of the hierarchy were involved in the process of deposing an anointed king: some were coerced by understandable fear; others,

as events unfolded, reluctantly despaired of a peaceful resolution
of the conflict any other way than by deposition; and a few were
eager promoters of Isabella's plans. It is not easy to distinguish
between the first and the second categories: Reynolds could well
have belonged to both. The third category has been characterized
as queen's bishops, owing their promotion largely to her influence
and forming a party deliberately constructed by her over some half
a dozen years; but this view does not survive close scrutiny since
only two of the alleged party were even remotely indebted to
Isabella for their appointments.[13] The rest of the so-called queen's
bishops had all suffered acutely from Edward's tyranny, and even
some of the others had been the targets of at least his threats.
Stratford, a royal diplomat, had been provided to Winchester in
1323 against the wishes of the king and paid a heavy penalty for it:
his temporalities were seized and exploited for a year, and even
after they were restored Stratford was placed under recognizances
of £10,000 to the king (£2000 down and the rest conditional upon
his good conduct), £1000 to the Despensers, and 1000 marks to the
chancellor, Robert Baldock, a clerk for whom Edward had
intended the bishopric; moreover, Stratford was summoned to
answer in the King's Bench for his conduct of a royal mission to the
papacy. It is scarcely surprising, therefore, that even though he
was again on royal diplomatic missions to France, in 1324–5, and
in 1326 backed Reynolds's excommunication of the invaders, he
soon recognized a *fait accompli* and gave his support to the
queen.[14] Orleton was charged in 1324 on account of his association
with Mortimer in 1321, and despite his protest against the
competence of lay courts – the assizes at Hereford and afterwards
parliament itself – to try him, his lands and goods and even his
register were seized by the king.[15] Burghersh, bishop of Lincoln,
had been promoted in 1320 when his uncle, Lord Badlesmere, was
among the king's favourites, but the bishop's fortunes and
affections changed when his uncle was hanged and his brother
imprisoned. Edward had seized the temporalities and sold off the
stock of Stratford, Orleton and Burghersh. Five bishops during
the course of 1326 suffered such confiscation; four were under
similar threat for the way in which they had earlier filled their royal
offices. The loss of their lands was a blow not just to episcopal

prestige and income but also to episcopal management and the pastoral care of a diocese; it cannot have been reassuring to any bishop to see how often temporalities were at the risk of malicious accusation or expedient suspicion. Hotham, bishop of Ely since 1316, was simply disenchanted with the regime of the Despensers and Baldock. Ayermine, who acquired Norwich in 1325, was a royal chancery clerk of long standing and, although he may have owed something to the queen's patronage, he should perhaps be ranked with the disillusioned, as indeed should Bicknor, since 1317 archbishop of Dublin. By the end of his reign Edward II had alienated too many prelates to enjoy more than minority support from them. Even so, it is a signal testimony to the mystique and power of kingship that men like Melton, Hethe, Gravesend, Ross and Reynolds held loyal to Edward until his cause was past hope.

The defections of the bishops has led some historians to denounce them as unscrupulous and leaderless. That, however, is to ignore the efforts of several bishops over many years to secure some lasting settlement between a wilful king and his resentful subjects; the lateness of their conversion to deposition – under duress or in despair – is rather to their credit than otherwise; as for the fiercest episcopal opponents of the king, their experience gave them good grounds for believing that the church's liberties would be better protected under another king. That the bishops were not united reflects adversely neither upon their integrity nor upon their leadership.

Vital as was the role of the prelates in Edward's deposition – so delicate a novelty could hardly have been accomplished without them – their participation was more ceremonial than formative. There is little evidence to support a view that Isabella or Mortimer embarked on invasion, conquest and dethronement under the influence, or by the counsel, of any bishop. The mission to invite Edward to come to parliament was prompted by Melton's protest against condemning the king unheard and unseen; the sermons of Orleton, Stratford and finally of Reynolds were not the spontaneous initiatives of these prelates, but clearly part of an opportunist programme coordinated by Mortimer and his allies. In short, the deposition only serves to underline the limitations of ecclesiastical initiative and power in politics. The notion that this is attributable to having a former royal servant, Reynolds, as archbishop instead of an authoritarian idealist like Winchelsey is to overvalue the role of individuals, of Winchelsey in particular; for all his principled vigour, Winchelsey had failed to ensure long-term security for the clergy, or much beyond transient relief even during his own pontificate. Clerical *gravamina* had been as easily evaded or thwarted under Pecham and Winchelsey as they were under Reynolds. Primates and prelates exercised political power most effectively when they were moving in support of magnate opposition; against united barons they were impotent. Aware of this fact, both king and barons conceded little to clerical demands. Undoubtedly these evasions were possible because among the clergy as a whole were many who served the king and depended upon his protection against the rigours of canon law, and because the pope, in his defence of the monarchy, undermined the independence and confidence of the prelates. The collusion of Clement V with Edward I and Edward II had surely jeopardized the political integrity of any future archbishop. This lesson lurked behind the events of 1327 and was even more evident in Richard II's reign.

Scottish Warfare

English politics throughout the fourteenth century and especially during Edward II's reign were crucially influenced by Scotland. Edward I had died on the Solway Firth when about to lead another expedition against the Scots. His son, seeking to staunch the outflow of money on the Scottish war, quickly arranged a truce, but it could offer few hopes of long-term disengagement. Several leading nobles by this truce lost control of, and revenues from, estates which they had possessed in Scotland: they were naturally inclined to emphasize its temporary nature. Meanwhile, the cessation of major hostilities left the northern English border exposed to endemic raids and marauding: the northern magnates looked to the crown for help to repulse and extinguish these threats. By 1310, therefore, when Edward moved his court and government to York in order to escape the inhibiting surveillance of the Ordainers, he did so ostensibly to combat the Scottish menace.

In the next few years, with nobles divided among themselves and often hostile to, or suspicious of, the king, efforts to resolve the Scottish problem proved as unavailing as they were costly and fitful. The nadir was reached when at Bannockburn in 1314 the English army was annihilated by the Scots under Robert Bruce. The circumstances of the battle are less important than its result which discredited the king and restored support for the earl of Lancaster and the advocates of the Ordinances. Now, however, the Scots were more audacious and belligerent than ever, and Lancaster was the heir to Edward's problems, particularly as the earl raised quite as many qualms and suspicions as the king did; there was even talk of him allying with the Scots in order to defeat his English enemies. From 1316 when Lancaster's power was at its height, until 1323, when Edward once again had full control of the government and the thirteen-year truce was concluded, Scottish forces ravaged northern England almost as far south as the Humber, plundering and impoverishing the clergy no less than the laity of that region.

A vivid impression of these destructive years emerges from contemporary chronicles and episcopal registers. In 1315 when the four northernmost counties were raided and Carlisle was besieged, Archbishop Greenfield, independently of the king, held two 'parliaments' – at York and Doncaster – of barons, knights and clergy in order to decide upon defence measures.[16] The following year the Scots penetrated as far as Swaledale and Richmondshire, burning villages and seizing or killing resisters: on this occasion Holme Cultram abbey lost livestock valued at £500. Two years later, in 1318, the Scots captured Berwick after twenty years in English possession and then advanced southwards almost to Pontefract: while burgesses of Ripon escaped the sacking of their town by payment of a thousand marks, just a few miles away the monks of Fountains abbey were similarly purchasing mercy from the invaders. Meanwhile, in the north-west, Carlisle cathedral and neighbouring houses were burnt to the ground so that the clergy had, as one chronicler put it, nowhere to lay their heads. The bishop of Carlisle was so impoverished by Scottish raids – his goods being carried off and his fields left uncultivated – that he petitioned the pope for licence to appropriate Horncastle church, in Lincoln diocese, for his relief. When in 1319 Berwick was the target of an English siege, led by the king, the Scots countered with a devastating expedition – allegedly of some 15,000 men – to Myton on Swale. There they were met by a force mustered from local people by Archbishop Melton, Bishop Hotham of Ely (who was chancellor of the realm), the dean of York, and the abbots of York and Selby. The carnage which ensued cost many lives, the chroniclers offering totals of 1000 killed and 3000 drowned in the Swale. Among the dead, apart from laymen like the mayor of York, were many priests and clerks, both seculars and regulars; among the captured was William Ayermine, chief clerk of the chancery, who was ransomed subsequently for 2000 marks and lived to become bishop of Norwich in 1325. For a while after that, the Scots were satisfied and the English forces discouraged and anyway distracted by domestic politics.

By the summer of 1322 Edward felt secure enough at home to embark on a final solution of the Scottish problem. In July he led a great army against the Scots, but their Fabian tactics and 'scorched-earth' policy defeated his efforts even to relieve Berwick; he returned to England 'with nothing done worth writing about', as one chronicler put it, and disbanded the major part of his army.[17] Soon after Michaelmas, however, Bruce descended with his own considerable force into England, defeated the king at Blackhowe Moor (near Rievaulx abbey) and almost captured him in Byland abbey, which along with Rievaulx was then sacked. The earl of Richmond was captured, Ripon and York were raided and many laity and clergy were killed; even Beverley was within the range of the Scots, but there the burgesses and canons saved their lives by paying a ransom of £400. A few miles to the south-west of Beverley the Scots raised their standard on the beacon at Hunsley, which marks almost the southern end of the Wolds and looks out across the Humber to Lincolnshire and across the Vale of York towards Selby and Doncaster. On 15 October hastening back from Berwick, the king, the earl of Kent, Hugh Despenser the younger, and the rest of the court arrived at Bridlington priory where they spent the night before retreating to Burstwick, in Holderness. Up on the Wolds, the Scots were looting and killing at Malton and around the villages of Kilham and Rudston; shrewdly the prior of Bridlington sent a Scottish-born canon to Malton to negotiate for the safety of his house, while at the same time the priory prudently removed all its muniments, vestments and precious relics (a piece of the true cross among them) to Goxhill, in Lincolnshire, and left only eight canons with one chalice in Bridlington. From Malton the Scots sent no fewer than nine men and eighteen horses to Bridlington to take as much bread, wine and beer as they wished in exchange for a somewhat qualified immunity. A fortnight later, on 22 October, the Scots withdrew northwards and soon after that the Bridlington community returned from Goxhill with their treasures. In the new year a renewed truce brought some respite to the north.[18]

Accompanying and often preceding this destruction there was taxation. To establish his credibility against the Scots, in the years from 1313 to 1316 especially, the king needed money on a considerable scale. To pay for the force raised to repel invasion in 1313, Edward extracted loans, varying from 300 to 500 marks (roughly £200 to £350), from his bishops: Swinfield of Hereford, for example, was asked for £200, though he refused because of his great costs and slender income.[19] In 1314 the northern clergy were asked by the king for an 'aid' for his projected campaign against the Scots, a request repeated to them and the southern clergy in 1316. By then, however, such was the devastation of churches and church lands that although the York clergy granted a tenth, which was to be collected in two instalments during 1317 (a delay eloquent of their difficulties), they successfully insisted on a revised valuation of their livings: instead of the tenth being levied on the 1291 valor, compiled before the Scottish war began, it was to be calculated according to the true current valuation of livings, a reduced level which endured for the rest of the Middle Ages. This relief, it may be added, was matched for a while by the exemption of some forty villages in the West Riding in 1319, and of 128 villages in the North Riding in 1322, from lay taxes because of the scale of their poverty resulting from the Scottish raids. Increasingly the Scottish war and the defence of the north had to be financed by taxes from the southern clergy and laity.

Edward's desire to rid himself of the burden and embarrassment
of Scotland was shared not only by his subjects but also by the
pope, whose concern for peace in England, a prerequisite for a
crusade, was once again evident. In 1317 he sent two cardinals to
mediate between Edward and Bruce, who was regarded by John
XXII as a pretender. After talks with Edward, and having
survived robbery with violence in Durham diocese, the cardinals
found themselves excluded from Scotland by Bruce. Returning to
London eventually, and still attempting to arrange the peace for
which they were empowered, they stayed on for a second year,
accumulating benefices and sustained by clerical procurations
meanwhile. From there in Michaelmas 1317 the cardinals promulgated a two-year truce, but since they would not recognize Bruce's
claims to the Scottish crown he ignored their pronouncements and
prepared to launch another attack on the north of England. In
response the cardinals excommunicated Bruce and all the Scottish
people before withdrawing to Rome. By their venality as well as by
their failure, these papal emissaries left behind them no very
happy impression among the English of aliens or cardinals.

When in 1320 the pope summoned Bruce and the Scottish
bishops to answer in Rome for their obduracy, Bruce sued for
peace, having selected or agreed to the king of France as mediator.
Two years later, however, with negotiations still incomplete,
Edward embarked on his abortive campaign with the results
described above. It was after that that Edward gratefully accepted
the thirteen-year truce which Bruce offered on less than favourable
terms. Perhaps the terms rankled, for when in the following year
Bruce sued at Rome for the lifting of the interdict Edward II sent
envoys, the chronicler Adam of Murimuth among them, to oppose
such a relaxation, a task in which they succeeded. Both antagonists, however, were by now either too weak politically or too
preoccupied to resume serious hostilities for the moment. Now the
pope had a new anxiety over the English crusade, threatened by an
Anglo-French dispute in Gascony.

The Scottish war added a dangerous dimension to the internal
politics of Edward's reign, impoverishing crown, clergy and laity,
embarrassing in turn both king and barons by humiliating defeats
or abortive campaigns. The clergy of the north were so deeply

afflicted at all levels by the fighting, the destruction and the taxation that one crucial consequence of the Scottish war in this era was the permanent reduction in the tax assessment of the northern province, and therefore in the tax yield with which the king was able to meet his war costs. The agonies of the north, both for the local populace and for the king and realm, were by no means at an end yet, but in Edward II's reign they reached a scale unapproached before and not exceeded afterwards.

Taxation and the Establishment of Convocation

The huge debts which Edward inherited from his father were not redeemed until the last four years of his reign when a lengthy if fragile truce with Scotland, together with reform and refinement of treasury administration, and ruthless exactions from the Contrariants and any other offenders, enabled Edward II to leave, as no subsequent medieval king was to do, a solvent crown to his successor. Before 1322, however, because of his often fraught relations with the magnates, Edward relied heavily upon the church for essential funds.

It is a remarkable fact that although Edward II received almost £240,000 in taxes from his clergy, for three quarters of that amount he was indebted to the papacy; Edward managed to get his hands on 92 per cent of the papal tenths imposed on the English clergy in his reign.[20] An outstanding papal tenth from his father's reign was collected in December 1307; in 1309 a triennial tenth was ordered and in 1313 a sexennial tenth. Of nearly £200,000 which was raised by these mandatory papal levies, the king received almost £180,000. Usually two bishops were appointed as papal collectors, and in 1313–14 London and Lincoln paid the proceeds of the last triennial tenth directly into the exchequer and wardrobe or to royal officers and creditors; arrears were to be paid to the exchequer. In that same year the first instalment of a sexennial tenth was also collected, and from it, after taking the cross, Edward received a loan which he never repaid. From June 1313 to April 1314 the clergy had yielded about £40,000 in such taxes. The regularity and the mandatory nature of these papal levies caused one chronicler to lament that the pope made 'greater exactions from the clergy, than the emperor himself from the laity'.[21]

In fact, the king had some difficulty in extracting grants directly from the clergy. At the beginning of his reign in the parliament of 1307 they assented to a fifteenth, but seven more years passed before the clergy again conceded any more: York province offered a small sum to ward off the Scots in 1314, and Canterbury reluctantly, and upon certain conditions, granted a tenth in January 1315. In 1316, however, the southern clergy met three times before they finally capitulated towards the end of the year and authorized the collection of a tenth; even then, it was to be delivered in two moieties, one in 1317, the other in 1318. Furthermore the clergy extracted as a *quid pro quo* some deceptively reassuring royal answers to their grievances, the answers known as the *Articuli Cleri* or 'Articles of the Clergy'. In 1319 a royal request for a grant was referred by the clergy to the pope who eventually allowed a tenth. These modest successes apart, the king faced refusals of taxation in 1311, 1313, 1314 (twice, though he finally got a positive response), 1315, 1322 and 1324. Without papal assistance, crown finances would have been in even more desperate straits than in fact they were. Although it is certainly true that papal levies were one spur to clerical refusals of the king, the clergy conducted a vigilant campaign to defend their rights and immunities with regard to taxation. On some occasions, as in 1319, they invoked the bull *Clericis Laicos*; on others, they raised various objections to the procedures adopted by the king, sometimes protesting against the writ of summons, sometimes against the venue, sometimes against the presence of royal lay councillors in their assembly. Edward II's reign saw a battle not just over royal taxes of the clergy, but about the body which should assent to these taxes. Between 1313 and 1322, with the help of Archbishop Reynolds, Edward II tried to extract grants from the clergy by means of their parliamentary proctors, but so obstinate were their objections and so counter-productive, politically as well as financially, were these attempts that by 1322 the king was content to seek subsidies through clerical assemblies and not parliament.[22]

It was in the king's interest to tax the clergy in parliament, which was a national and indisputably royal assembly, the king's high court. Clerical representatives, after all, sat in it almost as often as their lay counterparts who consented to lay subsidies: in seventeen out of the nineteen of Edward II's parliaments to which knights and burgesses were summoned there were also clerical proctors present. The clergy, however, preferred to discuss these matters in provincial clerical synods where they governed the procedures and priorities. In May 1314 they maintained that they could be taxed only in their own assemblies; when Edward tried to proceed through parliament he often found himself thwarted – as in January 1316 – by the inadequate attendance of the clergy. As an alternative, he tried on occasions to tax them in assemblies which were not parliaments nor yet independent clerical gatherings, but he alarmed the clergy either by the writs which he used then or by the presence of his lay councillors at the meetings. The king's writ ordering the archbishop to convene such an assembly contained the phrase *mandamus . . . venire faciatis*, 'we command you are to make them come', which was the wording of a common law writ used to compel attendance in a law court, before a royal judge. Acquiescence in, or acceptance of, this wording would therefore imply that convocation, too, was another royal court at the mercy of royal directions as to its procedure and business. Protests against the writs were lodged in 1314, 1315 and 1316. Objections were also raised (as in 1314) to being called to meet in Westminster, the usual venue of parliament, instead of at St Paul's, the normal place for gatherings of the southern clergy; in 1322 the southern clergy objected to a summons to meet at York in the northern province; in May 1314 and April 1316 objections were raised to the presence of lay councillors of the king. On several occasions – as in January 1316 – a grant was frustrated by the absence of many of the proctors who should have been there. After 1322 the king dropped the offending phrases and recognized that the clergy would have to be taxed in their own assemblies, initiated by, but otherwise independent of, himself. While Archbishop Reynolds and some other bishops and royal clerks colluded with the king, the lower clergy presented stout resistance, precisely as they had done in 1294 when they were also invited to pay for the tune played by the prelates. It was the lesser clergy who frustrated the king's attempt to smudge the distinctions to his own advantage, so that by 1322 parliament was virtually eliminated as the place to raise clerical subsidies, and convocation was no longer summoned by the offending writ. The institutional, legal and procedural definition of convocation had not been clear in 1307 nor was it finally resolved by 1327: the clergy were struggling to free themselves from the enveloping quicksand of parliament, the king's high court, and to reach the firm ground of an autonomous clerical assembly, no part of the king's court (with all that that implied) and free from the intimidating presence, or intrusion, of those royal councillors who were laymen. Parliament was an assembly over which the clergy had no theoretical control, however much weight they might wield within it in practice; convocation was a provincial – not a national – assembly, and, though often summoned on the king's nod, it met by, and laid down, its own procedures and determined its own composition.

Convocation, by 1327 no longer confusable with parliament, was assimilated to the clergy's own provincial synod. In January 1326 Reynolds recorded that he had not convened a council of prelates and clergy since 1323 because the king had expressed his wish that none should meet without his consent, even though by canon law provincial synods should take place annually. This identity of provincial synods with convocations was strengthened because such synods were seldom assembled thereafter except on the king's initiative and for the principal purpose of consenting to royal taxation. No doubt this was for the good practical reason that as royal taxation became more frequent separate and additional councils for the church's own business became more inconvenient: there was a limit to the number of times the clergy could be summoned from their parishes and livings to provincial assemblies in London or elsewhere. In any case, many royal clerks would see no sharp distinction between royal and church business or between clerical taxation and clerical reform, both of which were relevant to the well-being of the church: for many clergy, as indeed for Winchelsey, the solvency of the crown was part of their responsibility for the Christian commonwealth. If the clergy had gained – and continuing practice had yet to confirm this – the right to be taxed in their own assemblies rather than in parliament, they had exposed those gatherings to royal attention, intervention and considerable control. The price which the clergy paid for exemption from taxation in parliament was the encroachment of the king upon, and the dominance of his business within, their own provincial synods. The independence which they had won was qualified, and in the long run the king lost little by this switch: he could still tax the clergy – and did so frequently – and he could convoke them when it would have been impolitic to convene the laity in parliament.

Prelates, of course, continued to be summoned individually to parliament, and the representatives of the clergy attended parliament long after they ceased in 1322 to assent there to clerical taxation. Although the presence of the proctors was probably in order to assent to the lay taxes which fell upon the clergy's temporalities, from 1341 at least they were no longer *required* to attend; they were still summoned, but their absence from parliament was not deemed prejudicial to the king, no doubt because it could no longer delay or frustrate clerical taxation which was now in the hands of another body.

Of all the varied assemblies, other than parliament, through which the king attempted to elicit taxation, that of the clergy alone endured. This is surely to be explained by the paramount corporate and legal sense of identity which the clergy enjoyed and by the institutional roots which convocation had in the church's own provincial councils; the assembly of merchants, for example, was nothing like so well established or defined.

Anglo–Papal Relations

The suspicions which Englishmen voiced about papal intervention in the realm had various roots, but one of them was surely the disproportionately small representation of the English church in the Curia.[23] Between 1309 and 1376 there were only twenty-four English curialists when Spain had fifty, the Empire sixty-nine, Italy five hundred and twenty-one and France over fifteen hundred; under Clement V (as Anglophile as any pope in this era) only one Englishman was a member of the papal Curia; under John XXII no more than nine. As for cardinals, after Kilwardby's death in 1310 there were no more English bishops among them until Langham in 1368 and only four others – three Dominicans in this reign and Adam Easton later – before 1378, compared with fourteen Italian and one hundred and twelve French cardinals. It is not surprising, therefore, that Edward II felt it necessary to deluge the pope and the cardinals with letters informing them of his circumstances, hopes and needs: in the course of his reign he sent nearly eighty letters a year to the cardinals; in the first year of John XXII's pontificate no fewer than 306 royal letters were addressed to members of the college of cardinals. Without influential subjects serving about the pope, the king had to enlist the utmost support which he could muster among the cardinals in order to shape the papal response to his demands. Yet letters by themselves were inadequate instruments and of limited effect without the advocacy of royal ambassadors: from 1305 to 1334 at least twenty-five royal delegates were sent to the pope. These emissaries often bore gifts as well as eloquent words: since at least the early thirteenth century royal pensions were granted to promising or influential cardinals – to eighteen at least of the seventy-two who there were between 1305 and 1334, to six alone in 1309 when the royal mission secured papal backing for Gaveston's recall. The importance of the papacy and the college of cardinals for internal English politics – not to mention foreign relations – could hardly be more eloquently attested.

This evidence does not include the many English benefices which cardinals and curial officials obtained and mulcted. Some of these livings they were certainly granted by the influence of English churchmen and the king, eager to retain representatives at the Curia, but the majority seem to have been acquired through papal provision: the pope was remunerating his servants out of the English church's endowments, much to the growing fury of English patrons and politicians. During the pontificates of Clement V and John XXII (1305–34) twenty-nine cardinals claimed some one hundred and three livings in England, especially canonries and prebends in the cathedrals of York, Lincoln and Salisbury; moreover, sixty other papal officials were beneficed in England, some at the instigation of the crown. Curial clergy who displaced local candidates and took abroad native revenues did so with royal approval or acquiescence.

Throughout Edward's reign papal policy towards England was dominated by a concern for peace within the realm. Clement V provided Reynolds to Canterbury so 'that peace might be preserved to Edward and his realm': Reynolds was ordered to conduct affairs differently from the contentious Winchelsey 'so as to temper the rancour between the king and his nobles, hoping to benefit the church thereby'.[24] John XXII repeatedly expressed the same hopes in his correspondence with Reynolds. This concern of both popes was voiced and manifested by the frequent nuncios and legates whom they sent to arrange peace between the king and his barons, or between England and Scotland, or between England and France. In 1312 Clement V sent his vice-chancellor of the Curia and his chamberlain to resolve the conflict over Gaveston; in 1316–17 another mission was involved with the realignment of parties; and in 1326 the pope gave his backing to the queen only after his envoys had failed to achieve an Anglo-French peace between Charles IV and Edward II. The most vigorous intervention concerned Scotland, but its success by no means matched its efforts.

Edward II particularly profited from the almost unctuous service of Pope Clement V: he it was who absolved the king from Archbishop Winchelsey's curses and from his own various oaths; it was Clement who appointed Reynolds, the king's chaplain and treasurer, to Worcester and translated him to Canterbury to the exclusion of the eminently qualified capitular candidate, Thomas de Cobham; above all, Clement alleviated Edward's poverty with papal subsidies. It is sometimes implied that all this changed when that shrewd lawyer, John XXII, became pope, yet he readily promoted a number of Edward's episcopal candidates; moreover, from John, no less than from Clement, Edward II received the bounty of papal taxation of the clergy. John, like Clement, worked hard to secure the king at home and abroad so that he might one day embark on the crusade: the barons, the Scots, and the French were all pressured by John on Edward's behalf. Edward elicited these favours despite remarkable effrontery towards papal jurisdiction and patronage: in pursuit of royal rights of patronage at the expense of papal claims and expectations, Edward II was even more blatant than Edward I had been, and in 1309 and 1317 papal grievances went unregarded and unanswered.

Once again pluralism was the subject of papal revision, but this time no conflict with the crown ensued. By the bull *Execrabilis* in 1317 John XXII revoked all dispensations for plurality granted by previous popes and required the resignation of excess livings. Something over two hundred vacancies resulted in the immediate aftermath and a trickle of further resignations followed for some years to come. Half these benefices, however, were filled by their lay patrons, and of the rest most devolved, in consequence of alert and vigorous episcopal action, upon the diocesan bishop rather than upon the pope. No vast increase of papal provisions ensued as a result of this bull; nor did much royal embarrassment, still less the end of pluralism. Probably the king's enterprising patronage in other ways and his need of papal financial and political support help to explain the want of any crisis then in contrast with 1279–81. Although John cancelled his predecessors' grants, neither he nor subsequent popes abstained from issuing new dispensations to pluralists.[25]

Appeals to Rome were apt to receive from Edward II the same vigorous attention as from his father when they touched on royal interests. Prohibitions of such appeals in the thirteenth century had often cited for their authority a papal indult of 1231 in which Gregory IX had conceded that the magnates and barons of England should not be summoned in litigation beyond the sea, a privilege subsequently generalized to all the king's English subjects and soon known as the privilege of England. By the early fourteenth century, however, both king and pope were embarrassed by this: Edward I and Edward II because they preferred to invoke royal prerogative and national custom; the pope because he was anxious to disown, tacitly at least, any such concession. After this reign no more was heard of the papal basis for barring appeals to, and litigation at, the Curia.[26]

Bishops and Bishoprics

Out of twenty-eight appointments to bishoprics in Edward's reign, some of these made while Clement V was pope, no fewer than thirteen resulted from provisions by John XXII. Six of these enjoyed the king's blessing and it is noteworthy that the number of royal clerks holding bishoprics markedly increased after John's accession in 1316. Yet when he wished, John could act with adamant disregard for the king's will or interests; six bishops were provided despite the king's fierce objections, while some of the king's favourite candidates were ignored. On the one hand John promoted Adam Orleton in 1317 to Hereford against the king's express wishes. (One may note that in 1327 John translated Orleton to Worcester against Mortimer's opposition, and in 1333 to Winchester in defiance of Edward III.) On the other hand Edward II tried in vain to get Robert Baldock provided to Lichfield in 1321, to Winchester in 1323 and to Norwich in 1325; Baldock never did become a bishop. Of course, a web of complex circumstances operated in each of these appointments against the royal will: both Orleton and Stratford, who were among John's favoured candidates, were also royal diplomats. Subsequent popes would exercise their right to provide far more often and much more widely than John did, but never again would a king of England be quite so impotent in the choice of his bishops.

John XXII's independence came as a shock to Edward II, for no pope could have been more obliging to the king than Clement V, himself a former royal clerk. We have seen how Clement saved Edward I by papal taxation of the clergy and by suspension of Archbishop Winchelsey. Edward II began his reign by recalling Winchelsey in disregard of Clement's advice; when the archbishop sided with the Ordainers against Gaveston and the king, Clement commented, 'the truth is contained in the book of your experience.'[27] Popes, especially such as Clement, found men like Winchelsey – all inflexible integrity and principle – a political embarrassment, and what Clement sought was a unified realm ruled over by a king who was prepared to go on crusade, assisted by a primate who would readily raise the papal taxes to pay for it. When Winchelsey died in 1313, therefore, pope and king colluded to ensure that just such a successor was appointed. The monks of Canterbury chapter elected Thomas de Cobham, canon lawyer, theologian and royal diplomat. Cobham, however, smacked too much of the schoolroom, having already achieved distinction as a

writer about confession: learning, especially when tainted by
theological or pastoral concern, was by now seen to be a dangerous
thing in an archbishop. Cobham might adorn a diplomatic mission
but would surely mismanage a key political post such as that of
Canterbury's archbishopric. When Edward delayed his consent to
the election, Clement, whose own preference was for Walter
Langton, reserved the see, but in October 1313 translated Walter
Reynolds from Worcester to Canterbury where he remained until
his death in November 1327.

Walter Reynolds has been condemned as an illiterate and
unprincipled time-server, lacking in strength of character and
nobility of vision. By comparison with his three immediate
predecessors – Kilwardby, Pecham and Winchelsey – he may well
appear near illiterate, and, except for Hubert Walter in the 1190s,
he was the first archbishop to combine the primacy with the
chancellorship of the realm, which tended rather to compromise
the first than the second office. However, although he was not a
graduate – let alone a doctor – his library, his sermons and his
correspondence bear witness to his literacy, his reading and his
biblical knowledge; his liberality with licences for study while he
was bishop of Worcester, his concerned letters to the masters of
Cambridge University while he was archbishop, his interest in
Merton College, Oxford, and his encouragement of the Benedictines to go to Oxford all demonstrate the value which he placed on
learning. Nor can the charge of time-serving be wholly accepted of
a prelate who was on good terms with John XXII, who protested
against the king's retention of the Templars' lands, and whose
piety was esteemed by contemporaries. That he opposed Winchelsey earlier only aligned him with popes and realists; that his
appointment to Canterbury involved both the exclusion of a
saintly scholar and expedient intervention by the pope was hardly
of his doing or proof of his unsuitability; that he readily undertook
to secure taxes from reluctant clergy only looks unprincipled
against the background of thirteenth-century prelates who had yet
to adjust to the vast needs and new methods of kings everywhere.
It has been said that he provided no leadership and lacked control
of the episcopate, and it is clear that he waited on events in 1326–7,
only casting his lot with Isabella and Mortimer when the king's

cause was obviously lost. Leadership, however, is not to be thought of only in terms of resistance to the crown. What happened under Winchelsey in 1297–1305 endangered both church and realm, threatening to sever them so sharply and deeply that the church would end up a wholly dependent, deeply suspected and despised branch of royal government. Reynolds worked to win the church political esteem and influence through its contributions to affairs of state. That he could not command the bench of bishops into a unified stance on political affairs reflects less upon him than upon the variety of episcopal origins and experience: royal clerks may have been increasing among the bishops, but it is a mistake to regard them as if they were all identical in background and outlook. In any case, not all bishops had sympathized with Winchelsey, whose tactless and blundering adherence to principle divided the bench. Reynolds sought to unite them by avoiding unnecessary controversy.

Reynolds's role in the deposition should be regarded as creditable rather than shameful, for his oath and loyalty to the king were sustained until the cause was obviously lost; at that point his concern for public order, for the good of the church and the realm, dictated his choice of acquiescence instead of futile hostility. In 1326–7 he was not a king-maker (or -saver), partly because a legitimate heir was to hand, but possibly because he could not muster the opposition of prelates generally to Edward II's removal. When pope, barons and many bishops, as well as the queen and apparently the royal heir, were largely agreed, Reynolds could not hold back the tide of change. He was indisputably a loyal servant of Edward II, but he was not the will-less, visionless opportunist which his skilful pragmatism may suggest. Better than recent holders of Canterbury, he recognized the new realities of church and realm relations in the era of chronic war and royal taxation.

Prominent among the king's clerks was Walter Stapledon who became bishop of Exeter in 1308 and eventually paid with his life for his loyal service to the crown.[28] As a civil lawyer he was much employed in diplomatic business, but in the 1320s he was twice appointed treasurer and spent his time in that office supervising and organizing the more efficient collection of taxes, fines and forfeitures. The hostility which this aroused, as well as his role as royal guardian of London, resulted in his death at the hands of a furious mob and he thus became the first bishop since Becket to be murdered. Other prelates were to repeat his experience before our period ended, but significantly in each case, as in his, the murder was occasioned by service to the crown and not by defence of the church. It has been calculated that while Stapledon spent just under half his time before the 1320s in his diocese, once he became treasurer barely a tenth of his time was passed at Exeter; he relied instead upon the machinery of deputies to maintain his authority and execute his wishes there. The more royal clerks – whether administrators and diplomats or chaplains and confessors – became bishops, the more typical was Stapledon's apportionment of his energies and travel, and the more vital became the presence of professionally competent agents fulfilling the roles of vicars-general, officials principal, commissaries, and sequestrators in the diocese. Episcopal registers amply attest the development of this system.

The Suppression of the Templars

Largely as a result of machinations and pressure by the king of France, the Order of Knights Templar was subjected to papal scrutiny in 1308 and condemned to dissolution in 1312. Their lands, which had been seized by the crown in 1308, by papal decree should have been transferred in 1312 to the Order of the Hospitallers, but in England this transfer was not carried out for some years, during which the king continued to profit from the estates.[29] The Templar lands were declared to be lay fee and therefore forfeit to the crown on the dissolution of the Order; any attempts to challenge this were soon quashed by writs of prohibition. The king enjoyed their fruits either by direct exploitation or by granting the lands out for political reasons to some of the nobility – Lancaster, Pembroke and even the Despensers, for example. The Hospitallers, backed by Archbishop Reynolds, protested, but not until 1324 did a statute grant the land formally to them. Even after that statute, however, it was probably not until 1338 that the king yielded up nominal, let alone actual, possession. Since the lands of the Templars in England were worth nearly £3000 annually, the reluctance of Edward II, no less than of Edward III, to surrender them needs no great explanation. In this the English kings were no doubt encouraged by the similar practices of the French king as well as by the knowledge that the pope himself thwarted the hopes of Hospitallers in respect of some lands.

Apart from the gains in revenue and patronage, the seizure of the Templar lands has another significance. Although it might be construed in England as a joint papal and royal dissolution of a religious order and its houses, the statute of 1324 in waiving the king's rights over the forfeited property omitted all mention of a papal grant to the Hospitallers and thus left on the statute book an impression of autonomous royal action. The king and his judges were already acting on the assumption that all ecclesiastical endowments within the realm were originally held by and from the crown, to which they should therefore revert if and when a church failed of its purpose. The idea of 'patron paramount', implied in respect of the king's regalian rights, had a commodious significance. Already Edward I had briefly confiscated the property of alien religious houses, and Edward II's seizure of the Templars' lands – neither acknowledged nor perhaps intended to be permanent – was strikingly similar to his father's action in essence. By the time Edward III finally divested himself of the Templar lands, in 1338, he had already resumed the alien priories for the duration of the war and was thus compensated for any losses resulting. Indeed, the statute of 1324 coincided with an earlier seizure of alien priories by Edward II and may itself have been intended to palliate that action. Thus from 1308 until the end of his reign, as a consequence of French and papal connivance coupled with resolute disregard of the letter of the law, Edward II enjoyed a welcome addition to his revenues and patronage. To a large extent the Templar lands served to tide the crown over until the alien priories, briefly confiscated in 1324–6, were seized again from 1337 until 1361.

The King's Clerical Servants

During Edward's reign, and particularly in the 1320s, government administration and bureaucracy grew in scale and complexity.[30] To a large extent these developments were stimulated by the king's desperate need for finance, but his exploitation of the political defeat of the Contrariants also involved a massive administrative operation: both factors explain why the expansion largely took place in the treasury and exchequer. From 1318 new compendium rolls were ordered which involved a vast collection and collation of information from justices and others; even before then, exchequer summonses had tripled in number; furthermore, in the spring of 1321 a record was started of all royal gifts dispensed since the beginning of the reign. As a result of reforms ordained at Cowick in 1323, pipe rolls (which recorded the shire revenues of the crown) grew to be triple and quadruple the size they were under Edward I; rolls and writs of the treasury of receipt increased by five or six times; for the extensive Contrariant lands separate memoranda were compiled; new calendars were introduced to record estreats, matters despatched at the exchequer and accounts to be rendered. As a consequence of these changes alone, four new clerks and an additional baron were added to the exchequer staff, but further developments were yet to come. In 1325 escheators were made responsible for keeping duplicates of inquisitions of *diem clausit* and of returns to chancery; in 1326 a calendar of Contrariant lands was begun, a roll of serjeanties in various counties compiled and further auditors were appointed. Such a formidable enlargement of business and records entailed a corresponding increase not only in the responsible officers listed above but also among the common clerks who wrote and shelved the records. Yet what was going on in the exchequer and treasury was only symptomatic of changes throughout government, from chancery to wardrobe and chamber, from the great seal to the privy seal. This is the background to the ever fiercer competition between king and pope for patronage in the church of England.

Some idea of the importance of clergy in sustaining royal administration can be gained by a survey of the secular cathedrals of the realm. The proportion of absentee canons at each is a good indicator of royal exploitation,[31] which obviously was directed at the better endowed prebends. Whereas in Exeter cathedral, where endowments were modest and equally divided among the chapter members, only a quarter of the twenty-four canons were non-resident during Edward II's reign, in the cathedrals of York, Lincoln, Wells, Salisbury and Lichfield between two thirds and three quarters of the canons were occupied elsewhere. At York in 1321, thirteen king's clerks occupied fourteen of its thirty-six prebends; among these royal servants were the keeper of the chancery rolls, three chancery masters, various chancery clerks, the keeper of the privy seal, a baron of the exchequer and the keeper of the wardrobe. At Lincoln in that year ten prebends were in the possession of royal clerks; at Salisbury and London seven in each were held by royal clerks; at Lichfield five, and at Hereford four. Of the nine secular cathedrals in England, the deans at York, Lichfield and Wells were royal clerks, and out of fifty-two archdeacons sixteen were king's clerks – three out of five at York, four out of eight at Lincoln. That year William Ayermine, a senior chancery master, held canonries in six cathedrals and at four of those one of his fellow canons was Roger Northburgh, keeper of the wardrobe, who held two more prebends elsewhere: both soon after this became bishops. Collegiate churches were just as vulnerable to royal exploitation, especially if they were one of the royal free chapels – e.g. Windsor or Hastings – which resembled colleges of royal officials rather than religious foundations.[32]

Bishops who themselves were, or had been, royal clerks often commended to the king's service their own clerks and servants, and equally often found benefices for royal king's clerks. Under the first three Edwards when the government was located in York in order to conduct the war against the Scots – or to evade political constraints at Westminster – the archbishop of York's household became an important source of royal clerks, especially during Melton's tenure of the see (1316–40); these Yorkshire clerks dominated the chancery of Edward II and were also influential in the exchequer and wardrobe. With some justification Dr Grassi, who has studied this particular recruitment, has concluded that at this time 'the road to Westminster passed through York'.[33]

Royal patronage was by no means limited to cathedral and

collegiate prebends, which were often too valuable to be suitable and were also plundered by the pope for his servants; parish livings, too, were increasingly invaded by the king's men. In twenty-five years Edward II promoted his servants to more than 1400 benefices of all kinds.[34] His patronage was extended not only by the forfeited estates of Lancaster, Badlesmere and the Contrariants but also by the confiscated temporalities of bishops such as Langton (at the beginning of the reign) and Stratford, Orleton and Burghersh (at the end). The acquisition of Templar estates and of alien priories likewise enlarged the openings for royal clerks. Meanwhile, Edward exercised his regalian rights in vacant sees even more forcefully than his father had done. Not merely did he claim to present to livings retrospectively in his own reign but even to vacancies which had occurred *sede vacante* in his father's reign! Under Edward II judges increasingly followed the precedents set earlier, notably with regard to the definition of vicarages as temporal. Thus Hartburn vicarage which in 1284, during a vacancy of Durham bishopric, had been regarded as spiritual and left alone by Edward I, was in 1311 declared temporal and claimed by Edward II.[35]

Since the days of Henry III at least, kings had claimed from each newly elected bishop and from some monastic superiors a living or pension for a royal clerk. This particularly applied in the hundred or so religious houses of royal foundation but by the early fourteenth century the king was extending the custom to the newly elect of other institutions; not less frequently he requested a corrody (or board and lodging) for an ageing royal clerk or household servant. Throughout the realm the burdens of government which were borne in this way were substantial. Even before he became king, Edward sent out some ninety-four letters to religious superiors asking for benefices, pensions and corrodies for his clerks, and in the course of his reign over four hundred and fifty requests for corrodies, addressed to over two hundred houses, have been counted in just the *Calendar of Close Rolls*; between 1308 and 1327 Worcester priory received no fewer than fifty-one royal requests on behalf of royal servants.[36] There should be borne in mind the pressures exerted upon, or anticipated by, religious houses to use their resources to please the king even between elections. This was the context in which John XXII told the king *c.*1318 that 'the state of ecclesiastical dignity is in the realm of England more notably depressed, or rather its liberty crushed, than in all other parts of the world'.[37]

Lost Opportunities

It is difficult to point to any area where the church gained at the expense of the monarchy in Edward II's reign. It is true that the liberties of the church were proclaimed in a number of public documents – the Ordinances of 1311, the *Articuli Cleri* of 1316 – but these assurances were as vague as they were hackneyed and ephemeral, and in practice the king exploited the church even more ruthlessly than his father had done for revenues, patronage and manpower.

While the clergy successfully defended their claim to be taxed in convocation and not in parliament, this really made little difference to the king's income or, indeed, to the vulnerability of the clergy before his demands.

If papal provisions worked in some instances under John XXII to the disadvantage of the king, the pope endeavoured where he could to satisfy the king's wishes, so that at the end of the reign far more bishoprics were occupied by civil servants than in 1307. The alliance of king and pope ensured that no more Winchelseys became archbishops.

By further eroding the definition of *spiritualia*, the regalian exploitation of episcopal vacancies was now so extended that Edward claimed to fill livings – vicarages as well as rectories – emptied during an episcopal vacancy retrospectively, even if it had occurred during his father's reign. The impetus for these practices came from the need to remunerate the rapidly expanding number of clerks in royal service. A crucial result was that cathedral and parish clergy were increasingly infiltrated by men whose loyalties looked more to the king than the pope, to the realm rather than to the church.

Even the papacy under John XXII, who is so often contrasted as the strong man to Edward's weakling, gained little if any significant advantage to the detriment of the king. John needed Edward as much as Edward needed him, and no pope in that age would be eager to overthrow a king and encourage anarchy. Nor was there any issue between pope and king large enough to suggest such a notion. Only when Edward's unpopularity at home threatened to scuttle the crusade to which he was – somewhat loosely – committed, did John acquiesce in deposition; and then he was assured of a decent monarchical substitute in the person of the young Prince Edward. For the rest of the time Edward gained from John financial support through clerical taxes, and personal and political aid through the provision of some of his clerks to bishoprics and canonries. Both Clement V and John XXII sought to bring internal harmony to the realm by throwing their weight behind Edward and not his baronial opponents. Only at the end, when John saw the futility of this, did he countenance the opposition's cause.

3
Edward III (1327–77)
War and the Church

Edward III began his reign at the age of fourteen as the protégé of the queen mother and her ambitious collaborator, Mortimer, but their grip on affairs was quickly loosened by the manner and policy of their government. Mortimer, who dominated the council, wielded power with no more tact and delicacy than had the Despensers or Edward II; Henry of Lancaster, Mortimer's erstwhile ally, was excluded from policy-making in 1328, and in 1330 the earl of Kent was accused of conspiracy and summarily executed, much to the alarm of the other nobles. The loyalty of the nobles, as indeed of the people generally, had already been tested by the humiliating treaty of Northampton in 1328, by which Mortimer and Isabella bought peace with Scotland at such a price as to recall the sickening defeat at Bannockburn fourteen years before. Among churchmen, even those few bishops who had given enthusiastic support to the coup of 1327 had done so largely out of exasperation with the Despensers' greed on the Marches or with royal failure to defend the north against Scotland: such personal links as they may have had with Isabella and Mortimer were strained both by a peace which left the north exposed and by Mortimer's ruthless venality. Isabella and Mortimer could scarcely hope to survive long in power: neither had a claim to the throne but ruled in the name of Edward III; their authority was thus precarious and, given that Edward was in the Plantagenet mould, destined to early extinction.

In September 1329 Edward sent a yeoman of his household, William Montague, to enlist the aid of the pope in the matter of appointments 'not only for our own needs but for the advancement of the people of our household and for others'.[1] When the pope asked for some sign by which he could tell 'which requests are

important to us and are dear to our heart, and which are not',
Edward indicated early in the new year that he would mark such
requests with the words *Pater Sancte*, written in his own hand,
but he promised that these requests would be employed with
restraint – 'only as we can and ought'. This arrangement, known
only to Montague and to the king's secretary, Richard de Bury,
was designed to protect a vital area of the king's patronage and
power, namely his household, from control or manipulation by the
regents. The letter is remarkable testimony to the importance of
ecclesiastical patronage for the king's government. The stratagem,
however, was not in operation long, for later that very year the king
became master of his realm.

Montague, encouraged by king and nobles, masterminded the
arrest of Mortimer and Isabella at a great council meeting in
Nottingham castle in October 1330; Isabella was consigned to
comfortable retirement, but Mortimer, soon condemned for
notorious offences against the crown, was executed in November.
Like most of his other supporters, the bishops associated with
Mortimer were pardoned.

During the course of Edward's long reign the English crown
attained what, according to one historian, amounted to sovereignty over the English church. How far this was so in fact and how
it may have come about are important themes of this and the
following chapters. Even more important is the need to delineate
and explain the growth in anticlericalism and antipapalism which
was so marked in the second half of the century and which so
drastically modified the relation of the church to the realm. This
change, in itself, is hardly to be wondered at in a century which
saw such dramatic features as large-scale warfare and recurring
visitations of the plague: the consequences of both affected society
as a whole, the church included.

War

Even before Edward assumed independent control of his own
crown the Scottish throne was again in contention. Because David
II, the new infant king, or his regent reneged on some of the terms

of the treaty of Northampton, Edward gave his support to the rival claimant, Edward Balliol. The early 1330s, therefore, saw the renewal of English involvement in Scotland and in 1334 David II and his wife fled to France for asylum, a development which in its turn seriously complicated England's relations with France.

Through the right of his mother, Edward had himself claimed the French crown when it fell vacant in 1328, but probably more in hope than expectation, for in the following year and again in 1331 he acknowledged Philip VI's lordship of Gascony; not until 1337 was his own interest in the French crown voiced again. By that time Philip had confiscated Gascony and was insisting that boundary disputes there could not be resolved without a settlement in Scotland. During 1336–7, faced by two interrelated problems and by an aggressive and ambitious French king, Edward, in moves reminiscent of his grandfather's strategy, recruited allies all round France's borders: the count of Guelders, the marquis of Juliers, the count of Hainault, the duke of Brabant and Limburg, but chief of all, Lewis of Bavaria, emperor. To them he promised to pay some £276,000, much of it by the recklessly optimistic date of February 1338; from them he gained promises of military aid whose fulfilment depended largely upon the payment.

By the summer of 1339 Edward was overdue on many of his commitments and had paid the emperor barely a tenth of the sum agreed; with disillusioned and now unenthusiastic allies, he only succeeded in spending yet more money on campaigns to no avail, first in the Low Countries, then in Cambrésis and Vermandois. In September 1339 his debts were reckoned at £300,000 and still growing, yet in January 1340 he readily promised £140,000 to James van Arteveldt, the ruler of Ghent, for his assistance. Apart, however, from the naval victory at Sluys, no further successes in combat followed that year, and the allies were clamouring for payment. In the autumn, overwhelmed by debts, Edward agreed to the truce of Espléchin which was to endure until midsummer 1342. Before then, in June 1340, Lewis of Bavaria deserted him and made peace with Philip; in June 1341 David II returned to Scotland and renewed border raids; James van Arteveldt began to alienate his Flemish allies; and the French were advancing in

Gascony. English intervention in Brittany in December 1341 and August 1342 produced no worthwhile success before a further truce was concluded at Malestroit in 1343. By that stage four years of campaigning had amassed enormous crown debts, put the English nation under strains unknown since the 1290s and dangerously divided the king and his ministers.

The first stage of the war, to 1343, had produced more problems and doubts than profits and successes; the second stage, from 1343 to 1356, was punctuated by glittering triumphs and extensive conquests, both of which helped to redeem some of the debts and to quell some of the doubts.

Since neither side was ready to concede what was necessary for peace, hostilities were resumed in 1345. In Gascony a long and desultory campaign, led by the Black Prince and the duke of Lancaster, culminated in a notable success only in 1347, by which time a new theatre of war had been opened in Normandy. A large force, which landed there in July 1346, proceeded eastwards in order to join up with the Flemings, routed the French at Crécy in August 1346 and captured Calais a year later. Against the Scots, meanwhile, in October 1346, northern English forces won a resounding victory at Neville's Cross and captured David II himself, effectively relieving pressure on that front. Thereafter in Brittany and Gascony sporadic fighting continued, though little significant success followed from it, except for the vanquishing of the Spanish fleet in 1350. In 1355 an expedition to Normandy led by the king proved unavailing, but in the next year the French forces were crushed at Poitiers and their king, John, was captured. Predictably serious negotiations ensued, if not for peace then at least for the ransom of King John; but several years of intermittent diplomacy and warfare passed before a treaty was concluded at Brétigny in 1360 and confirmed at Calais in 1361. This marked the end of English triumphs until the reign of Henry V, half a century on; indeed, the futile campaign of 1359–60 already signalled that the peak of English success was passed.

Both sides now were in need of respite; peace endured until 1369 when the French, refreshed and led by a new and able young monarch, Charles V, confronted the English whose king was on the verge of senility and whose government was divided. The final stage of the war under Edward was vastly more discouraging, humiliating and squalid than the earlier stages, but no less costly. By 1370 the king was little more than a debauched, ageing and apathetic figurehead; the Black Prince was already mortally ill, and government was largely conducted by John of Gaunt in alliance with courtiers and the king's mistress, Alice Perrers. Unfortunately Gaunt had claims on the Castilian crown which induced him to put these interests before priorities in France and at the same time drove the formidable Castilian navy into alliance with the French. By 1372 England had suffered a naval defeat at La Rochelle and lost most of the gains which it had made by the time of the treaty of Brétigny; in the following year much of Brittany was lost; in 1375 another spectacular naval defeat was suffered; and in 1376 and 1377 the south and east coasts of England were alerted under threats of invasion or raids. A large English naval campaign in 1372 had proved abortive, an expedition to relieve Brest in 1373 ineffective, a progress led by Gaunt from Calais to Bordeaux that same year a 'grandiose failure', and a costly expedition to Brittany in 1375 too late to achieve its aim of influencing peace negotiations at Bruges. There at Bruges negotiations, which had been initiated by the papacy in 1374, foundered on the issue of sovereignty over Aquitaine and produced only a succession of fitful truces until April 1377. Against such a background it is no surprise that when, in 1376, Gaunt was at last compelled to call a parliament in order to raise cash, his aides were discredited and displaced. Before the end of the reign he had recovered control of affairs, but at no little cost to the church.

Prayer, Preaching and Propaganda

The demands of the king upon the realm for sacrifices and contributions towards the war effort would have been much less effective even than they were, had not the church acted as a kind of ministry of information and propaganda. Edward I had exploited the church's national network to publish and justify to his subjects the reasons for his campaigns against Scotland and France; under Edward III this development reached maturity.[2] From the mid-1330s onwards scarcely a year passed without the issue of writs requesting archbishops and bishops to order prayers in every parish for the king; additionally, whenever an army set off on campaign – whether against Scotland or to the continent – prayers and processions were ordered, and each victory (Berwick, Sluys, Crécy, Poitiers, Najera) and even the capture of King John in 1356 was at once announced and celebrated with parish prayers. The mandate for prayers of thanks for the capture of Caen in 1346 also ordered the publication of the king's itinerary 'for the comfort and consolation . . . of the entire English people'.[3] Well might a poem of that time depict the good ship of state being blown along by the prayers filling its sails.[4]

Because prayers had to be stimulated and informed as well as ordered, the preaching role of the church was no less important. In 1338 the northern clergy were to instruct their parishioners about the crucial need for, and inescapable burdens of, defence against the Scots, so that the 'pious exhortations' of the priests might induce support for a united struggle against the enemies of the realm.[5] Since friars were the pre-eminent preachers of the time they were particularly enlisted to explain, in public and private sermons, the legitimacy of the king's claim on the French crown and to stress his almost superhuman efforts to avoid conflict; preachers were to elaborate on French treachery, exposing their 'derogatory lies'.[6] In 1346 Archbishop Stratford was ordered to read to the clergy and laity assembled in St Paul's churchyard a recently discovered Franco-Norman agreement (actually concluded in 1339!) to invade England; publication was to be accompanied by a sermon and a solemn procession, 'so that by this means the people of the kingdom might be roused to esteem the king more fervently and pray more devoutly for his expedition in order that he may keep the people safe from Gallic machinations'.[7] Sermons and prayers stressed the patience, humility and virtue of the English king: when people were exhorted to pray for the great expedition which Edward, together with the Black Prince and the duke of Lancaster, led to France in 1355, they were told that it was setting out 'to procure peace'.[8] In contrast with the patient and virtuous English, the French were portrayed as, at best, dissembling, unscrupulous and bellicose; in fact, the patriotic exuberance of some clergy so overwhelmed Christian charity that they had to be warned against making their prayers too bloodthirsty![9]

This propaganda role of the church was no mere cynical response to royal commands and requests; many of the clergy were quite as deeply imbued with a sense of national self-righteousness as were substantial elements of the laity: Edward III later recalled that Archbishop Stratford had persuaded him of the need for such a war, though the king also told a tale of Stratford's reluctance for war. Certainly in March 1337 the prelates in parliament joined the magnates and the commons in giving their explicit assent to the war against France, and later that same year the clergy in convocation voted a triennial tenth for the purpose.

How persuasive the propaganda was is clear from the Latin war poems which even monks were then composing: some of these items were so popular that they found their way into school books for reading and glossing.[10] Typical of these is the *Invective against France* which survives in several manuscripts: it depicts the French as effeminate, combining the characteristics of the lynx, viper and wolf; King Philip's fraudulent claims to the French throne and his unworthiness for it are elaborately exposed with biblical and legal references; by contrast Edward's victories, secured by his virtuousness, serve only to prove that God was on his side. Indeed, Thomas Bradwardine, philosopher and later archbishop, when preaching to a mixed audience after the victories of Crécy and Neville's Cross, used them to underline his view of the omnipotence of God and the impotence of man: victory in battle was conferred by God on the righteous, as St Paul had declared in II Corinthians 2:14.[11] Apart from the implications of this for prayers and strategy, it was a comforting thought – so long as one was winning.

After 1360 and more particularly in the 1370s the war went badly for England. There are several explanations for this but for contemporaries, nurtured on the torrential propaganda that victories betokened God's recognition of virtue, the chief explanation seemed to be England's loss of virtue. Thomas Brinton, bishop of Rochester, preached that the English defeats were punishment for their sins.[12] Other men raised doubts about the rightness of the war itself: the poet Gower spoke of 'this false war';

the chronicler Walsingham, no mean chauvinist in his day, by the 1380s referred to 'this useless royal war'. Still others questioned whether any war could ever be worthwhile or just when fought between Christian and Christian; the doctrine of Christian love, such as Langland voiced in *Piers Plowman*, seemed incompatible with war. Humiliating reverses and exorbitant costs combined to amplify the message of the pacifist so that by the end of Edward's reign wherever one looks disillusion with war has displaced the zestful and righteous belligerence of the earlier years; now preachers, poets, chroniclers and prelates utter words which are gloomy and despondent. Unfortunately those clergy who had so eagerly and diligently defended and justified the war were likely to be engulfed and damaged by the pessimism and disillusion which its failure provoked: pacifism was commonly embraced by the lollards.

To measure the significance and consequences of all this prayerful and homiletic effort for the crown is no easy task. The king extracted grants of subsidies only with difficulty and was forced to concede more than he would have wished to both clergy and laity in return. Even then, it was the desertion of allies, the failure of his Italian bankers, and the capture of ransomable kings which saved him from financial disaster. And all this favourable preaching and prayer was powerless to avert the hostile criticism and pessimism aroused in the 1370s by the bungling campaigns of English forces and the imminent threats of raids and invasion by the French.

The Clergy in Arms

In the desperate circumstances of Edward's war, especially in the last years of the reign, prayer was not always enough and the clergy had frequent occasions to become in a literal sense the church militant. Although clerks were barred by canon law from arms and bloodshed, and indeed were excommunicated for such offences in the thirteenth century, the pervasive propaganda mounted by the clergy in support of the king's wars served to overwhelm these inhibitions in the early fourteenth century. There had been the occasional martial bishops, of course, ever since Odo of Bayeux came across with the Conqueror, not least perhaps because of the knightly or aristocratic houses from which some prelates came, but also because the bishop was often the sole or wealthiest magnate present to defend an exposed region when so many others were away on continental engagements. Prominent among the martial aristocrats on the episcopal bench was Henry Despenser who had already fought in Italy for the pope against Milan before he became bishop of Norwich in 1370; his military career was to be resumed in the next reign, as we shall see. Of the second category of bishops as regional leaders, the northern prelates afford obvious examples: in 1346 Archbishop Zouche and Bishop Kirkby of Carlisle participated in the defeat of the Scots at Neville's Cross, while Bishop Hatfield of Durham rode into battle at Crécy; ten years later he, too, campaigned against the Scots, and in 1372 he offered himself as a mercenary in the pope's wars in Italy. Among the religious who distinguished themselves in combat was the abbot of Battle – that 'outstanding warrior in monk's habit', as one chronicler described him – who twice, in 1376 and 1377, defended the town of Winchelsea from French raiders.[13] A few years before and not far away, the abbey of Quarr, on the Isle of Wight, had been licensed to crenellate its buildings.[14]

Prelates of a less combative temperament were still to be found organizing defences or, like Gynewell of Lincoln, directly arming the clergy of their dioceses.[15] From 1368, when the war was being carried to England by the French as well as by the Scots, royal writs of array were issued ordering the clergy to muster alongside others of the king's lieges in order to resist his enemies. Bishops were commanded to array all ecclesiastics between sixteen and sixty years of age in the diocese, each armed according to his estate and means. In 1372 stipendiaries, and rectors and vicars with benefices worth 10 marks (or £3 13s 4d), were to come as archers with bows and arrows; those with livings worth more than £10 had to attend 'well armed'; if their living was valued at £20 they had to be accompanied by two archers, if £40 by two armed men and two archers, if £100 by five armed men and six archers. Although assembled in units separate from the lay force, the clergy were sometimes supervised by a layman, just as occasionally clerics had charge of the lay contingent. This obligatory military involvement, though a burden which some clergy would willingly have evaded, was for others doubtless a proud duty or welcome excitement; not many of those assembled actually saw battle, but their association with this medieval 'home guard' must surely have blurred the distinction between clergy and laymen, with ambiguous and some unfortunate results: more popular they may have been, but equally more vulnerable when sentiment turned, as it did, against both war and the clergy.

The Seizure of Alien Priories

Another war-time expedient adopted by Edward I, repeated by Edward II, and exploited by Edward III was the temporary seizure of alien priories. But whereas they had been held for just a few years by his grandfather and father, they were in royal hands for thirty-one of the last forty years of Edward III's reign, from 1337 to 1360 and then from 1369 onwards to the end of the century. Several considerations encouraged this move under all three kings: fears that the alien priories might engage in spying were commonly voiced in parliament, but probably the king was more anxious about enjoying their revenues and their patronage.

The financial importance of this seizure for Edward III has yet to be satisfactorily explored and calculated, though it was clearly considerable: there were just over a hundred cells or estates involved and in the financial years 1342–3 and 1345–6 they paid farms to the king totalling £5304. 7s. 7d. and £4181. 8s. 2d. respectively.[16] Nor must one exclude from the economic benefits to the crown's war effort the acquisition of funds which would otherwise serve to enrich French mother houses and very probably, through taxation, the French crown. Additionally the seizure had a psychological importance, since it offered opportunities for gain to many of Edward's subjects who subsequently acquired a vested interest in the estates and therefore in prolonging the war or, at least, concluding it in triumph.

By no means all the alien clergy were expelled in accordance with the wishes of successive parliaments. Usually the priors became proctors for the king, paying over to him a farm (or rent), but as these farms were based on a high assessment many houses or cells sold or leased their property in order to buy denization. In the 1370s lay custodians took control of houses and property as the original priors died off, or, indeed, as property was sold to the laity. Many farms were let out to royal clerks and lay servants – another aspect of crown patronage. Although, therefore, the seizure was not intended to be permanent, conventual houses were largely unmolested, and wherever possible existing religious were allowed to farm the alien priories, the protraction of the war and the intention of the king to profit from this source as much as possible led to the permanent secularization of some monastic lands, and the extended management and farming of others by laymen as well as by royal clerks. After 1337 no decade passed without laymen leasing, or acquiring full ownership of alien priory lands, an experience which undoubtedly whetted the public appetite for appropriating church lands, while it simultaneously provided a precedent for such forcible recovery. In 1346 Pope Clement VI rebuked Edward for a seizure which would imperil his soul, not to mention those of the sacrilegious laymen occupying church goods. Archbishop Stratford, however, ignored several papal letters urging him to resist royal encroachments on alien priories. By default on the part of the English hierarchy another pass was sold and the integrity of the church still further jeopardized as a consequence of war.

War Finance

With the laity, the clergy suffered from the levying of purveyances in the early years of the war, even though by the statute of Westminster of 1275, confirmed in 1309 and 1316, they had been exempted from this obligation. Northern clergy, especially, endured the billeting of troops: the prior of Tynemouth in 1341 claimed to be utterly impoverished 'by the coming thither of magnates and others making stay here'.[17] To add to these burdens, the 1340 tax of a ninth of corn, sheep and wool, from which the clergy had obtained exemption by their grant of a normal tenth, was nevertheless applied to them by many local officials at first acting on their own initiative, but after January 1341 on the king's orders. All clergy, moreover, who had an interest in wool production and sales were hurt by the manipulation of the wool market for the king's profit. All these impositions, legitimate and illegitimate, oppressed the clergy, but their burden and the king's gain were far greater from the subsidies granted in convocation.

Enthusiastic as some of the clergy may have been for war and seduced as they sometimes were by their own eloquence and propaganda for it, they were less eager about the burdens which it entailed. Convocations yielded large and invaluable subsidies to the crown in the course of the war, but they often did so grudgingly and upon condition that some of their grievances were redressed. From 1334 to 1343 the clergy voted for no fewer than eight tenths, or from the combined provinces – and at a conservative estimate – roughtly £140,000; in the next decade almost as much, seven tenths or some £124,000 were conceded; during the second half of the 1350s only two tenths were granted, £35,000; the peace of Brétigny brought a respite from royal taxation until 1370, after which until the end of the reign £100,000 was raised by traditional subsidies, £50,000 was sought as a special grant in 1371 (though little of this was effectively collected) and a graduated poll tax was imposed in 1377. In the course of four decades almost half a million pounds were produced for the king by clerical taxation, and in fact its burden was all the more concentrated because of the absence of demands in the 1360s. Few of these grants were easily elicited, some were decidedly difficult to extract, and occasional demands were flatly refused. In 1340 the clergy were careful to concede a tenth only upon the understanding that they would be exempt from the ninth then being discussed in parliament. In 1351 the clergy granted one tenth and, provided their complaints were redressed, promised another. In 1356, after a succession of fruitless campaigns (though just before some spectacular successes), the king sought in vain from the clergy a grant of a tenth for each of the next six years; the clergy refused to offer more than a solitary tenth because not only had some of their conditions attached to earlier grants been ignored but also they themselves were too impoverished by war levies of all kinds to afford greater liberality. In 1370, when the war had resumed, the clerical representatives would agree only to a grant of two tenths instead of the three sought; the prelates, however, had already conceded three tenths, and their pressure and that of royal delegations eventually coerced the proctors of the lesser clergy into acquiescing, once again in the expressed hope that their grievances would be remedied. When convocation met in December 1373 even the prelates were alienated from the crown, or at least from Gaunt and those who carried on the government in the king's name: the attempt to levy an unprecedented tax of £50,000 in 1371 had aroused great resentment, aggravated in the next year when, in an effort to speed its collection, all the bishops of the southern province had their temporalities seized. At the convocation of 1373, therefore, bishops led the refusal of any grant: Courtenay of Hereford openly opposed the demand. Bishop Sudbury of London managed this convocation, in the absence of Archbishop Whittlesey who was sick, and succeeded eventually in extracting a grant of a tenth. This success lies behind his translation to Canterbury in the following year; thereafter, until his death in 1381, he presided over a period of taxation the scale of which exceeded even that of the early years of the reign.

Clerical grants, although generally dependable, were never to be taken for granted; they had to be extracted from convocations – by promises of redress, by divisions caused among the clergy, by desperate appeals, forceful delegations of royal councillors, veiled threats, relentless pressure and astute management. A key figure for this last task was the archbishop of Canterbury, but not all were as reliable or as effective on the king's behalf as Sudbury proved to be: Islip (1349–66) had not secured the sexennial grant requested in 1356, although probably even Sudbury would have had problems with such an extreme proposal; and after Sudbury, Courtenay (1381–96) was not always obliging. On difficult and urgent occasions – in 1356, 1370, 1371, 1373 and twice in 1377 – the king sent lay councillors and magnates along to exert their pressure upon the clergy. Usually several attended: various justices and the earl of Stafford among others in 1356; the earls of Arundel and March and the duke of Lancaster in 1370; no fewer than four earls and the Black Prince in 1371; March, Salisbury and

Lord Latimer in 1373. Usually only one of the delegation addressed the assembly at large on the king's needs, but it is hardly to be believed that the remainder were content merely to be seen. Although lay delegates had been tried before – in the 1290s, for example – the frequency of their presence in six out of the last eleven assemblies of Edward III's reign added a new (and continuing) dimension to convocation.[18] Their presence was all the more sinister amidst the approaching thunder of anticlericalism. Idealistic friars now put their arguments for a propertyless church to the service of Gaunt and other laymen who simply wanted to avail themselves of church wealth for the relief of their own tax burden. In the parliament of 1371 two Austin friars argued that in a national emergency the prince who has endowed the churches may resume their property for the good of the realm;[19] about this time Langland was enlarging in *Piers Plowman* upon Holy Poverty, as were so many friars in their sermons; before the end of the reign Wyclif, spokesman for Gaunt, especially against his wealthy political enemy, Bishop Wykeham of Winchester, was denying the right of priests to hold any property. In future years a combination of religious idealism, naivety, political expediency and oppressive taxation for a failing war encouraged widely based attacks upon the church's wealth and added a new dimension to the relations of crown and convocation.

One other and not unrelated feature of these Edwardian synods deserves note. Convocation was rarely concerned now with reform; Archbishop Stratford in 1342 was the last primate until the sixteenth century to issue provincial constitutions in this body which for the rest of the reign was wholly concerned with royal taxation or with eliciting, in exchange for grants, relief from crown or lay encroachments on church liberties or property. The clergy were beginning to pay the price for assessing their own tax in their own assembly.

Burdensome as royal taxation was during the war, the clergy were mercifully free of papal taxation except on two occasions. During the first thirty-six years of the century the pope had taxed the English church to the tune of almost £450,000, of which some £360,000 was earmarked for the king, a sum more than three times the amount produced in that time by direct royal taxation of the clergy. Yet after 1337 no further papal taxation was levied until 1362. Undoubtedly a principal reason for this was the Avignon popes' expedient friendship with the king of France, whose clerical subjects the popes frequently taxed for his benefit after 1337. Another reason may have been the desire to end the war as quickly as possible, better achieved perhaps by financing one side rather than both. Added to these considerations, there was doubtless pressure from the French king, aware that the pope would not be allowed to levy taxes in England without their major part being assigned to the king. By 1362, however, hostilities had ceased and the French king was a prisoner of the English; papal taxation on this occasion was certainly destined for Edward's coffers, but this was to meet the ransom of John II: the English clergy were thus taxed by the pope to enrich the English king and spare the French taxpayers! There could have been little expectation, especially after the war resumed in 1369, that circumstances would again favour papal taxation: yet they did.

By a concordat at Bruges in 1375 Gregory XI – eager to return to Rome and fighting a war with Milan – secured permission to levy some £9000 from the English clergy.[20] In return for this concession the English government obtained a number of crucial episcopal appointments, not least the translation of Sudbury to Canterbury; moreover, the good offices of the pope were assured in the current peace negotiations; finally, some of the money would find its way back to the English crown for the ransom of the pope's brother, Roger Beaufort, who was then an English prisoner of war. These papal concessions, however, made little favourable impression outside Gaunt's circle, and they combined with an unpopular truce, spectacular military setbacks and the threat of invasion to provoke the crisis of the so-called Good Parliament in October 1376. Fierce hostility to the bungling conduct of the war since 1370 resulted in the impeachment of Gaunt's friends – he was too powerful a figure for direct attack. After parliament dissolved, Gaunt set about recovering the initiative and control by adopting a stridently popular antipapal and anticlerical tone: he employed Wyclif to denounce the papacy, the wealth of prelates and clergy, and the independence of the church. The threat of papal taxation once again receded from the English clergy for some years to come.

While the pope was thus able to tax the English church only by the will of the king, the king's taxation was no longer restrained by canon law or at the mercy of the pope or – to any great extent – of an archbishop. Royal taxation usually had to be for the defence of the realm, but this was no longer interpreted with the narrow precision attempted by Winchelsey, and clerical objections and conditions more often turned upon other considerations: redress of grievances, exemption from lay burdens such as the ninth and purveyances, or simple impoverishment. Royal taxation of the clergy was no longer a matter of law but of pragmatic politics, no more of meticulous definition but of the balance of pressures.

War and the Stratford Crisis

In July 1338 Edward had set out on campaign in Flanders, leaving the realm in the charge of a keeper, the eight-year-old duke of Cornwall, and a council, on which Richard Bintworth, bishop of London, and Robert Wodehouse, archdeacon of Richmond, sat as chancellor and treasurer respectively. Accompanying the king to the continent were Bishops Burghersh of Lincoln, Orleton of Winchester and Richard de Bury of Durham, as well as Archbishop John Stratford and Canon Kilsby. The chief responsibility of the keeper's council was to keep the king supplied with necessary cash, but no amount of good will and effort on their part could have produced it as promptly and as copiously as the king's needs demanded. Even before this time, the cost of war was beginning to sap enthusiasm for it: loans on wool and in wool, accompanied by embargoes and dubious credit arrangements, were testing the patience and loyalty of more than the merchants who assented to these measures; purveyances, now being collected with a frequency and ruthlessness to match the 1290s, were provoking deep unrest in wide sections of the community, lay and clerical; efforts to muster arrays for defence against the Scots and French antagonized the clergy when the requests for support were directed to diocesan, instead of provincial, synods.[21]

In October 1339 the king sent Archbishop Stratford and the bishop of Durham back to England to expound his urgent needs and to extract the necessary funds, but the commons in parliament insisted on first consulting their constituencies. In February 1340 Edward himself came back to secure what his commissaries had failed to get, but only in May was he able to return to the continent assured of a grant. From convocation he obtained a biennial tenth conditional upon the clergy's exemption from any parliamentary tax. From parliament he was promised a ninth on sheep, wool and corn for two years, a grant difficult to quantify and very easy, as it turned out, to overestimate.

By the autumn of 1340, still awaiting the fruits of these grants, deserted by Lewis of Bavaria and with only the naval victory at Sluys to encourage him, Edward was borrowing from his own archers and offering his commanders as hostages for his debts to his allies. The truce of Espléchin in September did nothing to quieten importunate creditors, and on 30 November, having sent a bitter denunciation of Archbishop Stratford to the pope, Edward – frustrated, desperate and furious – set out for England to wreak revenge and secure funds. By May 1341 all he had got out of parliament was a resolution to collect the rest of the ninth and an offer of an extra 10,000 sacks of wool; no new money was granted. Even to get this much he had had to agree to a number of statutes which he construed as so prejudicial that he vowed to repeal them as soon as possible. To some extent his interest in revenge had helped to thwart success over taxation.

When he returned at the beginning of December 1340 Edward had immediately dismissed the home council, Robert Stratford, who was bishop of Chichester and chancellor, among them; Archbishop Stratford, then held responsible for the home government's failure, was ordered to Louvain as a hostage for the payment of the allies, while the dismissal and prosecution of other ministers and officials – mostly clerics – was set in motion. The archbishop fled to Canterbury where he proceeded to deliver sermons and issue pamphlets against the crown's infringement of clerical privileges. Early in the new year, when the king ordered the ninth to be collected from the clergy despite their earlier exemption, the archbishop excommunicated the collectors who complied. Various accusations, including that of treason, were thereupon levelled against Stratford and attempts were made to exclude him from the parliament which met subsequently. Stratford responded by invoking Magna Carta's principle of trial by peers, which for him at that time meant trial by the lords in parliament. Thus, threatened for his alleged failings as the king's minister, the archbishop skilfully sought to lay a minefield of principles – clerical liberties and rights of peerage – before the king and his agents. The commons needed little encouragement to join his opposition to the king's demands, since further taxation was particularly unwelcome in the wake of recent extortionate taxes and purveyances; as for the lords, they were concerned over the question of peerage rights which the archbishop had so astutely raised. Clergy and laity jointly seized the opportunity to demand laws curtailing crown abuses. Not since 1297 and 1310–11 had such an alliance confronted the king. It became apparent that Edward could win nothing if he persisted against Stratford and refused reforms; in May, therefore, he adjourned the archbishop's trial to a committee of peers (which in fact he never convened) and assented to the reforming statutes. But in October 1341, relieved of financial pressure by the desertion of some allies and by the bankruptcy of his Italian bankers, Edward repealed the offending statutes, though it is significant that it was done with the advice and assent of the earls, barons and other wise men. When it was learned that Stratford was convening a provincial council to oppose or denounce this annulment, he and other bishops received writs of prohibition forbidding them to do so. Thus ended an episode of high drama, the excitement of which tends to distort its significance.

Archbishop Stratford had protested not only against the manner of his trial but also against royal abuses of the clergy. His obduracy on these issues could have been dangerous in the heated atmosphere of those early months in 1341. Some years before, he had founded in his home town of Stratford-upon-Avon a chapel in honour of St Thomas Becket and he was inclined to see himself in that tradition of defiance of the crown. The parallel, however, was more apparent than real: Becket, after all, had exchanged the office of chancellor for that of archbishop, while Stratford combined both on several occasions. He was even a far cry from Pecham and Winchelsey. They came to office unsullied by royal service or political intrigue, and with the political principles and ideas of the schools fresh in their minds, but Stratford had won office by his service to the crown; he was one of those who managed the early wool loans and spent the opening months of the French war recruiting allies and spies on the continent; he may have resisted and condemned the malpractices of tax collectors, but he did not protest against royal taxation, burdensome as it was, before these crisis years. The archbishop was too compromised to stand convincingly as a champion of the church against the crown. Even if Stratford did not have the character for martyrdom, it is certain that Edward was too shrewd to promote it.

Little danger as there was of another martyrdom, there was even less chance of the clergy satisfying their grievances at Edward's expense: the most significant thing about the legislation of May 1341 is how easily it was repealed five months later. It is a telling commentary upon parliament but even more so upon the church's limited political potency: at that stage, the clergy needed the support not just of the commons but of the peers as well in order to defend effectively their privileges and franchises; repeal was effected in the council and chiefly through the agency of the lords; when the prelates contemplated a riposte in convocation they were instantly quelled by writs of prohibition. Without parliamentary support, clerical liberties were peculiarly vulnerable to royal pressures, although the time was fast approaching when the reverse became true and the king would defend the church from the plans of the commons and lords.

Even more striking testimony, however, of the indissoluble and complex bonds between the church and the crown, or between the church and the realm, is the nature of Stratford's principal antagonist and the defender of the crown's position: William Kilsby, canon of York, and archbishop-elect there (though unsuccessful). The animosity between Stratford and Kilsby was to some extent personal, yet even where it was related to principles, they were set within revealing limits of assumptions, experience and motives. It is doubtful if one should talk of a church–state conflict here, but even if one could it was a battle fought between royal clerks, king's servants. Their public polemic, in the early months of 1341, about royal authority and ecclesiastical obligations, by its notorious and indecorous vehemence, has attracted much attention from historians, but the ideas enunciated are less notable for themselves than for signifying divisions among the clergy over church and state relations, an ambivalence even more sensationally witnessed in the Becket conflict in the twelfth century and in the Hunne affair in the early sixteenth. From time to time the tensions of clerical dualism erupted into fierce controversy, but in 1341 at least the eruption resulted in no marked shift in clergy–laity relations, not even with regard to the employment of clerical ministers by the crown.

From 1340 until his death in 1348 the archbishop never again held high office or exerted much influence in the king's government. After his brother, Robert, bishop of Chichester, was dismissed as chancellor in December 1340 the king resolved to do without clerical ministers and no other cleric held the office until five years had passed. This interlude, however, does not mark a phase of anticlericalism on the part of the king, for during it clergy, like Kilsby, were prominent in the royal household and council and in lesser offices of state. What is far more significant than Robert Stratford's dismissal is Dean Offord's appointment as chancellor in 1345, for by this the king emphatically confirmed the crown's crucial need for clerical ministers. Not only were they more cheaply remunerated – at the church's expense, mainly – and far more experienced in the business and technicalities of administration and negotiation, but their clerical status gave them a weight which most laymen could only acquire by aristocratic connections or by ennoblement; lay chancellors, to be of any consequence, needed political and dynastic links, which could also spell danger for the king. A common lawyer, as in the 1520s, might seem a better choice than either a noble or a cleric in an office so concerned with the law, but in the early fourteenth century common lawyers were regarded with some suspicion by the king – witness the attempts to get them barred from parliament – and by people whose complaints about the corruption of lay judges were frequent until late in the century. In any case, at that time the head of the chancery needed to be acquainted more with Roman law, or at least with canon law, than common law, for chancery was just then beginning to function as a court of equity, a notion unfamiliar in the common law.[22] The 1340–1 crisis, therefore, underlines the connections rather than the divisions between clergy and laity, church and crown.

War Diplomacy and Anglo–Papal Relations

Even before the French war began in 1338 papal envoys were sent to England to dissuade parliament and the clergy from endorsing the king's plans for combat. Pope Benedict XII was not only keen to reconcile Edward and Philip so that their planned crusade could go ahead, but he was also anxious to keep Lewis of Bavaria isolated from either French or English help. Once war had broken out, Englishmen were deeply suspicious of any papal intervention: the truces of Malestroit in 1343, of Calais in 1347 and of Brétigny in 1360 were regarded as betrayals and the papal role in securing them as deliberately treacherous. Partly this was explained by the location of the papacy on the borders of France, at Avignon, and partly by the fact that so many cardinals as well as popes were French. Papal actions, too, appeared to add further proof: after 1337, except in 1362 and 1375, popes no longer taxed the clergy for the benefit of the king in England, though at that time they were certainly enriching the French monarch by clerical taxes; and while successive French kings readily obtained papal dispensations which enabled them to contract politically advantageous matches, Edward on two critical occasions – in the 1340s and 1360s – was denied such benefits.[23]

Gregory XI, who became pope in 1370, at once initiated peace moves, following which negotiations were conducted at Bruges in 1374 and 1375; unfortunately, as much because of English obstinacy as of French, only a truce until April 1377 was effected, while all the time the French threat grew more menacing, with the consequence that papal efforts again incurred suspicion. Chroniclers and poets in their embittered criticism of papal initiatives for peace were scarcely less vehement than the lords and commons in parliament, and when at last, in 1378, an Italian pope was elected, an Englishman at Rome rejoiced because 'Previous popes and their cardinals had been greater enemies of the kingdom of England than the king of France himself.'[24] Simply in terms of sentiment, the Edwardian war had left the papacy seriously undermined in England; but the loss was not only a matter of ideas and emotions.

Patronage: Royal and Papal

Edward III's ecclesiastical patronage in the first twenty-five years of his reign was more than treble that of Edward I (in thirty-five years) and double Edward II's (in twenty-five years): the comparative figures, revealed by the researches of Dr Saunders, are 919 (Edward I), 1419 (Edward II) and 3182 (1327–52).[25] All categories of royal patronage had increased, especially opportunities arising from monastic estates in the king's hands – from 70 under Edward I and 219 under Edward II to no fewer than 1282 now. The lengthy seizure of alien priories provides an obvious explanation for this, but the Black Death, of course, also multiplied vacancies for all patrons to exploit.[26] Probably this accounts for the greater part of the increase in *sede vacante* presentations made by the king, but he and his clerks pushed their claims to the limit. Almost half of Edward's *sede vacante* presentations were retrospective, some dating back to his grandfather's reign, and most being based on fictitious entitlement; considerable temptations were open to unscrupulous candidates, armed with dubious history, to challenge the rights of sitting tenants. If the sitting incumbent – or his bishop – was obstructive, a writ of *quare impedit* would assign the matter to a local jury to decide whether the living was void or not; there is convincing evidence to show that such juries were often packed and demonstrably found falsely for the king's clerk. Were the bishop or incumbent to prosecute the question of voidance in the church courts, a writ of prohibition soon removed it to the king's judges. Once the issue was decided by them, the bishop would be ordered by the writ *admittatis* to institute the king's man; failure to do so would bring yet another, and a far more formidable, writ, the *quare non admisit*, whereby his temporalities were seized for contempt until he submitted, the king in the meantime enjoying access to the rest of the bishop's patronage! Episcopal resistance could lead ironically to yet more royal exploitation.

The king supplemented these sources of patronage with papal provisions on behalf of his candidates, but it sometimes happened that the royal clerk, with or without a provision, found himself forestalled in a benefice by another providee. On these occasions the king deployed his usual armoury of writs to install his candidate and thwart the rival. In 1343 Archbishop Zouche of York at first resisted the king's nominee for the deanery of York because Cardinal Talleyrand had already been papally provided; when the king's judges found against him, Zouche acquiesced in the royal candidate, rejected the cardinal and endured papal excommunication for the last four years of his life.[27] Could there be more telling evidence of the king's authority *vis-à-vis* the pope?

For the church this surge in royal patronage had damaging effects, pastoral and political. The novelty and often the downright dishonesty of claims by royal clerks to livings which appeared to be legitimately filled already led not only to vigorous litigation, but even more seriously to insecurity, bitterness and local violence. It was not uncommon, even by Edward II's time, for a benefice to be forcefully defended against a royal presentee, or for him to be physically assaulted. And because there were too many royal presentees for efficient records to be kept, it was not unknown for two royal clerks to be rivals for the same living. It needs no great imagination to gauge the effect of all this upon the church's pastoral mission, particularly when we bear in mind the numbers of royal presentations cited above.

The serious political consequence was that as royal patronage expanded not only were the voices of royal clerks multiplied but the morale and priorities of the clergy as a whole were in danger of being increasingly swayed by hopes of royal favour. This had repercussions for the papacy as well as for the parishes.

Papal Provisions

Provisions, or the process whereby the pope appointed directly to a benefice or dignity, overriding the local or usual patron, had its origin in an intent to reform the dynasticized chapters of the twelfth century and in a justifying theory of papal sovereignty – or *plenitudo potestatis* – over the whole church. By the thirteenth century the increasing need of the pope to find ever more rewards for his proliferating servants and bureaucrats had almost supplanted concern for reform, although in disputed elections papal discretion was sometimes deployed to counter less suitable promotions and to insert men of principle, vision and capacity – Pecham to Canterbury, for example. What we see from the mid-thirteenth century to the mid-fourteenth is a gradual extension of the papal right to provide. In 1265 by the decree *Licet ecclesiarum* the benefices of all clergy who died while at the papal Curia were reserved for papal provision. John XXII by his *Ex debito*, *c.*1316–25, included within this general reservation the benefices of all those who died within two days' journey from Rome, as well as of all cardinals and curial officers (who might not necessarily die near the Curia) and of all bishops consecrated in Rome or appointed by the pope; this last category encouraged the practice of translating bishops from one see to another. Furthermore, since it was asserted that such benefices were deemed vacant until filled by the papacy, time no longer ran against the pope as it previously had done. In practice John XXII (1316–34) did not confine himself even to these occasions, adding to his opportunities, albeit much less than was once thought by historians, by the decree against pluralism, *Execrabilis*, in 1317. Whereas Clement V (1305–14) had provided on average to eight English livings a year, John XXII filled around forty each year. Benedict XII (1334–42) reverted to the level of Clement V but was then succeeded by the most prodigal of all popes. No pope exploited provisions with more zest than Clement VI (1342–52) who on average provided to some sixty prebends and dignities as well as to forty-two parish livings annually in England.[28] He is reckoned to have provided to more than 1600 English benefices in the decade of his pontificate; indeed, over a third of this total occurred in his first two years, an immense increase on previous practices.[29] A particularly provocative novelty introduced by Clement was to provide a clerk not to one benefice but to as many as would collectively produce a specified income and to do this in respect of two French cardinals. Providees, however, were not exclusively papal protégés: various parties from the king downwards sought, with the help of provisions, to exploit benefices not otherwise in their gift or under their influence. After the accession of Edward III the number of royal requests for provisions and of royal beneficiaries markedly increased and continued to do so until the accession of Clement VI; even from him, however, Edward successfully solicited over sixty provisions (to swell his already extended patronage), and after 1344 all bishops were appointed through papal provisions mostly in answer to royal petitions.[30]

Like the king, nobles too sought provisions for their candidates: the Black Prince petitioned for 105 between 1342 and 1366, the duke of Lancaster for 98.[31] Bishops, as well as sometimes being authorized to make their own provisions, were often petitioners on behalf of their own men. From the 1330s, if not before, Oxford and Cambridge universities were also soliciting provisions and 'expectations' (that is, promises of provision to some unspecified benefice at some uncertain future date) for their able but ill-connected alumni: in 1343, 1362, 1363 and 1366 Oxford even submitted lists of desired beneficiaries; from later in the century extensive petitions from Cambridge are extant – for 75 candidates in 1370, 265 in 1389–90, and 109 in 1399.[32]

Provisions added a welcome flexibility to ecclesiastical appointments and were much appreciated – especially by the universities – for doing just that. Nevertheless, English reactions were ambivalent: on the one hand glad to exploit provisions, and on the other resentful of intrusions. Sometimes patrons were offended and aspirants frustrated, as local candidates could be cheated or even the providees find themselves in an unpromising queue. The patrons who chiefly suffered were the bishops, for provisions rarely if ever encroached on lay patronage, since the act of provision was an expression of the pope's sovereignty (*plenitudo potestatis*) over the clergy. Back in 1327 Bishop Martival had complained to John XXII that the great number of papal provisions to the chapter of Salisbury cathedral prevented him from rewarding his own household and diocesan staff. In 1342 convocation and Bishop Grandisson complained in virtually identical terms.[33]

To these legitimate laments were added others which have more to do with war and chauvinism. The outcry against aliens which had prompted the confiscation of alien priories also engulfed providees. It was commonly believed and repeatedly asserted that the Avignon popes were flooding English benefices with French cardinals and bishops, absent in Avignon or at the French court. After the outbreak of war a strong suspicion grew in English minds that even if the pope was not exploiting the English church for the direct benefit of the French crown and French clerks, the English war effort was certainly not helped by the drain of much-needed capital to a Curia which appeared to be at best indifferent, at worst hostile, to English interests. In fact, recent research impugns the notion of aliens swarming over English benefices: even Clement VI filled no more than ten dignities and fewer than two parish churches a year with aliens, and some of these would have been especially useful to English suitors at the Curia and to the king himself both for litigation and for diplomatic contacts. Unfortunately Clement did nothing to dispel misconceptions when he provided two French cardinals to a string of English benefices.[34]

More substantially founded was the resentment at papal income from provisions. Since 1326 providees below the rank of bishop or abbot owed the pope annates (or their first year's income from the benefice); accounts survive for the years from 1349 to 1378 which show that annates yielded some £600 or £700 annually, a sum which would presumably have seemed modest in the opening years of Clement VI's pontificate. Bishops, on provision, owed services – some of which was shared among the curial cardinals. Nominally these services amounted to something over a third of the gross income of the bishopric: among English sees this ranged from 12,000 florins for Winchester, and 10,000 each for Canterbury and York, down to 1000 for Carlisle; 7500 were due from Ely, 5000 from Norwich, Lincoln and Exeter. The abbots of St Augustine's, Canterbury, Bury St Edmund's, St Albans, Waltham and Westminster were also liable to services. In the first half of Edward's reign the pope received (or was owed) nearly 200,000 florins for services.[35] Clearly fears about papal profiteering were not without foundation in the 1340s. That services fell by 20,000 florins, or 10 per cent, in the second half of his reign is less significant – a couple fewer archiepiscopal vacancies, for example, would account for this – than the absence of any sharp increase after 1344 when all bishops came to be provided to their sees.

Convocation expressed concern in 1342 about provisions; in April 1343 the commons and temporal lords protested against alien benefice holders and followed this in May with a letter of complaint to the pope. In 1344 an ordinance to stop the introduction of bulls of provision was approved by the king, who also ordered the arrest of all who brought into the realm letters which threatened his patronage of any church: ports were watched, and suspected or known papal agents were searched for offending documents. That same year Edward wrote to the pope deploring how Christian worship and the cure of souls were imperilled, and royal treasure removed from the realm, as a consequence of such provisions. Further parliamentary pressure followed, but the king responded with calculated caution. When in 1344 parliament asked that the ordinance be converted into a statute, Edward not only declined but even assured the pope that rumours of antipapal legislation were unfounded. In 1347 the commons complained again that there was still no statute against provisions, even the enforcement of the ordinance was being waived. Not until 1351 did provisions become the subject of a statute.

That the king should be less than enthusiastic about the measures was undoubtedly because he profited from provisions when he wanted to and effectively frustrated them when they threatened his own interests. Bishops on the other hand were at the mercy of papal anathema when they were not coerced by royal writs and the seizure of their temporalities: the fate of Archbishop Zouche makes their dilemma and vulnerability abundantly plain. Moreover, Edward was considerably less alarmist about aliens and services and annates than his subjects were. He did, however, recognize both the need to placate his subjects and the expediency of putting pressure on the pope.

The king's fluctuating support for parliamentary measures appears to correlate closely with his diplomatic endeavours.[36] In 1343 he was seeking to extend his influence in the Low Countries by marrying his heir, the Black Prince, to the Hainault heiress; because of affinity a papal dispensation was required for such a marriage, and the pope prevaricated. It seems likely that Edward seized on the parliamentary protests in order to coerce the pope by the threat of reduced annates. The 1344 ordinance was carefully applied with sufficient finesse and flexibility to threaten but not provoke Clement VI. By 1347 the king was eager to enlist papal sympathy in the current peace overtures, and Clement had drastically reduced his use of provisions. By 1351, however, since peace – like marriage – appeared improbable, Edward was happy to yield to public outrage at the renewed increase of provisions which followed the Black Death, and he approved a statute at last; he was also yielding to a difficult political situation at home.

Yet the statute, like the ordinance, could only be a blunt and ineffective weapon diplomatically. Offensive as this curtailment of his patronage and income must have been to the pope, he had far more to lose from France than from England: not only was Avignon geographically vulnerable to French pressure, but Clement VI himself had previously served as the French chancellor and the college of cardinals was preponderantly French. Moreover, since the English king and many of his subjects were doubtless reluctant to extinguish completely a practice which worked so often and conveniently to their advantage, a pope might understandably conclude that the extreme rhetoric of the commons would not be matched in practice, or not for long; and so in the event it proved. Indeed, almost immediately after this statute was promulgated the king, the queen and leading courtiers were soliciting provisions for their clerks. Nevertheless, popes viewed the statute with particular dismay, and for the rest of this century and well into the next, by which time provisions were significantly curtailed, they worked strenuously for its repeal.

The statute itself was regarded by an earlier generation of historians as a turning point in Anglo–papal relations and the culmination of popular antipapalism. For this view the text of the statute appears to offer some support: after reiterating the statute of Carlisle of 1307, and noting that it had neither been repealed nor enforced, so that the pope 'taketh of all such benefices the first fruits, and many other profits, and a great part of the treasure of the said realm is carried away and dispended out of the realm by the purchasers of such benefices aforesaid', it reminded the king of his coronation oath to defend the law of the realm and remedy the grievances of his people; by virtue of this, when papal provisions threatened the rights of ecclesiastical patrons, the king, as advowee or patron paramount, was to intervene and make the appointment as though the benefice or dignity were still vacant, patronage reverting to the original founder or patron only at the next vacancy.[37] Lay patrons, who were only on rare occasions threatened by provisions, were given six months to exercise their rights in defiance of the pope, and the bishop was allowed one further month after that to appoint by devolution; should neither patron nor bishop defy the provision within that time limit, the king would do so. If providees were to seize possession of the livings or frustrate rightful candidates by litigation, they would run the risk of imprisonment until the king had been paid a fine, the offended party placated and any consequent suit at law by them wholly renounced; where such offenders could not be found – perhaps because they were abroad – they were to be outlawed *ipso facto* and their revenues forfeited to the crown.

The role of the commons in all this remains somewhat clouded. That persistent pressure for legislation emanated from them is indisputable, but so little lay patronage was at risk because of provisions that why they took up the campaign is not without mystery. Since convocation in 1342, and bishops before then, had complained about provisions, it is not improbable that the clerical proctors or the bishops introduced the matter into parliament in 1343, though they would have got nowhere without the sympathy of the laity who were probably yielding to their chauvinistic impulses. As for the king, he seems to have seized on an existing mood as an opportune diplomatic weapon. Even if initiative is rightly credited to parliament or the clerical proctors, the terms, timing and enforcement of the statute only serve to underline the king's independence and role in legislation: he resisted the statute until it was expedient and then omitted to enforce it.

What perhaps is more striking about the statute is the role which it assigns to the crown: the notion of the king as patron paramount, the original source of all ecclesiastical endowment, had been implicit in Edward I's exploitation of his regalian rights and was on the lips of a royal judge *circa* 1344.[38] Ostensibly the king was exercising royal lordship or dominion over the church in order to defend religion in England, a theme which was soon to excite explicit affirmation in the writings of John Wyclif. Provisors legislation thus joined the statute of Mortmain as one of a number of authoritative texts, widely published and known in parliament and outside, which claimed or implied royal lordship over the English church. Herein lies its importance: in changing the attitudes of Englishmen yet to come, rather than in any immediate practical consequence. Men's minds more than men's actions were altered by it, for in practice the statute was no more consistently enforced than had been the ordinance which preceded it; its reaffirmations in 1365 and in Richard II's reign witness to this, and after 1351 until the end of the reign papal provisions averaged around a hundred or more a year.[39]

Praemunire

Not dissimilar from the statute of Provisors in its origin and importance was the statute of *Praemunire*, enacted in 1353. Ever since the time of William the Conqueror, kings of England had restrained appeals to Rome which threatened their interests, and a writ of 1306 expressly stated that 'according to the custom obtaining in our realm, no one of our subjects may be drawn out of our realm in a cause'.[40] During the early fourteenth century writs of prohibition were commonly sued out by subjects wishing to frustrate such appeals: E. B. Graves counted no fewer than 110 examples even in a cursory survey of records between 1307 and 1353. Nevertheless, in 1343 the king granted a commons' petition for the arrest of all who appealed or sued, against patrons or presentees, in any court prejudicial to the king's regality. Next year the commons renewed their demand and sought perpetual imprisonment or exile for such offenders. The king approved an ordinance to this effect and gave assurances that it would be converted into a permanent statute; in fact, nine years passed before this happened, and then there were significant differences. The statute of 1353 decreed that all who appealed to a court outside the realm on matters pertaining to the king's courts, or against judgements in them, were to answer for their contempt before his judges and to do so within two months of a writ of *praemunire facias* being issued; should they fail to do so, they were to suffer outlawry and forfeiture of all their lands and goods, the matter of the appeal then being concluded in the king's court.[41] The writ of *praemunire* had long been available and was by no means confined to ecclesiastical causes, let alone issues of provisions; what this statute did, however, was to ensure that those who embarked on the offending appeals in order to thwart the intentions of the statute of Provisors *should answer personally and promptly* for their offence or suffer severely for failing to do so; the penalties were not for making an appeal, but for failing to answer the charge of doing so. The statute did not mark a new direction in policy – it was usually applied only where the king's interests were threatened – and it neither defined new offences nor extended old ones. Its content as well as its timing suggest that it was intended principally as menacing propaganda to reinforce the ordinances and statute of Provisors, perhaps to jog the papal memory and twist the papal arm. What it did do was to write into the statute book claims previously advanced only in petitions and writs.

Pluralism, Provisors and Fiefdom

In the early 1360s, following the treaty of Brétigny, both England and France set about consolidating their positions. Edward looked for a match between his son, Edmund of Langley, and the heiress of the count of Flanders, and once again a papal dispensation was an inescapable prerequisite.[42] Urban V, however, was no less Francophile than Clement VI twenty years before, and no more obliging to Edward III. Nevertheless, the pope was particularly exposed to pressure over his measures against pluralism, a reform dear to his heart and an opportunity which the king was unlikely to disregard.

In 1363 in order to encourage and support more graduates, Urban issued his bull *Horribilis* which banned the holding even of sinecures in plurality.[43] Such a measure which would have impoverished all the king's clerks was unlikely to get sympathetic reception at any time and least of all when the king was trying to coerce the pope into a crucial dispensation. When that was refused in December 1364, the English response to *Horribilis* was more obstructive than ever. Thereupon the pope singled out England for another bull, with tighter procedures, to curb such pluralism; but this bull, *Consueta*, was also frustrated not only by its own ambiguous wording but also by English resentment which was manifested in evasive and half-hearted compliance with the order to list benefices held in plurality. Even had the bulls been better drafted and no question of diplomatic matches been at risk, it is inconceivable that the pope could have succeeded in a reform which threatened such disruption to the governmental machine and to so many sinecure holders. A far graver crisis of Anglo–papal relations might have ensued if incompetence and tactlessness had not invited and facilitated evasion.

Edward was never one to be content with simple combat: just as he mustered allies all round France at the opening of the war, and exerted pressure on Clement VI by the measures against papal provisions in the 1340s and 1350s, so in 1363–6 he applied all the screws he could find to bend the pope to his bidding. After years of neglect, and now on royal initiative, the statute of Provisors was re-enacted in parliament in 1365. This time, however, it was to be retrospective and activated on individual initiative, thus exposing numerous incumbents to harassment – at the very least – by rivals and enemies. *Praemunire*, too, was re-enacted. Once again, as in the 1290s and 1340s, the ports were closed to the ingress of papal bulls and the egress of money for the Curia; now official searchers (*scrutatores*) were appointed at the ports, and by the end of the decade they had become permanent officers.

Finally, Edward turned his attention to the tribute of 1000 marks which was due to the pope annually. This had fallen well into arrears by the time of Edward's accession, and a promise in the early 1330s to pay had yielded nothing in practice, but popes continued to expect the resumption of payments and the clearing of arrears. In 1366 the king extinguished these hopes for good. When Edward consulted parliament on the matter of the feudal tribute, he was advised by the prelates, dukes, earls, barons and commons that John's original cession was invalid because such an act required and patently lacked their consent; furthermore, it violated the king's coronation oath.[44] Of course, John could hardly have consulted parliament in that form before it was in existence, yet in Edward I's reign the principle was clearly enunciated that the king's coronation oath bound him to seek the consent of his parliament in matters touching the crown. Edward III could afford to entertain this notion, limiting though it was to the concept of royal lordship. Not only did this move further curtail papal income from England – albeit by a modest and irregular amount – but it also violated and was intended to rescind the feudal subordination of England to the papacy. In practice, however, the tribute had not been paid lately and the feudal dependency of England had been ignored and tacitly renounced ever since the demise of Henry III: no realistic pope, certainly after Boniface VIII's pontificate, and certainly not one located in mid-century Avignon, could have expected this feudal tie to amount to more than an annual rent, if even that. It is true that a certain 'special relationship' obtained between popes and the English monarchs in the fourteenth century: John XXII's episcopal provisions and his legatine efforts for internal peace make that clear. Edward III's secret letter to him in 1330 shows the other side of their relationship; but after the thirteenth century no homage or fealty was done by an English king, and no king succeeded to the throne by favour of the pope; even the special relationship must have been in doubt after the pope's partiality during the war with France. The feudal tie was a dead letter; its rejection in 1366 was little more than a rude gesture, hurtful, insulting and trivial – and in fact, like all the measures at this time, futile. In 1367 Urban granted the French king a dispensation to contract a Flemish match.

Clerical Grievances and Redress

On five occasions in the reign, the clergy submitted a list of grievances to the king for his action.[45] Because of his desperate need of money, the clergy had hopes of extracting the desired reforms. Yet, in fact, some of the grievances were ignored by the king and only a few of them were translated into statutes. A vital calculation for clergy and king alike was the attitude of the laity in parliament. When, in April 1341, clergy and laity were briefly united in their aims and submitted joint demands, statutes did result but they were repealed by the king a few months later, after the abatement of the crisis had dissolved the alliance. In 1344, with a grant of a triennial tenth, the clergy 'purchased' remedies for all their seven grievances; in 1352 twelve articles of complaint yielded a comprehensive statute *Pro clero*, but in 1376 out of ten articles only three items received any response at all. By then, however, the laity were stridently anticlerical.

The substance of the *gravamina* and of the remedies was often merely procedural, and sometimes both were simply repetitions of petitions and answers in earlier years; frequently they were hackneyed to the point of monotony. The principal concession by the crown came in 1344 when the king ordered the revocation of the commission by which since 1341 royal judges had been investigating not only the way in which crown officers used or abused their power but also complaints against officers of ecclesiastical courts and administration. Originally a vindictive response to Archbishop Stratford's resistance to the king, it revived memories of 1285 and its reversal was a matter of great importance to the church. The integrity and independence of clerical jurisdiction received further confirmation that year from measures which would restrict prohibitions and leave the courts Christian to decide on certain technicalities in cases of benefit of clergy. Other concessions to the church then included the reaffirmation of their immunity from purveyances and the protection of bishops from criminal charges which lacked royal authorization. All of these measures, however, addressed earlier abuses of the laws by reassertions of those laws rather than by offering new solutions or much, therefore, in the way of reassurance. On the vexed matter of regalian rights exercised during the vacancy of a see, the statute of 1344, by which the king abandoned retrospective presentation to such livings more than three years after a bishop was appointed, was never observed in practice, although it was repeated in 1352. Similarly a promise by the king in the same year, that he would not fill or claim vacancies which occurred *sede vacante* before his accession in 1327, was not fulfilled. A possibly more significant concession allowed that those who defaulted on payment of the clerical subsidy should be tried in the church courts and not in the king's, for this left the administration of clerical taxation firmly in the hands of the church.

In 1351 the clergy coupled a grant of a tenth with a list of *gravamina*, implementation of which would secure another tenth: the result was the statute *Pro clero* of 1352.[46] Although it touched on criminous clergy and on unspecific charges against bishops, its principal concern was to restrict abuses of patronage. Firstly the king agreed that he would no longer exercise it in virtue of those vacancies which had occurred in an earlier reign, although he insisted on his right to present to livings vacated up to three years ago; even so, his title to use another's advowson was to be carefully examined; moreover, the question of whether a living was already filled or not – the matter of plenarty – was to be answered in the church courts, not the king's. Aggrieved patrons or beneficed clerks were granted the protection of various writs, while bishops who were the targets of the writ *quare non admisit* were no longer to incur the loss of their temporalities but were to suffer fines instead. This statute went some way towards limiting the worst excesses of royal patronage and jurisdiction, yet statutes were seldom proof against the king's need or convenience.

In 1376 and 1377 little was gained by the clergy beyond some limits to prohibitions being again attempted and the conferment of immunity from arrest of priests celebrating divine services or carrying the host to the sick. But to weigh against this, parliamentary pressure had extracted a definition of *silva cedua* (cut wood) tithes more favourable to the laity than the clergy.

As a result of clerical grievances Edward III made no fundamental shifts in his ground and the church made few secure, and no large, gains. Many of the clerical *gravamina* met with no positive royal response and most of those that were positive, and even those enshrined in statutes, were disregarded whenever they proved inconvenient. Kings, after all, had amply demonstrated with the statute of Mortmain, and were to do so still more blatantly and spectacularly with the statutes of Provisors, their capacity to waive or ignore the letter of the law virtually at will; certainly legislation to restrict royal patronage or jurisdiction was seldom proof against the king's needs or convenience, and the clerical grievances and statutes of Edward's reign, by their repetition, afford some evidence of this. Such grievances expediently put forward by the clergy and expediently granted by the king when he needed their money, offered but fragile protection to the church's liberties. Temporalities, for example, were still seized and never more cynically than in 1372 when all the bishops of the southern province suffered the king's attempt to accelerate the delivery of the subsidy.

One should not conclude, however, that these issues seriously poisoned relations between the crown and church, for the clergy were principal beneficiaries of royal writs, particularly clerks in royal service who by this time were coming to dominate the episcopate. Moreover, as with so much else then, clamour far exceeded abuse: frequent assemblies of parliament and convocation, confronted by a king desperate for subsidies, encouraged complaint and its repetition, invariably based upon impressions not on measured or objective observations. All along the shifting boundary of temporalities and spiritualities, of the king's matters and the church's preserves, these disputes were common, but, except in radical, eccentric or academic quarters, parties on neither side proposed abolishing the boundary. At least, that was true until the next reign.

The Episcopate

Edward's bishops were characterized by three features: their remarkable competence, their increasing scholarship or expertise, and their amenability.[47] Following a trend already apparent in his father's reign, Edward used bishoprics especially to reward his administrators; thus, in the 1350s Islip and Thoresby, two former keepers of the privy seal, occupied Canterbury and York respectively – and incidentally brought to an end the chronic dispute over ceremonial precedence between the two sees; altogether fourteen of his bishops had been keeper of the privy seal before their promotion to bishoprics. Election, however, did not put an end to secular duties: nine bishops became chancellors, ten became treasurers; only eight chancellors and seven treasurers were not bishops. Even when holding neither of these offices a bishop was often preoccupied with royal business: in 1334 Archbishop Stratford was off to France on a diplomatic mission only a fortnight after his enthronement, and from July 1338 to October 1339 he spent 456 days abroad on royal service.[48] Of the eighty-five bishops of Edward's reign, only ten secular clerks who were without royal or household links held English sees, seven more held Welsh ones; for the most part these ten were elected by chapters rather than provided by popes on royal prompting. Only fifteen religious became bishops, eight of these in Welsh sees, and six in sees where they were members of the monastic cathedral chapter. By far the most remarkable was Simon Langham, if only because he was the last religious to occupy the see of Canterbury. The number of papal protégés on the episcopal bench was predictably small: ten only had served at the Curia, including Archbishop Sudbury who was an auditor there; but of these men, only four were promoted primarily because of their standing with the pope. Although no bishop was appointed without a papal provision after 1344, by then legislation constrained the popes who were anyway keen to placate a king whom they had to disappoint on other, more sensitive political affairs.

It has been said that the episcopate was tamed under Edward III, a fact largely borne out by the figures given above.[49] The significant increase of graduates among them when compared with Henry III's reign a century before, 70 per cent contrasted with 50 per cent, in many ways reflected this docility, for whereas theologians had not increased, lawyers were very much more numerous, and men distinguished for their scholarship were few indeed. To take simply the most important see, that of Canterbury, of seven holders appointed by Edward no fewer than five were lawyers, qualified in civil and canon law. Of the two exceptions, Thomas Bradwardine, whose tenure lasted less than a year because of the plague, not only was a celebrated mathematician, astronomer, moral philosopher and theologian, variously known as Doctor Profundus or Doctor Solemnis, but had also served as a royal chaplain with the king in Flanders from 1338 until 1347 and had been one of the commissioners who treated with

Philip VI in 1346.[50] Bradwardine's appointment affords a vivid illustration of the king's control not only of personnel but also of procedure. When John Stratford died in 1348 the Canterbury chapter elected Bradwardine without even seeking the king's *congé d'élire*, confident that they were electing the most distinguished scholar in England and a trusted and proven royal servant: Edward at once overrode this dangerous innovation and obtained a papal provision for John Offord, then chancellor of the realm and previously keeper of the privy seal and king's secretary. Offord, however, was already, or very soon afterwards, paralytic, and when he succumbed to the plague even before he had been installed and consecrated, Edward readily entered Bradwardine's name on the *congé d'élire* which the chapter now sought in line with normal procedure. It was the greatest irony that Bradwardine, too, should die of the plague a few months later, but Edward had made his point.

The other exception to the sequence of lawyer prelates was Simon Langham, who was probably a theologian by training.[51] Having caught the king's eye as a commendably vigorous and efficient abbot of Westminster, he was employed first as treasurer of the realm before becoming bishop of Ely in 1362, and then as chancellor before moving to Canterbury in 1366. That he should be the last monk to hold that see is scarcely more revealing of royal priorities than the manner of his departure from it. In 1368 when Langham was appointed cardinal (an office which aroused deep suspicions among the English at that time) Edward seized his temporalities and compelled him to resign; contrast the promotion of Kilwardby under Edward I when the pope elevated him to the cardinalate on the assumption that this would *ipso facto* entail his vacation of Canterbury. Although Langham was again elected by the Canterbury chapter when the see was next vacant, in 1374, it then suited both king and pope to keep him at the Curia and to promote instead Simon Sudbury, a former curial official who, as bishop of London, had demonstrated his loyalty to the king.

Sudbury's translation was part of a deal in 1375 whereby the pope was allowed to tax the English clergy in return for provisions which moved Courtenay from Hereford to London (rather than to Canterbury), Gilbert to Hereford, Erghum (who was Gaunt's chancellor) to Salisbury, and Wakefield (keeper of the king's wardrobe) to Worcester where he displaced the prior whom the chapter had elected.[52] Although few episodes better illustrate the value of provisions to the king and the grip which they gave him on the episcopate and the church, it is noteworthy that the pope acquiesced so readily only because he urgently wanted a *quid pro quo*: provisions were not by themselves an assurance of royal dominance, and although the king could always invoke the statute it was a weapon whose credibility would be weakened by excessive use. With or without provisions, however, the king could not be an arbitrary patron: the aspiring sons of noble houses – Courtenay, Neville and Arundel during the 1370s – could not be denied episcopal rank. The king's lordship in theory was not always matched in practice.

At the other metropolitan see, York, on Melton's death in 1340 the king backed his current servant and favourite, William Kilsby, but the chapter elected a former royal servant and their dean, William Zouche.[53] After two years of appeals to Rome the king's representations for Kilsby and resistance to Zouche proved unavailing. In 1352, however, on Zouche's death, the king succeeded in getting his chancellor, a civil lawyer and a former keeper of the privy seal, John Thoresby, translated from Worcester. Thoresby reminds us that royal nominees and the crown's grip on appointments did not inevitably – or indeed mainly – result in the promotion of unsuitable men. As well as serving as chancellor from 1349 to 1356 and guardian of the realm in the king's absence during 1355, Thoresby was an especially active archbishop, commissioning an English translation of, and commentary upon, the Lord's Prayer, the Creed and the Decalogue; in addition, he initiated and funded new building at York Minster and showed his further pastoral concern in his diocesan letters and constitutions.[54] His successor in 1373, the aristocratic Alexander Neville, was a graduate and a student of civil law as well as a royal clerk, but his tenure is less reassuring about royal prelates.

The preponderance of graduates, especially in law, among Edward's bishops reflects the growing professionalism of church and crown administration; it does not signify the advent of a fiercely independent episcopate, but rather the contrary. This development was certainly assisted, though by no means begun, by the crown's constraints upon papal provisions; the Provisors legislation did not result in a monolithic prelacy, although the king usually controlled appointments to key bishoprics and the occasions when prelates defied kings on crucial issues were few indeed in the rest of our period. The episcopate, led as it was so often by civil lawyers who were royal ministers, became vulnerable to the gibes about 'Caesarian' bishops levelled against it by Wyclif and others.

John of Gaunt and the Clergy

Hostilities with France had been resumed in 1369 at a time when the king's interest in affairs was proving fitful and government was increasingly dominated by his second son, John of Gaunt, duke of Lancaster. Gaunt conducted the war largely with reference to his own Castilian interests, at vast expense and with gross incompetence.[55] Partly in order to secure the replacement of royal ministers by his own, and partly to cow the clergy and cajole the laity into defraying the costs of the renewed hostilities, Gaunt encouraged the expression of anticlericalism and first provoked, and then sponsored, antipapalism as well. In 1371 he and his friends contrived the dismissal of the chancellor, the treasurer and the keeper of the privy seal, respectively Bishop Wykeham of Winchester, Bishop Brantingham of Exeter and Canon Peter Lacy of Lichfield. The anticlericalism of parliament in 1371 was doubtless fanned by the address of two Austin friars;[56] that assembly was certainly informed by Gaunt of the officers' mismanagement and failure to make the crown solvent even in years of peace, although the chancellor and keeper were appointed only in 1367 and the treasurer as recently as 1369. All three clerics were replaced by laymen and not until 1377 were these offices again in clerical hands. By then other problems had arisen for Gaunt and for Wykeham.

In the early 1370s, in order to enlist papal support for his own Iberian ambitions, Gaunt allowed a papal tax to be collected in England to pay for the pope's Italian wars; for the same reason he encouraged papal efforts to negotiate an Anglo–French peace which, although it would have pleased the more disillusioned subjects of Edward III, only outraged others; accompanying the peace negotiations at Bruges were discussions to resolve Anglo–papal disputes, a tentative agreement on which was reached in 1375. In the autumn of 1376 Gaunt's need for money compelled him to summon parliament where hostility to all these developments was manifested in renewed support for Wykeham and in the impeachment of Gaunt's principal agents. The 'Good Parliament', as it is known, established a continual council to oversee government and clamoured for the enforcement of Provisors, which the recent agreement at Bruges had threatened. However, as soon as parliament was dissolved, Gaunt followed the familiar precedents of kings and began to reverse its decisions and to win friends. The continual council was abolished, Wykeham was charged with corruption (committed back in the 1360s), and Wyclif was encouraged to give voice to popular anticlerical and antipapal sentiments. Gaunt's hostility to the clergy was opportunistic and shallow, as became clear in 1377 when he not only replaced the unpopular lay chancellor and treasurer with the bishops of St David's and Worcester but also completed the Anglo–papal concordat. By this the pope agreed to restrain his exercise of provisions and expectations in return for relaxation – not repeal – of the statutes of Provisors; while for his part, the king agreed to limit his exercise of regalian rights and to abandon the writ *quare impedit*. At that stage, however, neither pope nor king could long deliver these promised benefits.

During these last years of the reign, John of Gaunt had cynically stoked the fires of anticlericalism and antipapalism with reckless disregard for their control: they were fires not easily or soon to be extinguished.

Sovereignty

The statute of Provisors may be seen, in one light, as an issue of sovereignty, papal and royal. Yet the 1351 statute was never intended to exclude all or most papal appointments in perpetuity: it was a crude piece of blackmail applied or disregarded in response to affairs essentially unconnected with patronage and jurisdiction. The king himself would have been the chief sufferer had the law been strictly enforced, because he needed papal assistance in order to fill the episcopal bench largely in accordance with his own wishes. Since the capitulation of King John at the end of the Langton affair, no king could legally override a free election except at considerable political risk and cost; he could withhold temporalities and bully chapters only for so long without provoking formidable opposition at home and appeals to the Curia: it was the pope who had sovereignty over the electors, and the king acknowledged this both by the restrictions which he placed upon provisions and even more by the way in which he waived them. After the appointment of Trillek to Hereford in 1344, the pope played a necessary role in almost all subsequent appointments to English sees (up to and including Cranmer's promotion to Canterbury in 1533), the few exceptions occurring during the Council of Constance, 1414–18. Nevertheless, although first the ordinance and then the statute enabled the king to pressure the pope into congenial provisions, by no means all subsequent appointments were of the king's men. In the end, the statute of Provisors undoubtedly tightened the king's grip on his church through enlarging his influence upon the character of the episcopate, but even this gain had its limitations: not all sees fell vacant in one reign, or at convenient moments in it, and royal power over promotions was bound to fluctuate; the king himself was subject to pressures from magnates, courtiers, councillors, bishops, monasteries and popes, and circumstances compelled him to acquiesce in someone else's priorities from time to time. The episcopal bench from the middle of the fourteenth century may not have had a Pecham or a Winchelsey at Canterbury, but it certainly had a Courtenay and an Arundel; it varied in docility and character from reign to reign and within reigns. The king's lordship in theory was not always matched in practice.

As for sovereignty, it was no more securely achieved by *Praemunire* than it had been by William the Conqueror's ban on appeals in the eleventh century or by Henry II's in the twelfth. Edward III's statute pertained only to appeals in certain cases and was addressed to the problem of forcing offenders to appear in court; appeals to Rome had already been at the mercy of writs of prohibition long before 1353. The real significance of these statutes lies in their public criticism and curtailment of the exercise of papal authority: the realm, gathered in parliament, had attempted to set limits to the papal *plenitudo potestatis*. Not only was this legislation published in parliament, in the courts and at the ports, but it was also a matter of record acknowledged by reiteration or by dispensation. The more it was repeated and enforced, the greater was the stimulus and appeal to popular antipapalism.

Sovereignty might seem to have been more significantly advanced by the abrogation of the feudal tribute due to Rome since the early thirteenth century, but that obligation had been more honoured in the breach than the observance. Moreover, not since Henry III's time had either pope or king regarded it as involving anything more precise than a ceremonial payment; not even Boniface VIII – quick to claim lordship over Scotland – sought to make further capital out of the English tribute. After him, popes were well apprised of the emptiness of such feudal claims – perhaps even of the irony of a papacy in exile attempting to enforce its lordship. The renunciation of tribute and vassalage in 1366 was more significant emotionally than constitutionally.

Papal claims to tax the English clergy had always been at the mercy of royal restriction, in practice if not in theory. Usually such levies were only attempted in order to finance a royal crusade and with great regularity successive kings creamed off, or were granted, part of the revenue for their own political purposes. Papal taxation was not barred by the king after 1337 but stopped by Avignon popes eager to avoid financing Edward's war effort. When a pope did resume taxation, it was in order to pay Edward a ransom which otherwise the French would have had to find! The attempt by Gregory XI in the 1370s to levy a tax for his Italian wars was allowed by the grace of the duke of Lancaster but proved unprofitable and unpopular. Papal taxation was rare thereafter, but even before then it had always been levied subject to royal collusion.

On appointments, on appeals and on taxation, it is hard to discern significantly new limits imposed by Edward III. The king had certainly enlarged his role in episcopal promotions by the statutes of Provisors, but only at the price of acknowledging the indispensable role of the pope in these appointments. At a lower level of patronage the king's sanctions usually overrode the pope's, as the example of Archbishop Zouche makes clear, but bishops had long been vulnerable to the crown's confiscation of their estates, and in Edward I's time Archbishop Corbridge of York had felt the full weight of royal power for defending a providee. After *Praemunire*, appeals were no more restricted than before. Particularly during the 1340s and 1350s certain papal bulls were barred from entry to the realm at the ports, and money due to the pope from services and annates had been halted, but all this had been anticipated before Edward's reign. As royal tax needs increased, there was little likelihood that papal demands upon the clergy would be tolerated except where they redounded to the profit of the king: this was clear enough even in Edward I's reign. As for the rejection of the feudal tribute, this was more a financial loss to the pope than a practical gain for the king. Insofar as the sovereignty of the crown over the church was qualified by papal authority within the church, it is hard to see that any substantial advances had been made by Edward III. A different picture emerges of his relationship with the English church.

The clergy, like the laity, became accustomed in his reign to frequent and often oppressive royal taxation. They had little hope of, and during much of the reign perhaps no desire for, protection from a pope so closely identified with the enemy; in any event, the circumstances of war offered few grounds for invoking *Clericis Laicos* again. Although the clergy exercised some discretion in their responses to royal demands, from time to time exacting a *quid pro quo*, or refusing extreme requests – for a sexennial tenth in 1356, for a third tenth in 1370, and altogether in 1373 – they were only very seldom able to resist royal pressure. This took many forms: propaganda (in which the clergy themselves collaborated), personal appeals, veiled threats, menacing delegations of councillors, and astute management by archbishops such as Sudbury. As a result, the church made a crucial contribution to the crown's war revenues to set beside their administrative and propaganda role. One by-product of this taxation was the firm establishment of convocation in the constitution of church and realm.

The king supplemented his clerical subsidies with the revenues of alien priories which he seized for the duration of the war. So extended was this that by the end of the reign increasing numbers of laymen were accustomed to farming or acquiring ecclesiastical endowments. This secularization of the church's property coincided with the gradual extension of the crown's ecclesiastical patronage, a process begun well before this reign but in it reaching such an extent that it jeopardized clerical independence, morale and discipline. Opponents of royal patronage were crushed beneath a battery of writs, corrupt juries and ferocious sanctions from which not even an archbishop threatened by a pope was immune. Although Edward yielded redress on some of these issues when the clergy submitted corporate complaints, it was niggardly and seldom observed for long in practice. With an episcopate increasingly composed of royal clerks, Edward could take even greater liberties than his predecessors, yet there were limits and these were imposed more by political expediency than by legal constraints. In this context, the strains which the war – as well as other events – put upon traditional loyalties and habits within the church and the realm were to exert rather greater pressure on the clergy henceforth than the legislative and jurisdictional developments of the reign. By the end of the reign the clergy had more to fear from the laity than from the king.

The king's relations with his church afford two further observations on his authority. Firstly, throughout his reign and beyond, antipapal and anticlerical legislation repeatedly reminds us of parliament's limitations in obtaining from the king the laws which it desired when it wanted them. Provisors and *Praemunire* emerged as statutes only after years of campaigning by the commons, and even then were applied selectively when applied at all. Secondly, the king's tightening grip on the English church occurred just at the time when his feudal lordship over his lay subjects was beginning to suffer the inroads made by enfeoffments to use (virtually trusts) and when his ability to summon the feudal host was little more than a memory. It would be absurd to assert that the king was deliberately redressing the balance by affirming more strongly than ever his lordship over the clergy and their lands, and it would certainly be difficult at present to prove that he gained on the ecclesiastical roundabouts what he was losing on the feudal swings; but in effect the king was raiding the church to recoup his loss of resources elsewhere in the realm. The consequences for church discipline and pastoral effectiveness were considerable and they exposed the clergy to a rising chorus of popular criticism.

4

Plague and Disruption

In 1348 the Black Death arrived in England and by 1350 it had visited all regions, though by no means all communities. While the term refers to bubonic, and to the even more lethal pneumonic, plague, it probably trailed in its wake secondary infections such as typhus, measles, scarlet fever and influenza. Further wide-scale visitations followed in 1361–2, 1369, 1375, 1379, 1390–1, 1393 and with diminishing frequency and extent on into the sixteenth century; in addition, there were many localized or less severe outbreaks even in the fourteenth century. Although adults, especially the elderly, were undoubted targets of the plague, children and youths seem to have been the most conspicuous victims in 1361–2 and 1390–1, with obvious implications for the long-term effects. The visitation of 1390–1 compared in virulence and mortality with the first arrival in 1348, probably because it followed four years of famine and dysentery.[1]

So dramatic was the impact of the plague upon contemporary witnesses that their accounts probably exaggerate the decimation even beyond its actual horrific scale. However, recent attempts, particularly by the medical historian J. F. D. Shrewsbury, to discount most of the appalling statistics and to suggest that only 5 per cent died of the plague do not bear close scrutiny.[2] Yet neither are claims that the overall mortality figure reached as much as 60 per cent wholly convincing.[3] Most historians today, on the weight of all the available evidence – which is neither complete nor statistically satisfactory, and is often circumstantial rather than direct or precise – would opt for a figure of between a half and a third of the population, with the general consensus inclining to a third. Yet even a third on a scale to transform society, aggravating old tensions and creating new problems. The overall mortality figure is an average which was far exceeded in some communities and scarcely approached in others, so that any national picture is necessarily inadequate and misleading in respect of many local conditions. For example, St Albans lost its abbot, prior and forty-six monks within a few days in 1349, and at Meaux, in East Yorkshire, thirty-two out of forty-two inmates died, while Hickling priory, in Norfolk, was emptied; yet at Christ Church, Canterbury, only four monks succumbed.[4] Similar variations are discernible among lay communities. Of course, the effect of the plague was cumulative as each fresh wave reversed incipient recovery and even struck – as in 1361–2 and 1390–1 – at the potential child-bearers of the next generation: we might reasonably expect, therefore, the impact of the Black Death to change with the passage of time.

The astounding horror and panic upon the first arrival of the plague is easy to appreciate: prayers, processions and flight were commonplace; graveyards – as at Newark in 1348[5] – were quickly filled and new ones had to be dug; monastic houses were emptied, an archbishop struck down, manors cleared of their tenants, vills, towns and parishes depopulated. Yet demographically and economically what is most striking about the first visitation is the speed with which the deceased were replaced: Dr Bridbury has stressed how quickly vacant holdings on manors were reoccupied, and it was long ago revealed by A. H. Thompson and A. Jessop how over a thousand vacant benefices in York diocese, and more than eight hundred in Norwich, were filled in one year, eighty-three of Norwich livings being filled twice, and ten, three times. It is indicative of the reserves of manpower that in Lincoln diocese, where normally around two hundred vacancies occurred in a year, during 1349 over a thousand institutions were recorded.[6] Although it was once thought that this merely underlined how overpopulated with clergy England then was, it is now clear that the laity swarmed in equally excessive numbers on the eve of the Black Death. Yet, while some parish churches were united after the plague because of a local shortage of clergy, or of a reluctance on their part to serve in afflicted parishes, unions were also brought about by a dearth of parishioners, as at Great and Little Collington in 1352 where there was 'scarcely maintenance for one priest, so much has plague reduced the people and impoverished the land'. The bishop of Winchester's register records that 'Since the plague many churches are destroyed, and in many there are no parishioners or only a few and through want of parishioners many rectors lie in penury, and the churches are in ruins.'[7] All this strengthens the view of other historians that, notwithstanding the famine and cattle murrain of the years 1316–24, England was abundantly, and for its resources excessively, populated in 1348. Because the incidence of plague in 1348–9 was uneven and some communities were much more savaged by it than others, there were many new opportunities for enterprising individuals – clerks as well as laymen – to extract an increased reward for their labour. In 1349 an ordinance, and in 1351 a statute, sought to stifle this opportunism among the laity while Archbishop Islip applied similar restraint to the clergy.[8] This was the beginning of a sequence of measures to maintain the *status quo*, and wage-restraint legislation continued to be passed into the fifteenth century – eloquent testimony to the accumulating pressures of the intervening decades. These measures had the unfortunate effect of rehearsing in their preambles, in official and widely published instruments, ferocious condemnations of the greed of the hired, wage-earning clergy, the unbeneficed chaplains. In his constitution of 1378, for example, Archbishop Sudbury declared that

> priests of the present time, of our city, diocese, and province of Canterbury, are so tainted with the vice of cupidity that they are not content with reasonable stipends but claim and receive excessive wages. These greedy and fastidious priests vomit from the burden of excessive salaries of this kind, they run wild and wallow, and some of them, after gluttony of the belly, break forth into a pit of evils, to the detestable scandal of all clergy and the pernicious example of clerics.[9]

Not dissimilar criticisms prefaced decrees about clerical stipends in 1349, 1362 and 1388, yet such savage condemnation, emanating from the prelates and the well-beneficed, helped to identify these dignitaries as greedy predators in society. Such legislation drove a firm wedge between the ranks of the clergy as each denounced the venality of the other and thus fuelled and confirmed the anticlerical sentiments of the laity. Laymen who resented clerical wealth would find widespread support for their views, no longer just among those seculars who were jealous of the religious, or among the friars too self-preeningly rigorous in their definition and advocacy of poverty, but also among the lesser clergy and in episcopal and official proclamations.

The relationship of clergy and laity, however, was decisively shifted by the plague in other ways. No one nowadays maintains that the Black Death initiated the collapse of serfdom, but opportunities for villeins to obtain manumission or to flee from serfdom were undoubtedly increased as a consequence of the disruption which resulted. Serfs did not disappear, but in many places they were supplanted by leaseholders; a shrinking labour force encouraged lords to evade the expensive consequences and to lease out their land. The later years of the fourteenth century, despite all efforts to maintain the *status quo*, were a time of unprecedented opportunity and enfranchisement for many Englishmen, and it would be surprising if some did not regard obligatory tithe payments to the clergy as among those customary dues which were on their way out: the claims, championed by some friars and by some less orthodox and less disinterested advocates, that payments of tithes to the parish clergy should be free-will offerings dependent upon the moral or pastoral worth of the incumbent were in harmony with the growing disappearance of manorial obligations at that time.

As the successive visits of the plague took effect, social disruption increased, so much so that by the 1390s the population of whole villages had been transformed by the influx of new landholders. J. A. Raftis has shown what tensions resulted between the 'natives' and the 'aliens' of a community and how violence was magnified and multiplied.[10] Even where immigrants were not involved, or were not dominant among new tenants, so many new families acquired holdings that the stability of communities was often drastically undermined by the plague, so that at the end of the century there was a rootless air about many of them:

typically in one Berkshire village a 64 per cent turnover in tenants occurred between 1379 and 1394.[11] It may well be a reflection of all this development – as well as of the mobility of society at large – that in the late fourteenth century beneficed clergy were exchanging their livings with scandalous frequency, so much so that Archbishop Courtenay attempted to restrain the practice by a decree in 1392.[12] A great many reasons explain individual exchanges, and historians have shown them all; it was predictable, too, that agents or agencies should spring up to negotiate such transfers and then, for greater profit, begin to initiate and promote them.[13] Of course, beneficed clergy, so often pluralist or absentee, had always had a loose attachment to their parishes, but the scale of exchanges by this period clearly includes many incumbents who were not among the graduates and career men, and there is a qualitative difference between waiting for an opening and impatiently contriving one, often within weeks or even days of being inducted into a living. About the beneficed clergy of this age there is a frenetic rootlessness reflecting that of many of their parishioners. This had consequences for their pastoral role and responsibilities, but in the context of this study it is significant for marking yet another slackening of the communal ties between clergy and laity. In fact the pace of exchanges did not slow down, despite Courtenay's decree, until the 1440s, and when we know more in detail about the economy of the fifteenth century we may find that a social and not an administrative explanation is called for.

The psychological impact of the plague was doubtless the earliest and most dramatic effect, but it is the one hardest to define and grasp. Much has been written about the excess of fervour stimulated by the plague, but England did not witness the flagellant extravagances of some European areas, and Dr Wood-Legh has shown how chantry foundations were gathering impetus well before 1348; indeed, they probably have more to do with the wider diffusion of wealth which enabled a larger number of inhabitants to endow prayers for themselves and their own.[14] Those ghoulish cadaver tombs which are sometimes associated with this event are in fact very few, by far the most celebrated and numerous dating from a much later time; nor is the Dance of

Death encountered in English art until well into the fifteenth century. The prescriptions for simple funerals and the loathing of the flesh recorded in some wills probably had roots in contemporary Flemish piety as much as in English experience, yet it would not be unreasonable to discern among the survivors of the plague not only the greedy materialism of the newly enriched but also a pessimistic horror of worldly wealth.

Obviously the initial result of the plague would have been to intensify pessimism and panic and to prompt Edwardian men and women to greater efforts in order to secure their souls, if not their bodies, from disaster. Yet it may be that the survivors (especially of several visits) who looked back on the dramatic events of the disease gained new insights into the world and cosmology of which they were a part. In 1348 Archbishop Zouche issued indulgences, and in 1369 his successor, Archbishop Thoresby, ordered prayers and processions, to avert death and sickness, exhortations which were intended to be circulated, published and implemented throughout their province.[15] Both prelates emphatically proclaimed the commonplace that plague was divine retribution for sin. What then should people make of the seemingly arbitrary judgement upon Archbishop Bradwardine (himself, ironically, an advocate of the total omnipotence of God), or upon clergy and monks as well as upon laymen, regardless of all priestly efforts to avert its coming or its return? Implicit in all this was surely an omnipotent God beyond all the restraints, recommendations and pleas of the clergy; perhaps one might also conclude that if the sinful were punished with a plague which fell upon prelate, cleric and layman with no clear differential, there must be another church than the visible institutional one, a church invisible of the saved, the predestined saved. When Wyclif argued this a little later, contemporary experience appeared to support him.

We are dealing with the intangible and the immeasurable when we consider post-plague psychology, and we must certainly forswear any temptation to assign an extravagant scale to this phenomenon or to believe that contemporaries succumbed to all these emotions and attitudes consistently or with any self-awareness. We should, however, remember that the confessional enquiries to which they were subject and the sermons which they could regularly hear – quite apart from the books which increasing numbers of them could read or listen to – would have made them far more sensitive than we are to all the ramifications of sin and salvation. That more than a few were changed by their plague and post-plague experiences is surely borne out by the remarkable influence which Wyclif and his disciples exerted in the last decades of the century.

5

Learning and Literacy

Although most centuries can boast some significant advance in the spread of learning, and despite the fact that in histories of this kingdom the literate layman 'rises' almost as often as does the middle class or the gentry, the fourteenth century can nevertheless claim a special significance in the social history of English education. For the first time the graduate begins to dominate the administrative echelons of both state and church, and academic scholars profoundly influence popular ideas. Almost more strikingly novel in its way was the emergence of the English vernacular as a language to be written and read, fit for epic, romance, satire and the scriptures, a channel for the transmission of ideas and ideals across time and topography. The church both contributed to, and was profoundly affected by, these developments which realigned the whole nexus of cleric and layman. There were certainly other developments – war and plague among them – pressing in the same direction, but we shall surely fail to understand the changing relationship of church and realm in the later fourteenth century unless we also consider matters of learning and literacy.

The multiplication of legislation, the extension of taxation, the organization for war and negotiation for peace led to a massive increase in government bureaucracy. Under Edward I, the *Quo warranto* proceedings and the Mortmain applications would alone have entailed additional staff to cope with more records and new procedures. In Edward II's reign, and still more under Edward III, taxation as well as the raising and provisioning of armies and ships could not have been accomplished by relying upon a skeleton staff, nor indeed upon staff who were literate, without being mentally organized. In the 1320s Stapledon's treasury reforms necessitated the searching and keeping of records on an unprecedented scale, so that it is not surprising to see clerks and graduates displacing knights in the exchequer then. The emerging parliament, too, created records which made educated clerks indispensable. Diplomacy, all the more frequent as a result of war, required not only skilful drafters, but also prestigiously educated and cultivated agents. Non-graduates – even laymen – continued throughout this period to serve the crown in central as well as local administration, and among the most illustrious and capable non-graduates were Archbishop Melton and Bishop Wykeham, who head a considerable list; but they themselves depended upon the service of graduates about the king and in their dioceses.

The church itself recognized the value of graduates for its pastoral and pedagogic mission as well as for its administrative and jurisdictional machinery, and in 1298 Boniface VIII by the constitution *Cum ex eo* enabled beneficed clergy to absent themselves, with episcopal licence, for up to seven years in order to study at a university. Those graduates, however, who as a consequence of their degrees began serving a bishop and the church, not infrequently came to be commended by that bishop to the king's attention and ended up in the king's service, as we have seen happened at York during Edward II's reign.[1] Such a graduate would be commonly rewarded with abundant fat livings. The higher dignities of the church thus came to be very largely the preserve of those men who had degrees: between 1307 and 1499, 68 per cent of deans and 72 per cent of archdeacons were graduates of Oxford or Cambridge; in the fourteenth century just over 60 per cent of bishops were graduates, compared with 36 per cent in the thirteenth and 91 per cent in the fifteenth.[2] Very largely such ecclesiastical offices were filled by men inevitably preoccupied elsewhere, but this only meant more – if humbler – employment for graduates deputizing for their superiors. Bishops had vicars-general, archdeacons had officials, and so on: it was from the lower limbs of the administrative tree that some graduates climbed to the top of it.

During Edward I's reign Oxford University had acquired four new colleges (two for the religious orders), bringing its total to five; Cambridge had only Peterhouse, founded in 1284. But in the next century the endowment of colleges, halls and students gathered momentum and by 1380 five more colleges had been established at Oxford and seven more at Cambridge. Not the least revealing aspect of this expansion is the character of some of the founders and their wishes. Edward II founded King's Hall, Cambridge, to train clerks from the chapel royal; the college was maintained from exchequer funds, the warden was appointed by the king, and the fellows by writ of privy seal; most notably, the emphasis was upon the study of civil law.[3] Royal servants were prominent among the patrons of universities and students in this period. Bishop Hotham of Ely, treasurer and later chancellor, played an important part in the foundation of King's Hall. Bishop Stapledon of Exeter, Edward's most notable treasurer, endowed Stapledon Hall at Oxford and planned Exeter College, Oxford, which was completed by Grandisson, another bishop of Exeter: this college also was to train not theologians but lawyers. (Stapledon, like many of his fellow bishops, was also lavish in his grants of licences, under *Cum ex eo*, to beneficed clergy.) A chancery clerk, Adam de Brome, endowed the college of St Mary, later Oriel, at Oxford in 1324, the very year in which a chancellor of the exchequer, Harvey de Staunton, was founding Michaelhouse at Cambridge. Roger Northburgh, bishop of Lichfield and keeper of the wardrobe, planned halls at Oxford for students of logic and theology. What might be deemed the climax of all this endowment came in 1379 with Bishop William of Wykeham's New College, Oxford, and its attached grammar school in Winchester. New College was to provide for seventy students from Wykeham's diocese and episcopal estates; at least twenty of the inmates were to read law, and in practice nearly 70 per cent did so. There can scarcely be more eloquent testimony to the contemporary valuation put upon university education than that a man whose lack of a degree had in no way prevented his rise to pivotal authority in politics and the church should choose to commemorate himself by so extravagant an endowment of a university college. What made his foundation the more remarkable was its provision rather for undergraduates than, as was previously characteristic of colleges, for graduates; subsequent colleges and older institutions took up this lead. In the wake of large endowments followed innumerable gifts and extensive patronage. By no means all this generosity was intended to provide administrators for crown or church, but all benefactions implicitly acknowledged the practical importance and social usefulness of learning.

Some 15,000 graduates from Oxford and around 7000 from Cambridge have been identified from the period 1307 to 1499, and it is generally recognized that these figures are very far from affording a complete picture of the student body; so many have undoubtedly eluded the extant records (themselves far from complete) by departing from the university without proceeding to a degree or without entering upon a clerical career (in which they were far more likely to leave some biographical trace).[4] Except among the smaller number of religious, the graduates were overwhelmingly lawyers, civil even more than canon, although a goodly proportion had doctorates in both kinds. Theology seemed to open fewer opportunities in absolute numbers, but both church and crown had need of doctrinal experts and confessors. Lawyers had obvious utility: the canon lawyers in the church courts, civil lawyers in secular and especially diplomatic realms. Yet lawyers, like theologians, were often employed in roles wholly irrelevant to their specialism and it is quite clear that what was valued increasingly about the graduate was his trained mind – much like classicists in nineteenth-century England.

Academic training was encouraged by, and itself stimulated, governmental development; although the source and motivation were initially ecclesiastical, so interlocked were church and realm that the crown, too, and its servants promoted the growth of universities and exploited the expansion of graduate numbers. Without these copious 'fountains of clergy in this realm', as a parliamentary petition in 1401 described the universities,[5] it is doubtful if the king's government could have coped even as adequately as it did with the increasing demands made upon it by the complex developments of society and politics in the fourteenth century. The inns of court and chancery, whose pre-history has now been traced back into the early fourteenth century, were no doubt effective in producing common lawyers, but necessary as these were in the wake of parliamentary legislation, laymen were

costlier to remunerate than clergy and were hardly a match for the
civil and canon lawyers who conducted diplomacy for the king's
foreign antagonists and allies. The universities were ecclesiastical
institutions, but they were increasingly exploited to train the
king's servants until such time as laymen could be found in
sufficient numbers or sufficiently cheaply to supplant clerical
graduates. There were undoubtedly some lay students – most
easily identified when the sons of the aristocracy – and some
graduates and other students who turned subsequently to lay
careers (as we shall see below).[6] Some men proceeded to university
in minor orders only, and emerged from it in them still, able
therefore to pursue quite legally an entirely secular career; some
left for various reasons – poverty, disillusion, inability, succession
to an estate – without waiting to graduate even in arts, let alone
with a higher doctorate. Beyond the graduate and the cleric is a
well-nigh incalculable hinterland of laymen who had sojourned at
the universities.

Universities, however, were places of learning as well as places
of training and already by our period Oxford and Cambridge were
distinguished centres of scholarship. Much of this was esoteric and
technical, philosophical and theological, but that did not mean
that it was irrelevant to, or uninfluential in, contemporary society.
Kings and other politicians were not slow to see the value of
employing an intellectually renowned advocate for their policies:
did not Lewis of Bavaria employ Marsiglio of Padua and William
of Ockham, graduate of Oxford and Paris? At the opening of the
Hundred Years War Ockham produced a scholastic brief for
Edward III, defending his right to seize the church's property to
support a war.[7] Furthermore Edward III employed Bradwardine
over many years in diplomacy and war preparations. Still more
notably, during the king's dotage, John of Gaunt enlisted the
polemical skills of Wyclif, first and briefly as one of the team
negotiating the concordat at Bruges in 1374–5, later – in the
parliament of January 1377 – to denounce the episcopal hegemony
of Bishop Wykeham. After that, as we shall see, Wyclif's influence
was to be still more widely and fiercely exerted against pope, friars
and the institutional church and for the vernacular scriptures.

The link between crown and learned polemicist is easy enough to grasp, but to measure how or by what means academics influenced the unlettered or un-Latined is at first sight a puzzle.[8] One solution to it is to regard the sermons which on many public occasions were addressed by these scholars to the populace as a form of adult education;[9] two Austin friars preached in the parliament of 1371, Wyclif to Londoners *circa* 1376, Bishop Brinton at Rochester, Paul's Cross and in parliament during the 1370s and early 1380s, and Thomas Wimbeldon at Paul's Cross around 1388. Another solution to the puzzle of transmission is to note how the arguments and conclusions of rarefied academic debate were vulgarized and mediated to a popular audience by fellow scholars deliberately simplifying in the vernacular – as happened with Wyclif's ideas. There are many less contentious examples of this, not least in the vernacular literature of the period. Langland especially reveals an audience familiar with many of the issues of current theological debate; this is evident from *Piers Plowman* which has been described as an epic survey of current theological preoccupation. In fact, Langland, though not apparently a graduate, almost certainly was a student at Oxford who left without a master's degree and took up a chaplaincy in London where his spiritual concern and informed exposition were surely much appreciated by an audience which doubtless included some university-educated laymen. Modern research suggests that Langland was one – albeit among the most articulate – of a whole army of men who though they boasted no degree had nonetheless ordered and enriched their minds at one of the universities. Their writings, sermons and conversations were key bridges from the world of scholarship and controversy to the ordinary parishioner. Not least would the influence of the clergy be felt through the dialogue of the confessional in which the sinner encountered at close quarters the trained mind and the consequences of academic theology and law. Wyclif's popular influence would be quite unintelligible without this background; but no less essential to this understanding is some knowledge of the advances in schooling, and especially in the mastery of the English language itself, in the later fourteenth century.

In 1281 Archbishop Pecham published the decree *Ignorantia sacerdotum* ('The Ignorance of Priests') which laid down the minimum instruction to be given by the clergy to the laity in matters of faith, through the medium of quarterly sermons.[10] In fact Pecham was simply spelling out the implication of the Fourth Lateran stipulation that the laity should confess and communicate at least once a year, at Easter; in order to confess adequately, the parishioner needed to be properly informed about the tenets of his faith and about sin. For this purpose the clergy, too, had to be adequately instructed; Pecham's decree was thus no small stimulus to the growth of schools where aspiring clerics could learn to read and write, beginning with simple English and progressing to Latin by way of prayers learned in both languages.

Schools, of course, existed well before 1281 and for a variety of purposes,[11] but the reforming and pastoral zeal which was communicated from the Fourth Lateran to England during the course of the thirteenth century led, as Pantin has shown, to a massive and varied endeavour to save the souls of men through instruction and confession.[12] Along with the transmission of doctrine went also a concern in some quarters to inculcate fervour; hence the emergence in fourteenth-century England of a mystical or devotional literature alongside the pedagogic, pastoral-legal guides for the clergy. School foundations were but a part of a multi-dimensional mission which embraced sermons and treatises, prayers, hymns and art. While Orme could trace only thirteen schools in the whole of Lincolnshire, Nottinghamshire and Yorkshire in the thirteenth century, he was able to identify thirty-three in the same area in the fourteenth; these were located in villages as well as in county towns, and out of the thirty-three no fewer than twenty-five were explicitly revealed as grammar schools; these taught Latin and presupposed the existence of schools or teachers imparting the elements of vernacular reading and writing. In the country as a whole, a total of 105 fourteenth-century schools are listed by Orme. In York diocese alone, however, Moran has identified almost fifty schools of all kinds in the fourteenth century, and from her analysis we can gauge the overwhelming extent to which they were religious in their aims.[13] Two features should be remembered about these schools in that century: firstly, only a small minority were permanently endowed institutions, most schools being better described as schoolmasters (usually charging for their services); secondly, few endowed schools before the fifteenth century were founded by laymen (burgesses or gentry) or prescribed only secular studies for their pupils. It is indicative of their character that many of the masters of such schools were funded as chantry priests who were to sing masses for the founder as well as instruct a few pupils. A still more telling comment upon them is that the primer from which the pupils learnt their alphabet was a book of prayers. Many of those who bequeathed money to boys to study did so on condition that the beneficiary proceeded to holy orders. That Moran locates the most significant growth in the late fifteenth and early sixteenth centuries does not diminish the importance of earlier developments when growth is better reflected in literary works than in probate records which only become abundant in the course of the fifteenth century.

Not all schools, of course, fulfilled this religious end or were intended to do so. At Oxford John Cornforth, among others, was running courses in what we might call business studies: letter writing and accounts.[14] Towns probably had then – as some certainly did later – civic schools which were primarily intended to equip merchants and traders for their pursuits. Town schools, however, were much less frequently recorded and are therefore more difficult to identify than 'church' schools. Indeed, in some towns the church made efforts to restrict other teaching establishments: at York, for example, where there was a flourishing school (of some sixty pupils) attached to the Minster, the dean and chapter issued several decrees during the fourteenth century prohibiting other clergy and laity from keeping schools, a pattern of affairs repeated in London in the next century; the very act of prohibition, and its repetition, are eloquent testimony to the buoyant educational market which then obtained.[15] By no means every area, let alone every parish, had a school, and by no means every school was an enduring institution or free or open to all, nor yet were all schools religious in aim: but there is no room to doubt that in the fourteenth century a significant extension of schooling facilities took place as a result of religious ideas, social forces and ecclesiastical institutions. It might be argued that this is merely a reflection of the greater number of records generally which survive from that century as compared with earlier times – for example the progressively increasing number of wills – but these records themselves, for whatever reason they were made and kept, are witnesses of a growingly literate society, and there is a wealth of evidence to support these witnesses.

Not the least impressive evidence is the multiplication of writings for vernacular readers. English in this period becomes an acceptable vehicle for serious and common communication.[16] It supplanted French as the vernacular used when teaching Latin: a textbook of English grammar was compiled for school use in mid-century; English vocabularies appeared soon after; English chronicles followed. English creeps into official documents, not always yet permanently, but not less significantly: parliament, for instance, was opened in English in 1376; the law courts heard some cases in English (instead of French) in the 1380s; town records begin to admit English among the Latin in this period. The clergy cater for the new vernacular audience by devotional works in English – the poems of Richard Rolle pre-eminently; Archbishop Thoresby had the catechism translated into English verse for use by parish priests but also for layfolk to read to their children; Richard Caistor's famous devotional poem had its origin in the fourteenth century; Langland's masterpiece is in English; Chaucer and Gower, themselves laymen, wrote for the king's clerks and servants in English as well as in French and Latin; Chaucer, moreover, translated Boethius's *Consolation of Philosophy* into English; Trevisa translated works by Giles of Rome, Duns Scotus and FitzRalph of Armagh. Such was the context of the English Bible which followed later in the century.

The conclusion from all this is that towards the end of the fourteenth century, though it may be hyperbole to talk of a literate laity, it is certainly justifiable to talk of a laity better informed and more articulate than a century earlier; a laity encouraged by confessional instruction, homiletic guidance and devotional exhortation to take religion more seriously; a laity vouchsafed by literacy and translation direct access to some of the sources of their faith, and encouraged to view the clergy and the church with greater independence and growing impatience; a laity enfranchised from spiritual servility and complacency. By no means all laymen and women, of course, were in this category, probably no more than a small minority, but certainly more than society had hitherto experienced. Yet it was not only the laity who were gaining in literacy and learning, for many an unbeneficed clerk also profited from the easier access to schools and the assistance of translations and vernacular writings; some, like Langland, had tasted higher education. Alongside the learning of the graduate clergy and the literacy of the lesser chaplains, there had been a massive extension of education from cleric to layman during the fourteenth century, largely as a consequence of ecclesiastical initiative and clerical effort, and ironically this was the society to which Wyclif – cleric, scholar, and heresiarch – appealed.

6

Wyclif and Lollardy

The Prophet and His Message

In the last two decades of the fourteenth century anticlericalism, which had been fostered particularly by the stresses of the Anglo–French war, was enlarged, deepened and complicated by heresy which married academic speculation to popular moralism. The academic element was provided by John Wyclif.

Although the chronicler, Walsingham, regarded him as 'an angel of Satan and forerunner of Antichrist', Wyclif was remembered by several of his opponents as an eminent and justly celebrated scholar: to John Kenningham, a Carmelite antagonist, he was 'a wise clerk'; to Archbishop Arundel 'a great clerk'; to the chronicler, Henry Knighton, he was simply 'the most outstanding doctor of theology in those days, considered second to none in philosophy and unmatched in skill in the schools'.[1] Born probably in the 1330s in West Yorkshire, Wyclif was a fellow of Merton College, Oxford, by 1356 and, having been in turn associated with Balliol, Queen's and Canterbury colleges, he was the leading theological master in Oxford, if not in England by 1372. That year, in his inaugural lecture after obtaining his doctorate, he had questioned the papacy's title to speak in the name of Christ.[2] He was already a royal clerk in receipt of crown patronage, and in 1374 he was briefly a member of the diplomatic mission sent to Bruges to negotiate a concordat with the pope. Meanwhile he had been writing instalments of a theological compendium, a *Summa*, which from about 1375 took an increasingly radical and political direction, challenging the very basis of ecclesiastical authority and social organization. Book I of the *De Dominio Civili*, 'Of Civil Dominion' (or Lordship), finished in 1376, impugned the clergy's right to property. When in May 1377 the pope identified a number of errors in Wyclif's work, the author was driven to other radical assertions, encouraged by the anticlerical policies of the government and perhaps by his own disappointment over a papal provision in 1376; soon the papal schism, too, would add force to his polemic. Circumstances as well as ideas swept him onwards, further away from the shores of convention and tact. John of Gaunt's favour twice thwarted a formal trial of his opinions – at St Paul's in 1377 and at Lambeth in 1378. He earned and rewarded this protection by affirming in 1377 that 'the kingdom of England may lawfully, under the urgent necessity of her defence, withhold the treasure of the realm from being carried abroad, even though the lord pope require this on pain of censure and by virtue of obedience',[3] and by defending in 1378 the sensational violation of Westminster Abbey's sanctuary. Books II and III of *De Dominio Civili*, which followed closely upon the papal condemnation of 1377, demolished papal claims to jurisdiction and affirmed the obligation of the king to protect and guide the church of England. *De Ecclesia* in 1378 further assailed papal authority in England and returned to the issue of sanctuary. *De Officio Regis*, 'On the Office or Duty of a King', which was written *c.*1378–9, bitterly attacked papal claims and church liberties while vehemently advocating royal supremacy over the clergy. However, suspicions that Wyclif was a mere time-server are confounded by his treatise *De Eucharistia*, 'On the Eucharist': this pursued his logical premises to an heretical conclusion about the mass which alienated his earliest and most powerful patron and protector, John of Gaunt. It was one thing to denounce ecclesiastical and papal jurisdiction, but to question the doctrine of the Real Presence (as defined at the Fourth Lateran Council in 1215 and taught ever since) was an audacious move which cannot be regarded as calculated or self-interested. *De Eucharistia*, written about 1379, was followed soon afterwards by the Peasants Revolt in 1381, and these two developments threw Gaunt and the church together to defend orthodoxy and society. In May 1382 Archbishop Courtenay convened a council of doctors in London which examined Wyclif's writings and condemned a whole list of heresies and errors: no Lancastrian shield protected Wyclif now. The archbishop compelled Oxford

University to purge from its ranks the more notorious espousers of these views: Wyclif himself was banned from teaching, and he lived out the remaining two years of his life on his benefice of Lutterworth, whence a cascade of vitriolic pamphlets issued.

To extract some coherent system of ideas from Wyclif's writings which were so diverse in origin, purpose and provocation, which extended over a dozen turbulent years, and which were voluminous, impassioned and contradictory, is a task as necessary as it is arbitrary. Their unifying root is in his philosophical concept of realism whereby all things visible and all happenings spring from, and are manifestations of, a timeless idea (or 'reality') in the mind of God, who is eternal, having neither beginning nor end. The saved and the damned, therefore, were saved and damned from the beginning of time and will be to its end – supposing that it had either: salvation, in other words, was predestined. What, then, can be made of a church which claims by its sacraments to dispense the grace necessary for salvation and by its curses to deny and remove God's grace? And what, indeed, can we make of a church which sells its grace – through dispensations and in return for endowments – and which by excommunication withholds grace in order to protect its wealth? Wyclif's philosophical realism and pragmatic observations suggested disturbing answers to these questions. The church, co-eternal with God, was not the institutional *ecclesia* familiar in Europe then, but 'a community of the predestined elect . . . of which some are dead, some living and some yet to be born'.[4] The claims of the pope and bishops to bind and loose on earth and in heaven by excommunication and absolution were fraudulent, since that would suggest that the Creator's omnipotent will could be bent and bound by the crude and often dubious judgements of his mere creatures: that was preposterous in practice and inconceivable philosophically. The institutional church came to represent for Wyclif an impostor, a creation of the Devil, headed by that Antichrist, the bishop of Rome. The proof, source and basis of papal illegitimacy were its landed possessions and its jurisdiction, both of which Wyclif traced to the Donation of Constantine: church law was chiefly used to defend its wealth. Moreover, when one looked more closely at the earthly church, its jurisdiction was seen to be exercised on behalf of pope and bishops for whom there was no authority outside their own claims to it. Canon lawyers, of course, had built up a massive structure of supporting buttresses for ecclesiastical jurisdiction, but these buttresses rested on human – not divine – foundations. Not to lawyers, not even to canon lawyers, should one look for enlightenment, but to theologians 'who alone know what is contrary to scripture' and who 'state the case . . . according to the law of Christ'.[5]

If the church and its lawyers were rejected, guidance and justification for Christian acts must be sought in the scriptures, 'the charter of Holy Mother Church', in which 'all law useful to the Holy Mother Church is taught explicitly or implicitly'.[6] For Wyclif the Bible was not just a divinely inspired book or even the Word of God in our modern sense of the message of God; it was the Johannine *logos* – 'In the beginning was the Word' – the co-eternal voice of God, antedating the worldly church as God antedated it, anterior and of necessity superior to the institutional church, and now made audible, visible, unalterable, infallible and indestructible. By Wyclif's realism, the Bible became a measure, and not an instrument, of the visible church, a measure which revealed disquieting flaws in that body. Wyclif's fundamentalism did not delude him into the naive view that the Bible was an unambiguous and uncomplicated text equally accessible to all; he was too much of a scholar to fall into such simplicities. He acknowledged that one had to grasp the *sense* of words and that the early Fathers – who wrote before the Donation of Constantine and papal usurpation – must sometimes be enlisted for guidance.

Wyclif's view of the church is clearly a product of philosophical, theological, scriptural and historical premises. His view of the sacraments was similarly mixed in origin. Predestination impugned the role and efficacy of confession and excommunication; scripture provided no basis for ordination – not by Christ, at least – and history ascribed these developments to human (or diabolical) invention. The objections to current interpretations of the eucharist, however, were philosophical. By the definition established in 1215 the Real Presence in the mass was construed in Aristotelian terms: the physical appearance – or 'accidents' – of bread and wine persisted throughout the mass, but after the priestly consecration of these elements, the underlying reality – or 'substance' – was transformed into the very body and blood of Christ: transubstantiation had been effected. But for Wyclif his realism precluded the existence of 'accidents' without 'substance', since the former were the necessary manifestation of the latter; on the other hand 'substance' could and did exist without 'accidents', for it endured eternally and indestructibly. For Wyclif, therefore, the fact that bread and wine were still visible after consecration must mean that their substance was still present. Rejecting transubstantiation, Wyclif interpreted Christ's presence in the sacrament as spiritual. Wyclif had not denied the Real Presence of Christ in the sacrament but had redefined 'real'; in doing this he had rejected a solemn and crucial doctrinal definition. The finesse of his arguments was lost on the learned (like Courtenay), who were afraid, and on the ignorant (like many lollards), who unwittingly simplified and falsified.

Wyclif further complicated attitudes to the sacraments by arguing in some works that their validity (which in other works he dismissed entirely) depended upon the merit and virtue of the priest celebrating them: thus the salvation of souls was put in peril by vicious and unworthy priests who administered the sacraments. As an argument for indignation with, and reform of, the church, this was obviously powerful and urgent, and it had deep roots in the theological tradition of western Europe.

Perhaps the most menacing element in Wyclif's thought was his attack on the endowments of the church, not only because it justified so much current covetous attention to the temporalities of the church but also because – if followed to its logical conclusion – it imperilled all property ownership. Wyclif's objections to church property were partly moral-historical and partly theological. The notion that the present corruption of the church stemmed from its acquisition of territory through the Donation of Constantine implied that the church was purest when in its pristine state it had no property: reform necessitated a return to this imagined era of apostolic poverty. This was the theme of the mendicant orders and the cause of bitter controversy within them; Wyclif's ideas owed no little impetus to this polemical background, and a reprise in his work, from the earliest biblical commentaries onwards, was this restoration of the primitive church. Theologically he drew on the notion of grace to justify such a necessary disendowment. In the later thirteenth century Giles of Rome had defended papal jurisdiction by arguing that all dominion or lordship was dependent on grace – on divine will and conferment. Wyclif turned this on its head by declaring that as the pope and the clergy – that is, Antichrist and the sons of Antichrist – were clearly not in a state of grace, they were evidently unfitted to exercise lordship or to possess temporalities. Church lands were proof of sin, and since they were also the cause of sin they ought to be removed.

It was one thing to argue that the church would be better without lands and to declare that it should be disendowed; the next problem was to determine who should disendow it and to justify this both on a theoretical and a practical-legal basis. Wyclif concluded that the king was the only agent for this reform. The church under Antichrist was incapable of reforming itself; the king alone was able to lead it back to Christ. It never seems to have worried Wyclif that, according to his own arguments elsewhere, one could not be sure that a king was among the predestined saved and therefore fit to have lordship over property. It was one of the paradoxes of Wyclif's invisible church of the elect that the elect were difficult to recognize on earth since they might sin and still be destined to salvation while the damned might act virtuously; such a contention was a convenient way of separating the institutional church – and those of whom it approved – from the real and invisible church, which could thus outcrop in unconventional places; but it left the authority of all lordship in doubt. To Wyclif, however, the king was quite simply God's vicar on earth, obligated to defend the faith and – as in his coronation oath – the church. A further contradiction is evident here: that Wyclif has invoked the king to reform the familiar visible church, irrelevant as that is to salvation. Yet without these contradictions Wyclif could never have appealed to his contemporaries who were, for various reasons, eager to plunder and yet preserve the western church: he would have become simply the spokesman for a populist millenarian movement. He knew enough about the world to understand that reform needed the backing of governors. The basis of his proposals was a profound discontent with the condition of the contemporary church and a passionate concern to bring about reform. The irony is that he should be so obsessed with the abusive influence of the papacy that he pinned his hopes on the far more oppressive powers of the monarchy.

Once Wyclif had vested his hopes in the crown, he could call on a broad stream of precedents and traditions to give the practical proposal respectable and almost reassuring familiarity. Civil and canon law empowered all patrons to resume endowments where the conditions of the original grants had not been met over a period of at least two years, a notion embodied in the 1285 statute of Westminster and in several subsequent writs; when, for example, monastic houses fell into overwhelming debt, their endowments and finances were sometimes administered by, or on behalf of, the founder. The founder and patron paramount, the ultimate source of all land bestowed on the English church, was the king: Edward I asserted this, and the statute of Provisors in 1351 recalled it when describing the king as 'paramount and immediate patron of the men of holy church'. Parliamentarians had frequently spoken – and were long to do so – of the need to protect the interests of patrons who had endowed the churches in order to provide for their souls and the souls of others. Moreover, Magna Carta had imposed on the crown an obligation to defend the church – a body now redefined by Wyclif. Finally there was a well-established principle that the welfare of the realm could justify the sacrifice of church possessions: it was implicit in the papal bull *Etsi de Statu* of 1296, and in the king's outlawry of the clergy and seizure of their temporalities in 1297; it was explicit in the statute of Mortmain of 1279 and in the confiscation of the lands of alien priories for the duration of the war. Wyclif made the point with characteristic force when he wrote in the *De Officio Regis* that 'In a case where necessity threatens, it is permitted for the defence of a city to tear down a cathedral and construct a tower, to sell or melt down the chalices and give the money to the soldiers.'[7] None of this justifies the permanent disendowment of the whole church, but together all these strands form a rope pulled in that direction by Wyclif and his followers.

Not only did Wyclif give tongue to the growing habit of raiding church endowments in necessity, but he also articulated the nationalism of the English church. By his frequent reference to the precedents from common law and royal practice he underlined the unity and implied the insularity of the English church. He described the church universal as compounded of various national limbs, a kind of confederation of co-equal constituents,[8] and in 1377 he advised against exporting money to Rome because 'The secular lords of our realm gave all our possessions, from which the lord pope draws his money, not to any church whatever but to the English churches.'[9] He is speaking for, and addressing, of course, his own generation who experienced the increasingly nationalist fervour resulting from the war of the 1340s and 1350s and witnessed the increasingly partial leadership of the church from Avignon and its squandering battles in Italy. From 1378 the papal schism was to divide the church into two camps drawn up on political lines.

Wyclif's appeal was manifold: to scholars and politicians, to churchmen and laymen, courtiers and artisans, knights and burgesses. His message was the wider in its appeal because of its vigorous inconsistencies: logic was a vehicle which took him where he wanted to go and enabled him to visit and address sections of the community who might otherwise have been denied his message. The principal attractions of his programme were surely his advocacy of reform, his identification of this with disendowment, and his nationalist fervour: that these were interdependent added to the strength and appeal of each. He was the voice of savage and righteous indignation, of greed and envy, and of national identity; but he was also the heir of chronic polemics within the church and universities about the nature of the true church, as well as the spokesman of parishioners and clergy increasingly rootless and acquisitive in the wake of the plague visitations; in addition, although he wrote in Latin, he gave expression to the egalitarianism of the newly literate. He did all this with many contradictions, but the small print of academic treatises is apt to elude the sight of the people at large.

Transmission

There is little evidence that Wyclif himself set out to found a popular movement of dissent: he apparently wrote scarcely anything in the vernacular and his arguments were addressed to Oxford students, not to articulate artisans; moreover, he showed no enthusiasm for the Peasants Revolt; as well as being an academic, he was also a royal clerk, not an acquaintance of the poor or the proletariat; finally, proof that he sent out poor preachers in russet gowns is fragile in the extreme. It is true that he preached to London audiences in the 1370s and to parliament about the Westminster sanctuary case in 1378, but these were *ad hoc* responses to invitation or provocation. One historian has suggested that Wyclif did not aim for, or attempt to instigate, a popular movement of dissent because he realized that this was the wrong way to achieve reform which would more likely come by way of those laymen who could influence affairs – knights about the king's court and patrons of parish churches.[10] This theory has some appeal because seven knights at Richard II's court have been positively, and three more tentatively, identified as lollards.[11] Substantial figures as they were, however, they were noticeably few among Richard's court, which was markedly larger than his predecessors'. Moreover, their influence was local rather than national: Richard II was no tolerator of heresy and could usually be relied upon – as we shall see – to restrain parliamentary and popular anticlericalism, so much so that he earned from one chronicler the accolade of defender of the church;[12] only in the last years of his reign did he show unusual disregard for the church's liberties, but not even then for its doctrine. Apart from all this, Wyclif's message was broadcast by agents remarkably undiscriminating about their audiences. That Wyclif wanted to see his ideas translated into action can scarcely be doubted from the passion and vehemence of his arguments, but that he had a clear political or practical notion of how to effect that aim is not so evident: he was an advocate not an administrator, an academic not a politician, an opportunist not a planner; if he had such a horror of popular movements, he took no pains to keep his message from the people; were knights his prime target, he addressed them neither in

English nor in French and his Latin was scarcely accessible to those whose competence in it was principally confined to charters, writs and letters patent and close. There is nothing in the manner of his writing nor in the method of its transmission to suggest that he had a specific target in mind beyond his Oxford students and occasional parliamentary auditors. It is true that his antipapal and anticlerical message would have a strong appeal to greedy courtiers and commons, but it would appeal no less to the humbler members of society all too familiar with the failings of the local church and clergy. How Wyclif's message was disseminated and how it was received cast further doubts on Professor Wilks's suggestion that the knights were the key agents in a process descending from courtiers to the people, *de haut en bas*.

The radiation of Wyclif's ideas began naturally enough with his associates and friends in Oxford. Four in particular were responsible for transmitting the message further afield, both geographically and socially. John Aston, a secular clerk from Worcester diocese, preached and evangelized in the west country, where, despite a recantation, he relapsed into heresy and died a lollard around 1388. Working closely with him in the dioceses of Worcester and Hereford was Nicholas Hereford, another secular clerk, who had already attracted official attention at Oxford for his provocative sermon on Ascension Day 1382 and was active in the Nottingham area by 1387; he was reconciled to the church in 1391 and thereafter led a life of blameless orthodoxy and piety. Even more vigorously active in a career which lasted into the fifteenth century was John Purvey, a student at, though not apparently a graduate of, Oxford, and Wyclif's amanuensis. He spent some twenty years preaching in the Bristol area, and although he recanted in 1401 and was given a benefice, his later career is obscure and only doubtfully orthodox. The other notable Oxford convert was Philip Repingdon or Repton, an Austin canon of Leicester, who proselytized in that area until he abjured heresy in 1382, subsequently to become abbot of Leicester and bishop of Lincoln, in which office he vigilantly prosecuted lollards. The date of Repingdon's reconversion suggests that his message was largely that of moralistic Wycliffism rather than doctrinal or eucharistic in its focus. If that were so, it struck a chord with the preaching of

William Swinderby in the same Midlands area. Swinderby had been a wandering revivalist long before lollardy; he lived in Leicester until the women there threatened to stone him for his extravagant denunciation of their pride and weakness, after which he pursued a hermit's life in nearby woods, enjoying the patronage and support of John of Gaunt and the pious burgesses of Leicester. It would seem that he was soon recruited by Repingdon and joined a group of evangelists based on the chapel of St John the Baptist outside the city walls; among them were the chaplain Nicholas Waytestathe and the Leicester craftsman, William Smith. The latter taught himself to read and in due course composed heretical tracts which drew on the scriptures and the Fathers to advocate reform of religious practice and worship. From this centre the group evangelized surrounding market towns. The pattern discernible at Leicester can be matched or is hinted at in many other centres of heresy in England, and when one remembers how Oxford dispersed students and graduates as chaplains and incumbents to parishes throughout the land this is hardly surprising. There was, however, another route by which Wyclif's academic speculations impinged on the emotions and beliefs of the non-academic.

In the 1370s, as we have seen, Wyclif became the favourite anticlerical spokesman on behalf of the government, and in 1374 he was briefly a member of the diplomatic mission to Bruges. He was thus known to knightly members of the court circle, some of whom would find in his pronouncements echoes of, and justifications for, their own anticlerical and antipapal sentiments. That he enjoyed the favour of the duke of Lancaster and spoke about church wealth and papal greed with a vehemence easily matched in the sermons and declarations of orthodox and moralist bishops like Brinton could only have made the knights more susceptible to his appeal. Although his message had a strong political import, the handful of so-called lollard knights who have been identified reveal a pietistic and moralistic concern far more than any political interest. Of the seven confidently identified, several were of the Black Prince's circle and generation, one which was not only disillusioned with the papacy on political grounds but with the church as a whole on moral grounds, a church which in the 1370s was increasingly condemned for espousing a war between Christians and flaunting its un-Christian wealth. Several of these lollard knights composed wills which renounced ostentatious funerals and denounced the flesh in terms reminiscent of the then reviving piety of the Low Countries, the *Devotio Moderna*. One of them, Sir John Clanvow, was the author of a pious treatise, in English, on the life of virtue, entitled *The Two Ways*, heavily scriptural in its sources and ascetic in tone. Lollard knights, shadowy though they are, have more to do with spiritual idealism than political realism.

Their role in the diffusion of Wycliffism was not less significant because they were not themselves preachers. Although it is inconceivable that they did not influence or seek to influence their friends, their chief importance was as protectors of evangelists. It seems doubtful if they afforded much protection at the level of the court and council: the slowness of the government to take effective measures has more to do with the ambiguity of Wyclif's message and the ambivalence of the governors towards it than specifically with representations by these knights; that the king prevaricated over capital punishment for heresy is perhaps explained, if not by his humanity, as one historian has alleged,[13] then by his other preoccupations in the late 1390s. It was rather at local level that lollard knights defended and diffused Wycliffism. The chronicler, Knighton, tells of such a knight forcing neighbours to come and hear a wandering preacher in the parish church, and standing around with a sword to protect the heretic.[14] It was through their household and estate chapels and through advowsons that such knights sponsored heresy (although we must remember that some patrons may have been ignorant of their presentees' waywardness). Sir William Nevill sought the custody of Nicholas Hereford on his arrest in 1387 'because of the honesty of his person'; Sir John Montagu cleared the images from his chapel at Shenley and harboured lollard preachers; Sir Thomas Latimer was lord of Chipping Warden where he impeded the efforts of the bishop of Lincoln in 1388–9 to serve a writ on a chaplain who had allegedly made forty-five lollard converts; on his other estate of Braybrooke, Latimer (or possibly his widow) presented to the rectory there the notorious lollard, Robert Hook. After Latimer's death, his estate and church at Braybrooke remained an important lollard centre to which Czech scholars came in the early fifteenth century in search of Wyclif's writings, and not in vain. In the early fifteenth century Sir John Oldcastle first attracted official suspicions because of the preaching of clergy in his benefices. As patrons, as justices of the peace, and as members of county government and administration, knights and gentry with Wycliffite sympathies doubtless played a critical role in the spread and endurance of heresy, but their numbers were not large – or lollardy would have overwhelmed efforts to contain it – and their motives were much more religious than political. Furthermore, they were not the only protectors, for urban governors, too, fulfilled a similar role at Northampton and elsewhere.

Messengers, of course, are extremely ephemeral; their task is remarkably difficult and vulnerable without written messages, outward and physical evidence of inward and spiritual beliefs. Although measures were taken at Oxford in 1382, 1395 and 1407 to extinguish and suppress Wyclif's own writings, enough survived to make a bonfire at Carfax in 1410 and to fill several printed volumes today. Wyclif's ideas were communicated to the public at large, both by his own occasional sermons in English as well as those by others.[15] Over thirty manuscripts survive of a collection of nearly three hundred sermons in English which draw substantially on the heresiarch's teachings; the sermons were for Sundays, feasts and weekdays and were written in mostly handsome manuscripts obviously intended for public use. Also influential and widely circulated was the *Floretum*, a large theological handbook which under each topic, arranged alphabetically, cites among the usual authorities of the Bible, the Fathers, scholastics and canonists, lengthy passages from Wyclif. Such books were the *vade mecum* of aspiring preachers, and like the sermon collection mentioned above their importance can hardly be exaggerated in the diffusion of Wycliffism.

Of more immediate popular appeal would be the *Lay Folks Catechism*, into some manuscripts of which lollard interpolations were introduced. And then there were a host of vernacular writings disseminating the master's thoughts – and adding to them – which appeared both from 'official' organized scriptoria in

well-produced, careful and sometimes numerous copies, and from
individual scribes writing poor, hasty, *ad hoc* versions: sermons,
tracts and commentaries abound in these forms. Most numerous
of all, however, are the manuscripts of the English Bible.[16] There
were two versions of this, inspired, but not assisted, by Wyclif.
The first was a literal translation so crude as to be barely
intelligible; yet it was a necessary step towards something more
usable and survives in over thirty manuscripts. The second
version, completed around 1396, is much more comprehensible
and readable; it survives in over two hundred manuscripts, some
sixty of which date from after 1436. These translations, though
dubiously attributed to Nicholas Hereford and John Purvey
respectively, have nothing inherently unorthodox about them;
only nine copies of the later version contain the explicitly
Wycliffite 'General Prologue' and the few texts which include the
gospels unorthodoxly glossed are all early fifteenth century. The
Lollard Bible, therefore, until 1407, when restrictions were placed
on translations, could well satisfy the orthodox and disturb no one:
in 1401 Oxford dons were freely debating the merits and
procedures of translating the Bible. Most of these lollard versions
were heretical only by implication – because Wyclif had
counterpoised the scriptures to the authority of the church and
because by vernacular translations this challenge was more widely
sustained. In any event such texts provided ammunition for
heretical preachers and believers, and in the rest of lollardy's
history many extracts from the New Testament were copied,
distributed and pored over. If the Lollard Bible, save for a few
overtly heretical manuscripts, did little to spread lollardy, it
afforded important and encouraging support to those already
converted and to their efforts to proselytize others. Ironically, in
most of its manuscripts it would have given hope and depth to the
faithful too.

The Receivers

Most of the beliefs credited to lollards can be traced in the prolific
and contradictory writings of Wyclif, but shorn of his caution,

subtlety and restraint, and augmented by grievances of popular or other origin. Although Wyclif was often regarded as an authority and inspiration and even viewed by one fifteenth-century heretic – somewhat illogically – as a saint,[17] how his message was received and what parts of it were espoused depended upon the accident of transmission (with all the falsifying simplification which that involved) as well as upon the presuppositions and predisposition of the receiver. Not all lollards embraced eucharistic heresy; many were indifferent to Wyclif's views on the papacy; many more attacked pilgrimages, saint cults and images, though these scarcely figure in the master's writings. It is a peculiar characteristic of campaigners that they espouse causes and ideas in tortuous and highly selective ways. Probably Wyclif's ideas would no more command the whole assent and enthusiasm of a fourteenth-century lollard than a party political programme today enjoys the unqualified support of party members or of those who vote for it.

Wyclif's appeal lay to no small extent in the expression which he gave to the frustrations of the underprivileged who were increasingly aware of their condition. He conferred self-respect on men and women who, although outside the spiritual elite of the religious orders and lacking the status and authority of priests and prelates, were yet gaining ambition in the wake of literacy, freedom, land and prosperity. Yet his appeal was not just to those with social grievances or expectations. There were plenty of people, as parliamentary records make clear, who would have found encouragement in lollard denouncements of the pope as Antichrist. Equally, the heavily taxed laity were grumbling about monastic wealth and property long before Wyclif pronounced on them. There were clerics, too, who deplored the wealth and greed of their order, from pope to parish priest: the sermons of Bromyard, the visions of Langland, and the ravings of John Ball should remind us that much of Wyclif's message seemed to his contemporaries familiar, harmless, indeed salutary, and it graced their miscellaneous prejudices, clichés and emotions with an apparently logical framework and academic authority.[18] Men gave their assent and favour to Wycliffism for various and often highly selective reasons, and it need not surprise us that some – like Repingdon – grew out of their allegiance; some only gave it tentatively or recklessly in the first place. Wyclif could prove too disconcertingly nimble of mind for his followers; so copious were his ideas and voluminous his writings that few men were likely to encounter, let alone absorb, them all at once. No medieval scholar appealed to his contemporaries on so many radical issues. If he sometimes appears to be the naive tool of cynical politicians, his rapidly developing and multifarious thought soon left some of them wondering whether they were not the dupes. The doctrine of dominion, first employed for the support of the king and the laity against ecclesiastical privilege and demands, soon threatened the authority of laymen themselves. His assault on the possessioner monks, which had elicited approval from the friars, was soon extended to the friars themselves, once they opposed his version of the Real Presence. Wyclif posed, for Oxford students in particular, the same kind of excitement and dilemmas with which Marx and Soviet Russia confronted Cambridge men in the 1930s. Although authorities quickly acted to eliminate this threat in 1382, their success was hampered by questions of jurisdiction and ecclesiastical liberty so that not until early in the next century was lollardy effectively extinguished at Oxford.[19]

Diffusion and Survival

Within a decade of Wyclif's death lollards were detected on frequent occasions in an area extending from Nottingham and Shrewsbury in the north to Hereford, Bristol, Dorset, Hampshire and London in the south.[20] Early in the next century lollards are traceable in Sussex, Essex and Kent and are even faintly and briefly discernible in Newcastle and Northumberland. So far as the records – full of lacunae and hazards – tell us, the north of England was little affected, but we ought to remember that no less vigorous a proselytizer than William Thorpe claimed to have been active over many years in the north and Bishop Langley detected lollardy in Durham in 1422; when court books survive at York, and they do so only in the early sixteenth century, lollards are certainly visible there. We are conceded only one isolated, but extensive, glimpse of heresy in Norfolk, through the chance survival of trial records for the period 1424–8. Remarkable, therefore, as the available picture is, the true extent of lollard distribution must have been even more impressive.

Oxford, of course, was its earliest centre, but it also attracted most obviously the repressive attentions of the bishops and archbishops. During Arundel's archiepiscopate (1396–1414) lollardy was squeezed out of Oxford, but it had already played an important role in the conversion and sustenance of other lollard centres. Leicester, Coventry, Bristol and London all date their lollard traditions from the early 1380s; Northampton and Reading had lollard communities in the 1390s. The counties around and adjoining these towns were often deeply infected: Leicestershire, Northamptonshire, Derbyshire, Warwickshire, Gloucestershire, Herefordshire and the Welsh Marches show early signs of lollardy; Bedfordshire, Hertfordshire, Huntingdonshire and Buckinghamshire reveal infection by the first decade of the fifteenth century.

We know for certain that several of these centres survived all prosecutions and persecutions until the Reformation and it is likely that elsewhere the chance survival of a manuscript or the appointment of an energetic heresy hunter as bishop would have provided evidence of comparable endurance. Except at Oxford – Cambridge seems curiously unaffected – no lollard community seems to have been certainly extinguished by the efforts of the authorities or the rigour of the law. Coventry was a centre of heresy in 1383 and still in 1520 and intermittently between those dates. The village or township of Tenterden, in Kent, had its lollards in 1420 and in 1511, when fifty were prosecuted by Archbishop Warham. In Lincoln diocese Buckinghamshire had lollards from at least 1405 up into the 1520s.

It is well known that these groups or cells did not exist in isolation: prosecution records reveal connections and intercourse between them, partly a natural development of sharing common apostles originally, partly because of the enthusiasm of neophytes for meeting other like-minded folk, to some degree a reflection of the role of the itinerant artisans and journeymen of the cloth industry, and early in the movement's history the result of having in their ranks men with estates in different areas of the country.

When in the fifteenth century Sir John Oldcastle was on the run after his abortive revolt, he can be traced on his own and neighbours' estates in Kent and the Welsh Marches but also at innumerable lollard locations in between.

What Wyclif bequeathed to fifteenth-century society was a vast movement of dissent not dissimilar from some resistance movements in the modern world. It was a well-organized underground with safe houses – or in Oldcastle's time, even safe manors such as Sir Thomas Latimer's in Northants. There were also towns – as at Northampton – where favourable burgesses offered tacit security. Within those towns and villages household churches grew up where like-minded family and friends gathered to copy books, to read and hear them read, to listen to sermons and to discuss opinions. Anne Hudson has examined sermon and other manuscripts to expose the organization that went into lollard book production.[21] In 1415 John Claydon, a well-to-do citizen of London, hired a scrivener to work in his house copying out a lollard text, which he then had bound in leather and read to him – for he could not read – by a servant: the book was a favourite lollard tract, *The Lantern of Light*. Popular texts for copying were English sermons attributed, wrongly, to Wyclif, and gospels and epistles from the scriptures. Without the mutual support within groups and between groups and the encouragement of these multiplying tracts, even the absence of persecution would not have guaranteed survival on so large and long a scale. The indifference which some bishops showed towards the extirpation of heresy and the negligence of some secular officers certainly helped; during the early decades, the existence of protectors and sympathizers – not necessarily lollard in any, or in any large, degree – was important for the establishment of the movement: it took a while for some authorities to share Courtenay's or Arundel's perspicacious view of heresy. Undoubtedly some prelates and officials saw no cause for alarm in opinions so often – in the past and recently – voiced by the impeccably orthodox and responsible, opinions which they may have shared. It took the Peasants Revolt to alarm some sympathizers and the folly of Oldcastle's rebellion to alienate the gentry and squirearchy. After that, persecution strengthened the resolve of survivors by intensifying their isolation and mutual dependence and by providing them with occasional martyrs. This under-ground movement was to have its day in the reign of Henry VIII. Meanwhile, it survived the fifteenth century rather by quietism than by the radical enthusiasm of its early years.

Political Dimensions

Clearly Wyclif and lollardy were threats to the church, but did they also threaten the crown and the realm? Recent commentators have been inclined to play down the scale and importance of lollardy, but a subversive movement is not always accurately assessed by counting heads or by objective delineations of its power base: the impact of a development may be out of all proportion to its dimensions, being related more to what people thought about it than to ideological, statistical or social composi-tion. On ideological grounds Wyclif's ideas enhanced and enlarged royal authority over the clergy but contained within themselves seeds which could be destructive of the crown and of the social organization as a whole: if authority depended on grace, then it might not be long before people realized that logically this applied to kings no less than to popes or priests; and such a notion of grace might just as easily incite social rebellion. Archbishop Courtenay and the chronicler, Walsingham, believed, or encouraged others to believe, that the Peasants Revolt was rooted in the heretical doctrines of Wyclif. In fact, as we shall see, there is very little evidence to sustain such an interpretation and in this respect, at least, the political consequences of Wycliffism and lollardy must be declared negligible.

Lollardy exercised a more pervasive and far less measurable effect during Richard II's reign. First, it added to the problems and damaged the repute of the government; it was an embarrass-ment, too slender to cause its collapse yet too disturbing for comfort; it was an excuse for criticism and action by the enemies of the king, as in 1388 when the Appellants took measures against some lollard courtiers like Latimer. Secondly, it gnawed away at the political integrity of the church, leaving the clergy vulnerable to financial demands which it helped to justify and encourage among the laity. Thirdly, it made the church more dependent upon royal protection for which a *quid pro quo* might sooner or later be asked: at no stage was such a bargain struck or alluded to or perhaps consciously embraced, but political realism forbids us to believe that such calculations were not entertained, even if convocation did sometimes refuse or delay grants or couple them with conditions. During Richard's reign lollardy added significantly to the atmosphere of unrest, instability and incompetence.

Defensive Measures

As a consequence of the Peasants Revolt and Archbishop Courtenay's linking of this disturbance with the spread of heresy, from 1382 the chancellor was empowered, on application from a bishop, to commission sheriffs and other royal officers to arrest unorthodox preachers and their supporters and to detain them until they were cleared by canon law proceedings.[22] The beginning and the conclusion of this move rested with the church, but six years later the crown's role is more decisive. In 1388, commissions were issued not only for the seizure of heretical writings and the arrest of traffickers in them but also for the examination of such writings *before the king's council* and imprisonment of offenders *at the king's pleasure*. At first the commissions were granted to laymen, and only later to joint bodies of lay and cleric. The 1388 measures were introduced by the Appellants who had control of government at that time and with whom Bishop Arundel of Ely was closely associated; both his influence and their own concern to gain credibility explain their steps.

Moves to make heresy a capital offence were afoot during the 1390s and the subject of episcopal petition to parliament in 1397. However, the exile of Archbishop Arundel that year and other urgent preoccupations for parliamentarians and the king postponed a positive response until the next reign, when the statute for burning heretics was enacted in 1401.[23]

Wyclif's advocacy of the monarch as reformer of the church was not to be realized until Henry VIII – on quite different premises – stepped into the role. Yet royal power over the church, already extensive in theory and practice, was certainly augmented and encouraged by the threat of lollardy. Ironically, it was not in order to reform the church, but to defend it against would-be reformers, that the government intervened in its affairs; not to destroy it, but to eradicate the menace posed by Wyclif and his followers.

Richard II (1377–99)
The Clergy Under Attack

Although the new king was barely ten years old at his accession,
the appointment of a regent was thwarted by the suspicion and
unpopularity which the only feasible candidate, John of Gaunt,
duke of Lancaster, provoked. Instead, until 1380 government,
though nominally in the hands of the young king, was supervised
by a succession of continual councils comprising the principal
officers of the realm and representatives of the three estates. From
1380 Richard governed by officers of his own choice and an
informal council drawn largely from members of his court, men
such as Michael de la Pole, later earl of Suffolk, and Aubrey de
Vere, eventually duke of Ireland. From time to time the failure of
the regime to achieve long-awaited success in war, the burden of
taxation and the king's reckless patronage of his favourites led to an
alliance of commons and nobles intent on limiting the king's
freedom of action. During the 1380s a succession of reform
commissions or councils appointed in parliament to oversee
day-to-day government culminated in the Merciless Parliament of
1388 which convicted several royal favourites and agents of
treason. The alliance of commons and nobles, however, and even
the collaboration of nobles among themselves, usually faded
quickly once their aims had been achieved, and the initiative
reverted to the king. This happened in 1389 and from then until
1397 Richard controlled affairs, though he was careful to do so
with some restraint and tact, avoiding provocation and promoting
or indulging some of his erstwhile enemies. In 1397, however, he
took his revenge on them and ruled so arbitrarily and oppressively
as to provoke his own deposition two years later.

The early part of the reign had been overshadowed by the war
with France which brought with it a grave threat of invasion, but

this abated in 1389 when the first of a series of truces suspended hostilities for more than a decade; thus some financial pressure was lifted from the realm during Richard's personal rule. Throughout the reign, first Richard's enemies and then the king himself profited from the difficulties of the pope. A double election in 1378 resulted in a papal schism in which England and France and their respective allies supported rival popes, at first Urban VI in Rome and Clement VII in Avignon. This scandal not only linked the conclusion of the Anglo–French war with the solution of the schism but also made each pope desperate for funds and more patient with the expectations of his allies. In his last three years Richard fully exploited this advantage. Nevertheless, as the schism began to take on an appearance of permanence Richard and his subjects urgently sought ways to resolve it.

In Richard II the flaws in Plantagenet character overwhelmed the virtues. The pride which had led Edward I to claim Scotland's crown and Edward III France's was focused by Richard simply on his own sovereignty. The courage which Edward I revealed towards his barons and the pope was manifested by Richard at Smithfield in 1381 when he faced and pacified the rebels of the Peasants Revolt, but it was courage which soon declined into obstinacy in defence of his ill-chosen favourites, just as Edward II had protected Gaveston and the Despensers. Like all his predecessors, Richard could dissemble and wait, but rather to extract vengeance than to achieve political ends; indeed, his vengeance proved highly impolitic, leading as it did directly to his deposition. Richard's autocratic and vindictive lack of judgement was compounded by his intelligence and vigour which further disquieted his opponents. Even his piety exposed him to distrust, for his promotion of his courtier clerks to the episcopate and his repeated parrying of anticlerical blows against the church made as many enemies as friends. Richard's rule and fortunes were deeply affected by, and themselves greatly influenced, the church.

Poll Taxes

The political and financial strains of war, already apparent in the Good Parliament of 1376, became no less acute in the years that followed. For one thing, English armies still enjoyed no victory against the French which could bear even slight comparison with the last great English triumph, at Poitiers in 1356, almost a quarter of a century before; rather than by triumph, recent English expeditions, as in 1378, were distinguished by costly ineptitude. Moreover, the French were now carrying the war into England, intensifying dismay and spreading alarm by their sudden and destructive raids around the south coast. Nor was this all, for in the north the Scots were again in arms. All the greater then must have been the anger of subjects upon whom fell, ever more frequently and heavily, demands for money to support these hostilities.

E. B. Fryde has calculated that in the years 1377–81 some £217,740 was levied on the laity.[1] In those same five years the clergy were assessed for around £144,000, to which we should add the revenue yielded by the clerical poll tax in the last months of Edward III's reign, when each beneficed clerk paid one shilling and all others, friars alone exempted, paid 4*d*. Although in Richard's first year the clergy conceded a double tenth, by 1379 another poll tax was required. After a fortnight's discussion, convocation agreed to match the parliamentary grant of a graduated poll tax on the laity in such a way that each archbishop would pay £6 13*s* 4*d*, each bishop £4, and all other clergy with an income exceeding 500 marks per annum £3, and so on down the scale until all beneficed curates and parish and annual chaplains were charged 2*s*, and all unbeneficed clerks and poor religious (mendicants again exempt) were to pay 4*d*.[2] Reasonable as this graduation might seem, the poll tax followed so closely upon the earlier levies that it provoked widespread clerical protest and resistance. In the diocese of Carlisle, Bishop Appleby denounced it as an evil subsidy and not all of it was collected there; the clergy of Bangor and St David's resisted collection; even in the prosperous archdeaconry of Essex, in London diocese, it had still not been collected in 1380. Some of the few surviving diocesan returns show a yield far below that of the normal subsidy, evidence perhaps as much of effective evasion as of lenient assessment. Any shortfall in the yield was made good in 1380 when, in the wake of a lay subsidy of one and a half fifteenths, convocation granted a combined property and poll tax. This time ecclesiastical benefices which appeared in the 1291 valuation were to render a tenth while those benefices omitted from that valor and hence from subsequent royal taxation were to pay a tenth on two thirds of their value; all unbeneficed clergy, advocates, notaries, proctors and registrars were to pay 2*s*: only the certified poor and unable were exempt. Thus, as A. K. McHardy has pointed out, three separate taxes were combined here: the traditional tenth, a new assessment on the unassessed benefices, and a poll tax on the unbeneficed. As a consequence the yield, to judge by the returns of Salisbury diocese, was nearly 7 per cent up on the normal clerical tenth. Nevertheless, later in that same year the clergy, like the laity, were confronted by yet another poll tax demand. This time all beneficed clergy, monks, canons and nuns were to pay 6*s* 8*d*, and all the unbeneficed one shilling, but they were to do so in such a way that the wealthier should relieve the burden on the poorer; in practice, therefore, the diocesan rates varied. In London, beneficed clergy paid 6*s* 8*d*, religious and unbeneficed paid on a sliding scale from 5*s* 4*d* to 3*s* 4*d*, while some of the wealthier clergy paid a supplementary sum as well. In the dioceses of Carlisle, Lichfield and Salisbury other arrangements and scales obtained. The income from this tax was reckoned to be far less than for a normal subsidy, but this leniency has to be weighed against the cumulative effects of recent taxation as a whole, especially upon the unbeneficed whose burden rose from 4*d* in 1379 to 2*s* in 1380 (a 500 per cent increase) and to 1*s* or even 3*s* 4*d* in 1381. The recorded protests of 1379 may have come chiefly from the suspect areas of Wales, or from Essex where the laity were shortly to rebel, but in 1381 even in prosperous Oxfordshire the collector of the clerical poll tax in Bicester was beaten up for his pains. In view of all this, disgruntled clergy – like disgruntled laymen – must have abounded on the eve of the Peasants Revolt in the summer of 1381.

The Peasants Revolt

The rising which we call the Peasants Revolt began late in May 1381 in Essex and Kent, provoked by efforts to enforce the collection of the third poll tax. Like all such affairs its initial simplicity was soon overlaid with variety and complexity. Popular movements may have a single trigger but rarely a single motive; they may begin with a particular grievance but are seldom confined to that. Before the insurrection was defeated it had spread from Essex and Kent into East Anglia and to the other home counties and was matched by risings as far afield as Beverley and Scarborough; objections to the poll tax had been augmented by programmes to abolish villeinage, to reform the criminal law, to enforce egalitarianism under the king, to confiscate and redistribute among the laity much of the church's property. Often, however, local tensions and private quarrels were more important factors, while short-term gains rather than sweeping social reform provided the objectives.[3] Among the targets of the rebels were the great possessioner abbots of St Albans and Bury St Edmunds and the collegiate body of Beverley Minster; among the victims was no less a figure than Archbishop Sudbury. Yet to conclude that the rising was in any significant degree anticlerical would be mistaken. The clergy were attacked because of their privileges and policies as lords of estates and boroughs, not on account of their cloth: the abbeys of St Albans and Bury St Edmunds, and the collegiate church of Beverley, were not burned to the ground, nor were their inmates slaughtered; it was their deeds and court records which attracted the destructive attention of the rebels. Targets, indeed, and grievances varied with the locality.

The murder of Sudbury, the first of an archbishop since Becket's martyrdom, requires some comment. He had been provided to the see of London in 1361 and was translated to Canterbury in 1375; while the first appointment had been at the expense of a royal nominee, by 1375 he had proved himself a capable manager of the clergy's financial affairs on behalf of the crown. In 1371 and 1373, when Wykeham was in eclipse and Archbishop Whittlesey was ill, Sudbury of London presided over convocation and secured from a smarting clergy the desired taxes. Just such persuasive talents were needed at Canterbury. When Sudbury met opposition, he tackled it with inventive forcefulness. In February 1380, for example, faced by a clerical grant which seemed insufficient, he had induced convocation to impose a further levy of 2*s* on all unbeneficed clergy, proctors, advocates, notaries and registrars. That same year, when the commons had proposed a poll tax of £100,000 on condition that the clergy (who allegedly occupied a third of the realm) would contribute £50,000, Sudbury protested that it was not and never had been the role of parliament or of the laity to grant clerical taxes. He did, however, assure the king that the clergy would do its part, and so the third lay poll tax was matched by the clergy's. Sudbury had both forestalled a dangerous precedent and satisfied the crown.

Since January 1380, Sudbury had also been chancellor of the realm, an office which identified him so closely with an unpopular regime that it was to cost him his life during the rebellion.[4] His assassination was not a manifestation of anticlericalism, but of the people's fury and frustration at the unconscionable burdens which had been laid upon them for such meagre results. Sudbury was lynched because he was chancellor and the only leading representative of a hated government on whom the mob could lay its hands; had they been able to capture John of Gaunt, whose Savoy Palace they burned down, Sudbury might have escaped. No other bishops were assaulted, let alone killed, not even Brantingham of Exeter or Wakefield of Worcester, although both of them were deeply implicated in the crown's financial policy.

Clergy, however, were not only victims of the revolt, but also figured among the insurgents themselves, some undoubtedly acting as leaders, inciters and organizers.[5] The best known of these were William Wrawe and John Ball, whose radical voices were notorious long before 1381. On this occasion, however, Ball's preaching was directed against lordship, the continuance of villeinage and property rather than explicitly against the church and its temporalities, let alone against the status and authority of the clergy: Ball's message may have been antisocial, but even Walsingham, it seems, found nothing anticlerical in it, and it certainly owed little if anything to Wyclif.[6]

Sudbury's successor, Courtenay, who had for some time been trying to alert the nation to the perils of heresy, was quick to portray the revolt as the consequence of Wycliffism and on this ground to seek government aid to suppress the heresiarch and his followers. The alarm which gripped Courtenay is understandable in view of the murder of his predecessor, and perhaps already at this time, as certainly in 1390, he viewed recalcitrant tenants as though they were sinners in need of penance.[7]

The Peasants Revolt thus profoundly altered the response of church and crown to the challenge of Wyclif and the lollards, although in fact, as even Walsingham made clear, the uprising is much more accurately characterized as anti-lawyer than anticlerical.[8] Politically the most significant result of the rebellion was to force the government to abandon poll taxes. Indeed, immediately after the revolt taxation of any kind was kept to a minimum, but this only increased the crown's difficulties in meeting its military commitments and led in turn to new embarrassments for both church and crown.

Despenser's Crusade

One alternative to royal taxation arose out of the papal schism. Urban VI, in Rome, was willing to construe as a crusade any campaign against his rival pope, Clement VII, in Avignon, and Clement's adherents, chief among whom was the French king. A crusade could be partly financed by papal taxation and the sale of indulgences. Thus it was that in 1382 two possible expeditions were mooted as crusades: John of Gaunt, with his eye on the crown of Castile, was eager to lead his forces against the Clementist Castilians; Bishop Despenser of Norwich, whose lust for battle was evident during the Peasants Revolt, thought to win Urban more supporters in the Low Countries by taking on Philip of Burgundy there.[9] Since Philip by seizing Bruges had severely interrupted English trade and now threatened the Staple at Calais, Despenser's plan won ready support in parliament. Both men were prepared to bear some of the costs from their own resources, but Gaunt priced himself out of the running while Despenser made only a modest demand for cash aid. A full-scale expedition was ruled out both by the cost and by the insecurity which might result from the king's absence so soon after the rebellion. So it was that amid great publicity and with approval from the parliament and convocation, the backing of Urban VI and a flood of plenary indulgences, the bishop of Norwich led forth an army to strike a blow in Flanders for the pope, the crown, the merchants and the expectant people of England who had been for so long starved of satisfying success in warfare across the Channel. Carrying such hopes upon him, Despenser by failing to fulfil them soon incurred bitter recriminations. That he did fail is incontestable and was due to various causes: a lack of clear political and military priorities, the want of noble support, and too little money and too few men to conduct siege warfare. Put to flight by Philip of Burgundy, Despenser neither recruited new Urbanists nor chastised the French, and he left Ghent still isolated and Bruges still barred to English merchants; the few conquests initially made, he sold to the French as he retreated. In a few months this wealthy, vainglorious, belligerent prelate had raised and destroyed the hopes of a nation, frustrated Gaunt, discredited yet further an embarrassed papacy and impugned the notion of crusade by leading Christian against Christian. The crown as much as the commons felt cheated by him and their impeachment of Despenser was soon overtaken by royal prosecution.

The auspices for Despenser's crusade had not been good. Though he had shown himself an enthusiastic warrior against the rebels in 1381, he had given no sign that he was capable of outgeneralling Philip of Burgundy, although neither had Gaunt or any other English noble at that time. A slender force with slender means was not the best guarantee of success even with a brilliant leader, yet in the gloom of 1382–3 Despenser offered as much hope as anyone else, certainly at a lower price; fortuitous victory would have raised the morale of the nation and the repute of the crown, pope, bishop and church: failure damaged all these and made it clear that victory was neither to be had on the cheap nor to be sought through the church. The trial of Despenser united critics both of the clergy and of those currently directing policy at court. His adventure emphasized the lesson that war could not be effectively waged without extensive taxation; yet such taxation could not be raised without grave peril at home.

If the crusading ideal was not utterly discredited by Despenser's fiasco, it had suffered grievous harm. Its final demise among Englishmen came in 1396 when Richard II, as part of his efforts for peace with France and the reunion of Christendom, supported a crusade against the Turks which ended – through no fault of the English, it is true – in disaster at Nicopolis.[10] Never again did an English king espouse or give assistance to a crusade, though Henry V reputedly harboured ambitions to lead one of his own; as for the king's subjects, they remained profoundly unmoved by the ideal. And not even in Richard's reign had the pope been allowed to levy a mandatory tenth for the purpose of a crusade.

Convocation and Clerical Subsidies, 1383–9

The extreme reluctance of the commons to finance any extensive military campaign in the years after the Peasants Revolt not only ruled out hopes of a royal expedition and induced only limited support for Despenser's ill-fated venture, but also put greater pressure upon the church to contribute more to taxation. In November 1383 and again a year later parliament voted subsidies on condition that the clergy made matching grants in convocation. When Archbishop Courtenay protested vehemently on the second occasion – on the first he had other preoccupations – the laity spoke critically of the misuse of ecclesiastical wealth and menacingly about confiscating the church's estates.[11] However, the king was as eager as the archbishop to ensure that parliament should not formally determine when and how the clergy made their grants: he well understood, in the face of Courtenay's words, that unless convocation was placated he would get no clerical subsidy and consequently no lay one either: the hook had been cleverly baited by parliament. Richard denounced the parliamentary conditions and promised to uphold and even – so a chronicler alleges – to enhance the rights of the church: confiscation was clearly no option for a king recently reminded of the interdependence of church and realm. After these reassuring promises from the king, Archbishop Courtenay led convocation in granting two half tenths, the second of which was conditional upon Richard leading an army abroad before the end of June 1385.

On the first occasion when parliament had tied lay subsidies to a comparable grant from convocation, the archbishop had been more directly in conflict with the king himself. At that time, faced by a conditional parliamentary grant and eager to have it confirmed, Richard had ordered the archbishop to convene convocation on 12 November in London. Courtenay took exception to the inclusion of a precise date in the king's mandate, denounced it as unprecedented and instead called convocation together on 2 December. Apart from resisting any surreptitious moves to alter the conventions of the writ summoning convocation, Courtenay was also concerned to preserve what little independence in theory still remained to convocation *vis-à-vis* the crown and to forestall difficulties for his successors who might be intimidated by calculatedly unreasonable dates for the assembly. Once having made the protest and defied the order, convocation voted the desired subsidy, but followed parliament's example by making it dependent upon the king himself leading an expedition abroad for the defence of the realm – for which sort of expedition the combined lay and clerical grants were in fact insufficient!

Despite all this, in February 1385 Richard ordered convocation to be assembled in London on 17 April; this time the king was even more desperate and the clergy were even more adamant. Convocation had already granted two moieties to the king in December 1384, yet by January 1385 Richard was seeking another grant from them. Courtenay advised him to consult the laity first, but Richard dared not convene parliament, since in the current mood it would undoubtedly demand reforms in exchange for a subsidy. The archbishop ignored the stipulated date of 17 April and summoned convocation for 4 May, and when it refused a grant he happily dissolved it. Richard had no choice but to acquiesce, and he called for the collection of the earlier conditional grant on the grounds that he was about to lead an expedition against the Scots (not overseas against the French) in late July (after, that is, the term of the grant, 24 June, had expired); once again the wariness and the will of the archbishop were put to the test. Courtenay consulted his colleagues and concluded that the collection of the grant would be in order. This surprising decision seemed to imply that a conditional grant never lapsed but once granted was always available until, in suitable conditions, it was used; possibly the desire of the archbishop to be as obliging as he could was helped by the fact that although the expedition was scheduled for after the expiry date the request for collection was made before it. The clergy, of course, were under considerable pressure from parliament and the crown and were having to resist both as stoutly as they could while at the same time ensuring that they did not unite both against them; although on this occasion the clergy yielded to a somewhat dubious manoeuvre by the king, they had at least conceded no new grant. At the end of the year, however, they voted two more moieties, and yet two more in 1386 to be collected in the following two years. Altogether, since the Peasants Revolt, the clergy had contributed a full tenth in each year from 1383 to 1386, and a half tenth in 1387 and 1388. Two further moieties were approved in 1388, but specifically for a royal expedition abroad for the defence of the realm before Michaelmas 1389 and provided that no other royal impositions were made upon the church in that year. In fact 1389 saw the cessation of serious hostilities with France for the rest of the century.

The demands upon the clergy may have slackened since the Peasants Revolt, but they were still disconcertingly regular, more so than requests to the laity. In return for bearing this burden, however, the clergy had maintained something of their liberty and independence of parliament and the crown; by these grants they kept at bay the popular demands for expropriation and ensured royal assistance against heretics. It was an ominous development that convocation should meet to discuss taxation when no parliament was in session, as in April 1385, although this might optimistically be regarded as a sign of the independence of these two bodies; and on that occasion, in fact, convocation made no grant.

A similar though not identical pattern of burdens was borne during these years by the northern province, which from 1383 to 1389 collected one or two moieties in each year except 1386 and 1387. York province, of course, was very much poorer than Canterbury and was further impoverished by the Anglo–Scottish conflict which not only resulted in frequent devastation of the area but also in the frequent array of the clergy alongside the laity for the defence of the region. In April 1385 a York moiety was conditional upon the king personally leading a force against the

French or Scots 'and actually attacking them'.[12] In 1389 there were three conditions attached to the grant: first, that the king should lead a force to foreign parts sufficient to vanquish his enemies there; secondly, that the clergy should be free from any other royal imposition whatever; and thirdly, that they should be exempt from array except in respect of their temporalities and in the presence of the king. What these conditions did was to draw the attention of the king to the acute problem of the Scottish border and the devastation of the north.

What profit accrued to Richard from clerical taxation up to 1389 is by no means measurable. Some approximate figures for the amount collected may be gathered from the records of the period, but the political value of these subsidies is less obvious. It seems clear that by their meagreness they effectively prevented the king from conducting the war as vigorously as he might have wished; but the king was no less hampered by the even greater reluctance of the laity to finance his war effort adequately. At a constitutional level the king, on Courtenay's prompting, had successfully prevented convocation's subsidies being tied to parliamentary decisions, a far more important achievement than the royal success in 1385 in transcending the term of the grant. Certainly Richard had failed to establish his right to decide the day on which, or even the month in which, convocation should meet, but his right to call a meeting was unchallenged even when parliament was not sitting. Although three successive parliaments had refused subsidies, convocation did so only on one occasion. The cries among some parliamentarians, and even among some courtiers, for the expropriation of church wealth was something which Richard was unlikely to implement, but it put undeniable pressure upon the clergy to grant the king's wishes as often and as largely as they could. Nevertheless, it was one thing to grant subsidies, another to pay or collect them, and during Richard's reign writs of *de excommunicato capiendo* were sought in abundance against clergy excommunicated for defaulting on their taxes. Between 1371 and 1407 some 1500 clerics were the subjects of such writs.[13]

Opposition and the King's Revenge, 1381–99

As early as 1381, the commons blamed most of the current political ills upon the extravagance of the royal household, and set up a commission to examine its management and propose desirable reforms; but the commission proved impotent to impose any reforms and none followed. Although the king was compelled at least to dismiss from his court Thomas Rushook, a former Dominican prior-provincial and then a royal confessor, very soon afterwards Rushook returned and was even rewarded with the bishopric of Llandaff in 1383 and translated to Chichester in 1385. For some reason which is not quite clear, he in particular seemed to symbolize the abuses associated with the royal household, and in 1388 he was to suffer exile as a consequence. Other favourites, such as Robert de Vere (earl of Oxford, later marquis and then duke of Ireland), Simon Burley (Richard's tutor), Nicholas Brembre (a London merchant), and Michael de la Pole (soldier, courtier and from 1385 earl of Suffolk), offended the royal uncles, Gaunt and Gloucester, as well as such formidable nobles as the earls of Arundel and Warwick who found themselves effectively supplanted in the king's councils. A menacing alliance of the king's critics, however, was postponed by the differences between the commons and the lords over the decision to back Despenser's crusade rather than Gaunt's expedition; even when it did come about, the commons' suspicion of the nobles' retinues and expensive enthusiasm for war rendered such cooperation precarious.

During 1383 and 1384 tension between the king and his leading subjects mounted, not in the least helped by the recovery by the Scots of Lochmaben castle, the last English stronghold on the western marches. In the spring of 1385, at a meeting of the council in Westminster, both the lay and spiritual lords voiced criticisms of the king's favourites, but when Archbishop Courtenay carried this message to the king, Richard is alleged to have drawn his sword on the prelate; afterwards he evaded his opponents by leading, with Gaunt, a punitive expedition to Scotland. Any reconciliation between the king and Lancaster, however, was ended when they vehemently disagreed over tactics. The parliament which met in October 1385 granted a subsidy only upon condition that the king lived off his own (that is, ceased to raise taxes), stopped further gifts for a year, submitted crown accounts to parliamentary scrutiny and published in parliament the names of officials and ministers for the coming year. The king denied the right of parliament to interfere with his household and ministers, and once again when parliament was dissolved he ignored its prescriptions. A year later, however, circumstances had changed to his disadvantage.

In 1386 Gaunt departed to promote his claims to the Castilian crown and stayed abroad for three years. With him out of the way, his younger brother, Thomas of Woodstock, duke of Gloucester, emerged as the leader of aristocratic opposition to the crown. Gloucester lacked extensive landed estates and depended upon royal patronage in the form of annuities to enable him to maintain his station in society; all the greater then was his outrage as de Vere swallowed up the lion's share of royal grants. Moreover, de Vere's titles – the unprecedented 'marquis' and the previously royal 'duke'– were hardly calculated to placate his enemies; nor, indeed, was the ennoblement of de la Pole. Lacking Gaunt's vast landed endowments, Gloucester had less to lose and much more to gain from adopting an extreme posture. In addition to this, France was now preparing for a large-scale invasion of England which made the need for taxation urgent while at the same time it heightened tensions and emotions in all quarters. This was the context of the so-called Wonderful Parliament which met in October 1386 and proposed among other things to impeach the chancellor, de la Pole, in effect for failing to implement earlier reforms. A deputation of Gloucester and Thomas Arundel, bishop of Ely, which went to the king and demanded the removal of his chief ministers, met Richard's anticipated repudiation of these demands with a threat of deposition if he should ignore the counsel of his lords or the expectations of his people. Richard therefore acquiesced: Suffolk was impeached and imprisoned, being replaced as chancellor by Bishop Arundel himself; Bishop Fordham as treasurer was supplanted by Bishop Gilbert of Hereford; and various household changes were also made. The king moreover conceded the establishment of a reform commission of fourteen to supervise crown administration and finance for a year. On this commission served Archbishop Courtenay, Archbishop Alexander Neville of York, Bishop Wykeham of Winchester, Bishop Brantingham of Exeter, and the abbot of Waltham, jointly representing the clerical estate of the kingdom rather than any distinct political faction.

After parliament's dissolution, however, Richard left London and kept away from the commission; he released Suffolk from gaol, and soon won over to his side Archbishop Neville of York. More than that, when Richard consulted his leading judges about the legality of parliament's measures to control the crown, they condemned them in terms which implied that the king's opponents were guilty of treason. By the summer, while de Vere was gathering an army in Cheshire to support the king, Richard was confronted with resolute opposition from the duke of Gloucester, the earls of Arundel and Warwick, as well as the young earls of Derby (Gaunt's son) and of Nottingham. The last two, more political adventurers than anything else but less embittered and extreme than Gloucester, led a force which defeated the royalist contingent from Cheshire at Radcot Bridge (in Oxfordshire) in December 1387. It was after this that for a few days Richard was actually deprived of his crown by Gloucester and other lords until challenged by Derby on his return from the battle: most of the crown's opponents wanted to control the king, not replace him by one of their own number and least of all by Gloucester. Derby, as Gaunt's heir, particularly had little to gain by such an overthrow. Instead, a parliament was called for February 1388.

At this assembly, commonly known as the Merciless Parliament, several judges, favourites and favourers of the king were appealed of treason by Gloucester, Warwick, Arundel, Derby and Nottingham, who were henceforth known as the Appellants. Most of the accused had already fled to safety but Nicholas Brembre, Simon Burley and Chief Justice Tresilian (forcibly removed from Westminster's sanctuary) were among those caught and executed; Pole and de Vere were exiled, as were Archbishop Neville who was translated to the inaccessible Clementist see of St Andrews, and Bishop Rushook who was later moved to the equally unattainable Irish see of Kilmore.

By the autumn of 1388, in the Cambridge parliament, fissures were already apparent between the commons and the lords as the Appellants' promises of better government and more successful campaigns were seen to be unfulfilled. In the interval between the two parliaments the Scots had consolidated their hold on the Lowlands, executed devastating raids into Cumberland and Westmorland, and humiliatingly crushed an English retaliation at Otterburn in August 1388. Capitalizing on these embarrassments for his enemies and on their emerging differences, by May 1389 Richard was able to proclaim his personal control of government without provoking any resistance. In the same year Gaunt, returning from abroad with his ambitions slaked and his principal enemy at home, Suffolk, destroyed, added the stability which Gloucester patently could not guarantee.

For the next few years Richard governed tactfully, not to say shrewdly, by lavishing grants upon Gaunt, Derby and Nottingham and recalling Archbishop Arundel (who had succeeded Neville at York) as chancellor and Bishop Gilbert as treasurer when Wykeham and Brantingham resigned, respectively in 1391 and 1389. The king made no effort to rescue the Appellants' victims until 1392 when he vainly sought the end of exile for those still surviving. Moreover, in 1394 he formally pardoned the Appellants for their offences to him and in 1396 promoted Arundel from York to Canterbury on the death of Courtenay. The following year, however, he showed his hand when he arrested and appealed in parliament three of the Appellants: Gloucester, who was murdered while under arrest at Calais; Warwick, who was banished; and the earl of Arundel, who was executed. Arundel's brother, the newly appointed archbishop of Canterbury, was also appealed, banished and translated to St Andrews. Furthermore, at Coventry in the summer of 1398 Richard seized the excuse of a quarrel between Derby and Nottingham to exile them, and in 1399, on Gaunt's death, he confiscated the Lancastrian inheritance and extended Derby's ten-year exile to life. Very soon after this, Derby returned to claim not just his own lands but the crown itself; the earlier threats of deposition were at last consummated.

In all of these developments the clergy played a part, but rather as individuals or as representatives of their estate than as a party, at least until the late 1390s. During the 1380s the bishops were more distinguished as vital messengers and mediators or as essential members of the reform commissions than as formulators of policy or leaders of parties. Some, of course, like Rushook and Arundel, were undoubtedly partisan through pressure of circumstances; others, like Wykeham and Brantingham, were elderly and by now largely impartial administrators; most were concerned over the effectiveness of government, but even Courtenay who had several encounters with Richard over clerical liberties (including on one occasion the safety of his own person) recognized how much was at risk if the king were deposed or his authority seriously challenged. Courtenay was all too well aware that Gaunt had been among Wyclif's earliest patrons and that Richard was the clergy's shield against the anticlericals.

State Trials and Tyranny

During Richard's reign four bishops were tried for treason: Henry Despenser of Norwich in 1383; Alexander Neville of York and Thomas Rushook of Chichester in 1388; and Thomas Arundel of Canterbury in 1397. The first forfeited his temporalities though they were soon restored; Neville and Rushook were both exiled and, with papal assistance, translated to sees effectively *in partibus* – St Andrews and Kilmore respectively; and Arundel, too, was exiled and translated to St Andrews. None of them had committed their offences in defence of ecclesiastical liberties or privileges against lay or crown attack. Indeed, only Arundel could remotely be described as an opponent of the king; Despenser was impeached by the crown's enemies for mishandling the crusade to Flanders on behalf of the crown and pope, although it served the king to prosecute him in order to distance himself from the fiasco; Neville was tried patently because he deserted the parliamentary commission of 1386 and joined the king's side; Rushook, royal chaplain and confessor, was a scapegoat for the hated courtiers and household – in 1388 as he had been in 1381. Arundel in 1397 was arraigned by the king, ostensibly because of his collaboration with the Appellants in 1386–8, but perhaps more immediately because Richard was now busy dishonouring his brother, the earl, and dared not risk an alienated archbishop at Canterbury. Their trials – Despenser by impeachment, the others by appeal – took place, as befitted lords, before their peers in parliament, and their punishments observed the inhibitions on shedding clerical blood. No issues between church and state were involved in these trials; they simply underline how amphibious the clergy, and especially the higher clergy, were: creatures who swam in spiritual waters and walked on royal lands. Even their spiritual peers regarded, and responded to, their trials as to any other purely political affair and raised no points of order or principle because they were bishops; though it is doubtful if they all favoured the condemnation of their fellow prelates, they were certainly not moved to concerted defence of them.

Ironically the tensions in the relations of church and state were much more apparent and much more at risk when laymen were the subject of treason charges. The trials of de la Pole in 1386 and of de Vere and his associates in 1388 and of the three Appellants themselves in 1397 all involved judgement by the upper house of parliament, and because the accused were laymen and the charge treason the possibility of death sentences was raised. Now whether we count numbers, character, status, experience or connections, the prelates were a vital and formidable element of the house of lords and without their explicit assent any condemnation of defendants who were so controversial and so influential politically could prove hazardous and self-defeating. Yet it was well known that canon law barred the clergy from blood sentences. In 1386 and 1388 the spiritual lords withdrew from the trial proceedings in the upper house, though they were careful to assert that they were not intending thereby to surrender their rights as peers to sit in the upper chamber and to be tried themselves by their peers; moreover, they tempered their withdrawal by renewing their oaths of fealty and swearing to maintain the acts and judgements of the parliament.[14] This was the precedent which they proposed to follow in 1397 when the Appellants themselves were arraigned; but now the king insisted that in order to avert any subsequent doubts about the legality of the trials, the prelates should be represented by a proctor.[15] This stratagem would certainly enable the ecclesiastical peers to support the king in condemning the

Appellants without violating canon law and even without incurring any political odium. Some bishops, however, had already compromised themselves by consenting to Richard's revocation of his earlier pardons to the Appellants: when Richard claimed that he had granted the letters of pardon while under duress, only Arundel among the prelates expressed doubts on this. Most of the bishops concluded that although the king had freely granted a pardon to the earl of Arundel in 1394, what he had freely granted he could freely cancel – a view which even the royalist judges did not share and a measure of how Ricardian the episcopate then was.[16] There was never much doubt, therefore, that the spiritual peers would agree to a proctor consenting on their behalf to decisions which they could not take personally. Nevertheless, they still sought to preserve their liberties and privileges by the conditions to be attached to the appointment of their proctor, but after several days of argument and bargaining they acquiesced in Richard's rejection of these conditions and in his nomination of his household steward, Sir Thomas Percy, as their proctor; at least, they affirmed that while the proctor could bind them, he could not commit their successors. This was an assertion which afforded only limited security to Richard and ensured that a proctor of this kind would have no great constitutional future.[17] (It is even doubtful if a proctor could in law bind a principal to an act which was illegal for the principal: Richard's security, therefore, may well have been illusory from the start.)

After all this, Archbishop Arundel himself was accused, before the king in full parliament, of treason in that while chancellor he had aided, procured and counselled the establishment of a reform commission in 1386 contrary to the regality of the king and the dignity of the crown; furthermore, it was asserted that in 1388 he connived at the seizure of power by the same men and the arrest and execution of the king's loyal subjects. On 25 September the king declared that the archbishop had confessed before him and the lords, whereupon all the lay peers and Sir Thomas Percy as proctor of the spiritual peers adjudged Archbishop Arundel guilty of treason; he was ordered to leave the realm within six weeks of Michaelmas by way of Dover for France, and all the lands which he personally held when he committed the offences or which he had acquired since were to be forfeit in perpetuity to the crown.[18]

A few days later, before the high altar at Westminster, the prelates of both provinces declared that all the proceedings of this parliament should be inviolably observed by their subjects under pain of excommunication for helping, attempting or committing any contravention.[19] They swore – in the person of Sir Thomas Percy – on the altar of St Edward the Confessor and in the presence of the king to uphold and sustain all the acts of this parliament.

In January 1398, when parliament had adjourned from Westminster to Shrewsbury, the prelates – now represented by the earl of Wiltshire in place of Percy – swore again to uphold all the measures and judgements, doing nothing contrary to them, nor ever repealing, revoking, annulling or reversing them or suffering anyone else to do so.[20] Not satisfied with all these assurances, Richard also enlisted the aid of the pope who agreed not only to approve Archbishop Arundel's banishment and replacement but also to confirm the acts of this parliament and to excommunicate those who presumed to contravene them.

At Coventry in September 1398 when Richard banished the two surviving Appellants he demanded further oaths from his subjects: early in 1399 all abbots, priors, deans and other ecclesiastics were to swear to observe the acts of parliament at Westminster/Shrewsbury and the decrees at Coventry; the taking of the oath and the names of those sworn were to be certified to chancery. The sole diocese for which a return is extant is Salisbury where the task was completed only in June 1399, a mere month before the earl of Derby landed at Ravenspur.[21]

One earlier episode which, although it had caused the clergy some anxiety, proved in the end to be more alarming for parliament than for the clergy was the Haxey affair. In the parliament of January 1397 a bill was presented to the commons which was adjudged, by the lords and at the king's suggestion, treasonous.[22] Four matters were the subject of this bill but one in particular offended the king: it criticized the excessive cost of the king's household as a result of the numerous bishops and ladies gathered there.[23] The commons apologized abjectly and disclosed that Thomas Haxey was its author. As he was a clerk – he was present in parliament as proctor of the abbot of Selby – the prelates sought and obtained custody of him 'out of the king's free grace'. Although his provocative petition enabled the king to reaffirm the 1387 definition of treason, that Haxey was put up to it by the king has yet to be proved; and equally speculative is the suggestion that because of his earlier association with Arundel he was acting on this occasion as a covert spokesman for the archbishop. As for his charge about the bishops at court, it is only true if it is taken to refer to the number of royal chaplains who were promoted to bishoprics. The whole episode has less import for the church than for parliament, a fact which was recognized early in the next reign when the judgement on Haxey was reversed as being erroneous and against the liberties of the commons.

Jurisdiction

In Richard's first parliament the clergy presented a list of fourteen grievances or *gravamina*.[24] One asked that the king would employ only prudent men in his council and avoid extravagance in his household, so that taxes might be curtailed. Another sought and obtained a confirmation of all the church's liberties and franchises. Two concerned sanctuary rights which were endorsed by the king. Four dealt with prohibitions, to each of which the king's answer was to confirm customary usage. In addition, statutory limits on the trains and stays of royal officers sojourning in religious houses were to be enforced; violent interference with causes in the courts Christian was declared void and punishable; abuses of purveyance were to be subject to action by trespass because action for felony, involving as it did a blood sentence, was not open to the clergy; malicious summonses before the marshal of the royal household were to be remedied; tithe cases were only to be remitted from the secular to the ecclesiastical courts after clear demonstration of the grounds for doing so. Of all these petitions, only the first received no answer, but few of the others elicited anything like effective or positive replies.

Despite the confirmation of sanctuary rights, one of the most sensational attacks on church liberties occurred in 1378 when Robert Haulay, esquire, and John Shakel took refuge in the sanctuary of Westminster Abbey. Haulay and Shakel had been imprisoned in the Tower since October 1377 for refusing to hand over a hostage (captured at the battle of Najera ten years earlier) to John of Gaunt. In August 1378 they escaped and fled to Westminster, and soon after this the constable of the Tower and fifty men entered the sanctuary, slew Haulay and a sacristan and abducted Shakel. Archbishop Sudbury excommunicated the desecrators without naming them; Bishop Courtenay of London was more specific. In the parliament which met – at Westminster Abbey itself – in October 1378 the archbishop addressed the king and lords on the subject of sanctuary. He began by gratefully acknowledging the renewal of the church's liberties and franchises, then outlined the violation of sanctuary which had just taken place, and concluded by asking for due satisfaction and amends to be made to the church. Recognizing that the king was 'young, innocent, and guiltless', his appeal was directed especially to the lords; but their reply was a vehement tirade against clerical encroachment upon the king's regality and an avowal to repel any further developments of this kind. The lords denied that Westminster sanctuary should be extended to debtors (which in effect Haulay and Shakel were) and sought the sworn advice of some doctors of theology and canon and civil law. The doctors came with other royal clerks (Wyclif among them) to argue before the whole parliament the case against Westminster's sanctuary; the prelates were given another day on which to reply. Probably at this stage the commons joined in petitioning for a definition of Westminster's liberties. After examining the relevant charters with various doctors and judges, the king declared that sanctuary rights were valid only for felony and not for debt, but that out of his especial reverence for Westminster he permitted sanctuary to be offered to debtors impoverished by misfortune, thus excluding those who might simply exploit the haven in order to defraud their creditors; this was probably no more and no less than the original charters intended, and it seems to exclude Haulay and Shakel from its benefit.[25]

Ten years later, Westminster's sanctuary was again put to the test in an even more critical situation. Sir Robert Tresilian, chief justice, and one of those appealed for treason by the Appellants because of his 'royalist' answers to Richard's questions in 1387, took refuge in Westminster.[26] He was pursued there by the duke of Gloucester, violently removed, hauled before parliament, condemned and executed. Tresilian had claimed that Westminster's privileges had included immunity for treason (as indeed the charters of Edgar and Edward the Confessor implied), but this contention was overthrown by Bishop Thomas Arundel, then chancellor and ally of the Appellants. Arundel maintained that if traitors were protected in this way anyone could kill the king with impunity – an extreme and disingenuous argument to deploy with reference to Tresilian whose offence was not to contemplate or attempt regicide but to support too zealously Richard II's authority and independence. Arundel was not above political expediency and might be thought to deserve the king's later revenge. In 1387 Richard himself was powerless to take effective action in defence of his judge, although he approved the excommunication of those who abducted Tresilian from the sanctuary. 'There is not a bishop', wrote Westminster's chronicler, 'so jealous as he is for the rights of the church!'[27]

Sanctuary, however, even Westminster's, was never proof against a determined violator, least of all a government backed by force. Yet the principle remained inviolate, if only because it cost nothing to reaffirm sanctuary after an expedient breach, but more probably because where a charter, genuine or accepted as genuine, could be invoked, neither legally nor politically was annulment feasible. As a rule, the secular authorities and the church collaborated with surprising harmony. Most violations, if tragic for the victims, were more mundane and insignificant than the two considered above; some turned out to be fictional and farcical. For example, John Giffard in 1402 claimed to have been dragged from the sanctuary of St Mary Somerset, London, but was found by a jury to have been seized one Sunday night when on his way back to the church from a visit to the common privy, a hundred paces away, where he had gone to relieve his bowels.[28] Although sanctuary issued occasionally in great scandals, must have been a frequent source of grievance, and was undoubtedly an impediment to law enforcement, its importance in church–state relations should rank low in any list. There are two reasons for this: first, it was never itself the object of sustained or of primary attack, but always a short-lived incident in the course of a quite different conflict; and secondly, since sanctuary rights usually originated in some royal charter, any curtailment of them might be construed as an attack upon the king's regality, a consideration which may well have contributed to Richard's stout defence of Westminster, although he also had a deep personal affection for the abbey.

Richard's reputation as a defender of the church's jurisdictional rights appeared to be borne out in other matters besides sanctuary. When in 1377 the commons petitioned the king to ensure that penances should not be commuted to fines by the church authorities who should rather eschew 'the great ransoms taken from small people', this potentially combustible issue was simply answered by the king with an order to all bishops and ordinaries to give penalties according to the law of the church and not otherwise.[29]

Similarly in the same parliament a petition for the setting of a tariff of probate fees was met merely by the stipulation that these should be reasonable and considerate. A year later the commons set their own tariff by complaining of fees far greater than the 8d allegedly due, but again the response was that the ancient laws and statutes were sufficient, or, if it could be shown in certain cases that they were not, then due remedy would be ordained.[30] No further complaint or discussion concerning probate fees was heard in parliament during the rest of the reign.

Another chronic point of tension between lay and ecclesiastical jurisdiction was the subject of tithes of wood (*silva cedua*). Parliamentary petitions on this matter – particularly to secure effective prohibitions against clerical prosecution or to redefine what of this wood was titheable and what was not – date back to the thirteenth century, but during Richard's reign were presented with tiresome frequency, every few years, perhaps because on each occasion the response was that current usage should continue.[31] The 1391 supplication complained that divers bills had been introduced in several previous parliaments without any positive response, and none was forthcoming then; in 1393 the king did promise to discuss the matter with the prelates and to ordain a remedy in the next parliament, but almost predictably such discussion produced no solution which would satisfy the commons. On no other matter were king or council more consistently protective of the church's courts and rights.

Although at the very beginning of the reign some concern was expressed in parliament about religious houses evading the statute of Mortmain and enlarging their estates by acquiring the use of lands held for them by feoffees or trustees, nothing was done about this until 1391. In that year an act extended mortmain to cover land held to the use, or on behalf, of an undying corporation – now including guilds, confraternities, cities and boroughs. With respect to church lands, lollard and anticlerical pressure undoubtedly lay behind the measure, as well perhaps as a realization that mortmain was being extensively evaded by the employment of uses.[32] It was not only uses, however, which were the subject of suspicion and attempted restraint. Anxiety had been voiced in 1381 about churches inducing the king to buy land which he would then bestow upon them; although he promised self-restraint, Richard affirmed his prerogative right to purchase and give lands in mortmain as the spirit moved him.[33] Ten years later it was alleged that lands in mortmain were being augmented by the serfs of prelates and religious purchasing lands in fee or freehold, while in 1394 the fear was voiced that clerics were enlarging their holdings by marrying off their villeins to free women of property.[34] Such petitions seem to bear witness more to lay fantasies and animus than clerical devices.

Provisions and Praemunire Again

Since the beginning of the reign the commons had sustained a persistent campaign on the subject of papal provisions, believing that each such appointment deprived the king of loyal counsel, the realm of treasure (paid in fees, services and first fruits), patrons of their inheritance, parishioners of hospitality and alms, and finally souls of prayers. Until 1388 these protests had elicited sympathy but no action from the council and the king: existing laws were sufficient, so let them be enforced. But once the Appellants controlled government the matter of provisions soon attained sensational dimensions. Neville was moved to St Andrews, Arundel to York, Fordham to replace him at Ely, Skirlaw *vice* Fordham at Durham, Erghum to Skirlaw's vacated see of Bath and Wells, and John Waltham, keeper of the privy seal, was promoted to succeed Erghum at Salisbury; it was only in November 1389 that Rushook, exiled and translated to Kilmore, was replaced at Chichester by the courtier, Richard Mitford. These changes used to be construed as the demotion of nearly half the episcopal bench, but that would never have been in the interest of the Appellants who needed supporters not disgruntled enemies.[35] Most of the transfers were prompted by quite unpolitical considerations, were only questionably demotions, in some cases may have been initiated by the candidates themselves, and were doubtless welcomed by a pope desperate for money which the consequent services would yield. What began as a limited and political transfer of bishops ended as an extensive reshuffle which served to publicize the venal interest of the papacy.

Perhaps as an Appellant exercise in popularity, in the Cambridge parliament in September 1388 a statute declared that no one was to seek papal provision to a benefice in England unless they had first secured special leave from the king to do so; offenders were to lose the living so obtained and to suffer outlawry; the voided benefice was to revert to the patron – significantly, not the king.[36]

Moreover, in return for his collaboration over Neville and Rushook, Urban had been encouraged to believe that he would be allowed to raise a subsidy from the English clergy, although a statute in February 1388 banned the shipment of gold and silver out of the realm. Disregarding these obstacles, Urban reserved to himself all vacant sees and ordered the collection of the subsidy to go ahead. The king, however, on recovering full control of government in 1389, prohibited the collection.

That same year Urban died and was succeeded by Boniface IX, who at Richard's request translated John Gilbert from Hereford to St Davids, and thereby won royal consent for the collection of the papal subsidy. Parliament, disturbed at this new alliance of king and pope, in January 1390 revised the statute of Provisors in a form which can justly be called draconian.[37] It applied to any bishopric or benefice vacant on or after 29 January 1390: all who accepted provisions and were in peaceable possession before that date were unaffected, but any others then or thereafter who accepted, or abetted those who sought or accepted, provisions were to suffer perpetual banishment and forfeiture of all their lands and goods.[38] If any bishop sent to Rome, or even induced the king to send to Rome, in violation of the statute, he was to forfeit the value of his temporalities to the king for one year; a temporal lord would similarly lose a year's value of his estate; the candidate would lose the benefice involved and suffer a year of imprisonment. Whoever brought or sent into the realm any papal summons against those enforcing or observing the statute was to suffer imprisonment, perpetual forfeiture of all lands and goods, and risk loss of life or limb; any prelate who attempted to enforce such instruments was to lose his temporalities until he had made redress; lesser clergy were to be incarcerated until they had paid a ransom set by the council. Such ferocious terms immediately provoked a formal protest from the two archbishops on behalf of all their suffragans and clergy; in the full parliamentary assembly they explicitly dissented from any statute which restricted papal authority or subverted ecclesiastical liberties, and (with the king's full consent) they had their protest recorded on the Rolls of Parliament.[39] Their objection, no doubt triggered by the lollard antipapalism which surely informed the statute and its savage penalties, was unavailing. A month later, papal denouncement of the offending statutes only resulted in a joint remonstration by king and magnates against provisions. Furthermore, in 1391 all the king's subjects at the Curia were ordered to return home and forbidden to procure any bulls contrary to the law of the land.[40]

A concession by parliament in January 1393 allowing the king, in response to continued overtures from the pope, to modify the statutes of Provisors and negotiate a settlement with the pope,[41] is usually overshadowed in modern accounts by the far more sensational – but at that time much less noticed – great statute of *Praemunire* of 1393.[42] This spoke of papal plans to translate bishops out of the realm without the king's assent and even without their own prior knowledge, and it threatened anyone procuring or effecting such moves, or indeed anything else touching the regality or realm, with outlawry and loss of goods. It is nowadays argued that the measure was intended to exert pressure on the pope with reference to one specific current dispute. In this an alien cardinal, recently provided to a Wells cathedral canonry, had contended for it in the King's Bench against a royal candidate and lost, whereupon, so the rumour went, the pope was planning to excommunicate all who opposed it and to provide the king's candidate elsewhere – actions which the statute was well designed to quash. In support of this view is the absence of any sign that the statute was observed or enforced before the 1430s, and the equally remarkable silence about it in contemporary chronicles and from the clergy in parliament. However, when viewed in conjunction with the licence to modify the statutes of Provisors, it might also be seen as a calculated stick to accompany the carrot in ensuing negotiations.

In many ways the most remarkable feature of the great statute of *Praemunire* is the support given to its passage by the archbishop of Canterbury. In a barely qualified endorsement of the commons' petition which preceded the enactment, Courtenay on behalf of all the prelates declared support for the king 'in this and all other instances in which the rights of his crown are concerned' and acknowledged that papal translations without the royal assent were against the king's terrestrial sovereignty; he affirmed the established customs that disputes over patronage were justiciable in the king's courts and that excommunication of those who carried out the judgements of the courts violated the king's regality. At Courtenay's own request these avowals were entered on the parliament roll.[43]

That the prelates who protested against Provisors in 1390 should three years later support the *Praemunire* statute is perhaps to be explained by two factors: in both instances they were backing the crown's regality, against aristocratic restraint in 1390, against papal disregard in 1393; and on the latter occasion they were also protecting themselves from arbitrary translation by the pope. Insignificant as this statute of *Praemunire* may have been at first, its implications for royal sovereignty over certain aspects of the English church were extremely important: when bishops acknowledged 'the crown of England which hath been so free at all times, that it hath been in no earthly subjection, but immediately subject to God in all things touching the regality of the same crown, and to none other', they were paying hostages to fortune. They were also echoing contemporary references by Richard II to his imperial authority.[44] It is open to grave doubt, therefore, that they consented to these terms because they knew the ensuing act to be simply an *ad hoc* measure. That argues a degree of prescience and naivety which we can hardly credit to them: Courtenay above all was alert to precedent, liberties and dangers; Arundel was scarcely less so; and it is difficult to believe that the other bishops, with all their experience of royal and papal politics and government, could be blind to the implications of such ambitious words. Rather was it that for all their loyalty and service to the papacy, and to church liberties, they firmly believed that the king should have the last word in questions of patronage. That they should do so is a measure of how far things had shifted in favour of the king during this century.

Notwithstanding all this, the pope was still eager for repeal of the statutes and pressed on with negotiations to this end for the rest of the decade.[45] Richard exploited this opportunity to secure the provision of several courtiers to episcopal sees: thus Tideman, his physician, was provided to Llandaff and then translated to Worcester; Burghill, his confessor, also to Llandaff, and then to Lichfield; Mone, his clerk, to St Davids; and, above all, Walden, his secretary, to Canterbury when Arundel was translated to St Andrews. On this last occasion Boniface, more tactful than Urban had been earlier, permitted no chain reaction of episcopal appointments to occur.

In January 1397 parliament again authorized the king to modify the statute of 1390, provided that any resulting change was vetted in the following parliament.[46] Once again the archbishops on behalf of all the clergy reminded the king of their dissent from any restriction on papal authority touching provisions, though they did so saving their fealty to the king as well as the liberty of the church and their profession of loyalty to the pope.[47] Richard for his part consulted his judges and the clergy of each province about the threat to his regality posed by recent translations, even though they had all been at his own prompting![48]

A year later, in November 1398, a concordat was agreed, but

before it could be ratified and put into effect Richard had been deposed and the pope had to contend with a new king in entirely different circumstances: the struggle over provisions continued. Had the concordat operated, the king would have achieved almost absolute control of episcopal appointments, since the pope agreed to appoint only candidates recommended by, or acceptable to, the king.[49] Papal provisions to cathedral or collegiate churches were to be restricted during the next six vacancies and then were to cease, the bishop henceforth appointing; since bishops were so often royal servants or susceptible to royal suggestions and pressure, this would have ensured a continuing element of royal clerks among chapter personnel and a continuing reservoir of rewards for royal servants. With regard to other benefices in ecclesiastical patronage, papal provisions were due to cease at Easter 1400. Altogether, although this left the pope considerable patronage in cathedrals and colleges for some time to come and in certain parish churches for the next year or eighteen months, the concordat would have been a triumph for the crown and for the English antipapalists: it did not repeal the statutes so much as render them otiose. At that stage Boniface was doubtless seeking immediate gains rather than long-term ones, since the threat of an end to the schism was increasing year by year.

The Bishops

In the key appointments to the see of Canterbury both the restraints which acted upon the king's choice and the changes which had occurred since the early fourteenth century become visible. Sudbury, a papal servant and nominee, had been inherited from Edward III and was very much a royal collaborator. In 1381 after the assassination of Sudbury, William Courtenay succeeded to Canterbury. This could hardly have been the appointment of the young king – to whom Courtenay was in fact related – nor yet an arbitrary choice of his council. Courtenay had already served on the episcopal bench for over a decade and had progressed from Hereford to London; in the latter see he had won the respect and enthusiasm of the leading citizens of the capital; he was, moreover,

free from the political associations and embarrassments such as
afflicted older and eminent colleagues like Wykeham. Courtenay
combined experience with decorum and capability. Perhaps far
more important in the wake of the Peasants Revolt, he was a known
conservative who had tried hard to prosecute Wyclif in the belief,
which now seemed confirmed, that heresy and rebellion were
inseparably connected. None of his episcopal colleagues could
match his connections, his experience, his seniority, energy and
resolution, combined with his political 'innocence'. He was not
always a comfortable partner for parliament or king, but he
collaborated as much as he could and produced for the king more
grants than possibly a lesser figure would have done.

On his death in 1396 he was succeeded by Thomas Arundel,
brother of the Appellant earl of Arundel. Now only in his forties,
Arundel had been appointed bishop of Ely back in 1373 and since
1388 had held York; furthermore, he had been chancellor of the
realm in 1386–9 and again from 1391 until his move to Canterbury: he was thus a prelate of unrivalled political and administrative experience who could certainly manage the church in the
crown's interest. But for the link with the Appellants, Arundel's
appointment would seem unexceptional against the list of his
predecessors from Islip onwards. But since Richard was to charge
the earl of Arundel with treason and exile him only a year after the
archbishop's appointment, a question mark hangs over Thomas's
translation from York to Canterbury. Whether it was to lull the
archbishop and his brother into complacency or whether it was a
concession to a council still under the shadow of 1388 is uncertain,
but Richard would have needed very good reasons – and quite
alarming ones – to overlook the claims of Arundel upon Canterbury in 1396. Walden, who replaced him there, could not match
Arundel's qualifications; he was a courtier, the king's secretary,
and had held neither a bishopric nor a great office of state; his
direct appointment to the premier see of the realm only serves to
confirm how desperate, hurried and partisan his appointment was.
Yet his promotion fitted the recent pattern: among Walden's
suffragans, Ely, Exeter, Lichfield, Salisbury, Worcester and St
Davids were all occupied by former members of the royal
household, while Chichester, Norwich and Llandaff were held by

the king's friends. In the northern province all the bishoprics were
held by courtiers. Haxey's celebrated petition had some point to
it.[50]

King and Church

Among the accusations which were levelled at Richard II in order
to justify his deposition there were three which concerned the
church. The first alleged that he had impoverished monastic
houses by levying from them money, horses and equipment for his
Irish campaign. What is striking about the charge is its limits;
reference is made only to the circumstances immediately preceding deposition, the implication being that his accusers could find
no other more extensive extortions. The second charge is desperately and vaguely formulated: that Richard had violated Magna
Carta by issuing writs of prohibition in spiritual causes. Of course,
Magna Carta makes no mention of such writs, but it does
guarantee the liberties and franchises of the church; the remarkable feature of this charge, however, is that such prohibitions had
been commonplace and in many causes unexceptional since the
thirteenth century and were not some dangerous innovation made
by Richard II. The charge dates back to the *gravamina* of
Pecham's day and still begs a large question about the definition of
spiritual causes. The third charge, which concerns the king's
dishonourable treatment of the archbishop of Canterbury, obviously emanated from Arundel and was a political and personal
rather than a substantial grievance. A fourth charge referred to his
soliciting papal approval and confirmation of parliamentary
measures and acts, though this was concerned not with the king's
violation of church liberties but with his threat to parliamentary
authority and prerogative. In sum, these accusations seem to
imply that the king had been astonishingly successful in avoiding
offence to the church, or encroachment upon its liberties,
throughout most of his reign. Indeed, far from that being so, we
have seen how he responded to anticlerical petitions by defending
the church's rights and usages.

The first thing to note is that there were no great church–state conflicts during his reign. The impeachment and appeal of bishops arose from their political and not from their ecclesiastical roles; the issue of their presence at state trials concerned their peerage rights more than canonical inhibitions. Taxation was successfully reserved to convocation, and the clergy established their right to decide for themselves on which day it should meet; although the term of the grant was transcended on one occasion, this was done in such a way as not to open the door to serious abuses in the future. As for episcopal appointments, although Richard and his opponents made blatantly political appointments and dismissals, for the most part other factors operated and the majority of the translations seem not to have been so scandalously secular as was once thought.

Papal initiative was more effectively restrained in the matter of clerical taxation than in respect of provisions, but this was certainly neither an innovation nor unpopular amongst the clergy generally. Although the prelates recorded their opposition to the statute of Provisors, they did so in terms which suggest ambivalence or expediency. As for *Praemunire*, it was several decades before the full implications of its vague wording were realized; at the time it was more noticeable for the expression of support for royal sovereignty which it called forth from the bishops.

If Richard had not significantly advanced the grip of the crown on the church which he inherited from Edward III, he had saved it from the lollards and anticlericals eager to exploit its wealth. He had blocked their proposals and given the clergy assistance in discovering and arresting heretics. This was at the invitation of the church, but it had taken a significant step towards state responsibility for orthodoxy, always implicit in the idea of a Christian commonwealth.

When we turn to the influence exerted by the church upon the king's rule, it is found to be very little, the reason for which lies in the king's own person. Such was the nature of the episcopal bench that bishops reflected rather than led political opinion and assisted rather than directed secular policies. Archbishops appointed in order to manage the clergy responded to royal demands with just enough enthusiasm to keep the king quiescent and the church safe; they raised enough funds to keep him at bay, too little to make him effective. Rich in administrative experience, alert in preserving their privileges, informed by their aristocratic and political connections, and in the 1390s often promoted from his household, Richard's prelates had no great political ambitions of their own; if any large issue determined their actions, it was to contain the demands for the disendowment of the church. Had the church taken a determined and united line on royal policies – on war or taxation or provisions or translations, for example – the course of the reign would undoubtedly have been different. But largely because of the previous evolution of the English church and partly because of the rampant anticlericalism at the time, the clergy's influence was as muted as it was indispensable to the king.

Henry IV (1399–1413)
The Clergy and Usurpation

A successful usurper rarely has an easy reign, and certainly the glamour which attached to Henry of Lancaster soon deserted him once he was crowned. At first this is surprising, for few men before him reached the throne with greater political experience within England or wider political acquaintance outside; perhaps Edward I provides the closest parallel. Henry in his youth had been a jousting champion and the darling of tournament crowds; he had also been a valiant opponent of an unpopular regime which in the end had confiscated his massive Lancaster inheritance. It is true that by then Henry had shown a glimpse of very unchivalric treachery towards his fellow Appellant, Mowbray, but this was soon obscured when his ten-year banishment by Richard II was converted into disinheritance. When Henry landed at Ravenspur to claim his own, he appeared once again as a champion, this time of justice for all landowners. He had sat in parliaments, he had been on crusade, he was – for his class at that time – passingly well educated and conventionally pious, and he came in the company and with the blessing of an archbishop who had also been arbitrarily dispossessed and banished by Richard.

What Henry patently lacked for usurpation, however, was a clear title to the crown. Not only had Richard already named the earl of March as his heir, but there was also the obstinate fact that Richard was still alive and still king. Henry had to remove a living king and supplant an heir as well. The only precedent, Edward II's deposition, was not helpful: first, because while it was a precedent, people were nevertheless reluctant to see it repeated, to see the divinity which hedges a king violated again; and secondly, because in 1327 the claimant was the indisputable heir and was carried to the throne by popular revulsion from Edward II's regime, and subsequently from Mortimer's and Isabella's. Henry's accession involved chicanery.

Archbishop Arundel and the Change of Dynasty

In March 1399, while in exile in Paris, Henry of Lancaster was shorn of his late father's estates, and early in July that year he landed at the mouth of the Humber, ostensibly to claim his inheritance. He proceeded by way of Lancastrian estates and with the backing of the Percys to gather an army and by early August was at Chester. Richard, who had been campaigning in Ireland, returned and tried to muster his forces in Wales. By 9 August, having failed to raise a worthwhile army, he took refuge in Conway castle and there received emissaries from Henry. The earl of Northumberland, a Percy, was one of these and, according to an eye-witness, he swore an oath on the consecrated host that Richard's life and crown would be spared provided that he reversed his acts of dispossession, permitted the trial of five unpopular councillors, and recognized Henry's claim to be hereditary steward of the realm; in these circumstances, Henry would be content to remain duke of Lancaster and to continue a loyal subject to Richard. Reassured by this, though muttering to himself promises of vengeance (so we are told by a witness of the events), Richard was persuaded to leave the stronghold of Conway and to go and meet Henry at Chester. He was, however, arrested at Flint and put under pressure to abdicate, which he eventually did – or was alleged to have done – in the Tower of London on 29 September. The next day, lest anything of royal honour and dignity should still remain to him, he was deposed by the estates of the realm, whose proctors then withdrew allegiance and homage from him. Henry now claimed the vacant throne by right of his descent (horribly and deliberately garbled) vindicated by conquest, and all this was done before an assembly of estates which within a week was to re-form as Henry IV's first parliament and ratify the abdication and deposition. After another week had passed, on 13 October, Henry was duly crowned king.

Throughout this process of usurpation, from early August to

early October and beyond, the clergy and in particular the archbishop of Canterbury made a vital contribution to Henry's success.[1] Almost certainly Archbishop Arundel accompanied Northumberland to Conway, and was instrumental with him in luring Richard out of the sanctuary of the castle to meet Lancaster.[2] If, as a chronicler there present states, Northumberland swore on the host that Richard would retain his crown, then doubtless Arundel did too. So ambiguous and conflicting is the evidence that certainty on these points is impossible, but logic suggests that a senior magnate would be accompanied by a principal prelate – after the pattern of most diplomatic missions of the day and surely to convince Richard of Henry's serious intent. Moreover, Arundel is known to have been at Flint and Chester in the days before and after the Conway incident. If he was at Conway, there can be no doubt that he too perjured himself there. Of course, this raises difficult problems about the character and integrity of the archbishop, but alternative accounts of the facts are no less awkward to interpret: as we shall argue below, Arundel was committed to the usurpation from the moment he landed with Henry in Holderness.

Soon after the capture of Richard all the abbeys and major churches of England were instructed to examine their chronicles with especial reference to the state and governance of the realm from the time of the Conqueror up to the present, and to send the chronicles, under the common seals of the churches, to Henry and with them men who could speak authoritatively about their contents.[3] In September a committee of doctors, bishops and others (among them the chronicler Adam of Usk) was set up to consider how the usurpation might be legally accomplished, and they spent some time discussing the chronicles' evidence for Henry's claim by descent.[4] As well as historical evidence of this kind, the committee ransacked canon law for a text to justify Henry's seizure of the crown, or at least his removal of Richard.[5] They found what they were looking for in the sentence of deposition issued by Pope Innocent IV against Emperor Frederick II in the thirteenth century and in the canonists' glosses upon that sentence. What that precedent clearly necessitated was proof of Richard's incorrigible wickedness in government, and there resulted a long list of charges advanced against Richard by, or before, the estates of the realm.

These charges were read on 30 September after Archbishop Scrope of York and Bishop Trefnant of Hereford, as Richard's proctors, had announced his abdication, made and declared to them and other peers in the Tower on the previous day. Following the charges, the decision to depose him was affirmed and then conveyed to Richard by proctors representing each of the estates of the kingdom, the bishop of St Asaph's, John Trevor II, and the abbot of Glastonbury acting for the clergy; following the deposition the proctors withdrew the allegiance and homage of the realm. Both archbishops afterwards placed Henry on the empty throne and Arundel preached on the text 'This man shall rule my people' (I Samuel 9:17). A week later, now before the official parliament, Arundel delivered another address: he chose as his theme the words, 'It is incumbent upon us to provide for the realm' (I Maccabees 6:57) and expounded this as meaning the protection of justice, of the laws of the kingdom and of the degree or estate of each person.

At the coronation on 13 October Arundel anointed Henry with Thomas Becket's miraculous oil, a benefit which he had withheld from Richard.[6] This oil, contained in a phial in a golden eagle, was allegedly the gift of the Blessed Virgin to Becket especially for the consecration of English kings. Not heard of until 1318, it was not discovered until Edward III found it at Poitiers, and it was lost again by 1377 somewhere in the Tower. In 1399 it turned up once more, but Arundel refused Richard's request for a second anointing, now with the recovered oil. It was employed for Henry's crowning. Although there is little mention of the oil in the propaganda of the Lancastrians in 1399 or afterwards, and although its origin and legend antedate the usurpation, and despite the fact that it was later used by Yorkists too, one need not conclude that its use in 1399 was a matter of small moment for the usurper. Henry needed all the approbation he could get and this gift from the Virgin was literally heaven-sent. On the same day as Henry's first parliament had met, Canterbury convocation also assembled, and like parliament it was convened by means of an elaborate fiction. With neither an indisputable king nor an indisputable archbishop to convoke it, convocation was summoned by a mandate which was dated 3 September, nearly three weeks before Arundel was restored to his see, and issued from the prior and convent of Christ Church Canterbury, custodians of the vacant see, but sealed by an official of the court of arches, the archbishop's principal court. Explicitly called to promote the nation's affairs, to protect the laws and liberties of the church and the kingdom, and to deal with any other matters arising, its real purpose was to approve, justify and publicize the usurpation. Before it did that, however, a royal delegation came and declared that the king wished for no money from the clergy but simply their prayers, and that he would uphold the liberties of the church and extirpate heresy. After that encouragement convocation proceeded to draw up its own list of grievances to set beside those concocted in parliament against the erstwhile tyrant, Richard. Whereas parliament had confined itself to only five articles about Richard's exploitation or oppression of the church, convocation easily listed about twenty, mostly concerning violations of benefit of clergy, the unscrupulous use of writs of prohibition, and other malpractices of royal judges and officers. The clergy petitioned for the confirmation of all clerical privileges embodied in Magna Carta, *Circumspecte agatis* and Edward II's *Articuli Cleri*.[7] Finally mandates were issued to the province referring to Richard's unprecedented oppression and to Henry's coming like another Maccabeus, called by God to lead his people back to righteousness: one mandate ordered prayers and processions in every parish on behalf of this new Maccabeus. In the armoury of royal propaganda convocation was an invaluable instrument, reaching as it did into each parish of the kingdom. In 1399 parliament and convocation were complementary political agents for the installation of a new king and a new dynasty, and the returned archbishop marched perfectly in step with the *de facto* king and did all he could to make him one *de iure*.

There can be no doubt that when Henry and Arundel landed at Ravenspur they both intended even then to remove Richard II from the throne. It would have taken a fool to imagine in 1399 that Henry could have recovered his duchy and hold it securely, or Arundel his archbishopric, while Richard was still king. Richard had already amply demonstrated how long his vengeful memory was, and the duke's and archbishop's success would involve him in yet more humiliation, from the consequences of which they could not hope to be safe: Creton, an eye-witness, commented on Richard's intention to deal with Lancaster subsequently. It makes no sense to suppose that only at or after his meeting with the Percys at Doncaster did Henry resolve to seize the crown. Nor is it any more feasible to cast Arundel as a naive dupe who found himself allied to, and deceived by, an unscrupulous adventurer. Henry was no political novice, nor indeed was Arundel, son of a noble family, bishop for almost thirty years and chancellor of the realm for almost ten. During his exile he had gone to Rome and received assurance there that his translation was the result of misinformation and would be duly rectified; he had then joined Henry in Paris with, it might be reasonably supposed, the obvious intention of bringing this about.

That the archbishop needed Henry of Lancaster's help in order to recover his see is clear enough; but equally Arundel was vital to Henry's success and survival. To convince doubters of his claims to the throne and to convert opponents Henry needed the blessing of the church, and enthusiastic support from the clergy would be a major psychological advantage for the claimant: without it, or, still worse, in the teeth of clerical opposition, Henry would be severely weakened politically. The church could confer respectability and credibility upon the usurper and assist him in more tangible ways as well.

The key to the church's attitude and role was a forceful archbishop at Canterbury, but when Henry returned to England Archbishop Roger Walden was no such prelate. When Arundel had been thrust out of Canterbury, Walden was expediently and unprecedentedly elevated directly to it without holding any previous bishopric; the circumstances of his appointment were no more calculated to enhance his authority than was his origin as a butcher's son or his association with Richard's household; according to Adam of Usk he was 'better versed in things of the camp and the world than of the church or the study'.[8] As a former treasurer, Walden could be thankful that the Londoners who seized him soon after the coup in 1399 stopped short of the Stapledon precedent of

1326! Henry could probably have relied upon Walden for acquiescence if not cooperation, but nothing suggests that Walden could deliver, as it were, the clerical vote, least of all when supplies were needed.

Archbishop Scrope of York was certainly dignified enough by lineage, and experienced enough as a papal lawyer and royal diplomat, to be a powerful ally, and he was indeed linked with the Percys; but he was not a national figure who commanded much respect or support outside the north. It is inconceivable, moreover, that he could have been translated to Canterbury when that see already had two claimants who could point to papal provisions as their titles, one of whom before the end of September 1399 had been re-endorsed by the pope. Scrope's assent to the usurpation was undeniably important, but far from sufficient without a reliable and effective Lancastrian ally in Canterbury. Henry needed Scrope at York, and politically he had no alternative to Arundel at Canterbury.

Among the rest of the bishops there was a singular lack of experienced leaders of men. Wykeham, bishop of Winchester, and Despenser, bishop of Norwich, were in virtual political retirement and of a different generation from most of their colleagues, although Despenser was suspected – and acquitted – of involvement in an opposition plot early in Henry's reign. Beaufort, Henry's illegitimate half-brother and bishop of Lincoln, was too youthful and unpredictable to command wide support for or against the usurper. In fact, bishops openly hostile to Richard were as scarce as those prepared to oppose Henry. Only Thomas Merks of Carlisle is said to have spoken up for the late king on 30 September, but even that act is reported in a source more distinguished for its imagination than for its knowledge of events.[9] Merks was, though, to be officially identified as an opponent of the new king soon after this purported speech, as will be seen below. Most of the episcopal bench were administrators, confessors and diplomats rather than politicians, and they bent with the wind. Arundel made sure that they bent in the right direction.

In short, so far did Arundel excel most of his episcopal colleagues in birth, experience, vigour and resolution that without his support Henry might not have hoped to succeed. It is little wonder then that R. L. Storey has dubbed Arundel a king-maker. It might even be argued that Richard's greatest mistake was not to disinherit Henry, but to do so after dispossessing Arundel of the archbishopric.

Yet Arundel's services to Henry were by no means at an end with the coronation.[10] Although he ceased to be chancellor early in September 1399 – before the act of usurpation, in fact – he remained a member of the council until he resumed the chancellorship in January 1407; thereafter, except for his exclusion from office and influence during 1410 and 1411 (when the Prince of Wales and Bishop Beaufort dominated affairs), he sat on the council until the end of the reign. A diligent and enthusiastic bishop he undoubtedly was, but he was never out of touch with public affairs except for those two years. When he was absent from the council – as in September 1400 – a messenger was sent to elicit his advice on matters of importance.[11] Although accusations that he was involved in conspiracies in 1403 and 1405 were quickly recognized as baseless, they bear witness that he was still regarded as a figure of political consequence. Indeed, in 1405 Arundel himself underlined the fact to the king when he is said to have told him, 'I am your spiritual father and second to none after you in the realm and you should accept the advice of no one before mine if it be good.'[12] Not only was the archbishop a frequent attender at the council, but he was also present at all the parliaments in the reign and a trier of petitions in all those held when he was not chancellor – the chancellor was a trier *ex officio*.[13]

But by far his most vital service to the king was the management of the Canterbury convocation, from which he so skilfully extracted the subsidies which the king desperately needed in order to survive. The archbishop's presence there was essential if grants were to be made, and when in 1406 he was often preoccupied in the contentious sessions of parliament, convocation had to be adjourned no fewer than eight times to await his attendance.[14] Once there, he delivered subsidies with triumphant efficiency – sometimes prompted or even helped by strident anticlerical demands in parliament – and when he failed he still did his best for the king. In December 1404, for example, he wrote to inform the king that although he had made every effort in the last convocation to obtain a grant from stipendiary chaplains, and although the clerk of the rolls addressed the clerical proctors on three occasions, the proctors still unanimously declined.[15] Arundel suggested, therefore, that as the proctors refused and there was no way of convening the chaplains personally, a possible solution would be to urge the bishops to put pressure on the chaplains of their dioceses to make such a grant, and he added that 'I shall be ready to help.' When the king duly instructed his officers to write to the bishops letters under the privy seal, Arundel and other prelates on the council were consulted and suggested that a letter under the signet seal would have more chance of success with both the bishops and the chaplains.[16] On 2 May 1405 just such letters under the signet were sent to all bishops instructing them to ask all chaplains to contribute towards the defence of the realm – on this occasion without creating a precedent.[17] Arundel, thus involved at each stage of this affair, could hardly have done more, on behalf of the king, to circumvent the uncooperative proctors.

Nor was the archbishop unwilling to make sacrifices himself. In addition to the taxes which he paid, he lent the king £1675 in the course of the reign, a sum exceeded by only one other bishop – Beaufort – and only approached by one more.[18] In September 1405 he was given particular responsibility for organizing the collection of a general war loan from archdeaconries and counties, which was to be available to the king within three weeks.[19]

When in October 1404 the knights of the shire proposed confiscating the temporalities of the church in order to meet the king's war needs, Arundel reminded them that not only had the clergy granted tenths more frequently to the king than the laity had granted fifteenths, and had sent more tenants to the wars, but also 'they had offered more masses and prayers by night and by day for the prosperity of the king and all his household'.[20] Apart from the prayers ordered in 1399 to announce, and in effect to bless, the usurpation, Arundel sent out mandates for prayers whenever some imminent campaign required the Almighty's help or some saints' blessings, whether for expeditions against Scotland in 1402, or against the Welsh and Orléans in 1405, or to recover Aquitaine in 1412.[21] This traditional and perhaps inescapable (and maybe even sometimes involuntary) role of an archbishop should not be discounted from Arundel's services to the king.

However great Arundel's contribution to the revolution of 1399 may have been, one king-maker would not have been sufficient. Henry needed military support, and even with the church's blessing usurpation would have been a vain fantasy or transient wonder but for the aid of some of the nobles, not least of the earls of Northumberland and Westmorland. Henry also needed the support of the community of knights and burgesses, though he could be more sure of that when he was seen to have the backing of the prelates and nobles. King-makers, however, usually have a price to be paid and usurpers have to tread a narrow path between resentful enemies and expectant friends. It took Henry nearly eight years to escape from these perils, and although by then he was relatively secure, his health was also failing and all the king-makers had in some degree been disappointed, even Arundel.

Opposition and the Clergy

Almost the earliest, certainly the most protracted and by far the most dangerous opposition which Henry faced came from Wales. There in September 1400 Owen Glendower, descendant of Welsh princes and a product of the inns of court at Westminster, proclaimed himself Prince of Wales and raised a nationalist revolt which was to be a serious threat to Lancastrian stability for almost seven years and a potential danger for some time after that.[22] By 1407 Glendower had seen most of his allies defeated or divided, but until then his rising had been a constantly alarming and costly menace. English forces had had to be mustered against him in 1400, 1401, 1402, 1403 and twice in 1405. In 1403 he enjoyed the aid of the disaffected Percys and later that year Breton and French naval help; next year a Franco–Welsh alliance involved raids on the English south coast; in 1405 the Percys and Mortimer's friends planned a triple alliance and a tripartite division of England, and in July that year 140 French ships took some 2000 French soldiers to Wales. At various times Glendower's men controlled the castles of Conway, Carmarthen, Harlech and Aberystwyth, and threatened Caernarvon and Beaumaris. In

1406, however, the French abandoned practical help, the earl of Northumberland was defeated, and the heir to the Scottish throne was captured by the English which eliminated a serious distraction for the English forces. When France was divided and neutralized by the murder of Orléans in November 1407 the Welsh threat was effectively over and Glendower was reduced henceforth to sporadic and fruitless guerrilla warfare.

Apart from the dynastic, territorial and financial repercussions of this rebellion, it also had serious ecclesiastical implications.[23] In 1406 a plan was mooted with the French for the establishment of a separate Welsh church dependent upon the Avignon pope. Such a development would have deprived Henry of substantial patronage and a small but significant amount of taxation, neither of which he could at that stage afford and both of which were anyway disrupted by the rebellion meanwhile; four bishoprics would have been lost to the king and four dioceses would have been severed from the province of Canterbury and the supervision of the archbishop. In fact, the exploitation of the Welsh church by English kings during the fourteenth century and the subordination of it to alien and complacent rule from Canterbury were part of that general English arrogance towards the Welsh which fuelled and sustained Glendower's rising. Although the planned secession of the church, like the rebellion, proved abortive, it was no less alarming at the time. Glendower gave hope, aid and stimulus to all of Henry's enemies and immensely embarrassed the already difficult finances of the usurper-king.

Within England opposition, rarely without a clerical dimension, was sometimes purely ecclesiastical. The earlier opponents of the new king were largely motivated by a genuine attachment to the old one or to the principle of a *de iure* or legitimate monarch; the later insurgents and plotters were provoked by disillusion with Henry's government. Thomas Merks, the earls and the friars fall into the first category; the Percys and Archbishop Scrope into the second.

Even if Bishop Merks did not deliver the speech which one vividly imaginative chronicler attributes to him, he was indisputably Richard's most overt supporter among the bishops. A theologian and formerly a monk of Westminster Abbey, Merks had been appointed to Carlisle in the episcopal reshuffle of 1396–7, after which he served Richard in various ways – on a mission to the German princes, as the bearer of Richard's exclusion of Arch-bishop Arundel from the parliament of that year, on the king's Irish expedition, and as the executor of his will. Soon in disfavour and in custody in the new reign, he was accused, it seems, of complicity in the murder of the duke of Gloucester in 1397, and, though cleared of the charge, was returned to detention in St Albans in order, so the king said, to protect him from the hatred of the mob (*odium vulgi*).[24] By December, however, he was back in his old monastery of Westminster and soon implicated in the rising of the earls who had been demoted from their Ricardian dukedoms on Henry's accession. Merks was specifically accused of plotting with Sir Thomas Blount, Sir Benedict Sely and others in alliance with the king of France to kill Henry at Windsor where he was celebrating Christmas and Epiphany. On 5 January 1400 at Bampton, Wantage, Farndon, Cirencester and other places the conspirators unfurled their standard and rose up and captured divers of the king's men whom they robbed of the king's livery and other goods; at Wantage and elsewhere the rebels declared that all men should hold Richard for king.[25] The plot was betrayed and Merks was taken from Westminster on 10 January to await trial.[26] He protested his innocence and claimed the right to trial by his peers, but this was refused and later in the month a commission of oyer and terminer found him guilty. There were some arguments for the procedure adopted. Merks was a part of a treasonous plot to kill the king and restore Richard II; his hostility to the regime since September was well known, even if that knowledge was ill-founded; moreover, common justice and politi-cal wisdom demanded that he should be tried while the matter was fresh and other conspirators were suffering trial and death – most of the earls fled, were caught and lynched by mobs. Yet who or which court could try a bishop for treason was still uncertain. Impeachment, such as Despenser had suffered back in the 1380s, required parliament and all the unpredictable complications to which that could give rise; parliament would take time to assemble and could hardly be convened for, or confined to, just this cause. The court of the lord high steward in which peers were tried by peers had no established existence at this time. The court of chivalry, which despatched those it found guilty with Roman swiftness and savagery, had yet to be deployed against a prelate and usually operated, immediately after a battle, against traitors in arms. There seemed no alternative to a commission of oyer and terminer, but this certainly violated the clergy's view of their liberties.

At least Merks was not executed. Henry's political sense, if not Arundel's persuasion, surely explains why, out of respect for the bishop's orders, he decided to commute the death sentence. Instead, Merks was imprisoned for some months in the Tower and in June 1400, already deprived of Carlisle, he was sent back to the custody of Westminster Abbey until further notice.[27] Pardoned in November of that year, he thereafter enjoyed some royal favour and even attended the Council of Pisa on behalf of the English church and realm.

One other bishop was implicated in the rising of the earls, Despenser of Norwich, the elderly crusader and soldier, whose nephew, Lord Despenser, was executed for his part in the plot. The bishop was arrested and consigned to the keeping of Arundel to await judgement, but in the end the king exonerated him without trial and restored him to his bishopric, perhaps for want of evidence or to avoid a trial and judgement which would strain clerical loyalties still further. The suppression of the rebellion only tended to spawn new problems when the clergy were involved.

It was fortunate for Henry that the earls were able to enlist the help of no more influential prelate than Merks, bishop – and then only briefly – of a small and remote see, a Benedictine monk with little political or episcopal experience, and too evidently partisan for Richard. If Despenser was among their backers, his influence and political repute had been exhausted by his ill-fated crusade in 1383, and he stood isolated by temperament as well as age from most of his episcopal colleagues, which may be why Henry acquitted him. Yet even without more substantial support from the bishops, the plot of the earls was alarming enough, and an undoubted consequence of it was the demise at Pontefract shortly afterwards of the late king: by enforced or voluntary starvation, he was dead before 17 February 1400. That, however, was a difficult fact to advertise without arousing disturbing suspicions, and it proved all the more difficult therefore to convince people of it; long after this rumours of Richard's survival – in Scotland or Wales – focused discontent and motivated rebels.

In 1400, however, disillusion seemed to be afflicting even Arundel. In that year, so Adam of Usk recalls, Arundel called together his clergy and deplored 'how temporal powers fear not to violate the liberties of the English church and specially in seizing, imprisoning and in judging bishops, without distinction, just as they would laymen'.[28] This outburst cannot be referred to convocation, for there was none that year, and the burden of the complaint as well as the circumstances in which it was made seem to rule out the convocation of 1399: Adam speaks of no synod and his own recorded exchanges with Arundel suggest that the meeting was of a more intimate and less formal kind than a provincial assembly. It is not unreasonable to suppose that immediately following the trial of Merks, Arundel was beginning to fear that Henry was about to emulate Richard's example. Just a year later even Henry's confessor, Philip Repingdon, was writing a coded message of criticism to the king.[29] On 4 May 1401 he addressed a long letter to Henry, phrasing its most savage remarks in biblical quotations and adopting the confessor's tone of reluctant critic: 'Faithful are the wounds of a friend, but the kisses of an enemy are deceitful' (Proverbs 27:6). He spoke of the 'great desolation in the hearts of the prudent' because 'law and justice are banished from the realm' where 'thefts, murders, adulteries, fornications, extortions, oppressions of the poor, hurts, wrongs and much reproach are rife; and one tyrant will doth serve for the law'. After more in this vein Repingdon continued: 'we hoped that your wonderful entry into the realm of England, which I doubt not was the work of the hand of God, would have redeemed Israel', but 'now our harp is tuned to mourning' (Job 30:31) and there is a danger that the commons will rise up and 'the despisers of the law shall be confounded'. To avert this disaster, Repingdon prayed that 'God, the sun of justice, [may] take away the veil from your eyes' and that the Holy Trinity would teach and lead the king. In this long and diffuse letter there is much rhetoric and little detail, as well as an emphasis more on social than political grievances; there is certainly no reference to royal encroachments on church liberties or privileges. Yet that such a letter of anxiety and disillusion could be written by the king's own confessor and friend so early in the reign – and even just a few weeks after the statute for the burning of heretics – is indicative of the strains which Henry was putting on his kingdom at large and of the hopes which were not being fulfilled by the new regime.

In 1402 Repingdon's dire predictions looked like being realized. The king sent a letter to the authorities in the south-western counties warning them that some of his subjects, in various parts of the realm, were spreading lies in taverns and other meeting places to the effect that he had not kept his coronation promises; he gave orders that such rumours were to be contradicted and the preachers of this sedition arrested and imprisoned.[30] Late in May 1402 nine inmates of the house of Franciscan friars at Leicester, the prior of the Augustinian canons at Launde (Leicestershire), two secular priests, and two Dominican friars (from Cambridge and Winchelsea) were arrested and charged with treason.[31] Seven of the Leicester friars were convicted in a secular court and executed along with the prior of Launde and some others. Two Franciscans who initially escaped arrest were later caught near Lichfield by Prince Henry and beheaded there. The accusation was that the ring-leader, Dr Frisby, had despatched his friars to London and Wales to stir up sedition, to collect donations for the aid of Glendower, and to spread rumours in taverns. In their sermons they urged people to believe that Richard was still alive and the true king; they even enjoined some penitents to seek Richard in Wales. Others were instructed to raise a force of 500 men from Scotland and to swell a gathering of laymen and clerks on Oxford Common on 23 June, where they would be joined by forces mustered by Richard himself.

The seriousness of this affair lay not least in the extent of its seditious network, which the preaching, begging and travelling friars were so well able to construct and sustain. Some idea of the area and locations affected can be gauged from the destinations to which the traitors' heads were sent for display: first at London Bridge, and then on tour, as it were, until the end of 1404 by which time they had been seen in Anglesey, Coventry, Northampton,

Nottingham, Oxford, Leicester and Stamford.[32] Chronicle evidence also implicates Franciscan houses at Cambridge, Ware, Norwich or Walsingham, and we have already seen that a Dominican from Winchelsea was involved as well.

Apart from the extent, however, there were the Welsh and Scottish dimensions. The Welsh connection was particularly important and may have triggered the whole affair. The Franciscans at Llanfaes in Anglesey had been executed and the house seized by the crown in 1401 for abetting Welsh incursions across the English border; one of the community was only put to death early in 1402 for declaring that he was exceedingly glad that Richard was still alive and that Henry was duke of Lancaster and not king. The fate of their Welsh brethren was likely to find a sympathetic response among the English Franciscans, and Glendower at that stage offered the best hope of effective aid against Henry. Scotland was much more remote, of course, but an obvious potential ally, and no one seemed quite sure whether Richard was in Wales or Scotland.

Beyond the extent of internal hostility and the enlistment of external enemies, the most significant feature of this Franciscan conspiracy was its stand upon constitutional and legal principle – precisely where Henry was most vulnerable. When Frisby, the leader of the Leicester friars, was examined in June by the king himself, Henry was driven to exasperation by the remorseless logic of the answers that he got. Frisby declared that if Richard were still alive he would be the true king; his abdication could not be valid because it was made under duress while in prison; if he had not abdicated, Richard certainly was not deposed, for one could not depose a rightful king except by usurpation. As for the election of Henry to the crown, any such election was necessarily void if the crown was not vacant. The final provocation to Henry was Frisby's assertion that if Richard were dead, it was because Henry had killed him or had him killed, an act which invalidated any legal claim of Henry's to the throne. (Apparently the canon law arguments for deposition were not put to Frisby, but then they were only tentatively advanced by the canonists themselves in 1399.) In his speech before execution Frisby emphasized that the aim of the conspirators was not to kill Henry and his sons, 'but to make him Duke of Lancaster, which is what he ought to be'.[33]

At the provincial chapter of the English Franciscans held in August 1402 all members of the order were prohibited from uttering a word against the king, on pain of life imprisonment. John Zouche, the provincial minister who presided, was currently trying to force upon the province an austerity which was unwelcome and stoutly resisted by his subjects, and he certainly won the king's support in this by his measure at Leicester in 1402. When, however, Zouche threatened to split the province by his zeal and when he had lost the backing of the minister general, Henry averted a menacing development in a dangerous order by promoting him to the bishopric of Llandaff in 1407.

Although religious were implicated in two other plots in the years after the Leicester conspiracy, the friars were not involved again. In April 1404 the abbots of Beeleigh, Colchester and St Osyth's, the parson of Tendring, and several other clerics and laymen were arrested with Maud de Vere, countess of Oxford and mother of Richard's late favourite.[34] They all came from the same area where her estates and influence were dominant. Maud was suspected of negotiating with the duke of Orléans and the count of St Pol to land a French force in Essex in December 1403, at just the time when Glendower was also enlisting French aid. The abbots of Colchester and St Osyth's were persuaded to believe that Richard was alive in Scotland and would come south when Orléans and St Pol brought his queen from France to Essex. In the event, St Pol had had enough after a fruitless landing on the Isle of Wight in April and Maud's plot was betrayed by a servant. The accused were tried for treason in August but were eventually pardoned, not acquitted. Their scheme was reckless and futile, naive and opportunist, narrowly local and personal, and the pardon is perhaps an index of how scantly the king regarded its threat.

Even less cause for concern arose from the report made by two thieves on trial in Huntingdon in December 1405.[35] They claimed to have delivered money to Glendower and accused various persons of contributing £7000 for the Welsh rebels. Among those named were the abbots of Bury St Edmunds, Warden, Woburn and Lavendon, and the priors of Huntingdon, Newnham, Thet-

ford and Ixworth, as well as three former members of parliament
and other laymen. All the accused were in due course exonerated
and the story may have been an attempt by the thieves to save
themselves by false information against traitors, just as the sum of
£7000 smacks of exaggeration if not fiction.

The most alarming clerical opposition which Henry had to face
after 1402 occurred when the archbishop of York threw in his lot
with the aggrieved Percys in 1405.[36] Henry had vexed the Percys
some years before by denying them part of the profits of the
campaign which they had fought on his behalf against the Scots,
by withholding money due to them as wardens of the March, and
by refusing to ransom their relative by marriage, Mortimer. In
1403, therefore, the Percys, accusing the king of perjury and
usurpation, joined in league with Glendower, only to be defeated
in a battle which cost the life of their favourite son, Hotspur. By
1405, however, they were ready to try their fortune again; they
renewed the tripartite agreement with Glendower and planned to
raise the north, aided by forces which the archbishop would
assemble from York and its environs. After McNiven's analysis of
the insurrection, it is no longer possible to regard Archbishop
Scrope as the prime mover or leader of it; rather must he be seen as
the dupe of Mowbray, Bardolf and Northumberland, but a willing
dupe in a dangerous enterprise, and one who led some 3000 armed
men out to Shipton Moor to join with their forces. Scrope's
rag-tag, untrained and undisciplined army found itself alone on
the moor as a result of the earl of Northumberland being driven off
by an earlier failure in the plot. In these circumstances the
archbishop was easily persuaded to dismiss his force, after which
he was seized, summarily tried and executed. Mowbray was also
captured and executed, but Northumberland and Bardolf escaped
and lived on in Scotland until they returned to fight and to die at
Bramham Moor in 1408.

That Archbishop Scrope should join such an adventure may be
a reflection upon his political naivety, as well as upon his family
connections with the Percys and his identity with the north, but
more than that it reflects upon his idealism. He was acutely aware
of the threats and hardships posed by Scotland and the penury
resulting from Scottish incursions, compounded by royal taxation

which was levied in defiance of the king's bland promises of 1399. He was equally conscious of Henry's violations of clerical liberties, not only by the imprisonment of Merks and Despenser but also by the employment of laymen and secular judges to enforce the collection of subsidies from the clergy – a grievance raised at York convocation in 1404. In May 1405, however, the manifesto which was circulated by him, or in his name, addressed itself to a wider audience than the clergy.[37] It condemned the king for his perjury against Richard II, for the slaughter of nobles (with Hotspur and the earls, no doubt, in mind), for the loss of territory in Wales, Aquitaine and Ireland, and for the vast spoliation of the people by taxation. Ecclesiastical grievances included, of course, excessive taxation, but also the restriction of papal provisions to the detriment of Oxford and Cambridge graduates, and the arrest and execution of many clerks, even including bishops. The document declared the aims of the insurgents to be the restoration of the true heir to the crown, peace with the Welsh and Irish, and the cessation of all unjust exactions from the people of the realm.

By May 1405 when the Northumberland-Scrope rising occurred, Henry IV must have been severely embarrassed and immensely discouraged as his good intentions were disregarded and his necessary actions much resented. Was there no end to this turmoil? Would he never hold the throne securely? Already the ambitious Prince of Wales was becoming a focus for loyal opposition. As the strains of government mounted, Scrope paid the full penalty for adding to those strains. Clemency in the past had produced few fruits that could still be tasted in 1405. We can hardly be surprised that the king for once acted imperiously and shunned caution and finesse when he ordered Scrope's execution.

Desperation was no doubt coupled with anger that Northumberland and Bardolf should have repaid earlier leniency with further plotting and have escaped again; Scrope and Mowbray, the only prominent rebels captured, were bound to pay for Northumberland and Bardolf. There is no doubt, too, that anger was directed personally against Scrope who had shown hitherto no cavils about the accession of Henry. Scrope after all was no discountable abbot or friar or bishop of Carlisle, but the primate of England, leader of the northern province, principal prelate in a highly sensitive and delicately balanced part of the kingdom, who might have been expected to know better and act more wisely. To Henry the archbishop's irresponsibility and naivety must have appeared outrageously dangerous and intolerably treacherous. Simply to encourage his successors in the see to take their political duties more seriously, Scrope ought to be executed: not translated to some bishopric *in partibus* or to some Scottish see, but executed.

Henry's chief worry about the execution might have been the fear of Scrope becoming a latter-day Becket. Indeed, by April 1406 embarrassingly large crowds were congregating at the archbishop's tomb in York Minster, and when in the following year the city serjeants tried – on royal orders – to discourage people from making offerings at the tomb they were expelled from office, such was the local sentiment for Scrope whose cult was later to win expedient favour from the Yorkists.[38] Yet significantly, Arundel, who had protested at the death of Scrope, threw his weight behind royal efforts to thwart popular canonization. The circumstances of Scrope's death, after all, were very different from Becket's. The archbishop of York had taken up arms and not been struck down while praying at the high altar. Henry IV was too obviously a pious protector of the church against heresy and anticlericalism. Popes of the Great Schism lacked the stature and aura which those of Becket's time enjoyed in the wake of Gregory VII. And Becket was certainly not the tool of some opportunistic magnate family. No thunderous decrees echoed round England against Henry IV because Archbishop Arundel – in the interest of public order – decided not to publish the bull of excommunication, and the most effective action which the pope could take was to make difficulties over Henry's episcopal appointments, which indeed he did do, especially over York itself. If the papal condemnation of the act was not widely known, still more surreptitious was the absolution which reached England in December 1408: it was read before the high altar in Newark parish church – on the very edge of York province – and then affixed to the door of Lincoln cathedral.[39] That Henry was anxious to give the matter of his absolution as little publicity as possible attests to the general indifference of the church and the realm – at least outside York – to his execution of the archbishop. When at the beginning of that year the bishop of Bangor was captured on the field of Bramham Moor, he was spared the fate of Scrope, probably because the papal absolution was still awaited and long-vacant bishoprics had still to be filled; Henry was less squeamish about the abbot of Halesowen who was not so lucky as the bishop of Bangor.[40]

Scrope's influence is sometimes viewed as more long-term, seeing that barely a month after the execution Henry suffered his first seizure. Although the king quickly recovered from this, he was to suffer more and his health deteriorated erratically but progressively.[41] There has been some speculation that the cause of this breakdown in the king's health was his sense of guilt either at the death of Scrope or over his perjury in 1399 and the realization in 1405 that all had been in vain. Yet the pressures of the recurring crises and multiplying problems and hostilities of his first six years would have been enough to tax any man then approaching middle age even without a burden of guilt. Whatever the cause, the consequences were most certainly serious. Soon after 1406 his mobility was greatly hampered by a leg condition, and such a handicap was critical for any medieval king, especially for one still trying to win the confidence of his people.

In these circumstances it was natural that his eldest son, the Prince of Wales, should take a keener interest in government and in the preservation of what should be his due heritage. The prince had his father's ambition and early vigour, coupled with youth and greater ability. He became a focus for the hopes of those Lancastrians who despaired of his father solving his problems. Prince Henry's intimate companion was Henry Beaufort, bishop of Winchester, his half-uncle and former tutor and a man of great wealth and ambition.

Fortunately for the king his political problems did subside, quite suddenly, in 1408. By then his major external enemies had been neutralized and his desperate need for money and for parliamentary grants had somewhat abated. With the lessening of royal demands, opposition receded and became almost an affair of the royal household. Henceforth disputes were over the emphases and direction of foreign policy, and they arose between the king and Archbishop Arundel on one side, and the Prince of Wales and Bishop Beaufort on the other.

Crown Oppression

(i) Financial Demands from the King

The declaration by his emissaries to convocation in 1399 that 'it was not the wish or intention of the lord king to make henceforth any exaction of money in his kingdom, except for great necessity of wars, and of inevitable necessity' was soon put to the test by these and other events.[42] A multitude of problems quickly engulfed him, some of which were not to subside until the reign was half-way through. When Chief Justice Thirnyng explained to parliament in January 1401 the king's need for taxes he listed the following causes: rebellions within the realm and in North Wales; wars in Ireland and Scotland; the defence of Calais and its march; the defence of Guyenne, now annexed to the French crown and assigned to the Dauphin; the return of Richard's queen, with her jewels and dowry, to France; and the great borrowings which must be repaid.[43] Even then he had not commented upon the extravagant grants by which Henry had secured his usurpation nor upon the fall in customs revenues – in the taxes on wool especially – as piracy in the Channel interrupted trade. To these expenses should be added the costs of the marriage negotiations by which Henry sought to elicit European recognition of his title. And soon serious rebellions – in 1403, 1405 and 1408 – and dangerous Welsh alliances were to compound the king's shortage of money. Well before all this, before Henry had been king for six months, he was compelled to seek a loan from the lords and prelates of the realm. Thereafter, in a reign considerably shorter than Richard's, he taxed the clergy (as well as the laity) even more severely: twenty-one half tenths from Canterbury province, seventeen from York, and special subsidies (or additions) in 1404, 1405, 1406 and 1408.[44] Twelve of the twenty-one half tenths from the southern clergy were collected in the first seven years of the reign, as were five of the York subsidies.

Although the king avoided asking for clerical taxes until 1401, he collected a property tax on spiritual peers in 1400 (agreed at a great council) and a tenth granted by York province to Richard II and still unlevied at his deposition. After that his financial needs overwhelmed his earlier assurances to the clergy. To an increasing degree he lived off loans for which clerical subsidies provided important collateral, security which was all the better because the clergy neither refused subsidies when asked for them nor attached to them the embarrassing demands for retrenchment and reforms which parliament made. Although the clergy generally stipulated that their grants should be used for the defence of the realm, and occasionally that the church should administer the collection and no other grant be sought until the current one was collected, they yielded on these points under pressure. In November 1403 a new grant was to be collected in the southern province even though an instalment of a previous one was not due for collection until the following February. And in January 1404 that November grant was diverted from defence to defraying the costs of the royal household. The proctors of the lower clergy in Canterbury province may have refused a demand for a tax on stipendiaries, but Arundel, as we have seen, advised the king to order the bishops to put pressure on the chaplains.[45] In 1406 some levies were certainly made from the unbeneficed in both provinces, although York chaplains had already been taxed in 1405 on the assurance that it would constitute no precedent. In 1410 when a further request was made for a tax upon the York stipendiaries, it was refused. Not only were chaplains taxed by Henry but so too were benefices previously exempt from the assessment: in 1404 all those exempt benefices worth £5 or more in the southern province; in 1405 all worth £10 and over; in 1408 *all* the exempt churches in the northern province.

War, however, took its direct toll of church benefices: in 1406 fifty-one parish churches in Hereford diocese were certified as too impoverished by the effects of war – against Glendower in this region – to pay any subsidy at all; and in the north in the previous year the churches, granges and tenancies (with all their goods and chattels) which belonged to Hexham priory had been almost destroyed by the Scots.[46] In all areas, however, collectors frequently encountered resistance and the yield invariably fell short of the assessment.[47] A half tenth from Canterbury province ought to have produced around £8200, but usually the sum collected was more like £6500. A half tenth in York province was assessed at £922, but rarely anything like that figure was collected so many were the licensed exemptions on account of impoverishment in a region so torn by strife. And no diocese was ever without a list of often substantial arrears long overdue.

Although convocations rarely acceded to the king's demands on the nod and frequently only did so in the presence of a battery of royal agents (clerical and lay) to press the king's needs, the clergy were certainly more obliging than the laity in making grants to the king, and there are several reasons for this. First, Archbishop Arundel's influence was undoubtedly vital; not by any means a Caesarian prelate, his obliging role reveals his sharp sense of reality and ends. The great danger was that anticlericals who were proposing various degrees of expropriation of the church would exploit any chance to bring this about, and a king disillusioned with the church or a king at the mercy of his parliament for financial aid might provide just the opportunity. The parliamentary manoeuvres against the church in 1403, 1404 and 1410 were thwarted: they were years in which convocation proved particularly prompt to make a grant. Another consideration which must have weighed with all the prelates was the knowledge that their own and other clergy's loans to the king, and even their own expenses incurred in the king's service, were from time to time secured on forthcoming clerical subsidies.

The king's need for loans from his subjects – not an innovation of Henry's reign, of course – increased with the urgency of defence. Subsidies were rarely sufficient in themselves and seldom to hand when required, collection being a slow and inefficient operation; for immediate cash the king requested advances of money from his leading subjects who were scarcely able to refuse. On no fewer than five occasions the king turned to the clergy for cash advances, and the Prince of Wales sought similar aid for his Welsh campaign in 1405. Barely five months after his accession, Henry asked the clergy for cash. In February 1400 at a great council, called to avoid the necessity of a parliament, all the peers present, spiritual and temporal, agreed to an aid; the spiritual lords granted a tenth – to be levied in all haste – which would gain them exemption from payment of the next clerical subsidy, should there be one. It was also agreed that letters under the privy seal should be sent to all abbots inviting them to act with similar generosity.[48] In April 1403, because a parliamentary subsidy was not due for collection until Pentecost and the king was in desperate need for the defence of the kingdom against Scottish, Welsh and overseas threats, a loan was demanded by letter from bishops, abbots, priors, knights and others, the money to be sent in all haste to the war treasurers in London and to be repaid from the next instalment of the clerical subsidy.[49] On this occasion the bishops of Durham, Exeter, Lichfield, London, Salisbury and Winchester advanced a total of some £3500, of which £1100 came from the bishop of Winchester. From thirty-two heads of religious houses almost £6500 was sought, including 4000 marks from the abbot of Glastonbury and 500 from the abbess of Shaftesbury. Ten other clergy – wealthy parsons, graduates and dignitaries – yielded nearly £1600 between them. In all, at that time, the clergy lent the king over £11,000, but when more loans were requested in 1404 for the defence of the Welsh castles, the clergy were once again prominent lenders; among them the abbot of Glastonbury advanced £100, the heads of Tavistock and Torre £40, and of Milton Abbas £20.[50] Notwithstanding all this, in the following year two more loans were raised: one for the Prince of Wales from the abbot of Glastonbury and some lay notables; and one for the king, to be paid within three weeks to the war treasurers at Worcester.[51] This second one, from lay and clerical subjects, was to equal half the usual yield of the lay fifteenth and the clerical tenth which were due for collection later in the year and from which, it is implied, the loan would be repaid. Seven years later when cash was sought for Thomas of Lancaster's expedition to Guyenne, eleven bishops offered around £3200, two abbots £300, two dignitaries over £350 and the master of the clerks of chancery 1000 marks – a total of well over £4000.[52] Altogether the church was a capacious and accessible purse for a hard-pressed king.

(ii) Royal Writs and Menaces

In line with his promise in 1399 to uphold all the liberties of the church, Henry in 1402 reissued the statute *Pro clero* of 1352. This among other things had limited the king's power to fill benefices retrospectively and to present in the right of another patron, to seize bishops' temporalities for contempt or to indict bishops on unspecific charges of extortion. The re-enactment was granted by Henry in return for the clergy's loyalty to him and 'the great charges' which they had borne for him since his coronation, he wishing to be 'a gracious lord to them in their affairs'.[53] However, such assurances of 'gracious lordship' appear less effective when we learn that as late as 1409 some judges were ignorant of the re-enactment and some could recall no mention of it in the courts![54] Reassurance might be derived, though, less from the judges' knowledge than from their frequent punctilious regard for the church's rights and their evident good relations with the prelates themselves.[55] It was in fact neither the king nor the judges who posed the gravest threat to church liberties – which indeed the king frequently reaffirmed – but rather the individuals who invoked the laws inappropriately or unscrupulously: not a few of these individuals were clergy.

It was now a common practice to insert into indictments of clerks, or of those who might claim to be so, the phrase 'highwaymen and marauders' (*insidiatores viarum et depopulatores agrorum*) which cancelled any benefit of clergy. A statute now insisted that the phrase was to be used only where that offence was the subject of the charge, and even then benefit of clergy should still apply.[56] In return for this protection, the archbishop promised that convicted clergy would be securely kept by bishops in accordance with the decree of Archbishop Langham in 1351, and that such clerks would suffer additional penalties at the bishop's discretion; furthermore, no purgation would be available to them where the law did not permit it.[57] In actual fact the church was giving little away by this measure, but it did make notable gains, for the offensive phrase had probably been used to curtail the growing army of offenders who successfully claimed benefit of clergy.

The difficulties which confronted an incumbent when a royal presentee claimed his benefice was the subject of repeated legislation in the fourteenth century and further statutes under

Henry IV. A debate in 1399 about the proper use of writs of prohibition in these cases drew from the king a bland assurance that he wished such usage to conform to the law.[58] In 1402 an aggrieved incumbent was now permitted to sue for his rights at any time after the clerk's induction and was no longer confined to doing so within a year.[59] This amendment did nothing to lessen the burden but something to enlarge the hope of those displaced.

Although writs of prohibition still aroused protest and indignation,[60] their efficacy was often frustrated by writs of consultation. In this way, for example, it was complained in the commons in 1401, incumbents who sued for tithes of *silva cedua* and were stopped by prohibition simply trumped the prohibition with a consultation writ and went ahead, much to the injury of those who wanted the timber for ships and war and trade and had to pay so much more for it; therefore it was decreed that writs of consultation were not to be allowed in these cases.[61] Another instance of the problems created by these two writs comes from Winchester diocese. The bishop prosecuted in his own court the mayor and bailiffs of Southwark for assaulting a clerk; they sued a writ of prohibition, which he then countered with a writ of consultation.[62] In view of the hazards and uncertainties arising from their use, prohibitions lost favour among litigants who increasingly turned to the writ of *praemunire*, based on the statute of 1353 and not yet on that of 1393. *Praemunire* had several advantages: it was immune from writs of consultation, more harassing in its consequences for the defendant, and more generous in compensation for the suitor.[63]

The king's own deliberate encroachments on church liberties were not so frequent or so grave as the alarmist utterances of Arundel, Repingdon and Scrope might suggest. The trial of Merks and the trial and execution of Scrope were pragmatic and legal responses to isolated cases and not part of some calculated or continuing policy. No doubt the role of lay judges in extracting subsidies from the York clergy in 1404 did violate custom, but the circumstances then were desperate and the laymen were not so employed again – perhaps a victory for Scrope. The curtailment of provisions caused anxiety because it particularly hampered the universities in their efforts to benefice their graduates, but restraint on provisions was nothing new or anticlerical in the fifteenth century. The limitations which, as we shall see, were placed on papal dispensing powers – for appropriation, pluralism, non-residence, tithe exemption, etc. – were intended to redress grievances as deeply felt by the clergy as by the laity, and were not contrived principally to clip papal wings.

It was in the area of appointments that a king was most likely to infringe clerical liberties, particularly in appointments to bishoprics. During Henry's reign there were some protracted vacancies and the temporalities were on occasion withheld unduly. Desperate as the king's financial needs were, however, they do not explain his long retention of some temporalities. This was either the result of a genuine dispute with the chapter or the papacy about the elect, or because of royal indignation over the elect: York after Scrope's death was clearly a special case and the rival candidates for London, Bath and Wells, and Durham sufficiently account for the length of those vacancies; at Carlisle and Norwich the offensive local choice of Strickland and Tottington, respectively, undoubtedly prompted Henry's reluctance to concede their temporalities. In these last two cases, the violation of church liberties was plain enough and not the less because financial gain was not the motive; that both candidates did nevertheless secure full possession of their sees in due course reveals the restraints upon Henry's power and resolution.

At a lower level of appointment his regalian rights were still on occasions pushed to extremes by the king's greedy protégés, as when one claimed Sandiacre prebend in Lichfield cathedral on the grounds that Edward I had presented to it when the see was vacant in his reign; a few years later, in 1411, another claimant sought another prebend in Lichfield because Edward III had appointed to it![64] But of the king himself advancing or defending these claims there is no evidence.

If, however, Henry was above chicanery, he was certainly not above using threats – as the imprisoned Tottington of Norwich could vouch. When Henry recommended his secretary, William Pilton, for promotion to the first vacant prebend in Hexham, the prior and convent of Durham were told that if they hoped for future favours for their church, they should heed this request and

give credence to the king's esquire who was the bearer of the letter
– and who, no doubt, could enlarge upon the favours to be
conceded or withheld.[65] Yet kings and patrons generally would
have seen little amiss in the vehement expression of his wishes
here.

Crown Defence

(i) Measures against Lollardy

Even before his promise to the convocation of 1399 'to destroy
heresies, errors and heretics as far as he could', Henry had on 1
October enjoined sheriffs and mayors to forbid support being
given to 'certain evil disposed preachers, holding diverse nefarious
opinions, and detestable conclusions, repugnant to the canonical
decisions of Holy Mother Church, and redounding to the offence
and discredit of the Orders of the Mendicant Friars'.[66] This relates
rather to Franciscan disputes than to lollard errors, but a few
months later he ordered sheriffs to proclaim that no chaplains,
except parochial ones in their own parish churches, were to preach
without episcopal licence;[67] clearly directed against lollard
preachers, this mandate, in fact, merely added weight to existing
canon law. By far his most notable act against heresy, however,
was the introduction of capital punishment for it.

In the 1380s and 1390s bishops were referring obdurate or
relapsed heretics to the king's council for sentence, usually of
imprisonment and forfeiture. They were doing nothing new,
therefore, when in February 1401 the bishops in convocation
referred the relapsed lollard, William Sawtry, to the king and his
council. On 26 February the king ordered Sawtry's burning in an
open place in London, and this was carried out on 2 March at
Smithfield.[68] Both the sentence and the execution antedated by a
matter of days the promulgation of the statute for the burning of
heretics. Already in 1397 the bishops had petitioned for such a
measure, but on that occasion in vain. In 1401 they petitioned for
royal officers in each diocese to receive from the bishop all
recidivist and obstinate heretics 'and do what is incumbent upon
them in that matter'.[69] The commons, too, had prayed that

convicted lollards should receive an exemplary punishment. The statute interpreted these euphemisms as the petitioners undoubtedly intended, and so at long last England adopted the continental defence against heresy: death by fire at the stake.[70]

Strangely enough this fearsome innovation did little to contain lollardy or to expunge it from the land. In the first place it was for use only against those who refused to recant or who were caught twice, and many heretics were tried in Henry's reign who fell into neither category: lollard contempt for oaths made abjuration acceptable and even sensible, and men and women who escaped once were especially wary of discovery again. Apart from Sawtry, only one other heretic, John Badby in 1410, was burnt during Henry's reign. The other provisions of the statute had little more practical effect than the death penalty. The clergy in their original petition had stressed their inability without help from the king to contain and suppress the multitude of false preachers and teachers. The principal problem was the ease with which offenders escaped capture and correction by crossing into neighbouring dioceses. The clergy also wanted the king to penalize those who preached without licence, or who published – in books or schools or meetings – any unorthodoxy, or who favoured such malefactors, and to enforce the surrender of suspected writings before a set date. The statute banned such offences and empowered bishops to imprison offenders until they were canonically purged or abjured and had paid a fine to the king. The problem of flight from the diocese was ignored. The collapse of lollardy as a serious threat to church and realm was not brought about or even hastened by the statute *De Heretico Comburendo*, the significance of which lies elsewhere.

Although the church gained less than it thought by this legislation, the king could count some profit. He elicited a clerical subsidy and promoted reserves of good will for the future; moreover, he was authorized to employ, albeit on the church's prompting, the ultimate sanction against some fanatical menacers of the peace. The importance of the statute to the king is evident enough when it speaks of heretics and their teachings as threatening 'not only the destruction of the church in England and peril to souls but also many more other hurts, slanders and perils, which,

God forbid, might come to this realm'. Perhaps, though, an even more notable aspect of the act was its involvement of parliament in the defence of doctrine: a century hence, this interest was to assume a new significance.

Only one other statute in the reign dealt with lollardy and this resulted from a petition introduced into the parliament of 1406, in December, by the Prince of Wales on behalf of the lords spiritual and temporal.[71] This proposed that lollards or those who moved people against the Catholic faith, the sacraments, or the temporal possessions of the church, in violation of the laws and customs of the realm, should be arrested and taken before the chancellor in the next parliament to answer the charges and await judgement. Furthermore, an obligation was to be placed upon all peers, judges, justices, sheriffs, mayors, bailiffs and others having rule, to arrest such persons and investigate charges. The prince petitioned that this statute should be proclaimed with all haste, taking effect from 6 January 1407, and that all writs necessary to its enforcement should be granted 'without any difficulty'. The king consented and decreed that it was to be enforced until the next parliament; as this met in October 1407, the law had only a short life, for it was not renewed. Despite its brief operation, however, considerable significance attaches to it.

The petition was probably intended as a riposte by the lords to the confiscation proposals put forward by the commons in the last parliament: the preamble enlarges upon the threat to society and the realm at large contained in those proposals. The petition seems particularly concerned to show the orthodox flag in order to rally conservatives and alert them to profound social dangers. It was also, no doubt, a calculated publicity stunt by the Prince of Wales, adding political and theological leadership to the generalship which he had already displayed on the battlefield. Yet it not only reveals something of the notions of society and kingship which inspired the future Henry V but it also foreshadowed the important arrangements which were to be adopted against heresy in his reign. On the first matter, more will be said below. On the second, one should note that secular officers in the kingdom were obligated – briefly and somewhat vaguely, it is true – to act upon their own initiative against heretics, judgement being reserved to parliament, or at least to the chancellor in parliament. The statute of 1414 was to develop this lead much more precisely and effectively, but the principle is clearly present in 1406. In fact, though, the eventual containment of lollardy resulted less from the secular laws introduced in Henry IV's time than from the decrees of the then archbishop.

At a specially convened provincial synod which met at Oxford in December 1407, Archbishop Arundel promulgated thirteen articles designed to stifle heresy; they were confirmed in the convocation of January 1409.[72] These constitutions reaffirmed earlier restrictions upon preachers, limited those who could discuss doctrine, banned the reading of Wyclif's works, regulated the translation of scripture almost – but not quite – to the point of proscription, and severely inhibited arts and grammar teachers in what they could teach to whom, and students in what they could read without licence; college and hall principals or wardens were obliged to conduct a monthly search for erroneous material circulated by the inmates. The very holding of the synod at Oxford was designed to cow the university authorities and teachers, and it coincided with the exclusion of Oxford's franchises from those generally confirmed in parliament that year.[73] Arundel was not yet finished with Oxford. In 1410 he appointed a commission to examine faith and correct and extinguish errors there, but it met with such obstinate resistance from some members of the university that the king's help had to be enlisted. In October that year Henry IV denounced false doctrines and ordered the arrest of their maintainers at Oxford who were either to be imprisoned or sent to the king for punishment.[74] Much of the opposition – ostensibly at least – was not doctrinal but constitutional, and the leader of it was no lollard but Richard Courtenay, chancellor of the university, member of a noble family, and so much a *persona grata* at court that he obtained a bishopric early in the next reign. In 1411 Courtenay led others in an appeal to the Prince of Wales to defend the liberties of the university against interference by the archbishop. Once more Arundel had his authority upheld by the king, who again excluded the university franchises from his confirmation of ecclesiastical liberties that year.[75] Courtenay was deposed as chancellor and the proctors were imprisoned; the university apologized and sued for Arundel's pardon.

Arundel, however, and still less the king, must not be seen as the potent cause of Oxford's intellectual decline in the fifteenth century, its academic freedom crushed under the alliance of church and state. To do so would be to confuse coincidence with cause. Some years ago Gordon Leff observed that an equally marked deterioration occurred at Paris University in the fifteenth century.[76] It may even be thought that the decline itself is an illusion arising from the scorn of humanists and Protestants, as well as from the neglect of later scholastic writings by modern scholars. In fact, the English universities showed some significant advances in the course of the century, not least from a desire on the part of patrons to counter lollardy with educated clergy. Before 1461 five new colleges (including King's which was for seventy poor scholars) were established in Cambridge, and three (including All Souls and Magdalen) at Oxford where also a new divinity school was completed and notable libraries, founded with benefactions from Humphrey, duke of Gloucester, and Bishop Grey of Ely, opened windows, however slightly, on to humanism. What Arundel did was simply to sever lollardy from its academic roots, in itself an important achievement.

Outside the universities, Arundel's restrictions on preaching did little more than reaffirm those that had already long existed. It was a measure which seems to have had minimal effect upon the survival of lollardy, though it has sometimes been credited with stifling preaching endeavour of the orthodox clergy; that was the contention of Thomas Gascoigne, relentless and orthodox critic of his contemporaries, who depicted with some satisfaction Arundel's death by choking – as he had choked the preachers![77] The charge, however, is denied by the wealth of sermon manuscripts which survive from throughout the century.

Far more serious in its consequences was the restraint upon vernacular scriptures which deprived an increasingly literate and articulate laity of their key religious text so that henceforward they could get it only from unorthodox sources, a fact which was to confer upon these an appeal and an authority which they might otherwise have lacked. More than this, it hobbled the parish clergy whose Latin was often unfit for extended biblical reading and

deprived both them and the laity of a book which could have
deepened their piety, strengthened their orthodoxy and improved
their morale. In England, partly because of Arundel's restraints, a
credibility gap grew between the church and the questing layman.

In a number of ways during the reign of Henry IV lollardy
stimulated a long-term shift in the balance of church and state and
of clergy and laity, and it is a deep irony that some of the efforts to
expunge heresy were in the end the more injurious to the church.
What is of immediate importance here, though, is how ineffectual
were royal measures, despite all their good intentions and earnest
appearance. The king's defence of the church proved more
valuable against the designs of the radicals upon its property.

(ii) Church Lands Saved

In October 1399 the commons elected Sir John Cheyne as their
speaker.[78] The next day Archbishop Arundel denounced him in
convocation as an established enemy of the church whose opinions
and feelings were especially dangerous; and who would miss no
excuse to inveigh against the church and its clergy; indeed,
Arundel asserted that there were a number of parliamentary
knights who, far from wishing the clergy well, were fiercely hostile
to the church. To forestall this threat the archbishop persuaded
convocation to curtail the excesses of pluralism and non-residence,
after which he procured the dismissal of Sir John Cheyne. The day
after he had been presented to the king and accepted by him as
speaker, Cheyne resigned from the office on the grounds of ill-
health. It is difficult to explain this sudden change except by
archiepiscopal intervention with the king. Perhaps Cheyne was a
lollard, but if so it is remarkable that Henry IV sent him to Rome
in 1399 to elicit papal approval for the usurpation, and again in
1406 in order to secure the promotion of John Prophet and other
royal clerks. In 1404, 1406, 1410 and 1411 Cheyne was a royal
envoy to France, often in the company of Henry Chichele, bishop
of Bangor and later archbishop of Canterbury and no lollard
favourer. Perhaps the king was prepared to employ men regardless
of their orthodoxy so long as they were useful to him; certainly
after Arundel's protest of 1399 Henry cannot have been in any
doubt about Cheyne's standing with, or his attitude towards, the

church. Two years later, at a great council held at Worcester, when the king was desperately trying to raise money for a campaign against the Welsh rebels, the bishops pleaded that they were too poor to help, whereupon some knights and esquires suggested that the prelates' horses and money should be seized and the prelates themselves be forced to go home on foot 'so that the needs of the king's household could be met from their abundance'.[79] According to one chronicler, Arundel replied to this with great vehemence, threatening that before the knights snatched anything of his they would first suffer some hard blows. The king, it seems, remained above the strife, but he earnestly besought the bishops for some benevolence, a plea – perhaps coupled with the lay threats – which sent Arundel off to exact a subsidy from convocation. This episode clearly resulted from the exasperation of the knights, of the sort which was paralleled in the crisis of 1297, well before lollardy. Once again the strain put upon clergy–laity relations by war is revealed, and this time an insight into the character and tensions of Archbishop Arundel himself. A little later he faced a more considered and serious threat.

In the parliament which met at Coventry in October 1404 some knights, described by one chronicler as 'laymen in faith and doctrine, and less wise than pagans of any nationality', proposed the seizure of the church's temporalities for the king's use for one year.[80] Arundel sprang to the defence of the church by reproaching the knights for their effrontery when they were living off the leases of alien priories, and he underlined the generosity of the clergy in taxation. Another bishop reminded the knights that their proposal would violate Magna Carta, for which they would incur excommunication. Apparently cowed by these retorts, the knights asked for the archbishop's pardon and dropped their demands. An Act of Resumption of crown grants was passed in that year, and in order to tide over the period until it produced any fruits the commons had proposed the surrender of a year's income from all royal lands let out to farm and a year's moratorium on the payment of all pensions conferred by Richard II and Henry IV. In the light of this, the proposed seizure of the temporalities of the church for one year seems not to be specifically or maliciously anticlerical.[81] Nevertheless, as in 1402, the clergy were quick to grant a subsidy when they met in convocation shortly afterwards.

A far graver and more overtly anticlerical proposal was aired at the parliament of 1410. A group of knights, clearly lollards or their sympathizers, outlined a plan for confiscating the lands of the bishops and wealthiest religious and seculars in order to provide the king with £20,000 a year for defence costs, and the realm with an additional 15 earls, 1500 knights, 6200 esquires, 100 almshouses, and 10,500 (or in some sources, 15,000) priests and clerks who were to receive £2 and food and clothing, or else £2 13s 4d a year; 5 (or 15) universities were to accommodate 15,000 clerks.[82] There is no formal record of this plan, but it survives in several chronicles, albeit with varying figures and precarious calculations. Even the year in which it was mooted is in doubt, though the weight of probability is in favour of 1410. The figures were obviously designed to convey a sense of earnest responsibility, just as the comprehensive range of constructive proposals was intended to enlist correspondingly wide sympathies. Following close upon these plans came conventional lollard denunciations of worldly clergy.

The scheme had no chance of success, but was simply an impudent and notable exercise in kite-flying on the occasion of the kingdom's foremost public assembly. Possibly the sponsors of this document sought to take advantage of the departure of Archbishop Arundel from the chancellorship and the council in December 1409, but if that was so, they gravely miscalculated. The Prince of Wales joined the king in strong condemnation of the plan and one of the king's close associates, Sir John Norbury, even declared himself ready to join a crusade which he urged the archbishop to mount against these 'enemies of the cross'.[83] The London chronicles assert that the king prevaricated and deferred a decision, but that seems unlikely, for the proposals attracted no official comment or record which might signify royal toleration.

Ineffective as the 1410 scheme proved, its significance may lie precisely in its failure: the realization may well have dawned then upon a certain member of the lords that revolution, not petition or legislation, provided the only hope of reform; taking his seat in the upper house for the first time was Lord Cobham, formerly and better known as Sir John Oldcastle, leader of the revolt of 1414.

That all these proposals came to nothing owes as much to Arundel as to the king. Arundel was quick to get Cheyne replaced in 1399 and to repulse the radicals at Worcester in 1402 and at Coventry in 1404. While Henry obviously collaborated in 1399, he seems to have exploited the situation for his own advantage in 1402, and at Coventry he was hardly in a position to protect the church from parliament when he was having such a hard struggle to protect himself. In 1410 – if we accept the year given in the St Albans chronicle rather than by the London authors – royal defence was prompt and vigorous: it may be that so detailed a scheme alarmed too many with vested interests in the *status quo*.

Some church lands, of course, those of the alien priories, had already been seized by the crown and many were occupied – as Arundel pointed out – by the laity who were vociferously urging further confiscation. John Cheyne himself had acquired extensive property in Gloucestershire, Herefordshire and Lincolnshire which once belonged to the alien priories of Beckford and Newent and the Norman houses of St Barthe and Beaubec.[84] From these he derived an annual income of some £230 and by virtue of them he was a lay rector well before the Reformation: in neither respect was he unusual among the holders of alien lands. The enjoyment of the church's temporalities was a widely shared experience among the gentlemen of later medieval England, and it is no wonder that many of them – and not just lollards – thought that the rest of the church's lands might be used for their tax relief, if not more directly for their profit. By 1410, however, the farmers of alien lands, perhaps foreseeing a possible conclusion to the war, were eager to convert this temporary, if protracted, arrangement into something more permanent: that year the commons petitioned that the king's lieges might travel to the mother houses in France in order to purchase ownership or lease of the lands after the cessation of hostilities.[85] About the same time Bishop Langley, perhaps to forestall such laicization, appointed an agent to seek the assent of the French houses to the permanent severance of their English lands so long as they were put to pious uses, a reminder that some of the lands were already leased to religious houses in England – the cell of Citeaux in Scarborough, for example, to Bridlington priory.[86] Such arrangements would have threatened the crown's advantages even if licences had to be sought for these deals; it is doubtful if licence fees would adequately compensate the king for the loss of revenues which in 1408 substantially contributed to his household expenses and in the following year yielded much of the 10,000-mark dower for Queen Joan. The logical solution for both parties would have been for the king to make permanent his seizure and their leases from him; the trend was clear.

Schismatic Popes and the Usurper King

The freedom of the papacy to exercise its sovereign authority – its *plenitudo potestatis* – over the English clergy was always subject to royal qualification, and the king, for his part, like all kings, treated papal demands and interventions with pragmatic flexibility.

It might be thought that Henry IV's licence in relation to the pope was somewhat greater than that which many of his predecessors had enjoyed. After all, the papacy was in schism: there were two popes clamouring for recognition and dividing not only the loyalties but also the fruits and resources of western church. In 1401 the lords and commons petitioned the king to do all he could to end this cause of grief and desolation to the church and to restore unity and concord, but they were at pains to stress that this should not be done 'at great charge and cost' to his subjects.[87] In 1407 the king's envoys, already on their way to Rome when Innocent VII died, were instructed to wait and see whether the cardinals would proceed to an election or would delay until the schism was resolved; if the former, the envoys were to be neither the first nor the last on behalf of a Christian prince to extend recognition to the newly elect.[88] In fact, Gregory XII was elected, but by now there was pressure on the rival popes to resign simultaneously and make way for a pope elected in a general council; king, emperor and cardinals were agreed on this plan, though there remained unsettled questions of how to compel the present popes into resignation and whether reform should precede a new election or follow it. In the event, the council held at Pisa in 1409 only succeeded in producing a third pope, Alexander V, as Gregory and Benedict refused to withdraw.

Before then, however, Henry's relations with popes had not markedly differed from those of previous kings for the best part of a century. Henry's independence of the pope was qualified by a number of factors, not the least of which was a genuine attachment to the very idea of papacy. Scarcely less important was England's historical attachment, since 1378 when the schism began, to a Roman pope, as against his Avignon rival who was favoured by France and her allies; England's allies likewise lined up behind Rome. Not only, therefore, would desertion of the Roman pontiff entail diplomatic and military complications and dangers, but it would also aggravate affairs at home as Englishmen, the lords and commons of parliament especially, were suddenly asked to realign their loyalties or even espouse a French pope. Henry could not be too cavalier, therefore, in his treatment of claims and demands emanating from Rome, not least because he himself required papal blessing upon his own precarious regime. The pope on his part badly needed money, which gave the king some leverage; this may explain why he was reluctant to withdraw obedience in order to force resignation but preferred, unlike Arundel and others, to reduce funds to the pope.

So far as solving the schism was at issue, Henry IV's approach had largely been shaped by his diplomatic alliances and needs. It was with the emperor and the call for reform before a new pope was elected that he sided. The Council of Pisa, however, solved nothing and at Henry's death the Council of Constance had not assembled. King, churchmen and university scholars were united upon the need for a council and for reforms, although they differed slightly on procedures; the schism was not, therefore, a dividing issue between the English king and church, and if the England church was weaker at his death than at his accession, this was not the direct outcome of the schism.

While the convocation of 1399 petitioned for the statute of Provisors to be set aside because of its adverse effects upon graduates, the commons in parliament 'of their own free will' authorized the king with the consent of 'such wise men and worthy persons as in this connection it may please him to call on for counsel' to modify the statute and even, should it seem necessary 'for honour and profit' of the crown, the realm and the people, to 'quash, repeal, delete and wholly annul the said statute'.[89] This motion, no doubt on royal prompting despite the disclaimers, freed the king's hands when bargaining with the pope: similar authority had already been accorded to Richard II on an earlier occasion. Within two years, however, the commons sought the exclusion of any provisions in favour of cardinals or other aliens.[90] In 1407 the commons successfully petitioned for the confirmation of the Provisors legislation of Edward III and Richard II 'in all points . . . the moderation of the said statutes notwithstanding' and for all elections to be free from apostolic interference and royal.[91]

Yet before the moderation and after its withdrawal Henry IV continued to apply the statutes with as much and as little rigour as his predecessors had done. Around 1401 he banned aliens from coming into the realm bearing bulls or letters which were prejudicial to the king or his realm, and while in 1405 he ordered a monk of St Augustine's, Canterbury, who was then at the Roman Curia, to return '*a toute celeritee en le roiaume Dengleterre*', he also appointed Dr Richard Dereham his special nuncio and proctor in Rome for securing the provision of royal clerks to vacant benefices.[92] In the very year of the forceful renewal of the statutes of Provisors, Chichele and Cheyne were on their way to the Curia to obtain the provision of John Prophet and other royal clerks.[93] No king worth his salt was going to neglect papal assistance in the promotion of his clerical servants, and when Henry IV gave his consent to the 1407 petition, he did so carefully, 'saving his earlier liberties'.

Regardless of parliamentary authority to modify or even annul the legislation, and apart from his own arbitrary disregard of it for his own convenience, Henry followed the example of previous kings and licensed his subjects to contravene it or pardoned them for having done so. For example, Dr John Ixworth in 1405 petitioned for a royal licence to accept papal provisions to benefices in Salisbury and Chichester cathedrals, and in 1410 John Mont-fort, a royal clerk, sought a licence for his provision to Bossall church in York diocese.[94] No fewer than fifty-four such licences were granted in 1406, the peak year of his reign.[95] Occasionally recipients founds themselves in conflict with, and often thwarted by, men whom the king had presented directly to the living. John Franceys, licensed to use a papal provision to any prebend in Lincoln cathedral, found the king had already granted the one he coveted to John Macworth, chancellor of the Prince of Wales; Macworth sued Franceys for violation of Provisors and won – a licence which was not for a specifically named benefice rarely prevailed against another claimant or incumbent.[96] Indeed, a statute of 1401 had voided all pardons and licences where the providee disturbed a sitting tenant, and the king had agreed to grant no more licences in such cases.[97] From 1406 licences were only valid for benefices which were empty on the date of issue.[98]

After 1407 provisions and expectations on the one hand, and licences to use them on the other, both fell sharply and parliament evinced no further interest in the subject for the rest of the reign. Pope Alexander V, on his election in 1409, sent envoys to obtain the repeal of Provisors, but Henry explained that he would have to consult his parliament on the matter, which he never did.[99] Although the king aroused the suspicions of parliament and observed its measures with flexible resolve, the statutes were nevertheless enforced with impressive effectiveness. The early latitude which the king enjoyed to annul or alter the statutes was surely bait to entice the pope's approval of the *coup d'état*. The licences which Henry sold were designed to gratify his subjects, powerless against his own candidates and often ineffective against current incumbents even before statutory reforms made them so; and they declined after 1407. At the end of the reign Henry made no effort to accommodate papal wishes for repeal; by then he could hardly have expected, nor perhaps did he wish, parliament to be as tolerant as in 1399.

It was not only bulls of provision which were proscribed or curtailed in Henry's reign. As a result usually of parliamentary pressure and of genuine and often justified fears of religious and pastoral consequences, the papal dispensing powers were limited by statute and occasionally the subject of royal appeal to the pope. In 1401 members of religious orders were banned from seeking bulls which exempted them from the authority of their superior or, in some cases, of their bishop, as well as bulls which permitted them to hold monastic offices for life or in plurality.[100] That same year papal bulls were nullified which exempted Cistercians from payment of tithes even on their own lands which were farmed out or occupied by others, and whoever tried to purchase such bulls incurred the penalties of *Praemunire*; moreover, the king was to write to the pope asking for the revocation and cessation of such licences.[101] The same parliament wanted a complete ban on appropriations, but it was not until 1402 that a statute dealt with this matter too.

Papal licences for appropriations had multiplied during the pontificate of Boniface IX (1389–1404). He is known to have granted 155 dispensations for this purpose, 130 of them to religious houses and 56 of these permitting a religious inmate to serve the parish church annexed.[102] This last concession violated the statute of 1391 which insisted that a properly endowed vicarage should be established in such churches. Furthermore, of all Boniface's authorizations, the vast majority were conceded in the five years 1397–1402. In 1402, however, a petition by some Cornish parishioners no doubt prompted legislation on the subject.[103] Men of Liskeard, Linkinhorne and Talland complained that their vicarages had been appropriated by the rectors, namely the prior and the convent of Launceston, even though there were only fifteen canons in that house which had an annual income of, so they alleged, £1000. Convocation had successfully secured the revocation of the bulls authorizing this action, but the convent was contesting this development in Rome and spending great sums of money there for the purpose. The parishioners petitioned parliament for the termination of the suit at Rome and for compulsion upon the convent to provide vicars, divine services and hospitality in all three parishes. When the king promised parliamentary remedy, he doubtless had in mind the statute which followed. This commanded that vicarages should be ordained in all churches which had been appropriated since 1391, on pain of annulment for failure to do so, and that all vicarages which had been annexed since then should be disappropriated; it further stipulated that henceforth only secular clergy should act as vicars.[104] The measure seems to have been swiftly effective: not only did bishops enforce it, but Boniface IX in 1402 annulled all bulls granted by himself and his predecessors which had not yet

taken effect, and thereafter issued no further bulls of appropriation.[105] The next year the king, with the advice of a great
council, sent a letter asking the pope to revoke all appropriations.[106] In 1404 parliament reaffirmed its earlier legislation
and declared null all letters patent to the contrary.[107] By 1406,
when a new pope reigned, an English proctor at Rome obtained a
bull of appropriation for Rochester priory to annex Boxley parish
church, but he observed that the pope rarely granted such bulls
nowadays.[108] A concerted effort by king and parliament had
quickly reduced a serious and growing threat to pastoral welfare,
even if appropriations were not quite at an end.

Not only did these restraints on dispensations diminish papal
authority but they also reduced papal revenues. There was an
unfounded suspicion in parliament that the pope was trying to
make good this loss by exacting excessive levels of annates and
services from newly appointed bishops, and a statute of 1404
attempted to stop this by making forfeit to the crown any excess
over customary sums. The measure, however, was based upon
either a misconception or false information, and in any case it did
not define 'excess'.[109]

A more important source of papal revenues would have been
taxation, but that was rarely attempted and never collected in
Henry IV's reign. Gregory XII sought free-will offerings from the
prelates in 1407 and John XXIII imposed a mandatory triennial
tenth in 1411, but there is no sign that the king acquiesced on
either occasion, still less that any money was raised as a consequence.[110]

The pope's critical role for the king was now played in the
appointment of bishops. Faced by an inherited episcopate more
acquiescent than enthusiastic, Henry needed above all to
strengthen his hand by promoting his own proven servants, but
this did not happen quickly or without difficulties, and most
remarkably not one see fell vacant in the last six years of his reign.

In 1400 Carlisle and Rochester were vacated, but they were not
rich sees calculated to honour a rising civil servant or political
crony. Before Merks was tried for treason in January 1400,
Boniface IX had translated him from Carlisle to a bishopric *in
partibus* and provided a local son, Strickland, to the see. No doubt

the pope was eager to undo the wanton appointments made to gratify Richard's wishes in 1397 and felt confident that the new king would not object, nor yet the chapter, which was Augustinian, to the departure of a Benedictine. But when, in March 1400, the king learnt of this provision he sent off a furious protest, reminding his holiness of his express declaration, when restoring Arundel, that no bishop was ever again to be translated against his will.[111] Henry was not prepared to jeopardize his control of the episcopate simply in order to gratify his personal animosity. Although he did not succeed in nullifying the provision, he did keep Strickland waiting almost a year for his temporalities. Rochester meanwhile, being virtually in the gift of the archbishop, was filled with Arundel's chaplain, John Bottlesham.

Elsewhere in April 1400 Bath and Wells was vacated by death and within a fortnight the king's candidate, Henry Bowet, one of his favourite servants and allies, was elected. A month later, however, the pope provided Richard Clifford, keeper of the privy seal. To Clifford's papal support was added that of the lords and commons in parliament; they pleaded with the king to let Clifford's provision to Bath and Wells stand, despite the statute of Provisors, 'considering that the greater part of the prelacy of the realm so occupied and occupy their benefices and dignities by papal provision, notwithstanding the said statute'.[112] But while the king acknowledged Clifford's good service to him, he declared that Bowet had risked great peril on his behalf, had been duly elected by the chapter at Bath and Wells and had received the king's assent, and Henry could hardly be expected to grant that see to two people, much as he would have liked to assist both. Nearly a year later a solution was reached whereby Bowet was provided to Bath and Wells while Clifford was translated to the vacant see of Worcester.

Three years passed before another episcopal vacancy occurred. In 1404, with the king's blessing, his half-brother, Beaufort, was translated from Lincoln to Winchester, where Wykeham had died; Repingdon, a royal confessor, was provided to Lincoln on the same day. That same year another royal confessor, Mascall, succeeded Trefnant in Hereford. There were no problems about these appointments. At London, however, the king tried in vain to get his chancellor, Langley, appointed, but the pope insisted on the former archbishop, Walden. In the aftermath of Scrope's execution, the king tactfully gave way and then strove to get Langley into York against the papal candidate, Hallum, a scholar and conciliarist. Not till 1407 was the issue settled by the translation of Bowet to York, and the provision of Langley to Durham and Hallum (against a royal candidate, Bubwith) to Salisbury. When London fell vacant on Walden's death in 1406, pope and king amicably promoted the king's clerk, Nicholas Bubwith. In that same year the king favoured his clerk, Richard Dereham, for Norwich but the chapter there elected its prior, Alexander Tottington, who then secured a papal provision and resisted all the king's efforts to force his withdrawal.[113] When the king heard that Tottington was seeking the temporalities of Norwich by virtue of certain bulls (of provision), he expressed his astonishment and ordered the prior to take no further action or he would suffer the penalties incurred for violating Provisors.[114] In fact, Tottington was imprisoned in Windsor castle for a year until Arundel at last persuaded the king to acquiesce in the election. Dereham's chance, alas, had passed. Another loser was John Prophet, keeper of the privy seal and the only one to hold that office in this reign who failed to get a bishopric. He seems to have been squeezed out by the pressure of men already bishops who wanted further advancement, and although in 1407 royal ambassadors were sent to Rome to secure his promotion, by then episcopal vacancies were at an end for the rest of the reign.

Eighteen English vacancies – that is, excluding the four Welsh sees and Walden's removal from Canterbury – were filled by only fourteen men; six of these were translated to second sees, and one more, Bubwith, to a second and a third; Clifford technically held three sees, but gained full possession of only two. There were no purely papal candidates: all who were provided to sees had local backing and were usually suggested locally – by the archbishop, by the chapter, or most frequently by the king. While the king by no means had a free run of the vacant bishoprics, all his candidates save two did eventually land respectable and appropriate sees. Even those whose promotion the king resisted and impeded were for the most part royal servants: only at Carlisle and Norwich –

and then only after a fight – did a *persona non grata* to the king secure a bishopric. These two instances might signify the occasional value of provisions in protecting capitular free elections, but they both occurred when the king was under pressure from other troubles – recognition and rebellion in 1400, the wake of the Scrope affair in 1405. Sometimes the pope advanced a royal servant in the teeth of royal resistance, but rarely without the backing of the chapter – as at Durham in 1407. The combination of pope and chapter was difficult to defeat, as Henry undoubtedly discovered; patently the free capitular election still occurred, but it needed papal protection to withstand the king's resolution and wrath. However, frustrating as these episodes were and as the pope's obstinacy on occasion could be, Henry could hardly complain if only two out of eighteen appointments resulted in bishops whom he would not have thought of himself; even they were not political opponents. Without being servile, the popes had certainly been sympathetic and responsive for the most part.

In sum, the reign of the first Lancastrian saw few significant royal encroachments on ecclesiastical liberties: the trials of Merks and Scrope, and the fate of the latter, were isolated incidents and were to remain so, not part of some calculated policy; royal taxes were burdensome but only ineffectually novel; seizure of the alien priories was renewed, not introduced; Provisors and *Praemunire* were not yet extended, although restrictions on papal bulls for the exemption of religious and for the appropriation of benefices were introduced. Bishoprics were filled on the initiative of pope and king, and variously at the expense of either, even though usually by mutual agreement. Nevertheless, a distinct shift in the relationship of church and state came about through the eagerness of Henry to prove his king-worthiness by his defence of orthodoxy and suppression of heresy. The presence of lollardy, accompanied by raucous anticlerical demands for the confiscation of church property and wealth, emphasized to the clergy their dependence upon the crown for protection and encouraged their collusion in the king's departure from his accession promises.

Henry V (1413–22)
Defender of the Faith

To discover Henry V's conception of kingship we can do no better
than look at the petition against lollardy which, as Prince of Wales,
he presented to parliament in 1406.[1] It was submitted on behalf of
all the temporal lords of the realm because they were threatened,
so it claimed, by the proposed seizure of the church's temporalities: since the church held its lands by as good a title as any under
the law, to breach that tenure would be to encourage a similar
assault upon the estates held by secular lords and that would spell
the destruction of society and the realm. The organic relationship
of church and society was a medieval cliché, but it was rarely so
forcefully particularized as on this occasion. The petition is
noteworthy, too, because in this affair Henry was the identified
leader of the nobles; he shared and was seen to share their concern
about the integrity of their property – perhaps a not unintended
contrast with Richard II. More striking than this, however, are
the opening words of the petition which allude to England's earlier
kings 'who had had such famous victories over their enemies as are
known through the whole world' and who 'were obedient to Holy
Church, and firm in the Catholic faith, and maintained and
defended this faith and the sacraments of Holy Church'. The
implication that the defence of orthodoxy and of the church
(which must include its lands) was the basis of military and
political success was a notion (at least as old as Charlemagne)
which still informed Henry's words, deeds and policy when he
became king. For him and for his reign the bond of faith and
politics was as intimate and fundamental as that of the soul to the
body. It is fitting, therefore, that this chapter should pay
particular attention to Henry's piety, his defence of orthodoxy,
and the role of prayer, since for the king and his contemporaries

these were the *sine qua non* upon which his more spectacular, and to modern eyes more engrossing, achievements rested.

It is generally agreed that Henry was one of the most successful kings of medieval England: when he came to the throne he was already precociously and extensively experienced in war and politics, and when he left it he could boast a list of achievements which none of his predecessors or medieval successors could match. He had crushed a lollard rebellion, stifled a noble plot, played a decisive role in ending the schism, defeated the French, colonized Normandy, secured – on paper at least – succession to the French crown, founded two notable religious houses, forced the Benedictine monks to attempt reforms, revitalized royal administration, and died if not actually on the battlefield at least near it on campaign. He amply filled – and perhaps suggested – the framework of the ideal king which was commended to his son later in the century: just, pious, vigorous, valiant and triumphant; a hero in his own time, a legend soon and for long afterwards.[2] It is true that some modern historians have voiced doubts about the wisdom of his aims, the integrity of his methods, and even the significance of his achievements, but Oxford historians, following the earlier lead of K. B. McFarlane, have recently mounted a vigorous defence of his kingship and statecraft, leaving us once again confronted, if not intimidated, by a paragon.[3] An examination of Henry's policy towards the church and of the contribution of the church to his general political success may lead us some way towards a resolution of these conflicting appraisals.

The Warrior King

Henry's brief nine-year rule was dominated by war; when he was not fighting, he was preparing to do so by negotiations designed rather to provoke and justify hostilities than to avert them. He had already shown, when in charge of his father's council and government in 1410–11, an eagerness to exploit French divisions in order to recover the French crown and kingdom. At that time, he had backed the duke of Burgundy against the Armagnacs, a policy which his father unprofitably reversed in 1412. The

Armagnacs, however, did not dominate, as Burgundy did, the Flemish markets so vital for the English cloth and wool trade, and while they promised Henry large concessions in Aquitaine, these were no more than might be expected from Burgundy which in fact was closer to capturing Paris and the French king. On his accession, therefore, Henry V renewed the Burgundian alliance and then put pressure on the French. In August 1414, when he was already raising money by subsidies and loans for war, Henry's emissaries – the earl of Salisbury and the bishops of Durham and Norwich – were sent to France to claim the recovery of what was tantamount to the old Angevin empire of the twelfth century as well as 2,000,000 crowns for the match of Henry to the French princess. One of the principal sticking points for the French then and in resumed talks in February 1415, by which time English demands had shrunk a little, was the demand for half of Provence which was not France's to give and more than recent history justified. Although bargaining continued, it was soon overtaken by hostilities as Henry landed in Normandy in August 1415 in order to claim his own and to extract by force the just settlement which the French had denied him in negotiation. The chancellor, Bishop Langley, informed parliament some years later that the king had been forced into war by necessity not desire, and had often and earnestly sought peace through his ambassadors before the war began.[4]

Whether or not Henry harboured a grander and nobler ambition than possession of the French crown is open to some doubt notwithstanding the repeated assertions in the *Gesta Henrici Quinti* that he was planning to conquer France in order to unite Europe in a crusade against the infidel. The author of the *Gesta* was probably a royal chaplain and writing at the king's prompting *circa* 1416–17; at that time the king was still angling for the effective support of the emperor, whose chief concern was the Turkish threat to his south-eastern border. In any circumstances the conquest of France alone was a mammoth task and one of questionable wisdom; as a prelude to a general crusade, it becomes preposterously unlikely, for such a crusade would have put any triumphs in France at risk.

The first expedition of the war was to Normandy in August 1415 and by the end of that campaign, in November the same year, the exertions of the nation had been rewarded with the great victory at Agincourt. In August 1416 a truce was signed. A year later, however, the duke of Burgundy, one of the signatories, was advancing on Paris and Henry himself had embarked on his conquest and colonization of Normandy which was more or less complete when Anglo–Burgundian pressure resulted in the French signing the Treaty of Troyes in 1420. By this, Henry was to marry Charles VI's daughter and their son would combine the two realms under the Lancastrian crown. There was a snag in that the Dauphin still controlled much of France and was hardly likely to acquiesce in any plan to disinherit him. Nevertheless, the union of the crowns was at last acknowledged by a king of France, and in December 1420 Paris was taken. Henry spent the early part of 1421 in England and then returned to France to resume the campaign against the Dauphin, but he contracted dysentery during the siege of Meaux and died some months later, still abroad, on 31 August 1422.

Each stage of the war was costly but at each stage alluring prizes were won: Agincourt in 1415, Norman lands for colonizers by 1419, the French crown prospectively in 1420 and the realm perhaps thereafter. Henry had certainly had his luck: the Agincourt battle resulted from a chance encounter; in 1419 menacing negotiations for an alliance between Burgundy and the Armagnacs were aborted when the Armagnacs assassinated the duke of Burgundy, thereby driving his successor into a further alliance with England. In the medieval mind, however, luck was generally a synonym for providence and served not only to encourage but also to justify support. Trial by battle took place between realms as well as individuals. And if anyone should doubt that God was on the side of Henry, they had but to look about them and listen for reassurance as royal propaganda was heard and seen not only in parliament and in the city but in each parish and church throughout the realm.

The Devout King

Although piety was an expected virtue in a medieval king, the examples of Henry III and Henry VI have caused historians to doubt its usefulness for the practice of kingship: Henry V triumphantly demonstrated its relevance. Like several of his aristocratic and knightly contemporaries, he had a devoutness that was more than superficial, a concern for worship, prayer, austerity and simplicity – which indeed led some knights to espouse or favour lollardy. Soon after his accession he set about fulfilling his father's promise to atone for Archbishop Scrope's death by founding three religious houses. It is an eloquent testimony to his own values that he chose to establish a Carthusian house at Sheen, a Bridgetine house on the opposite bank of the river, at Syon, and a Celestine house alongside that.[5] His Charterhouse was the last of nine founded in England during the Middle Ages; as seven of these dated from later than 1340 and six even post-1370, two as recently as 1397–8, there was no doubting the king's fashionable piety. The Carthusian Order was celebrated for its ascetic humility and appealed especially to knightly and aristocratic founders looking for the prayers of worthy religious. As for the Bridgetine house, this was the first and only example in England of an order characterized by a dual community of men and women and notable – as Syon certainly was – for exalted spirituality and learning. The third order which attracted Henry's sponsorship was the Celestine, a fiercely ascetic group of Benedictines established in Paris, but the king's negotiations with the mother house proved unsuccessful or else another unique foundation would have flowered on the banks of the Thames. Although Sheen and Syon received their charters early in 1415, the Celestines were suspicious and spurned his overtures, fearing that such an establishment would become yet another alien priory subject to royal confiscation at the whim of parliament and very likely cut off from its mother house by the war if not also by the schism. Ironically Sheen and Syon had largely been endowed from confiscated lands of alien priories, a notably religious reinvestment.

Incomplete though the realization of his plans may have been, there were hardly two more noble and exemplary houses in fifteenth-century England than Sheen and Syon. Towards the end of his reign Henry tried in 1421 to extend spiritual ambition to more mundane houses; he summoned a general chapter of English Benedictines, addressed it himself and shaped its initial proceedings towards reform; that in the end the results were predictably anodyne may have as much to do with his preoccupations and death in France as with the inertial recoil of the monks from any drastic change in their way of life.

Henry's attachment to the life of prayer is borne out by the author of the *Gesta* who records how the king elaborated observances and ceremonies in the chapel royal and how, once he had begun to listen to a service or to offer his own prayers, no one, not even a noble or magnate, was allowed to interrupt him, however briefly.[6] The same author recounts that when Henry learnt how the fleet waiting off Winchelsea to go to the relief of Harfleur was delayed by unfavourable winds, he spent the evening in prayer and the next day enlisted the hermit of Westminster Abbey, the Charterhouse at Sheen (soon put to good use!) and others, too, to make supplications 'continuously and untiringly' for favourable winds.[7] No doubt the writer was fully aware of the propaganda value of his words, but that makes them all the more revealing about the public and political impact of the king's devotion.

Heresy Repulsed

About Henry's theological expertise we know little, but there is a tradition that he attended Oxford University and engaged in disputations at Paris in his youth. He was certainly eager to reason with the heretic Badby at the stake and showed himself a keen defender of the faith in several ways. Not the least of these was his assault on lollardy. Soon after his accession he was tested by the great lollard uprising led by Oldcastle.[8]

Sir John Oldcastle, of Herefordshire, served in Henry IV's army against the Scots in 1400, and in various campaigns with Henry, Prince of Wales, against Glendower's forces in the following years. In January 1404 he was a member of parliament for his home county and two years later he was sheriff there. A second marriage, in 1408, brought him through his wife the title of Lord Cobham and a summons in 1409 to sit with the lords in parliament. In 1411 he was one of the captains of the expedition sent to France by the Prince of Wales. Long a friend of the prince, he was described by a contemporary as 'one of the most valued and more intimate members of his household'. All this time, however, Oldcastle had been leading a double life which only gradually came to light as two of his Kent chaplains (in churches which he acquired by right of his wife) in 1410 and 1413 attracted the attention of the archbishop by their unorthodox preaching. Moreover, in 1413 a search of an illuminator's shop in London uncovered some heretical manuscripts belonging to Oldcastle. At first he was able to satisfy his friend and patron, the king, that there was an innocent explanation for his connection with these books, but accumulating evidence and the archbishop's persistence eventually aroused the king's distrust and he allowed Oldcastle to appear before an ecclesiastical assembly which duly condemned him for heresy. The king was still reluctant to disown his former friend and insisted that forty days should elapse until the death penalty should be exacted. On 19 October 1413, however, before the forty days had expired, Oldcastle had escaped from the Tower and by the end of the year had hatched a *coup d'état*. For this a group of conspirators disguised as mummers were to seize the royal family at Eltham while a nationally raised force of lollards was to assemble on St Giles Fields ready to seize London. The aim, according to the official charge, was to kill the king and his brothers, along with prelates and some magnates, and to expel the religious from their houses and confiscate the endowments of all the realm's churches; apparently Oldcastle was to become regent. Whatever the real aims of the rebels may have been, they were frustrated – as were so many plots against the first two Lancastrians (Henry IV may be thought to have started this fashion with his revelations about Mowbray in 1398) – by betrayal; defeat was ensured by the ludicrously small numbers who gave Oldcastle support, no more than three hundred in all. On 10 January 1414, the day of the assembly in St Giles Fields, the conspirators who arrived were rounded up, and within two days seventy of them were tried and condemned and of these forty-five were promptly executed; significantly only seven were burnt as heretics as well as hanged as traitors. Meanwhile the king had already sent out commissions to twenty shires and to London and Bristol for suspects to be traced and for the evidence against them to be collected; those who were arrested were to be held until the king and council had decided their fate. Oldcastle eluded capture and when a general pardon was issued in March for any who sued for pardon he spurned it. Those who had been condemned but were not yet executed found themselves detained for a year and were then handed over to their bishops to purge themselves of heresy, as indeed the pardoned also had to do. Hiding in safe houses and on safe manors in various parts of the kingdom, Oldcastle was not captured until the end of 1417. Then, although already a convicted traitor and heretic, he was interrogated in parliament, where his garrulous impudence and his lofty dismissal of any earthly judges only served to confirm his fate. He was hanged and burnt on 14 December 1417.

From this distance the rising led by Sir John Oldcastle, alias Lord Cobham, appears as a contemptible fiasco easily suppressed and never again attempted. It seems clearly to mark the end of serious lollard threats to the political community and the alienation of the gentry and knightly class from its ranks and favourers. To contemporaries its significance was not so evident. In the first place, Oldcastle, a *persona grata* in the highest places of the realm, was revealed to be a secret lollard with a network of safe houses and a chain of communication at his disposal, and with London scriveners – the medieval forerunner of the printer – and countrywide recruits as his allies. It must have been as alarming and shocking then as the defections of Burgess and Maclean were in recent times. That the numbers involved were almost negligible, even though some of them had to be lured by wages and rewards, was hardly likely to prove reassuring when the leaders were so prominent and influential and the links and structure so menacing; in any case, medieval people were almost congenitally unable to count and measure accurately. Genuine lollards may have been very few even among those who did turn out, but all risings attract a wide variety of opportunists and what is important here was that a lollard was the instigator. This rebellion was yet further proof that heresy was as much a threat to society as it was to the church, a fact soon to be underlined as Bohemia, where Hus had imported Wycliffism, dissolved into civil war. Gratitude and not complacency followed Henry's defeat of Oldcastle, whose conspiracy was no derisory affair but a national crisis surmounted by a hero-monarch who defended the faith and was himself defended by God.

Henry's response was, in the end, firm and decisive and in marked contrast to the dilatory action of Wenceslaus of Bohemia where the Hussite problem quickly got out of hand.[9] Oldcastle himself had been in correspondence with Hussites in 1411 and at that stage a nationwide rebellion was not inconceivable in England. Here, however, the appeal of heresy – aside from the opportunity which it afforded Welsh optimists – was not to nationalism but to dynastic factionalism, which had not been allayed either by the death of Richard II or by his ostentatious reburial at Westminster Abbey in December 1413. Just over a year after the fiasco at St Giles Fields and on the very eve of the king's departure for France in 1415, the earl of Cambridge, Sir Thomas Grey and Henry, Lord Scrope bred a plot to depose Henry V in favour of Richard II or, failing him, the earl of March. It was foiled by the loyalty of March who betrayed it to the king. Futile as these conspiracies proved in practice, and weak though their popular support was, their occurrence early in the reign – when Henry had yet to captivate the public imagination by his triumphs in France – opened up alarming possibilities. Yet by their defeat and especially by the subsequent measures which he took against lollardy, Henry significantly strengthened the Lancastrian monarchy and notably augmented the powers of the crown and the role of the laity in matters of religion.

Simply by surviving, Henry gained prestige: 'A just and merciful God, who allows no one to be tried beyond his strength but always provides a way of escape for His elect in a time of temptation' had decided in the king's favour.[10] Henry further proved himself one of the elect by the statute which he promulgated in the Leicester parliament in May 1414.[11] Henceforth, 'to the honour of God, and in conservation and fortification of the

Christian faith, and also in salvation of his royal estate, and of
the estate of his realm', all royal officers, from judges down to
mayors and bailiffs of cities and towns, and all others having
governance were to swear an oath when they entered on their
office that they would use all their powers to 'put out, cease and
destroy all manner of heresies and errors, commonly called
lollardies' and assist bishops and their officers when called upon
to do so. All judges, justices and JPs were empowered to
enquire into anyone holding errors or favouring those who did,
and into those who wrote books, preached sermons or held
schools and conventicles which were at all suspect. Justices of
the Peace were so instructed by the terms of their commissions.
Whoever was indicted as a result of these enquiries was to be
promptly arrested and to be delivered for examination within
ten days. In franchises where the king's writ did not run, the
franchise holders were similarly empowered. Thus was orthodoxy made the subject of routine and obligatory vigilance and
investigation by the secular governors of the realm. The crown
and all lay officers in the kingdom now assumed responsibility
as of course for the defence and enforcement of orthodoxy, a
responsibility which was not relinquished until the eighteenth
century. The definition of true faith was still in the hands of the
professional theologians, the clergy, but the state could now on
its own initiative compel observance and had elaborate
machinery to do so.

All this did not mean, however, that Henry discounted the
role of the church in the prosecution of heresy. In 1415 all
bishops were charged by the king's council to take steps to resist
the malice of lollards in their dioceses.[12] Possibly as a result of
this, as well as of the statute's implications, Archbishop Chichele in July 1416 ordered that in every deanery and parish
diligent enquiry was to be made at least twice a year for heretics
and their favourers.[13] This mandate was copied into several
bishops' registers where frequent action is recorded against
lollards. The prelates were certainly not allowed to relax or left
to their own devices; for instance, when some lollard suspects
purged themselves in the bishop of Bath and Wells's court in
1417 the crown demanded a certificate of all that was done

there.[14] No wonder that lollards themselves dubbed Henry 'the prince of priests' (*princeps presbiterorum*).[15]

War Efforts

(i) Prayer and Propaganda

It is not surprising that the prince who so defended the faith, prayed into the night, and called upon his local hermit and his own Charterhouse for their suffrages on behalf of his fleet should employ the whole church of England to pray for his plans and success. Nor is it surprising that the prelates responded eagerly to these calls from the

> piler of our feith and wareyour
> Ageyn the heresies bitter galle.[16]

Every stage of his campaign was mounted on the wings of prayer and every parish church in the land was commanded to hold special masses and say special collects on Wednesdays and Fridays for the king's success, or for his health, or for fine weather (for his fleet or army, no doubt), or for the unity of the church (one of his aims would unite the English and French churches), or for the justice of his cause, or for a profitable outcome of negotiations, or in thanks for his victories. Parishioners were encouraged to attend and pray by the lure of forty-day indulgences, if by nothing else. In fact, though, it seems that so frequent were the calls to prayer that zeal waned under the pressure of demand and both clergy and laity were accused of negligence in these matters. In each year from 1415 to 1419 inclusive the archbishop of Canterbury issued mandates, sometimes more than one in a year, for such prayers, and much the same was happening in the northern province. In 1416 and 1417, however, the mandate had to be repeated because of the lamentable indifference of the clergy and people to these commands. In August 1416 Archbishop Chichele wrote of his recent order meeting only a lukewarm response: 'notwithstanding the testimony of the Saviour and the Scripture as to the efficacy of fervent and uninterrupted prayer, for the people conquered while

Moses prayed but were conquered when he put down his hands.'[17]

The archbishop urged his bishops to incite the faithful to pray 'even more devoutly'. Yet in May 1417 he complained that despite three times ordering the clergy and laity to pour forth prayers for church unity, royal and national prosperity, and fine weather, the clergy and laity alike had rather ignored than obeyed these mandates. Even this rebuke was unavailing; in the following spring the bishop of Lincoln was moved to reproach the inhabitants of that city for their 'great neglect' of prayers and processions for the royal and public weal. Popular enthusiasm for Henry's campaigns appears to have been sagging under the burden of intercession which he placed upon it, but there were other signs in these middle years of his reign that the demands of war were not welcomed: the raising of money and troops both occasioned concern about this time. All the more necessary then were the public reminders of the king's needs and achievements which prayers and processions afforded. On Palm Sunday 1419 the bishop of Hereford preached on the need for prayers for peace between Henry and the Dauphin after the fall of Rouen.[18] Around Michaelmas that same year supplications and ceremonies were bidden throughout the province to protect the king against necromancy and evil spells, and a month later the king acknowledged that these prayers had prevailed against the black magic which had menaced his person.[19] Additionally a stream of victories provided accumulating evidence of the effectiveness of all this invocation of divine aid.

It was not just at home, however, that the clergy prayed for the king. Those who accompanied him on campaign, 'the clerical militia', joined in these suffrages and fell upon their faces in prayer. One of them sitting on horseback at the rear of a battle in 1416 prayed privately that God would 'not suffer the supplication and tears which the English church had poured forth, and in this very hour and in her accustomed processions did undoubtedly pour forth on our behalf, to come to nothing'.[20] The sense of a united nation and of a united effort which these words reveal surely had no small significance for the morale of Henry's forces.

Of course, the saints too played their part, and gratitude to them provided recurring opportunities for public celebration of the victories which they sponsored. In 1416, on the king's command, the feast of St George, patron and protector of the English nation and patron of the Order of the Garter, was promoted to a 'greater double' which required the cessation of all servile work, and attendance as for Christmas itself.[21] Later in the year the lesser feasts of St John of Beverley were specially commended to the realm: not only the deposition of the saint on 7 May but in particular his translation on 25 October, which was the day of the battle of Agincourt 'where St John demonstrated his special patronage of the English people' and on which day, so Chichele told convocation, his tomb exuded oil.[22] That same year the feasts of St David, St Chad and St Winifred were also commended to the people in gratitude for their assistance.[23]

Prayers and processions to avert political (as well as other) disasters and to procure victories kept the people informed and served to elicit – or at least claim – their support. There was nothing novel about this by the time of Henry V, nor were prayers the only vehicle of propaganda deployed by a king whose victorious entry into London[24] was a landmark in the development of pageants in England, and whose advocates included the civil-servant poet Hoccleve and the household chaplain who wrote the *Gesta Henrici Quinti*. Yet few kings of England before Henry, if indeed any, had brought the nation in so short a time so often to its knees, and few were so quick to exploit the saints or left their mark so heavily upon the liturgy and public devotions. Henry was as resolute and methodical in prayer as he was in administration. In his reign the nation at prayer was the obverse of the nation at war; prayer was part of the sinews of war. More, however, was demanded of the church than prayers.

(ii) Money and Men

The financial burdens of the war were massive: in a mere nine years Henry V raised just about as much from his subjects, lay and clerical, as his father had in fourteen years. Canterbury clergy voted Henry V ten and a half tenths in the course of his reign, two in each of the four years 1414–17: only in 1414 was there no collection of tax from the southern clergy, and in 1416, 1417 and 1420 there were two collections in each year.[25] The two-year moratorium which convocation had stipulated as a condition of its grant in 1414 was wholly disregarded. The tenth which was due to be collected in November 1417 was replaced by one and a half tenths in February and another half tenth in April of that year, followed by yet another tenth in February 1418. The November 1417 tenth was eventually levied in February 1420 when a further moiety was added as well as a tax of half a mark on chaplains and stipendiaries who were earning at least 7 marks a year or £2 with food. The grants collected in 1416, 1418, 1419 and 1420 were levied also on some beneficed clergy who were normally exempt from paying subsidies. Not since the late 1370s, and before that the 1330s and 1290s, had so much been demanded from the clergy as in the middle years of Henry V's reign.

It was about this time that mandates for prayers were falling on deaf ears and there are signs that tax demands too were being met only reluctantly by the laity at least; the modern editors of the *Gesta* believe that the work may have been written in the winter of 1416–17 precisely to dispel growing apathy or hostility in the nation at large. The propaganda or the military triumphs apparently worked, for after 1414 the clergy of Canterbury province attached substantial conditions to their grants on only one occasion. In 1421 they insisted that no clergy paying the tenth were to be charged for the lay tax in respect of their private lands and goods; clergy who were prepared to make loans to the king were to get preferential repayment; all exemptions and allowances were to be respected by the exchequer, and no attempt was to be made to collect the grant earlier than agreed. Despite these conditions the clergy's tenth in 1421 was more than welcome to the king; the laity had been spared a demand in 1420 but had proved reluctant to yield to one in May 1421; convocation's grant in that same month enabled Henry to postpone further approaches to parliament until December 1421 when, having enjoyed almost two years without tax grants, the laity were more forthcoming. Not till early in the next reign was a tax demand refused by convocation which then claimed, in 1424, that benefices were too impoverished to attract clergy let alone support taxes.

York province, too, was just as regularly raided as Canterbury in Henry V's reign. While it had yielded eight and a half tenths to

Henry IV, it provided his son with seven and a half tenths, five of them as full tenths. The condition attached to the 1415 grant, that there should be no further tax demand for two years, proved as ineffective as Canterbury's moratorium. A week's debate in January 1417 – it was unusual for York convocation to sit more than two days – proved equally unavailing, as did complaints about Scottish depredations, drought and murrain in 1418, and about rain and floods in 1421. Not only was the king implacable but from July 1417 the bishop of Durham was his chancellor, while the archbishop was that ageing Lancastrian servant, Henry Bowet; moreover, weighty voices in convocation were the royal holders of several dignitaries and prebends in the minsters of York, Ripon, Beverley and Southwell. Pressure on the northern convocation can be measured by the sinking thresholds to exemption: in 1415 from the usual £6 13s 4d down to £5; in 1418 down to £4; in 1421 raised to £5 6s 8d, still half a mark below the level of 1415.

In the interval between the granting and collecting of taxes the king found ready cash by means of loans yielded from individual subjects and various communities after negotiation and diverse degrees of persuasion. The comparative ease with which they were raised and the considerable extent to which they were promptly repaid by Henry V are striking indices of his administrative and political skills.[26] His leading subjects and councillors were perhaps the least able to refuse his requests and also the best placed to secure repayment with reasonable speed. Bishops, of course, both by their closeness to the king and by the resources of their sees, were considerable lenders – Chichele advanced some £1900, Bubwith £1700, Repingdon over £1000 – but unique among them was Beaufort. Beyond the sums which he lent by virtue of his bishopric, his notorious indiscretions exposed him to what was in effect blackmail by the king. Before Beaufort set off for Constance he lent the king some £14,000 as surety for good behaviour, and after he had accepted the cardinalate and the legateship he was compelled to buy back the king's favour by a further loan of £17,000, sums which the king felt no urgency to repay. By the time of Henry's death Beaufort had advanced over £35,000 to the king and had received repayment of less than half that total. No other cleric was so vulnerable to royal pressure or capable of advancing such sums. Apart from the bishops, well over a hundred abbots and priors were among the king's creditors, but the abbot of Glastonbury's £200 indicates the scale that applied here. Several deans of collegiate churches and more than a hundred parish clergy lent to the king. In fact, Henry enjoyed greater credit from the religious and the minor clergy (as from the gentry) than either his father or his son could command, and the clergy played a not insignificant role, too, in collecting the loans. Henry's successful appeal to so wide a spectrum of his subjects may indicate the importance of all those prayers and processions. Possibly Beaufort's unusual contributions enabled the king to pay off his other creditors to an extent which disguised how precariously poised the royal finances stood at his death; as Steel has written, 'the tension [*sc.* financial] snaps, almost audibly, upon his death bed'.

Prayers, taxes and loans comprised by no means all the war effort which the king required from the church. Twice in the reign the clergy of the southern province were ordered to muster with all possible speed – religious, secular, exempt and non-exempt – competently arrayed according to their status, so that they should be ready to repel any attacks upon the Catholic faith, the church or the realm.[27] In 1415, Bath and Wells diocese reported the array of 60 men-at-arms (a term usually denoting mounted lancers), 830 bowmen, and 10 hobelars (probably lightly armed cavalry); Lincoln diocese – vastly bigger – mustered over 3000 secular clergy and over 1500 religious equipped as some 500 well-armed men and around 4000 archers; in Rochester diocese the stipendiaries mustered as archers.[28] In that year eleven dioceses, those for which records are extant, arrayed some 12,000 clergy. In 1418 twelve dioceses returned lists totalling over 15,000 clergy, of which the sparse diocese of Hereford provided 79 men-at-arms and 433 bowmen.[29] In the northern province, where military threats were commonplace, arrays of clergy were more frequent; as well as in 1415 and 1418, others were called out against the Scots twice in 1417 and several times in 1419, and this was one reason why York hesitated over the granting of taxes.[30]

Although some bishops supervised these arrays personally, none seems to have displayed the martial zest of the late Bishop

Despenser of Norwich. True, one of his successors there, Richard Courtenay, accompanied Henry to Agincourt, but apparently his services were confined to those of a negotiator and an intelligence gatherer, in which respect perhaps his interest in astrology was not without its uses; he died in France, but of sickness, not in battle.[31] Benedict Nicholls, bishop of Bangor, who was also on that expedition, no doubt assisted morale by ceremony alone: when Harfleur surrendered in October 1415, Nicholls entered the town dressed in his episcopal robes and accompanied by thirty-two chaplains, before each of whom an esquire carried a lighted torch.[32] In 1417, when there were more prelates with the king, a future bishop, John Kemp, was employed to hear the army's confessions; in 1418 Kemp was holding musters at Bayeux, but by then he was the king's chancellor in Normandy.

The lesser clergy who accompanied the king to France were mostly his chaplains whose task was to fight the good fight with prayers, not arms. We have seen above how the clergy gathered near the army's baggage and threw themselves (almost literally) into prayer rather than combat. Robert Gilbert, dean of the king's chapel, was present at several of Henry's battles, but he himself killed and wounded no one: what troubled his conscience long afterwards was that he had rejoiced when the king's men had triumphed, and grieved at their reverses.[33]

Church Liberties

Henry V's deep piety was accompanied by no servile posture towards either the English church or the papacy. So far as the national church was concerned Henry well understood that, great as his need for money was, if it were pursued too recklessly his war aims would be jeopardized and not advanced; it was simply not politic for him to provoke conflict by disregard for custom and equity. While the king repeatedly confirmed the liberties and franchises of the church, it was the laity rather than the king who posed a threat to the church. The most obvious alarm was caused by Oldcastle and the lollards, and the king dealt forcefully with that. No one dared to suggest again in parliament the confiscation of church wealth or income apart from that of the alien priories; these were already in effect secularized, and now Henry seized the opportunity afforded by parliamentary resumption to employ at least some of their lands for religious ends again.

A more dangerous royal encroachment might seem to be implicit in the statute of 1414 which concerned prohibitions.[34] By the terms of this act, church courts were obliged to provide defendants with a full libel of detailed charges upon demand, as without it a writ of prohibition could not be obtained from the king. Some ecclesiastical judges had attempted to avert royal intervention in their courts by withholding or editing such libels when requested to provide them. Clearly this was an area where the clergy and not the laity had departed from law and custom. Writs of prohibition, however, were probably not issued as frequently or granted so lightly as was once thought or as earlier protests suggested; indeed in 1421 the care taken over the issuing of such writs was publicly displayed.[35] In that year the parson of Somersham, in Lincoln diocese, and the abbot of Ramsey, in Ely diocese, were in dispute in the court of arches where sentence was given against the abbot. He thereupon sought a prohibition to stop execution of the sentence on the grounds that it had been given without consideration of all the issues, as was demonstrated by the libel, which he produced. The suit was a complicated one about parish and manorial boundaries and the application of a papal privilege granted to the abbey of Ramsey.

> After great altercations and disputations which went on a long time in the Chancery, between counsels of the said parties, on the issues, and because the chancellor and the royal clerks of his chancery, on account of the complexity, could not quickly and rightly be advised what the law prescribed in this matter, the chancellor adjourned it to parliament, and referred the parties there to hear what might be determined by the advice of parliament.

When the chancellor had given the parliament a full résumé of the case so far, as had the parties' counsel, the duke of Bedford (then the guardian of the realm) ordered the judges of both benches and the chief baron of the exchequer to give parliament their considered view of the matter according to the law. After careful and mature consideration of all the arguments the judges and chief baron duly advised the guardian and the lords who then decreed that a prohibition did not lie in this case against execution of the sentence, nor could do so, and should not therefore be granted. What matters for us is not the technical reasons for this decision but the elaborate expenditure of time and effort in order to reach it, emerging as it did from consideration successively by the chancellor and chancery clerks, parliament, and the king's judges with the chief baron of the exchequer. It is perhaps of minor significance that the suitor for prohibition was – as so often happened – a cleric. Less reassuring for us is our present ignorance of what occurred in cases where the king or one of his clerks was a party.

The writ of *praemunire*, even more formidably menacing than the writ of prohibition, was also the subject of an encouragingly detached judgement. Nicholas Ryecroft sued out a writ of *praemunire* against Roger Lansell, clerk, for having cited him to answer in Rome on certain issues prejudicial to the king, the laws and the customs of the realm.[36] When Roger appealed and exhibited the citation before the council in October 1415, they concluded that the issue was purely spiritual and in no way harmed or threatened the king, and that the judges should proceed with the case as law and reason demanded; a writ was therefore denied. Although the council on that occasion comprised Archbishop Chichele, Bishop Beaufort (then the chancellor), John Wakeryng (then keeper of the privy seal and a month later elected to the see of Norwich), and only one layman (the treasurer), yet one could hardly expect Chichele, who was trained in civil law, or Wakeryng, who had made his way in the chancery, and still less the treasurer, to take an unreasonable or unfounded clerical line on this matter; Beaufort's approach alone is open to doubt.

Another hoary and contentious jurisdictional subject, the issue of tithes of wood (*silva cedua*), was raised again in the parliament in 1414.[37] On that occasion the king decided that it was so complicated and required such mature deliberation that it should

be adjourned to the next parliament when the clerk should bring it
again to the king's and parliament's notice. In fact, for some reason
he did not, perhaps because the petitioners had realized that the
outcome was much more uncertain than they had anticipated or
that the king was here engaged in evasion.

A quasi-jurisdictional matter was that of fees charged for
probate in ecclesiastical courts; this became the subject of
parliamentary complaints on three occasions in the reign.[38] After
the first complaint, in 1413, the king issued a stern warning to the
bishops to take the matter in hand or else he would provide a
remedy. When the complaint was repeated a year later, the king
extracted a promise from the bishops to issue a decree on the
subject within six months of the then vacant see of Canterbury
being filled. According to Usk, this was done in the October
convocation in 1414, when a tariff was set ranging from one
shilling where the value of the testator's goods totalled £5, up to ten
shillings per £100, with an absolute maximum charge of £20. This
hardly mollified the commons who in 1416 returned to the matter
with some passion: they recalled that under Edward III 2s 6d or 5s
was the normal probate fee and that now, by virtue of a
convocation decree of Arundel's time, £2 or £3 was commonly
charged, and they proposed the restoration of the Edwardian
levels and a fine of treble the sum received in excess to be levied on
all offenders. The duke of Bedford, as the king's lieutenant, gave
his assent to this petition until a subsequent parliament; but no
more was heard of the matter there.

The measure against excessive probate fees, harking back as it
did to levels current under Edward III, may be seen as part of a
wider effort to keep inflation down and to protect taxpayers from
extraneous demands. In 1414 a statute had already set limits to
clerical stipends.[39] Remarking that in 1362–3 legislation had put a
still disregarded ceiling of 5 or 6 marks upon annual clerical wages,
parliament now recommended that chaplains and stipendiaries
who claimed more than 6 marks or £5 per annum in wages should
pay the excess to the use of the king. He, however, after consulting
the lords and commons, moderated this and permitted ceilings of 7
marks for annual chaplains, and 8, or with episcopal permission, 9
marks for parochial chaplains, and any mention of sanctions or

fines was dropped. Even these new limits were evaded, so that in 1419 the commons were proposing that JPs should have powers to investigate and punish offenders who should pay double the excess to the king. The only response was that the existing statute should be enforced. In this, as on several other points, the king seemed to be restraining and moderating the zeal of parliament to curb clerical income and alleged excesses, notwithstanding the efforts to enlist his support by offering him in some instances the fines that should be exacted. If the extravagant anticlericalism of Henry IV's parliaments had vanished, there was still a residual resentment and even hostility, and the church still had more to fear from parliament than from the king.

Henry V, however, exercised his rights of patronage as firmly as any of his predecessors, though apparently without extravagant excess or extortionate zeal. The archdeanconries and deaneries of the kingdom were as full of royal clerks as ever and the appointment of one of these is especially revealing. The dean of the chapel royal, Dr Robert Gilbert – he of the tender conscience – became archdeacon of Durham in 1420, but only after the king had three times ordered his installation and finally threatened the penalties due for contempt; even then the bishop, who was the king's chancellor no less, first ordered an enquiry into the king's right to present, evidently with a happy result for the king and Gilbert.[40] Only a full-scale study of his patronage, however, will allow these impressions of fair but firm exercise to be replaced by certainty. In the next reign the king's exploitation of cathedral canonries and dignities was to recede as laymen supplanted clerks among his bureaucrats.

King's Bishops

Nowhere was the king's exercise of patronage more critical for the well-being of church and realm than in the appointment of bishops. Vacancies afforded opportunities for gain to pope and king: the pope especially by translations which multiplied vacancies and the services and annates which accrued from the subsequent provisions; the king by exploiting his regalian right and drawing income from the temporalities of an empty bishopric.

Of twenty-five English and Welsh episcopal vacancies during the reign, nine were occasioned by translation, fifteen by death, and one by Repingdon's resignation from Lincoln.[41] Seven of the translations were initiated by Pope Martin V, but there are no signs that they were unwelcome to the king who restored the temporalities without undue delay; for the most part they were men who had served him and Martin at Constance or at Rome, and since Henry was hoping for some papal concessions over the organization of the Norman church he was no doubt well disposed to concede some *quid pro quo*. Very few vacancies were protracted, and even then not always by the king: John Kemp, for example, who undoubtedly enjoyed the king's favour, had to wait eight months for his provision to Rochester and six more months for its temporalities in 1419, seven months for provision and six for the estates at Chichester in 1421, and three for provision and seven for the lands at London in 1422; except on the third occasion when the king was engaged on his final French campaign, the delays were caused at the papal end. There is little evidence that Henry was exploiting vacancies to fill his war coffers.

When we turn to the men who were appointed to fill these sees, the impression gained is one of disciplined and responsible exploitation. Of the sixteen men promoted to English bishoprics – sixteen to fill twenty-one vacancies – only one, John Wakeryng, had risen through the civil service; he had been a chancery clerk in 1395, keeper of the rolls in 1405, and was keeper of the privy seal in 1415.[42] Two other keepers of the privy seal who gained bishoprics – John Kemp and Henry Ware – had first served in the Canterbury ecclesiastical courts where they attracted the attention of an archbishop already in royal service and thus the notice of the king himself. Chichele, too, had prospered through diocesan service. A degree in civil law, and sometimes in canon law as well, admirably qualified them for diocesan jurisdiction and for the openings then abounding in royal diplomacy – negotiating with Burgundy or France or the Empire, exploring royal matches all over western Europe, or attending the pope or the Council of Constance. There were really only two court bishops: Stephen Patrington, a Carmelite prior-provincial, a formidable theologian who had participated in the Blackfriars Council in 1382, a well-known anti-Wycliffite, and from 1413 a royal chaplain and confessor; and Edmund Lacy, also an Oxford theologian, king's clerk in Henry IV's reign, and dean of the royal chapel at Windsor from 1414. John Chaundler, dean and then bishop of Salisbury, probably qualifies as a courtier – of Richard II, Henry IV and Henry V – but his election to Salisbury sprang very much from a local initiative. Richard Courtenay is difficult to categorize; he had a civil law degree, had been with Henry in his youthful campaigns in Wales and went with him to France in 1415, but became prominent as chancellor of Oxford University whose liberties he attempted to defend against Archbishop Arundel in 1411; with his aristocratic background, he was perhaps a courtier as much as anything.[43] There appear to have been three entirely independent candidates, apart that is from the doubtful case of Chaundler. Roger Whelpdale was a theologian and mathematician whose local connections won him the see of Carlisle. William Heyworth, abbot of St Albans, and John Langdon, monk of Christ Church Canterbury, appear to have gained Lichfield and Rochester respectively without royal or papal prompting.

Of the sixteen bishops, seven were lawyers, at least five were theologians. Nearly all were substantial figures on account either of their learning or their practical experience, or both. The papal candidates were no less worthy than the royal and had come to the papal notice either because of, or with, Henry's favour. Obviously the most important and critical appointment was to Canterbury, and there the king's choice exemplifies his decisive and sound judgement.

That Henry should have preferred Chichele to fill Canterbury rather than his uncle and long-standing colleague, Beaufort, bishop of Winchester, is only superficially surprising. Beaufort was an ambitious opportunist, too familiar with the king to be a comfortable tenant of Canterbury, as the episode over the legateship and the cardinal's hat was soon to show. Chichele on the other hand was already known to Henry for his administrative and diplomatic talents. A civil lawyer by training, a diocesan administrator by experience, bishop of St Davids by office since 1407, and royal diplomat, as well as a member of the Prince of Wales's council in 1411, Chichele had proved himself a solid, dependable negotiator, a firm executor of orders rather than an independent initiator; he was as predictable as he was diligent, as alert as he was unoriginal, and as tactful as he was resolute. Chichele made a worthy successor to Arundel and was not at all overshadowed or intimidated by an episcopal bench teeming with learning, ability and character. In fact the qualities of the archbishop and his fellows reflected not only the preoccupations of the reign but also the qualities of the king's own government which was, after all, maintained in no small degree by the episcopate.

For the most part the role which the bishops played in Henry's government was diplomatic, both before and in some cases after their elevation. Hallum, Bubwith, Catterick, Polton and Fleming were engaged for some of their time at Constance. Courtenay and Nicholls, already bishops, and Lacy, on his way to promotion, were with the king in France in 1415; others accompanied him during his second campaign. From 1418 John Kemp was the king's chancellor in Normandy and in 1419 he obtained the first of his several bishoprics. At home, the experienced Langley, holder of Durham, was chancellor and with the duke of Bedford, the king's lieutenant, kept the government running, sometimes being the only minister present in the council.[44] Archbishop Chichele played a more ecclesiastical role but one which was not less significant for the government: he managed convocation in the fight against lollardy and in the granting of clerical taxes, and he organized the nation's prayers. Episcopal membership and attendance at the council increased after the king's visit to England in 1421 when Bubwith, Beaufort and Morgan (of Worcester) returned home. Even from Normandy, however, the king mostly kept a tight hold on the government of the realm so that there was often little room for initiative or independent policy-making by the council and its episcopal members.

As for the diocesan responsibilities of Henry's bishops, these were by no means neglected, for – like the king in Normandy – they kept a close watch, even when distant, upon the working of what by now was a well-developed administrative machine for the rule of a diocese. The episcopal registers amply bear out the bishops' genuine and not unsuccessful efforts to serve a king and a diocese. The problems which beset the English church at that time were neither created nor neglected by the bishops.

Papal Relations

The Great Schism was, in its origin as well as in its solution, partly a constitutional problem about electoral procedure, but inevitably a moral question also intruded about reform and authority in the church, and running through it from beginning to end were political considerations of allegiance to, and alignment behind, one of the several claimants to the papal throne. When, in desperation for a solution, the Emperor Sigismund convened a general council of churchmen and statesmen at Constance in 1414 there was initially a problem of how to remove the three existing 'popes'; but the more obdurate they were, the more isolated they became, and in the event one resigned, one was deposed in 1415 and the third was deposed two years later. By then the question of whether to proceed with reforms before or after the election of an undoubted pope was exercising minds and wills.

Presided over by the emperor, attended by over five hundred prelates and theologians as well as by princes and nobles, voting by 'nations', and sitting until 1418, the Council of Constance became inescapably a clearing house for secular as well as ecclesiastical diplomacy, insofar as these were separable. The English delegation or 'nation' – very much a royal delegation – comprised the bishops of Bath and Wells (Bubwith), Salisbury (Hallum) and St Davids (Catterick); the abbots of Westminster and St Mary's, York, and the prior of Worcester; the earl of Warwick, Lord FitzHugh, Sir Walter Hungerford and Sir Ralph Rochford; and lastly the king's protonotary, Dr John Hovingham. All were intent on ending the schism, and while the clerics concentrated particularly upon reforms, the laymen were eager to negotiate an alliance with the emperor against France. An Anglo–Imperial treaty was signed at Canterbury in 1416 but the problem for Henry thereafter was to prise Sigismund away from Constance and get him on campaign. It was for this reason that on 18 July 1417, as the proceedings to depose John XXIII were approaching their conclusion, Henry V ordered his subjects at Constance to act with unity on his commands or to return home and answer for their disobedience.[45] Whereas hitherto the English 'nation' had favoured and promoted the introduction of reforms before proceeding to elect a new pope, it was now ordered to secure a papal election first, which the cardinals and the Latins were already advocating. Shortly afterwards Bishop Beaufort arrived, ostensibly on pilgrimage but actually to reconcile Sigismund to the English *volte face* and to an urgent election. This took place in November when Odo Colonna became Martin V. So sudden and effective a change of direction by the English delegation is eloquent testimony, as indeed is his letter, of Henry's priorities and of his vigorous and firm control of clergy and policies.

The reforming measures, which had previously been discussed by special committees of the council, were now implemented by individual concordats between pope and kings. With the triumph of the conservatives who looked to the pope rather than the council as a source of reforms, it was too much to hope that all the proposals so optimistically drafted by Oxford academics in 1414 would survive into the English Concordat of 1418.[46] This, indeed, like others concluded by Martin, was largely confined to uncontroversial matters, abuses which had justly aroused general criticism, such as dispensations for pluralism (which were now to be reserved principally for nobles and scholars) and licences for appropriations (which were now conditional upon episcopal enquiry and consent). The issues which pre-eminently affected royal–papal relations, that is provisions and taxation, were omitted, but then they were raised not long afterwards by the pope himself.

Martin proved to be an unexpectedly forceful pope, intent upon recovering as much as he could of the papal plenitude of power, especially with regard to finance. In England he pressed for the restrictions on provisions and papal taxation to be lifted and, with this clearly implied, in December 1417 and barely a month after his own election, he appointed Bishop Beaufort of Winchester a cardinal and legate *a latere* to England for life.[47] In fact, this was an extremely maladroit move which, had he known more of England or pondered a while upon Chichele's earlier appointment to Canterbury, he might have avoided. As Chichele was quick to complain to the king, legates *a latere* (or papal plenipotentiaries) had never before been appointed for life or, indeed, at all without great and notable cause; their powers rivalled and in some affairs superseded an archbishop's, and Chichele was doubly affronted by such a legate who was also one of his suffragans. Normally, the cardinalate entailed the resignation of other bishoprics, but in Beaufort's case the pope had licensed him to continue holding Winchester. Henry was no less offended than Chichele by the pope's move, and after making clear to Martin the unwelcome advent of a legate *a latere* and impounding the bulls of appointment, he threatened Beaufort with the penalties of the statute of Provisors if he continued to hold Winchester. In the end Beaufort was allowed to remain as bishop of Winchester (whence he derived the highest episcopal income in Britain) in return for abandoning any legatine authority and for a vast loan to the king. In the course of the affair Henry remarked to the duke of Gloucester that 'he had as lief set his crown beside him as see him [Beaufort] wear a cardinal's hat'.[48] Thus ended Martin's first step towards the repeal of the statute of Provisors, which as recently as 1416 had been reaffirmed in parliament. When in 1421 the papal collector, Simon da Teramo, approached convocation on this subject he was redirected to the king who promised to raise it in parliament when he returned from France. It was not done, and it is exceedingly unlikely that parliament would have responded favourably or that Henry even imagined or expected that it would.

Da Teramo was also authorized by Martin to collect payments of procurations overdue to the papacy, a task so beset with frustration that it can hardly have encouraged hopes of resuming papal taxes. Such a move would have strained relations with Henry still further at a time when he himself was only just managing to get all he needed from his subjects, and Martin wisely postponed any approach on this to Henry V.

The king's decisive repulse of Martin's endeavours and his expedient referal of Provisors to consideration by parliament – in effect, to the Greek Kalends – are as impressive as his distrust, humiliation and exploitation of Bishop Beaufort. Henry had very clear objectives and he pursued them with swift and calculated vigour, whether he was routing lollards, nobles, the French, a council, a bishop or a pope. Yet his exercise of power was never impetuous and can seldom be called cynical. He avoided a blood-bath and chronic resentment after the Oldcastle rising by his skilfully arranged pardons; he was judicious though not disinterested – no king dared be – in his episcopal appointments; he frustrated the pope by reference to the law and the estates of the realm; he allowed the overweening and over-wealthy bishop of Winchester to buy his way back to favour. If Henry exploited the liturgy and litany of the church to unite the nation in support of his war, he could at worst be accused of self-deceiving sincerity and not of detached or cynical manipulation, for he was as passionate a believer in the power of prayer as he was in the faith and doctrines of the church. Only at Constance, in church affairs at least, can he be charged with sacrificing principle to expediency, and yet in such an assembly the priority which some conceded to reform before election smacked of ineffective idealism, nor did the election preclude some necessary reforms; that council can no longer be condemned for the deficiencies of the fifteenth-century church. If Henry V's conscience, rather like Henry VIII's, accommodatingly confirmed his own changing needs, this was an aspect of his strength and resolution as a ruler: no self-doubt, no self-distancing, no humour even, gnawed at his confidence or hinted at his flaws, or encouraged others to do so. Intelligent, devout, cultivated, responsible, demanding, steadfast and successful, all these virtues shine through his reign and his deeds: the men, not least the bishops and churchmen upon whom he relied, bear witness to these qualities and to his judgement of men. His mastery of affairs and men is so plainly visible in ecclesiastical politics that one recent historian has described him as 'in all but name . . . the supreme governor of the Church of England',[49] and one basis of that supremacy was his role as defender of the faith.

Henry VI (1422–61)
Advance and Retreat

There can be no greater contrast than that between Henry V and his son Henry VI: the one all positive resolve and brilliant success; the other marked by vacillation and resounding failure. Few reigns in English history have been more disastrous than Henry VI's. With rare exceptions, failures rather than successes marked the progress of the years from 1422, when Henry, a mere nine months old, succeeded his father, until 1461 when he was driven from the throne by Edward, duke of York. Yet not all the responsibility should be heaped upon the king. Some of the troubles resulted from the legacy which his father left him: extravagant bequests, an exhausted people, a government divided among ambitious uncles, and above all a war in France the prolongation of which entailed crushing economic problems just as the conclusion of it would incur political ones, so that war with profit and peace with honour were equally impossible. Efforts to convert the terms of the Treaty of Troyes into reality committed the crown to expenditure and debts which seriously jeopardized its authority and the order of the nation. Problems were compounded by the long minority: it accustomed the nobility and others to factionalism and opportunism which they were reluctant to abandon when the young king came of age. Other difficulties were consequent upon the king's ill-health in 1453–5, while his failure to produce an heir until October 1453 further aggravated his insecurity. Unfortunately, Henry was more than usually ill-equipped by character and temperament to cope with such challenges. Deriving his piety from his father, the young king inherited the emotional instability of his French grandfather and turned out to be so irresolute as to earn the contempt of his subjects. Even Pope Nicholas V wrote in some anger in 1450 to remind him that constancy of purpose was an essential quality of kingship.[1] Ten years later Pope Pius II, though perhaps influenced by the Yorkists, spoke of Henry as 'a man more timorous than a woman, utterly devoid of wit and spirit'.[2] The vacuum at the centre of political affairs in the realm was filled in the 1450s by Henry's French queen, Margaret of Anjou. He had married her in 1445 at the price of surrendering the strategic county of Maine to the French, an act which provoked as much outrage in most Englishmen as did her later vigorous intervention in internal politics. Only a change of dynasty resolved these problems, but nearly forty years elapsed after the death of Henry V before this resolution occurred. Over the daunting hiatus reigned the luckless Henry VI.

The consequences of all this for government and society necessarily encompassed the church and churchmen, some of whom were deeply involved in the politics of the time. Yet by no means all significant developments in church–realm relations during this reign can be linked to its sensational instability.

The Era of Bishop Beaufort, 1422–47

(i) Politics

During the minority the government of the realm was in the hands of the council, presided over for the most part by Humphrey, duke of Gloucester, uncle of the king and intended by Henry V to exercise the office of regent in England, while John, duke of Bedford, his senior, was to act as regent in France where his military and political abilities would be crucial. This arrangement, however, was soon modified to leave Humphrey with the lesser role of protector, to be ceded to John whenever he was in England; the powers of the protector were so circumscribed that he was in effect little more than the chairman of the council, the composition and procedure of which were laid down, and later qualified yet further, to avert the danger of an uncontrollable protector. All this was scarcely to the liking of Humphrey, of course, but it reflected the concern of Bedford for his own authority in England and the unease shared by Henry V's old councillors about the reliability of Gloucester, whose dash and flamboyance appealed more to the populace than to sage councillors. Moreover, Henry V's plans had allotted no clear role to his own uncle, Henry Beaufort, bishop of Winchester. A son of John of Gaunt and for almost twenty years now a senior bishop of the realm, a man who had served as chancellor under Henry IV and Henry V, and a prelate who had the ear of the pope, Henry Beaufort was unlikely to be content with a modest role in the new reign; apart from any other consideration, there was his substantial financial investment in the Lancastrian regime as well as his powerful Beaufort relatives. The bishop, moreover, had his father's reckless opportunism and meddlesome ambition, perhaps even magnified by consciousness of his illegitimate birth and the patronizing legitimation by his half-brother, Henry IV. In the downgrading of Gloucester's role, Beaufort certainly played an influential part, no doubt for good reasons as well as from jealousy or animosity. For the rest of the minority and beyond, the antagonism between Gloucester and Bishop Beaufort was to be a persistent theme as each exploited the mistakes of the other in order to advance his own political fortunes and policies: in the process both the church and the realm were affected.

Humphrey very soon confirmed the justice of fears about him when in 1423 he married the heiress of Hainault and then in the following year set out to recover her inheritance from her previous husband; since the latter happened to be a vassal of the duke of Burgundy, this move constituted a serious threat to the Burgundian alliance which was crucial to English success in France. While the protector was abroad on this expedition in 1424–5, Bishop Beaufort became chancellor and effective leader of the council and government; when Humphrey returned from his abortive mission a power struggle ensued which led to armed confrontation with Beaufort and necessitated the return of Bedford from France to restore peace. In 1426 Gloucester resumed his office of protector, the council's powers were extended, and Beaufort discreetly accompanied Bedford back to France.

No sooner had the bishop arrived at Calais than he received the red hat which Henry V and Chichele had denied him almost a decade earlier. Martin V appointed him legate at a later stage, but legate to Bohemia, not England, to lead an army against the Hussites. It was in connection with this that he returned to

England in 1427, armed with powers to raise a crusading tenth and army. Predictably Gloucester challenged his cardinalate, or at least the retention of the bishopric of Winchester with it, and sought to charge Beaufort with violation of Provisors. The duke of Bedford, however, was at that time seeking papal approval for his ecclesiastical arrangements in Normandy and he also saw an opportunity to enlist the crusading force to campaign against the Dauphin and Joan of Arc. Gloucester's efforts being thwarted by the council, Beaufort was allowed to raise a reduced army – 250 lancers and 2500 archers instead of the 500 and 5000 of each which he wanted – provided it was first diverted to assist Bedford in France for six months. The crusading tenth was to be voluntary, not mandatory, the gold and silver raised being spent on provisions and equipment in this country, not abroad.[3] Beaufort, therefore, led his force to France and crucially relieved Paris in 1429, whereupon Henry VI was promptly crowned in order to counter the Dauphin's recent coronation at Rheims. With the protectorate ended by Henry's coronation, Gloucester acted instead as regent in England from April 1430 until February 1432 while Henry stayed in France.

Gloucester seized this opportunity to renew his challenge to Beaufort. Not only had the bishop retained the see of Winchester together with the cardinalate, which was unheard of and against the law and custom of the realm, but he had also – Gloucester learned – secured a papal bull back in 1418 exempting him from the jurisdiction of the archbishop of Canterbury, a flagrant violation, in the regent's view, of the statute of 1402 against such papal exemptions. Moreover, accusations of an offence against *Praemunire* and even of treason were being voiced against the bishop. The council prudently deferred any decision about the charges until the return of the king, to whom Beaufort convincingly avowed his loyalty. Henry VI had no qualms in granting Beaufort the pardon which he sought – perhaps because of a loan of more than £10,000 which the cardinal promised.[4] Opposition to the pardon was no doubt allayed, if not by the loan, by a licence for Beaufort to attend the Council of Basle on business of the church and the realm. For the rest of the decade the cardinal was abroad on diplomatic labours for the crown, first at Basle, then at Tours, striving for the peace. Gloucester meanwhile, particularly after the death of Bedford in 1435, was the dominant voice on the council where policy to a large extent was determined more by him than by the king.

In 1435 at the congress of Arras, presided over by two cardinals, Philip of Burgundy was absolved from his oath to implement the Treaty of Troyes on the grounds that it embodied an act by Charles VI of France which was *ultra vires*, the alienation of his succession; thus equipped, Philip abandoned the English alliance. Without Burgundy's help, the English were facing a bleak future in France, and the following years were spent vacillating between vigorous campaigns, which could be ill afforded, and peace overtures which divided the councillors. Since the direction of the king's influence was predictable only in its unpredictability, neither policy prospered as it should have done, and the loss of France became merely a matter of time.

At a conference near Calais in June 1439 Beaufort negotiated a long-term truce which envisaged the eventual abandonment of English claims to the French crown. Gloucester's unsurprising reaction was to launch yet another attempt to discredit the bishop, this time by producing a lengthy condemnation of his whole career and particularly emphasizing his violations of Provisors.[5] It was in vain, and some time after this the cardinal witnessed and probably engineered a crushing humiliation for Gloucester.[6] Beaufort and Archbishop Kemp of York on their return from the continent had succeeded in ousting Gloucester from the council; soon afterwards, in 1441, his wife Eleanor was indiscreet enough in her astrological associates to attract accusations of witchcraft. It was alleged that she had been trying by necromancy and astrology to discover – which was almost tantamount to plotting – when the king would die, a matter of no small interest to the heir presumptive, her husband. Three of her chaplains when arrested duly implicated her. Archbishop Chichele, together with Beaufort, Kemp and Aiscough (of Salisbury), conducted preliminary enquiries and recommended a formal trial. The bishops of London, Lincoln and Norwich conducted this before the council, where Adam Moleyns acted as prosecutor. Eleanor confessed, abjured, was divorced, condemned and sentenced to life imprisonment, eventually dying still in custody in 1457 in the Isle of Man. She was luckier than some of her chaplains who were executed, the quarters of one of them being distributed among various lollard centres and major towns. Her fate, however, was something of a coup for Gloucester's enemies, since the utmost delicacy of procedure was required to bring down the wife of the senior noble of the realm and the king's chief heir; the care with which the prelates went about their task and the fact that the final proceedings were conducted in the council confirm this. Eleanor, though, had made things easy for them, for she was undoubtedly reckless, notoriously haughty and consequently widely unpopular. Nevertheless, there is no doubt about the justness of the charges and of the sentence; the prelatical examinations were not cynical or manipulated, and their decisions were inescapable on the evidence. Eleanor had transgressed against propriety and orthodoxy in the interest, requested or otherwise, of her husband. Her condemnation effectively ended his political influence over affairs of state, for after it he was a broken man and a suspect one, but such was the popular esteem which he enjoyed that he could not be wholly disregarded by the peace party.

The peace overtures continued, resulting in 1443 in a match between Henry and Margaret of Anjou, which was completed with the marriage in 1445 and the cession of Maine in 1447, both agreements extremely unpopular and both contributing to the final collapse of English rule in France. The peace moves were supported intermittently with military campaigns as futile as they were costly. By 1447, therefore, Gloucester again seemed to pose some threat to his political opponents. The charge of treason which was now laid against him no doubt restored their peace of mind, for it probably precipitated his death. Beaufort, however, was not to prosper, for he too died that year. The rivalry which had separated Duke Humphrey and his uncle, the cardinal, endured in their political heirs, respectively Richard, duke of York, on the one hand, and William, duke of Suffolk with the Beaufort earls of Somerset and Exeter on the other. The departure of Bishop Beaufort, however, did have one considerable effect.

(ii) Finance

The cost of attempting to realize the terms of the Treaty of Troyes burdened the government with enormous debts, which by 1433 were reckoned to stand at £168,000 – two and a half times current annual income! In part they were compounded by the reluctance of clergy and laity alike to contribute to the expensive campaigns of the 1420s: parliament granted no subsidy until 1429, Canterbury convocation none until 1425, York convocation not until 1428. Canterbury refused a grant in 1424 because, it claimed, benefices were too impoverished by previous taxes to attract priests to fill them; four appearances by royal councillors and desperate pleading by the archbishop availed nothing, so that the assembly dissolved after five months without yielding a subsidy at all. The next convocation lasted from April to July 1425 with repeated adjournments and refused a grant until the very end when a half tenth was conceded, but with substantial exemptions. A much briefer assembly in 1426, which also authorized only a half tenth, was followed by another protracted meeting from July 1428 to December 1429, when, after prolonged debates and urgent appeals from royal councillors, a further tenth was added to the previous grant. Before the end of the minority, convocation proffered three and a quarter tenths, but the grant in the critical year of 1433 was achieved only with the greatest difficulty.[7] York convocation made no grant until 1428 and no more until 1433 (a quarter of a tenth – a mere few hundred pounds) and 1436 (two half tenths, one to be collected in 1437, the other in 1438).[8] By the end of the minority the clergy had contributed some £83,000 in subsidies while direct lay taxation amounted to about £209,000.

The government tried to enlarge the income from both lay and clerical taxes by various devices, few of them novel. The laity were confronted by an income tax as well as a poll tax; the clergy were pressed into conceding levies from chaplains in 1429 and 1435, in 1435 from those unassessed in the 1291 valuation, and later, in 1449, from those normally exempt. But these were all desperate measures which could only be employed occasionally and were rarely worth the trouble and odium which they provoked; they did little to bridge the gap between the crown's immediate commitments and its pitifully inadequate income.

One earlier solution to this dilemma was ruled out by the middle of the fourteenth century. When Edward III reneged on his debts

to his Italian bankers, the Bardi followed the Riccardi, who had
suffered similarly under Edward I, into bankruptcy and it was a
long time before the Italians were again prepared to risk their
capital on such a scale with English kings, not indeed until the
Yorkists ascended the throne. Of necessity the gap was filled by
indigenous lenders to the crown – merchants, traders, nobles and
prelates. By Richard II's reign increasing need led the crown to
request loans – or benevolences – from individuals, groups and
communities, among whom were the clergy. Whereas under
Richard the clergy altogether lent little more than £1000 a year
(barely a sixteenth of the total raised in loans by the crown then),
under Henry VI these levels soared: in the first decade of his reign
bishops alone lent nearly £6000 a year on average, in the second
decade this had almost doubled, but in the next two decades it
declined to around £4500 and £1100 respectively. The lesser
clergy and religious contributed in aggregate annually much less
than the bishops, yielding per annum only some £680 in the 1430s
and around £790 in the 1450s, for example.[9] Three points need to
be noted: first, the clerical loans had risen as a proportion of the
total quite markedly, from barely a sixteenth under Richard II to
nearly a third in the 1420s, over a quarter in the 1430s, a sixth in
the 1440s and a twelfth in the 1450s. Secondly, episcopal
contributions were immensely swollen under Henry VI by the
advances from Cardinal Beaufort, who in the 1430s lent £91,000 of
the clerical total of £110,000, and in the 1440s £25,000 out of
£45,000. On three occasions he advanced sums of £20,000 and was
rarely owed less than £20,000 by the monarch. The estates of the
bishopric of Winchester were an obvious source of Beaufort's
funds, but added to these were numerous grants from all three
Lancastrian kings of wardships, marriages, estates and lucrative
offices; furthermore, his own deals netted him additional
property, plate and jewels. He was just one of several magnates in
this reign who at some time held the crown jewels, or some of
them, as security for loans.[10] The scale of Beaufort's lending in the
1430s is underlined when it is learned that only Archbishop
Chichele even approached his total; yet Chichele lent a mere
£14,000 and only one other prelate, Lacy of Exeter, advanced
more than £1000. In the 1440s Kemp of York advanced £2000,

Aiscough of Salisbury £1600, Archbishop Stafford no more than £833. Nor did any lay magnate approach the cardinal's figures. Nevertheless, his liberality was not always voluntary. The crown repaid loans from the customs and from lay and clerical subsidies; although through his influence on the council, Beaufort could usually claim priority of assignments, occasionally circumstances – especially when manipulated by Gloucester – forced him, as in 1432, to lend still more in order to elude his political enemies and ensure the repayment of earlier advances. Most of the time there was political as well as financial profit for the cardinal from these loans. If, apart from him, the church was no eager backer of government policies, neither were most of the laity. There is no ground here, therefore, to construct some theory of discontent, or opposition, peculiarly clerical; like many laymen, the clergy were sceptical of pouring money into an increasingly unpromising war, especially when repayment was often late and incomplete.

(iii) Papacy
It was evident in 1417, when Martin V prematurely appointed Beaufort cardinal and legate *a latere*, that the pope regarded the bishop as a key agent in the reassertion of papal authority over the English church, particularly with regard to provisions and taxation. On that occasion, however, Henry V had effectively thwarted such plans by compelling Beaufort to renounce the red hat and the legateship. The question of provisions was referred by the king to a forthcoming parliament, which – though Martin failed to realize this – was a polite refusal. Papal taxation Martin either did not have time to raise with Henry V or dared not. The death of Henry, therefore, and the succession of a minor in whose government bishops, and especially Beaufort, might be expected to wield considerable influence must have encouraged new hopes in Martin. That he exploited provisions in the early 1420s in order to build up a papalist party among the prelates has been argued but not proven; what he certainly did was to make Beaufort a cardinal in 1426 and a legate, albeit this time to Bohemia, not England.[11] Ironically, this move could only make Beaufort's voice less effective in England.

Objections to Beaufort's appointments came predictably from

Gloucester and from Archbishop Chichele. Gloucester based his opposition on the retention of an English bishopric with a Roman cardinalate, pluralism for which there was no precedent in England and which Henry V had impugned. Chichele raised objections, as in 1417, not from any personal animus, we may believe, nor from antipapalism, but out of a keen regard for the constitutional position of the archbishopric in the English church. Not very long had passed since the chronic dispute between Canterbury and York about their respective precedence and authority had been laid to rest; no holder of Canterbury would welcome a fresh challenge from, of all sources, his suffragan in Winchester. His opposition now, and his offence to Martin over Becket's jubilee a few years before, provoked papal suspension of his *ex officio* legatine powers (more ceremonial than those of a legate *a latere*). By this means Martin cowed Chichele into an appeal to parliament for the annulment of the statutes against provisions. In the company of Archbishop Kemp of York, Chichele tearfully led the bishops' plea to the commons to revoke the antipapal legislation. It availed nothing in that cause, but the effort won from Martin full restoration of Chichele's authority. [12]

This was the last serious attempt by any pope to reverse measures which had substantially reduced papal patronage and, still more significantly, papal revenues. Eugenius IV, who succeeded Martin in 1431, was soon threatened not only by the shadow of a general council at Basle – it claimed to have suspended him in 1438 and to have deposed him in 1439 – but also by the approaching tide of Ottoman Turks before his death in 1447; none of his immediate successors before 1461 could afford the luxury of an uncompromising policy on Provisors. In the whole of his pontificate Eugenius successfully effected only eleven provisions apart from episcopal appointments, and in 1434 he was urging, not ordering, Bishop Grey of Lincoln to admit a papal providee to the archdeaconry of Nottingham; from 1458 to 1464 Pius II could boast of only four successes. [13] One consequence of all this was that annates (or the first year's fruits of a benefice) which had been levied since 1326 from providees below the rank of abbot or bishop now produced only a pitiful sum. Of course, episcopal appointments continued to be invariably affected by papal provisions, and in a year of several vacancies the papacy gained substantially from the services which were due. Thus in 1424 services produced over 10,000 florins, in 1425 nearly 22,000, and in 1426 just over 19,000, in 1452 no less than 38,867. On average, throughout Henry VI's reign almost 8000 florins per annum resulted from the levy of services.[14]

So far as the personnel of the episcopate was concerned, the pope had by no means a free hand, but had to negotiate, contrive, conspire and often concede. In 1414 when Martin translated Bishop Fleming from Lincoln to York, Fleming was forced to renounce the move or face the penalties of Provisors; Martin reluctantly acquiesced.[15] Three years later, when the pope ignored the capitular election at Salisbury and provided instead Beaufort's nephew, Robert Neville, he succeeded because the council favoured Neville too.[16] When in 1433 Thomas Brouns was provided by Eugenius to Worcester against the government's wishes, he received a royal letter, endorsed by the council, reminding him that he might not accept provision to Worcester 'nor obtain it by the laws of our land without our assent first had thereupon'. Brouns was ordered to certify the pope and king immediately of his intentions in this matter. Nine days later the council endorsed a royal letter to Eugenius recommending Bourgchier to Worcester and Brouns to Rochester, moves which were papally confirmed only in the spring of 1435.[17] A few years afterwards, Bourgchier was elected by the chapter and provided by the pope to Ely but he was frustrated by the council which forced through the appointment of Louis, archbishop of Rouen, who was to hold Ely *in commendam* with Rouen until his death in 1443, when Bourgchier was at last translated there.[18] Royal decisions about bishoprics were questions more of deciding priorities than principles. In practice no bishop in this period was provided in the teeth of royal (or conciliar) opposition, and few royal candidates were for long disregarded by Martin V or his successors. For the most part the government shrewdly sought candidates acceptable to the pope, but they were overwhelmingly men who justified their promotion by previous or later service to the crown. The irrelevance of the chapters in all this is nowhere more eloquently illustrated than at Durham in 1438.[19] R. B.

Dobson has revealed in detail the solemn farce whereby the chapter, on receipt of the king's *congé d'élire* containing the nomination of Robert Neville, proceeded by way of 'compromise' – in effect, appointment by a committee – but this time by a committee of one, the prior. He formally consulted some senior members and then announced the name of Neville, whereupon the chapter sought Neville's consent and the king's approval. The pope's acquiescence was already assumed.

As in the matter of provisions, so with Martin V's attempts to revive papal taxation of the English clergy, Beaufort's papalism and influence in England were unavailing. Martin's imposition in 1427 of a mandatory tenth for Beaufort's crusade against the Hussites met with prevarication from the clergy in convocation and a veto from the council acting in accordance with the statute of 1388.[20] The proceeds of indulgences which the council did permit for the crusade were subsequently employed to defray the costs of Beaufort's expedition to France.

In 1444 when the pope next demanded a mandatory tenth for a crusade, this time against the advancing Turks, the bishops of the southern province proposed a free-will offering which was to be considered in diocesan synods (even archidiaconal synods in London diocese) lest a meeting of convocation attract royal demands for a subsidy. The response was reluctant where it was not negative. York convocation, which did meet, voted *2d* in the pound – more than the southern bishops suggested, far less than the pope ordered. In the end little more than £1000 (barely one eighteenth of a tenth) was collected and that very slowly despite papal mandates and deadlines. When in November 1446 the king barred its onward transmission, three years had been vainly consumed by the pontiff's efforts.[21] Even after the fall of Constantinople in 1453 English resistance to papal taxation did not waver, as we shall see below.

Lollardy

Although the failure of Oldcastle's rebellion was critically decisive for lollard fortunes, this was not so apparent to contemporaries, and during the 1420s much effort was expended to contain a threat which was soon heightened by the progress of the Hussites in Bohemia. Convocation was busy hearing heresy cases in 1425–6; Bishop Fleming founded Lincoln College, Oxford, in the 1420s to train theologians in order to combat heresy; Nicholas Love, prior of Mount Grace Charterhouse, adapted an earlier devotional work, *The Mirror of the Blessed Life of Christ*, to satisfy the needs of simple folk for a knowledge of Christ; and Thomas Netter, Carmelite friar, brought to a conclusion his three-volume history and documentation of Wycliffism and lollardy. While the first two works were evangelical, Netter's was combative and repressive, and his volumes were presented by instalments to the pope in the years 1426–8.[22] In response to Netter's prompting and to Hussite triumphs, Martin V in December 1427 ordered the English bishops to publicize the Council of Constance's condemnation of Wyclif, the public burning of his bones and the scattering of his ashes. These alarms were echoed in convocation in the summer of 1428 which gave lengthy consideration to more effective legal procedures against heretics. At that time a large-scale lollard conspiracy, centred on Kent chiefly around Tenterden, was forestalled. However, this success only drove proselytizing fugitives into East Anglia, where during 1428–30 lollard activists, schools and cells were detected over an area which extended from Loddon and Ditchingham to Colchester and Chelmsford, and from Martham to Beccles. Altogether some 120 were prosecuted and many more implicated. A key figure, the priest William White, who had abjured before convocation in 1422, resumed his mission in East Anglia, attacking friars, the sacraments and the clergy's temporal possessions.[23] Clearly lollardy was not dead, even without aristocratic and academic support, and the ecclesiastical authorities could take no chances that it was. Indeed, when an infant king could give no lead and rivalries among the leaders of the government might induce further political-heretical rebellion, the church in England had no need of papal letters to stir it into vigilance and vigour. The heresy trials in Norwich diocese reveal both the hidden extent of dissent and the urgent concern of the church.

In 1431 a plot, led by William Perkins, was uncovered; it was based in Abingdon but had links in London and Salisbury. Meetings of the conspirators in London and distribution of seditious pamphlets in Oxford, Coventry, Northampton and Frome took place in the spring; in May overt attacks were made on Salisbury cathedral and Abingdon abbey, but the authorities, forewarned of trouble, soon dispersed the rebels and extinguished their hopes. It was alleged that they had planned to disendow the church after having removed such obstacles as the monarchy, the prelates and the secular lords; the hope was that 20,000 insurgents would gather in the village of East Hendred (Berkshire) and then proceed to seize the royal uncles, nine abbots and three priors, the dukes of Norfolk and York, and the earl of Huntingdon. None of this occurred and after investigation by a commission only thirty-eight were executed – thirty-one of them for treason, seven solely for heresy. Most of them were artisans – weavers, dyers, fullers – none was a gentleman or a priest or a graduate. It is true that three gentry including Sir John and Sir Thomas Cheyne were accused but their involvement was dubious and they escaped capital punishment. The rising itself by its extravagant plans and hopes betrays wild and reckless delusions rather than any substantial threat to church or realm. Although it had several centres and some distribution of propaganda, it lacked anything like the force of mind and character of the 1402 Franciscan plot, for example. No other heretical rising of any size or note occurred after the Perkins fiasco, but lollards continued to be discovered over their bibles and tracts throughout the fifteenth century, and the public were reminded of the threat which they posed by a steady trickle of public burnings for the rest of our period.

A measure of the panic provoked by heresy was afforded when in 1456–7 Reginald Pecock, bishop of Chichester, was tried for his unorthodox writings, for their whole purpose was to rout lollardy.[24] A graduate of Oxford University in Henry V's reign and an academic for some years after that, Pecock wrote numerous books to counter the lollards. Probably in recognition of this work, he was in 1444 promoted to the impoverished see of St Asaph's by Suffolk's influence, and in 1456 he succeeded the murdered Moleyns at Chichester. He was clearly one of the Suffolk party bishops along with Aiscough, Moleyns, Booth, Lumley and

Lyhert, so that when the political tide turned he was certainly vulnerable. What made him even more exposed was his cleverness coupled with his arrogance. His writings were in English, directed at the expanding literate laity; in an attempt to outflank the crude scepticism of the lollards, his arguments trusted more to reason than to the citation of authorities; and in his pursuit of rationalism he conceded in theory positions which outraged and alarmed his episcopal colleagues and others. In 1457, however, he attracted suspicions of unorthodoxy and on the authority of the king's council Archbishop Bourgchier set up a panel of twenty-four assessors who duly found the suspicions justified and reported back to the council in November 1457. Pecock abjured, his books were burnt (with the result that few of them are extant today), and he was suspended from office and imprisoned in Thorney abbey. When, however, he obtained papal absolution in 1458, his enemies charged him with violating *Praemunire* and forced the king to set up a new investigation of his works and acts; this found that he had violated not only orthodoxy but also the law of the realm (*Praemunire* perhaps, but the heresy laws too were no doubt in mind here) and he was induced to resign his see in the autumn of 1458 and retire to the abbey of Thorney, where he died *circa* 1461. This episode, in which a daring, able and well-meaning thinker was brought low by earnest, perhaps partial and doubtless plodding enemies, has little to do with politics for all that the council was involved and *Praemunire* invoked. The alarm against Pecock was raised well after the downfall of his patron, Suffolk. That it was raised also years after most of the offensive material had been written and circulated suggests malice and ulterior motives; yet the man who started the hue and cry against Pecock was Viscount Beaumont, a Lancastrian supporter, and Pecock's successor at Chichester was no Yorkist but the king's physician, John Arundel. The involvement of the council was unremarkable when the accused was a bishop of the realm; moreover, the council's role in heresy hunting dates back to Richard II's reign. The allegation that Pecock had violated *Praemunire* by his appeal to the pope was, by this time in the century, almost the least notable feature of the Pecock affair. As for the final verdict that he had violated orthodoxy and the law of the realm, either it refers to

the statutes concerning lollardy or it simply refers to the Premunire charge. The significance of Pecock's downfall lies in a
different sphere. That a man who was sincerely orthodox though
occasionally indiscreet and contemplated aloud what was unthin-
kable to others, who made an imaginative and enterprising attempt
to appeal to the laity in their own vernacular on theological matters
and to rout the arguments of the lollards with better and fuller
logic, that such a man was subdued, humiliated, disgraced and
deprived is a revealing commentary upon his fellows. More than
this, it stifled any subsequent attempts to enlarge the layman's
theological knowledge and deepen and consolidate his grasp of
orthodox doctrine: the restrictions and suspicions placed upon the
bible in English were now coupled with an equally stultifying
absence of vernacular theological writing to inform parish clergy
and literate parishioner alike. The church failed to recognize that
in the wake of literacy came intelligent scepticism and criticism
which could hardly be satisfied with the homiletic diet purveyed
by John Mirk's sermons or by the *Golden Legend*, or even with a
simple catechism or list of the articles of faith, all of which were
fairly commonly available. When Protestantism arrived in
England in the early sixteenth century, it encountered remarkably
crude and shallow defences, and those who accused and condemned Pecock share the responsibility for this with Arundel and
others.

Church and Government

(i) Clergy Supplanted

The public for whom Pecock wrote was educated at the multiplying schools, the expanding inns of court and chancery, or the
developing universities of Lancastrian England. Of all these,
arguably the most significant were the lawyers' inns. According to
Sir John Fortescue, writing in the 1460s, the four inns of court and
the ten inns of chancery equipped a very substantial number of
laymen with a training in common law and a liberal and social
education: each chancery inn comprised at least a hundred
students, and each of the senior four inns of court at least two

hundred, so that a total of around 2000 or more is implied.[25] It was a world in which laymen now were not only attending but ever more frequently founding schools, whose teachers, by the way, were often laymen. The demand for books was met in London by the scrivener John Shirley who ran what amounted to the first circulating library, while in Bristol and Worcester Bishop Carpenter established public reference libraries, albeit theological and primarily for the clergy. From the fifteenth century survive the first substantial collections of vernacular correspondence – the family papers and letters of the Norfolk gentry and lawyer Pastons, the business papers of the wool-trading Celys from Northleach and London. By the middle of the century English was increasingly challenging Latin as the language of wills and had already supplanted French in the proceedings of the court of chancery. Beyond those who could read were those who gathered round them – as in the 1920s people clustered round the early wireless sets – to listen: not only lollards hearing the scriptures, but a pious and raucous widow from King's Lynn, Margery Kempe, listening to her chaplain read from Bonaventura, St Bridget, Richard Rolle, Walter Hilton and more. It was no longer just the clergy who were informed and articulate. The audience and readers of William Langland were no isolated or passing phenomenon, as all those Wycliffite tracts and bibles sufficiently bear witness. Perhaps a consequence, undoubtedly a contemporaneous feature, was the shortage of recruits to the clergy in the opening decades of the century. Demographic constraints may have played some part in this, for certainly later in the century clerical recruitment recovered and reached levels previously unmatched. But R. L. Storey, who first exposed the recession, tentatively related it to the discouraging anticlerical atmosphere which prevailed then; possibly the prestige of the clergy was eroded as much by the loss of their earlier monopoly of literacy as by hostile criticism.[26] Yet whatever the cause, not only were fewer ordinands coming forward in the early fifteenth century, but increasing numbers of those who took minor orders turned their backs on the major orders (which would have committed them to a clerical life) and preferred to marry and establish a family. All this had repercussions for secular government as well as for the church.

In this period the personnel of chancery numbered something over a hundred: twelve masters, twelve secondary clerks, twenty-four cursitors (who worked only on the simplest of documents) and numerous writing clerks (who have been compared to a modern typing pool).[27] When some ordinances for the office were published in 1388, these men were overwhelmingly clergy, yet by 1461 they were predominantly laymen. This transformation occurred during the reign of Henry VI, although the regulations of 1388, and their repetition by Henry V, imply that already the clerical ice was beginning to crack, for they insisted on a minimum number of unmarried men in chancery employment. In Henry V's time five married clerks were permitted, but by the 1430s and 1440s this number had been far exceeded. By then many clerks who had entered the king's service in minor orders and been rewarded with ecclesiastical perquisites were opting instead to abandon clerical pretensions or ambitions in order to marry. One of the most remarkable of these was Thomas Haseley who entered chancery in Henry IV's reign. He was remunerated with a succession of benefices, which included a church, two chapels and a prebend; and yet by 1421 was calling himself 'esquire' and in the 1430s was sustained with grants of lands and annuities; by 1437 he was married with three children; at his death in 1449 he was a knight, under-marshal of England, JP for Middlesex, and a clerk of the crown in chancery! Among his colleagues in chancery were not only clergy who, like himself, had shunned holy orders and sought marriage, but an increasing number of other clerks who had entered chancery as laymen and were remunerated from the beginning of their service with lay offices, such as a customership of the port of Boston, or the constableship of Salisbury castle, for example. By the middle of the century many of the hundred or so chancery clerks styled themselves gentlemen.[28]

What was happening in chancery was matched and even slightly anticipated in other sections of the royal administration. Whereas at the opening of the fifteenth century all the major positions in the exchequer, the king's household and chamber, as well as the keepership of the great wardrobe and the clerkship of works were held by beneficed clergy, already by 1413 some of the holders were laymen, and by 1430 clergy were the exception. The five clerks of the privy seal office were all laymen by the 1440s. Even the Duchy of Lancaster's administration was changed similarly under Henry VI.[29] The signet office which served the king's private, or secret, seal was staffed almost wholly by clerics before it lapsed for Henry VI's minority; after its revival in 1437 its clerks were with rare exceptions laymen.[30]

It must be said that the principal offices in all the departments of government except the exchequer remained predominantly clerical, but that is partly explained by the fact that they were also graduates who were clearly recruited for their general or legal expertise. There was in fact an increasing separation between the clerical-graduate heads of departments and their lay staff.

The reasons for this development are complex. While it may certainly be that the anticlerical ethos deterred some men from taking holy orders and seduced others into affirming the legitimacy and attractions of married life, it is somewhat difficult to reconcile the chronology of major change with the peak of lollardy and anticlericalism. Moreover, when in the later part of the century ordinands abound, there are no signs of a reversion to clerical manning of the departments of state. It seems unlikely, too, that official policy provides an explanation, for a hard-pressed crown was put under even more financial pressure when it had to find annuities and remunerative offices, instead of church benefices, for its bureaucrats. Moreover, from the middle of the century even monastic and episcopal estate administration was being entrusted to laymen rather than to clerics.[31] Undoubtedly the availability of literate and well-schooled laity made the change possible, but the impetus must be sought elsewhere. It may have resulted from the genuine concern, expressed in a parliamentary petition in 1425, about the connection between absentee incumbents whose neglect exposed their parishioners to the lollard seductions.[32] This was a viewpoint which was bound to appeal to the prelates of the council during the minority of Henry VI and perhaps to the young king himself on his majority. Certainly as a consequence of the changes, not only did ordained clerks preoccupied with secular administration become rarer in the parishes, but also major offices of responsibility in cathedral chapters reverted to full-time residents: those lavish rewards prized by civil servants in the fourteenth century, the deanship and treasurership of York Minster, from the 1430s were more usually held by residents.[33] No longer were these and other dignities, together with innumerable parish livings, so commonly the subject of the acquisitive attentions of royal clerks with all the demoralizing and alienating consequences which flowed from that. If, as a result of these changes, the crown found its lay patronage put under ever-increasing strain, it no longer needed to subject the church to the remorseless exploitation which had characterized the government of the first three Edwards. The decline of friction was marked by a decline in the use of those resented writs of prohibition and of *quare non admisit*.

All of this was a mixed blessing for the church. Indisputably religion and the pastoral mission must have profited from the change; perhaps even the upsurge of clerical recruitment, which was a feature of the second half of the century, may have owed something to the increasing perception that the church in the parishes was not just another branch of the civil service. On the other hand the church's representation in the corridors of power was declining; this, of course, was not true of the major offices of state – even the treasurer was a cleric from time to time – but the ministers' office staffs now represented the voices and views of laymen. More than all this, in a vital area of government where the clergy had long enjoyed a virtual monopoly and provided almost exclusively an indispensable service, it was no longer doing so: a fundamental shift towards a secular government manned and shaped by laymen was taking place.

This change was reflected at a more elevated level by the almost complete absence of political theorizing by ecclesiastical writers in England after 1400. Such a remarkable indifference by the clergy to the nature of the polity in which they existed has been explained by reference to various factors – an unthreatening king, a perilous uncertainty about governing regimes, the growth of a lay-vernacular reading public.[34] There was no Ockham or Wyclif to advocate royal authority and priority, and no cleric took up the implications of usurpation or deposition for church and realm. Whatever were the reasons for it, this theoretical vacuum underlined the radical change observable at more mundane levels of government.

(ii) Clergy Promoted: Clerical Diplomats

This laicization of government was certainly masked to some
extent by the increasingly prominent role of bishops in the
Lancastrian scheme of things, in France as well as in England. As
under Henry V, many bishops served the crown in France before
and after their promotion: Beaufort and Kemp are obvious and
well-known examples. In 1430 Stafford, of Bath and Wells, and
Morgan, of Ely, earned themselves 700 marks each for accompanying the king to France as members of his council there; along
with them, as Henry's chaplains, went Master Richard Praty and
John Carpenter, respectively promoted to Chichester in 1438 and
Worcester in 1444. In 1442 William Lyndwood, better known
today for his canon law treatise *Provinciale*, who had served on the
king's council in France back in 1423, obtained the see of St
Davids, having been keeper of the privy seal since 1432.[35]

But apart from engagement in the government of English
France, many bishops and potential bishops were busy, especially
during the 1430s and 1440s, in the almost constant diplomacy
which war and peace efforts necessitated. The bishop of London,
William Gray, and Dr John Stokes, a lawyer, set off on an embassy
in 1428; Kemp, archbishop of York, was frequently abroad on
royal business and absent from his diocese in consequence, though
less notoriously so than was once believed; Beckington was
another frequently called upon for diplomatic services, as to
Guyenne in 1444; Moleyns of Chichester was a key negotiator of
the Anjou marriage and then of the cession of Maine.[36] Vivid and
not untypical evidence of the diplomatic employment of prelates
and senior clergy comes from November 1430; William Alnwick,
bishop of Norwich, and Dr William Lyndwood were among those
sent to treat for peace with emissaries from Castile and Leon; Dr
John Gentill negotiated at Bayonne with the ambassadors of
Aragon and Navarre, Dr John Stokes went on a mission to
Scotland, Dr William Sprever to Denmark and the Hanse towns,
and Master William Swan to the emperor.[37]

What was indisputably required of great embassies and at high
negotiations was ostentation. When Cardinal Beaufort joined the
peace conference near Calais in 1439 his tent, built of timber frame
covered with new canvas, was more than 100 feet in length,

encompassing a pantry, butlery, wine cellar, two chambers, a hall
– covered and lined with scarlet tapestries – which was large
enough to seat 300 people at table, and a kitchen. Nearby stood
'suitable' (*honesta*) tents for the archbishop of York, the bishops of
Norwich and St Davids, the duke of Norfolk, the earls of Stafford
and Oxford, and others.[38] It was for the purposes of diplomatic
prestige that Henry VI, disregarding earlier prejudices and
suspicions, in 1439 sought a cardinalate for Archbishop Kemp of
York. Kemp, in fact, was among the third batch of cardinals to be
promoted by Eugenius IV; when they were so prominent in
international councils and conferences of the 1430s, Henry VI saw
the wisdom of joining this bandwagon. Writing to thank the pope
for the speed of the promotion, the king remarked that it would
add greatly to the archbishop's influence when negotiating peace
with the French. Nevertheless, Kemp had hesitated to accept until
Henry persuaded him to keep his see and defy Chichele's
displeasure.[39]

Clerics, usually graduates, drawn from ecclesiastical administration or from royal service, sustained by benefices and
prebends, rewarded often with bishoprics and ministerial office,
had, of course, long been an important element in diplomatic
negotiations throughout our period, occasionally dominating
missions by their numbers, or by leading them, and bringing to the
business much-needed expertise in law and Latin. It has been
calculated that from 1327 to 1461 clerics were present on 491 (or 78
per cent) out of the 629 embassies sent to negotiate with European
princes, led almost half (48 per cent) of the total, and constituted a
majority of the delegation on 141 occasions (or 22 per cent of the
total).[40] From the start of Henry VI's reign that numerical role was
quite significantly increased, fewer missions than ever before
venturing abroad without a clerical component. Up to 1413 74 per
cent of diplomatic missions had clerics on them; during Henry V's
reign that figure rose to 87 per cent, under Henry VI to 93 per cent,
and whereas in previous reigns no more than 35 per cent had a
clerical majority, under Henry VI the percentage rose to 48.
Under Henry VI 69 per cent were led by clerics, compared with an
average of 48 per cent for the whole period from 1327 to 1461.

The explanations for all this are not easy to determine: certainly it is not to be explained by the business of the ecclesiastical councils at Pavia, Siena, Basle and Florence, for the clergy were just as often on missions to kings and princes – ranging from Scotland to Iberia and from Germany to Brittany – as they were on embassies to popes and councils. Nor can it be the work of that pious king, Henry VI, for the increase was evident even in the first years of his reign when he could hardly have influenced such decisions. Indeed, an increase in clerical incidence had already occurred, though not to the same degree, during his father's rule. M. S. Blust, whose researches have provided these figures, speculates that the growth after 1413 springs from the failing French of English lay diplomats who increasingly relied upon English rather than French as their vernacular, so that for international exchanges Latin-speakers became more urgent: hence the clergy. There is certainly some evidence, which she cites, that from 1404 onwards exchanges with the French were to be in Latin, and it is undoubtedly true that English was supplanting French as the vernacular of the English knightly and diplomatic classes. However, this was a slow and uneven process and far from complete by 1422; in fact many Englishmen were enlarging their grasp of French by settling in Normandy then. Moreover, at a time when aristocrats and princes were frequenting universities – in Henry V's case reputedly participating in a Parisian disputation – and when grammar schools were multiplying and the inns of court and of chancery were expanding, we cannot confidently assume that the 'diplomatic' laity were so ignorant of either Latin or French. In addition, the clergy do not seem to have been more intensively used only in negotiations with the French. It is possible that experience at the Councils of Pisa and Constance had already made the English self-conscious about the importance of learning and eloquence in international negotiations and propaganda and that a stronger clerical force on embassies was regarded as the best way to match rival delegations, but Henry VI's reign was to be well advanced before humanism exerted much influence and young clerics began to take themselves off to Italian universities in order to enhance their Latin and their prospects of advancement. A more probable explanation perhaps lies with Henry V: his deliberate preference for clergy in his administrative and diplomatic service may reflect both his piety and his aversion from the lollard-anticlerical ethos of the early fifteenth century; it certainly stemmed from his need for civil lawyers to manage the multifarious and crucial negotiations about territory and regality. The clergy whom Henry V appointed to ecclesiastical and secular government were dominant throughout the minority of his son: Beaufort, Chichele, Langley, Stafford, Kemp among them. With men such as these active on the council or in ministerial office or leading missions, it is not surprising that they should show preference for diplomats of their own kind and order. When Henry VI was at last able to influence decisions, he already had a pattern to follow which, in view of his own pious and clerical inclinations, he would hardly be keen to ignore or reverse.

(iii) Clergy Promoted: Episcopal JPs

The striking increase in the presence of clergy on diplomatic missions during Henry VI's reign is to some extent curiously paralleled when we turn to commissions of the peace. The office of justice of the peace from its emergence in the late fourteenth century had been the preserve of laymen, yet from the beginning of Henry VI's reign bishops are frequently and regularly appointed to the office.[41] During the first and second decades of the reign only nine counties were without a bishop serving on commissions of the peace; in the third decade sixteen counties fell into this category, but during the 1450s only three. There were never fewer than fourteen of the seventeen English bishops so employed, and while some shires had three on their list – the Gloucester commissions between 1437 and 1441 included Bath and Wells, Worcester and York – some bishops sat in several counties in one year, the bishop of Winchester outstandingly in Berkshire, Buckinghamshire, Devon, Hampshire, Middlesex, Oxfordshire, Somerset, Surrey and Wiltshire.

Whether they actually attended sessions, or did so frequently, is still a matter for research; although some could scarcely have done so in view of their other commitments, their commissions were usually located in shires where they had estates, which encourages a presumption that some at least did take their place on the bench. Where or when bishops were resident in their dioceses they were certainly called upon to perform a variety of important secular tasks on behalf of the crown, swearing in sheriffs and escheators, for example.[42] They appeared, too, among the numerous commissions which conducted government business in the shires, not only the routine but also special *ad hoc* commissions. Thus in 1434 the bishop of Exeter was named with three laymen to swear, in accordance with parliament's order, the shire and borough communities to eschew violence and in no way assist or encourage disorder.[43] Indeed, when the parliament of 1439–40 approved a triennial poll tax upon aliens, it fell to the bishops, as justices of the peace in their provinces and dioceses, to draw up a list of the eligible taxpayers, which was to be certified by the bishop and forwarded under his seal to the exchequer.[44] How effective their presence was is also in need of investigation, but it must be seen in the context of their magnate colleagues on the bench, and some doubt about their influence arises in the light of Bishop Beckington's pitiful pleas to the dukes of Somerset to restrain their loutish followers.[45]

In fact this new role for bishops may have had less to do with imposing order on an unruly society than with enhancing a bishop's local prestige and power. Since a bishop was usually appointed where he had estates, it gave him a further opportunity, however illusory it sometimes proved, to protect them from the unruly and the criminal. Yet it is equally possible that the advent of the bishop-JP was a deliberate counterblast to the anticlericalism of the time and a recognition of the role of JPs in heresy prosecution under the terms of the 1414 statute. The timing of their appearance seems best explained by those formidable prelates who dominated the council in the 1420s and were so anxious about lollardy.

Church and Lack of Government

(i) Bastard Feudalism

So little has been written about the church and bastard feudalism that it is tempting to suppose that the one passed the other by, yet such a view would be wrong. Not only could the church, *a priori*, hardly escape the impact of social and political changes going on around it, but there is also enough stray evidence to confirm this presumption. Until a full study is undertaken, all that can be done here is to sketch in the contours and suggest some possible consequences. First, however, a word is necessary about bastard feudalism itself.[46] In essence it was the exchange of money for services, whether these were knightly or of another kind, which in the past had been more usually purchased with land (or fiefs). By no means originating in the fourteenth century, this practice increasingly became the norm of social and military arrangements, and by the age of Henry VI was so widespread as to be credited by some historians with the collapse of the Lancastrian dynasty and royal authority. This explanation of the fall of the house of Lancaster is not widely accepted today, though no historian denies that order broke down under Henry VI or that bastard feudalism had by then developed pernicious features. It was particularly associated with the retaining of armies, royal and private, by money contracts, or pensions, and the clothing of these forces in the lord's livery. In practice, not only troops were so contracted or dressed, but all manner of men rendering specific services or even general assistance sometimes simply in return for the lord's good will or good lordship. Underlying these arrangements was the ancient and traditional relationship of patronage, and arising from them came the sinister emergence of private armies of thugs and the perversion of law courts and administration by intimidation or 'maintenance'.

Although we hear little in histories of the period of ecclesiastical magnates employing retainers, their existence is clearly illuminated by the example of the Staffords of Grafton. In 1449 Sir Humphrey Stafford was in receipt of fees not only from a number of lay magnates but also from the bishop of Worcester, the abbots of Evesham and Pershore, and the prior of Worcester. His son by 1451 was the beneficiary of the same abbots and prior, but also of the abbots of Bordesley and Halesowen and the prior of Studley.[47] The sums were modest in comparison with those delivered by temporal lords and some of the arrangements were shortlived, but there is nothing to suggest that either the Staffords of Grafton or their ecclesiastical benefactors were untypical. Clearly no ecclesiastical magnate of any consequence could risk alienating men of influence locally or nationally by not so enlisting their services, and since it often happened that both parties to the arrangement carried influence there were reciprocal advantages involved. The results must have been no more or no less menacing than the accumulation of directorships or consultancies by modern politicians.

Nevertheless, too much significance should not be placed upon those relationships, since the patron and retainer were often linked in other and earlier ways, whether as landlord and tenant, or as fellow members of commissions, or by normal patronage. One must not think of these retainers as armed mercenaries, nor of the pensions as the sole links between patrons and clients. Indeed, retaining was sometimes disguised in the form of specific employment: thus in the fifteenth century the steward of the archbishop of Canterbury's estates was often a layman nominated by the king and was paid £40 per annum in addition to expenses.[48] After Edward IV triumphed in 1461 two Kentishmen to whom he owed much for his victory were not only appointed treasurer and comptroller of the royal household but were also retained by Archbishop Bourgchier at £6 13s 4d each annually for their counsel.[49]

One of the features of bastard feudalism which most alarmed contemporaries was the distribution of livery (or uniform) to forces which were casually recruited and disbanded, mostly in order to intimidate or impress neighbours, courts, officers or enemies. Attempts to regulate this were made by Richard II in 1390 and by Henry IV in 1399, in statutes reaffirmed in 1406 and 1429. In 1390 prelates and clergy were debarred from giving any livery, unlike temporal lords who were allowed to confer it on their retainers for life or upon their war-time retinues. The statute of 1399 reversed this, recognizing the right of clergy and others to give livery to their household servants, their officers and their councillors learned-in-the-law. There is no reason to believe that the clergy constituted any special threat to order by their liveried retainers, though they were certainly at times the victims of such threats.[50]

The best and well-nigh the only study of the clergy's involvement in this practice concerns the reign of Edward III.[51] In 1333, the abbot of Crowland was granting livery and pension for life to the rector of Burton beside Lincoln for past and future services. In 1328 a man who was frequently on commissions of oyer and terminer received a pension and robe for past and future services and in 1334 joined the abbot's council. Another who served on similar commissions and in 1336 was knight of the shire for Northants received a pension and robe from the same abbot. More notably, in 1339, Simon Islip, then vicar-general of the bishop of Lincoln and in 1349 archbishop of Canterbury, no less, received an annual rent of 10 marks and half a cloth of livery of the abbey's clerks on becoming the abbot's good and faithful councillor, helping him with his business against everyone except the bishop and the abbot of Peterborough (to whom he was probably also contracted); were any dispute to arise between Crowland and Peterborough or the bishop, Simon would use his good offices to bring about a just solution. This sheds a remarkable sidelight on the conduct of diocesan business and management. In many ways it is more sinister than the granting of a pension of £5 for life to Simon Simeon in 1349, a favoured royal servant. Yet quite as menacing in a different way was the recruitment to the abbot's council in 1339 of no less a figure than Gustave de Folville, well-known between 1326 and 1330 as a gentleman gangster, murderer, kidnapper, robber and rapist; although he was paid an annuity for life of 20 shillings for his advice and aid, it seems more probable that this was simply the price of protection, either in the form of 'strong-arm' work or else in the form of self-restraint on the part of Folville.

These were by no means all of Crowland's retainers in that period. As can be seen, they ranged from local and fairly obscure clerics to episcopal officers, lay judges, royal clerks, and even a knightly thug. Their services, rendered in return for livery and pension, were clearly to advise, assist and protect a landlord inescapably exposed to quarrels and litigation arising from the abbey's extensive estates. Although much more research is needed on this subject, it cannot be doubted that what was going on at Crowland must have been a common necessity among all large ecclesiastical landowners then and well beyond the early four-teenth century. It has recently been shown how most bishops and religious houses retained common lawyers in the king's courts by the mid-fourteenth century, as in the thirteenth they had fee'd canon lawyers in the church courts – itself eloquent testimony to the shifting balance of jurisdiction. Among the earl of Devon's retainers in 1384–5 were eight clerks, four of whom were parsons.[52]

Far less formal and measurable than the bonds of retaining and pensions was simple patronage or clientage. This was obviously much older than the fifteenth century, but in this period it is not only better recorded in the sources but also acquires a term of art – 'good lordship'. In the circumstances of Lancastrian England, however, when crown institutions often failed to coerce the king's subjects, the term 'good lordship' took on a certain ambiguity. Margaret of Anjou, in a letter reeking of the polite imperative, sought the abbess of Barking's 'good ladyship' towards the king's squire and secretary, Robert Osbern, who dwelt near the abbey.[53] Even more explicitly, she urged the bishop of Norwich to use his influence with the mayor, aldermen and commonalty of Norwich to have one, T.S., a cousin of her squire, appointed sergeant of that city: 'that in this matter you will have the said T towards your good lordship especially recommended.'[54] This could almost be described as immemorial patronage: in late medieval England, as well as before and long after it, such intervention was regarded as normal and expected; such patrons were the medieval equivalent of modern referees. Moreover, in an age when bishops, even the best, commonly appointed their relatives to offices about their diocese or estates, no one thought in terms of free or impartial election or appointment. The test was whether such interventions could be resisted or perhaps diverted by the intrusion of other patrons. The forces which operated upon episcopal patronage were deeply embedded in the social fabric.

Maintenance was the name given to the intimidation of courts and juries by patrons, lords or friends of the accused in criminal prosecutions or a party in civil litigation. Parliamentary complaints and legislation against it extended from the early fourteenth century to the end of our period and beyond, though the legislation was often defeated by maintenance itself! If maintenance was not new in Lancastrian England, it was almost certainly more common and more spectacular, or more resented and reported. Back in 1402 the abbot of Newsham (Devon) had petitioned parliament for remedy against Sir Philip de Courtenay, knight, who had terrorized the abbey and kidnapped inmates, including the abbot. The frustration of the abbot in his attempt to get justice was vividly underlined in his petition:

> the said Philip is so great of seigneurie and maintenance
> in that county that the said suppliant could not move
> the common law against them without great charge and
> destruction of the said suppliant and of his house.[55]

Throughout the reign Fountains abbey and other northern monasteries complained that suits against them in the franchise courts of the north were compounded by the court's refusal to allow the abbots to be represented by proctors as was their right (or would have been in the common law courts), so that they were put to great expense and – so numerous were the suits which faced them – were forced to let many cases go by default.[56] In 1443 Sir John Neville was charged on pain of £1000 to keep the peace against Fountains, its servants and friends and to desist himself, and prevent others, from harming the personnel or goods of the house.[57] Just two years earlier the Cistercians had expressed to the king their fear that their obdurate and fugitive members might 'procure resistance and seek maintenance and not wilfully be reduced to religious observance without succour of your highness', the help of whose officers they now requested.[58] About that same time the archbishop of York's property was vandalized by the earl of Northumberland's men.[59] Not far away Bishop Booth of Lichfield was complaining in 1449 about the impotence of his officers in Cheshire to correct offenders against the law of God, in some cases because of the power and status of the offenders themselves, in others 'for cause of maintenance that they have of mighty men within the said county'.[60]

In the south-west, in 1444 Bishop Beckington of Bath and Wells wrote to John, duke of Somerset, about malefactors in Sherborne and Longport who prevented the clergy from saying divine service and celebrating the sacraments, vexed the poor and put people in fear of their lives: 'it is said that all this they do under boldness of you and your mighty lordship.' Beckington proceeds to make a tactful but stern appeal to the duke, reminding him of the doctrine of the two swords (which portrayed the laity in the role of defenders, not masters, of the church).[61] A few years later, however, the bishop was again having to appeal to the duke (now Henry, who had succeeded to the title meanwhile) to withdraw his support from vandals and thugs in the parish of Bekington:

> My lord it hath not been seen in my days such rule and governance as late hath been and yet is in the church of Bekyngton in my diocese, which by no power of the church, but by force and strong hand is now held and occupied by favour and supporting, as is said, of your highness.[62]

Against this background, which could be matched across England and not least in the Paston country of East Anglia, the wisdom of churchmen, bishops and abbots, themselves retaining magnates, gentry, justices of the peace, sheriffs, judges, royal clerks and household members, was no more than simple prudence. The dukes of Somerset were perhaps above hire, so in his letter to John, Beckington warned of divine vengeance:

> Truly, my lord, any true Christian Prince may well understand that whereas true obeisance is suffered to be withdrawn from God and his church, it must soon after, by God's rightful doom and punishment, be withdrawn from man that suffereth and helpeth it to be done.

Henry was reminded of his obligation as a Christian knight – 'the promise that you have made to the church by order of knighthood'.

In 1440 the abbey and convent of Bury St Edmunds asked the king to empower, under his great seal, the earl of Suffolk 'to support, maintain and defend your said monastery, your said chaplain and all your priests, his brethren, with all other things that of right belong to them, and correct such persons as be their misdoers and oppressors'.[63] What greater admission could there be of the partiality of the law enforcers from whom the abbey should have expected justice, than this appeal to the king to appoint (under the great seal) a local aristocrat as its defender? Not merely the church's liberties and franchises but even its pastoral role suffered from the lack of governance, as the case from Beckington makes clear. Yet it is not certain in the present state of research that this disruption was more frequent, as distinct from being greater in its degree, than it had been before and was to be afterwards. Nor, in view of the petition from Bury St Edmunds, should it be forgotten that the church exploited the system in order to repulse its worst effects.

(ii) Benefit of Clergy

The privilege whereby clerks who had committed crimes other than treason were tried and only punished by the church courts had been a contentious issue between crown and church since the time of Becket in the twelfth century. At that time the issue had arisen both from concern for the church's freedom from the lay power and from the increasingly hierarchical definition of clergy by the theologians and canon lawyers. Subsequently, in England, who was a clerk was ascertained by a specific and limited test of the offender's literacy. By the middle of the fourteenth century an accused clerk was tried first in the king's court and if convicted there was claimed by his bishop for further trial and sentence in the episcopal court. Too often, in the view of some critics, the clerk convicted by a jury in the royal court was exonerated by compurgation in the court Christian; even when found guilty in the latter court, the clerk would certainly escape the more savage penalties meted out by the king's judges. As literacy spread, more offenders claimed successfully to be clerks – labourers, wire-drawers, cordwainers among them – entitled to benefit of clergy, much to the outrage of some laity and the embarrassment of some bishops.[64] Those laymen who fretted over contemporary disorder and those who were motivated by anticlericalism were frequent petitioners on the subject in parliament. Bishops who suffered increased expenditure on prisons and prisoners as a result, and were fined for those prisoners who escaped, can hardly have welcomed the rising tide of criminous clerks, as frequent royal writs ordering the prelates to claim such offenders from the crown courts make clear. Bishops conceded nothing on the privileges of clerkship, although they can hardly have been unaware that such clerkship was often – because of widening literacy – little more than a legal fiction by now. As each fresh case involved two public trials and sentences, much common knowledge fuelled passionate resentment and anticlerical sentiments at large. In the fifteenth century the problem was aggravated in two ways.

In December 1429 convocation complained of false and malicious indictments made against clerks in order to profit maintainers and others, not for the advantage of the king or for the furtherance of the law. A similar complaint was addressed to parliament in 1439:

> Forasmuch as indictments in matters of trespass, rape, robbery and felonies often be not used to conserving of law, to execution of justice and to stabilizing of peace among the people, but rather such indictments in these days oftentime be procured to extortion of sheriffs and other officers, to lucre of maintainers of quarrels, and to enriching of jurors, which in these days in many counties be withholden of fee and clothing as men learned in the law.

This sentiment was echoed again in a petition in 1446 and in 1449.[65] On this last occasion, explicitly because convocation had granted a tax on stipendiary clergy, the king pardoned and acquitted all clergy of all manner of rape committed before June of that year and entitled each offender to receive a charter of pardon.[66]

The commons in 1449 retorted with a complaint about the increase in felonies of all kinds committed by clerks who put some of the proceeds of their offences into the safe-keeping of others in order to purchase compurgators for any resulting trial before the bishop. The commons went on to ask that clerks convicted in the king's courts should be denied purgation and be kept perpetually in prison by their bishop, on pain of £100 fine for failure to do so.

The king, however, simply asked the bishops to provide a convenient and suitable remedy.[67] In fact just such a remedy was already provided by canon law, which stipulated that convicted clerks who, after an obligatory enquiry by the bishop's officers, were found to be notorious offenders or of evil reputation were not allowed to proceed to compurgation. All this, however, did not impress or satisfy the commons who returned to the subject again in 1455, this time demanding that all convicted clerks, for whatever offence, should be deemed guilty of high treason for which no benefit of clergy was allowable. Somewhat illogically, the commons then went on to assert that if bishops refused or neglected to claim criminous clerks, the bishops would be fined and the convicted clerks executed. What seems to be occupying the commons most in all this is the burden that such clerks when unclaimed put upon the crown and other prisons. Arrangements were also prescribed for keeping local assizes and the King's Bench informed so that second offenders could be readily identified. In some ways the most radical proposal was that this act should have retrospective effect.[68] Once again the king prevaricated and agreed to take advice; that was the end of the matter until Edward IV ascended the throne in 1461.

All this concern about criminous clergy suggests that either there was a crime-wave amongst Lancastrian clergy, or false indictments were increasing, or simply that more literate laymen were claiming benefit of clergy. Both the accusations brought by the laity and the *gravamina* of the clergy bear further witness to the breakdown in order and morale which characterized England generally during this reign.

(iii) Excommunication

Even though Edward I and Edward II had not only withdrawn assistance from, but actually prohibited, excommunication of their servants and tenants-in-chief, by the late fourteenth century prelates had learned discretion (or lost courage) and the king, faced by heresy and its unpredictable fall-out, had learned to value excommunication, not least when employed to extract subsidy dues from reluctant clergy.

Since the time of Pecham a list of offences which incurred excommunication *ipso facto* had been published in the churches four times a year, or should have been. Stratford's enlargement in 1342 comprehended not only violators of ecclesiastical liberties but also felons, conspirators, maintainers, perjurers before the king's justices, inciters of false quarrels, and disturbers of the peace and liberties of the realm. This decree was reissued in 1431 and 1434. On the second occasion a revised and shortened version was to be proclaimed three times a year. Still those who violated church liberties or possessions, or withheld tithes, or espoused witchcraft, or disturbed the peace and tranquillity of the king and his realm, or unlawfully withheld any rights which belonged to the king were pronounced excommunicate. Once again felons, their inciters and maintainers were likewise condemned. The reissue in 1434 may have been prompted by a commons petition in the previous year that because of the 'diverse enormous and special crimes . . . inhumanly perpetrated in several counties' the clergy might be ordered, in accordance with a writ from Edward II's reign, to pronounce sentence of greater excommunication, in all churches on each Sunday and great feast day, against the offenders 'so that who does not fear the justice of human law' might at least dread the sentence of the divine judge. The king responded by promising to consult his council. In some manuscripts of John Mirk's *Instructions for Parish Priests*, then a popular manual among the parish clergy, under the general sentence were included 'all that destroyeth the peace of England and traitors that be false or consent to treachery against the king or the realm'.[69] In a sense the use of excommunication for the peace of the realm was only the obverse of prayers and processions for such a purpose, and those, we have seen, had long been employed.

What political effects, if any, flowed from these decrees (which were certainly implemented)[70] still await investigation, but they nevertheless stand as witnesses to the enduring paternalism of the church from Pecham to Chichele towards the crown and the realm. They further remind us that excommunication was not only a defensive mechanism of the church but also in an age of hazardous and intermittent law-enforcement another instrument, however frail, for the promotion of good government. At the very least, the general sentence of excommunication was a public reminder in each parish of the realm three or four times a year of the requirements of the law of the land as well as of the church.

It might be thought that this habit would soon degenerate into a perfunctory routine, solemn though its accompanying ceremony appears, yet there is evidence to suggest that the bishops at least took their role of law defenders too seriously for that. In July 1449, for example, Bishop Lacy ordered all the curates of churches and chapels in the city and diocese of Exeter to announce that unless those who had stolen money, goods and muniments from the mayor and bailiffs of Exeter restored them within fifteen days, they would incur excommunication. A year later the same bishop was acting similarly, though on a mandate from the archbishop this time, towards some Cornishmen who had seized and sold merchandise from a galley in Plymouth.[71] In fact, excommunication was used, rather like indulgences, to promote or procure benefits for the king's subjects and local communities as well as for the advantage of the crown and for the safety and welfare of the church.

(iv) Arbitration

When the power of the common law courts proved inadequate to resolve disputes, increasing resort was had to arbitration by some local magnate or dignitary. The clergy figure both among the arbitrators and the seekers after their judgements. In 1429, for example, William Heron and John Manners were under conciliar pressure to submit their dispute to three umpires – the priors of Guisborough, Durham and Tynemouth. Eventually the last two brought about a reconciliation of the parties and the end of a bitter wrangle in which the established law courts had failed to produce a solution acceptable to both antagonists.[72] A few years later, in 1443, the sheriff, mayor, aldermen and citizens of York, on the one hand, and the abbey and convent of St Mary's, York, on the other, were ordered to keep the peace and seek a compromise from such persons as both parties would agree to, or else to submit to the decision of the king's council. In the event they chose Lord Scrope to resolve their differences.[73]

Decline and Fall

(i) The Suffolk Crisis, 1447–50

The political heirs of Gloucester and Beaufort, respectively Richard, duke of York, and William de la Pole, earl and soon duke of Suffolk, inherited, if they did not actually create, immense problems. Campaigns had not ceased with negotiations or agreements and still drained copious funds from an exchequer fast approaching yet another crisis as revenue shrank and accumulating debts mounted further.[74] While York was dismissed from the lieutenancy of France to that of Ireland, Suffolk presided over a policy which involved the cession of the county of Maine to the French, an act which in the public mind symbolized retreat and despair. Gloom and outrage were deepened by the shattering loss of Rouen in 1449. At this point Richard of York intervened actively in English politics. As the largest landowner in the realm apart from the king, and as a descendant of Edward III with a strong claim to the throne while Henry VI remained childless, Richard was justly aggrieved with his earlier treatment at the hands of the Beaufort and peace party; he returned to England with some eagerness in 1449 to exploit the difficulties of his opponents.

In parliament in 1449 the king's closest councillors and advisers were arraigned and outside it they were assaulted. Suffolk was accused of treason by his enemies, banished to save his skin by the king, but lynched by sailors while crossing the Channel to safety. Bishop Moleyns of Chichester was murdered at Portsmouth on 9 January 1450. A few months later, in June when the south was in uproar, Bishop Aiscough of Salisbury was seized when saying mass at Edington (in his diocese), taken out to a nearby hill and put to the sword. About the same time the bishops of Lichfield and Norwich (William Booth and Walter Lyhert) and the abbot of Gloucester (Reginald Boulers, soon to be bishop of Hereford) were also attacked. That these prelates should attract such unwelcome attention had little to do with anticlericalism or animus against the church, for clergy were by no means the only victims then. Moleyns, who had risen from being clerk of the council to becoming a full member of it and keeper of the privy seal in 1444, and then bishop in 1445, was prominently involved in the arrangements for the Angevin match and the surrender of Maine, as well as in the truce negotiations during 1445–8; moreover, he had played unpopular roles in the humiliation of Gloucester in 1441 and 1447 and voiced Suffolk's criticisms of York. All this would have made him vulnerable to popular hostility in 1450, but he was apparently the victim of sailors in Portsmouth frustrated by the non-payment of their wages.[75] Aiscough, who had been provided to Salisbury in 1438, was making only his second visit to his diocese when he was murdered; almost certainly he was *en route* to the shelter of his castle at Sherborne, for there was no doubt of his unpopularity. The root of this hostility lay partly in his role as the king's confessor and still more in his solemnizing of the marriage of Henry with Margaret in 1445; to this particular animus and the general grievance in 1450 against the king's friends was doubtless added local outrage at his long absence from his diocese until he needed political refuge there. In 1446 a London draper had coupled Aiscough with Suffolk in the charge of dominating the king and keeping him from his wife, thereby preventing the conception of an heir! In 1450 a bitter political poem singled out Aiscough for special condemnation among Suffolk's associates.[76] Booth and Lyhert were respectively chancellor and confessor of the queen; Boulers a confessor and confidant of the king. These were not the only clerical supporters, or suspected supporters, of Suffolk who suffered accusation and harassment in 1450: the abbots of St Albans, St Mary Graces on Tower Hill, and Westminster, as well as Suffolk's sister who was abbess of Barking, also rank among the victims.[77] By the summer of 1450 the Kentish rebellion under the leadership of Jack Cade had given vehement voice to public grievances and its success encouraged others to acts of unpremeditated, if deliberate, violence. Not only the higher clergy were engulfed by the hostility which swept Suffolk away: John Squyer, parson of Alderton and chaplain to the duke, was 'piteously slain and murdered through great malice borne because of his said lord'; and in July 1450 the vicar of Multon, in the county of Suffolk, was almost decapitated in his vicarage by men allegedly linked with Cade.[78]

(ii) Changing Bishops

Of the bishops who were lynched or assaulted in 1450, Moleyns alone bears comparison (albeit only faintly) with Stapledon and Sudbury, for he at least had held ministerial office; the rest were courtiers. After the end of Henry's minority a gradual and significant change came over the episcopate which had important implications both for the monarchy and for the church.

Until the mid-1440s government and policies were dominated by prelates inherited from, or set upon their careers by, Henry V: Chichele at Canterbury, Kemp at York, Beaufort at Winchester, Stafford, Morgan and Langley. The chancellorship, for example, was held in fact until 1454 by such men, successively by Langley (of Durham), Beaufort, Kemp (of Rochester, Chichester, London and York), and then from 1432 to 1450 by John Stafford who had begun his career as keeper of the privy seal under Henry V and held the see of Bath and Wells until he succeeded to Canterbury in 1444. Kemp's return in 1450 (until his death four years later) witnesses to the fact that no one of comparable seniority of experience was then available.

The new bishops – Beckington, Carpenter, Aiscough, Moleyns, Lyhert, Waynflete, Booth, Beauchamp, Boulers, Chedworth, Stanbury and Hales – were overwhelmingly men without experience of administration in the great departments of state; predominantly theologians (rather than lawyers like Henry V's men), they served the king in his household as chaplains and confessors or assisted him in the foundations of Eton and King's College, Cambridge. Their role on the council, therefore, all too readily smacked of partisanship in the circumstances of the 1450s, and what is more they undoubtedly lacked the taste and will for politics which their predecessors had generally had. Politically they were lightweights, unable to command the respect, or offer the stability at the centre, which Henry V's prelates, ministers and councillors had held. They suffered, too, by their involvement in negotiations far removed in purpose and popularity from those which the earlier prelates had conducted. Henry VI and in her turn Margaret of Anjou loaded the episcopate with men who were often learned, pious, able and worthy, but were mostly lacking in administrative and political skills. In many ways they recall the household bishops of Richard II and emphasize the dangers which beset a medieval king (and the church, too) when he crowded the bench with candidates more notable for piety than for political wisdom.

When the duke of York controlled the government during the king's incapacity in 1454–5 and virtual captivity later in 1455–6, he had Thomas Bourgchier translated from Worcester to Canterbury and George Neville provided to Exeter. Bourgchier looks at first sight like a blatantly partial appointment, yet no subsequent attempt was made by the Lancastrians to get him translated to some backwater, as would have happened in Richard II's reign. In fact, he had been a bishop since 1433, when he was appointed to Worcester with the full backing of the council; and in 1443 he was translated to Ely, where Louis of Luxemburg had forestalled him some years before. Of noble family, with an Oxford background and with such considerable episcopal experience, by 1454 he was the obvious, if not the only, choice for Canterbury. If his brothers, Viscount Bourgchier and Lord Berners, were ready associates of York, there are few signs that the new archbishop was seriously engaged by politics; not until the protectorate and after his move to Canterbury did he occupy an office of state and then but briefly. George Neville, by contrast, was not only a newcomer to the episcopal bench but was also clearly promoted (before he had reached the canonical age) to satisfy his brother and then York's keenest supporter, Richard, earl of Warwick, at the expense of the queen's nominee, John Hales, who some years later was compensated with Lichfield. Neville, whose interests lay principally in the academic circles and affairs of Oxford, was not to hold a government office until 1460 when he became chancellor, but certainly he appears politically more eager and partial than Bourgchier, possibly as a result of his youth if not under the influence of his ambitious brother.

Only once in the whole period did a pope reject a suggested candidate. That occurred in 1448 when the king changed his mind about his nominee for London, Thomas Kemp, and tried to substitute Lumley, then at Carlisle and the treasurer of the realm; instead Nicholas V directed the rebuke to Henry which has been cited earlier in this chapter.[79] The rumour that two years before, in 1446, Eugenius IV had allied with the duke of Suffolk to intrude

Lyhert into Norwich against the king's wishes which were focused on Stanbury has been shown to be without foundation.[80] The episode of Hales in 1456 demonstrates the continuing limitations of papal authority in episcopal appointments: provided to Exeter in October 1455 on the queen's nomination, in February 1456 he was forced by York to resign and make way for a new provision in favour of Neville; however reluctantly, the pope acquiesced in this alteration even though Neville by his age was canonically disqualified. In 1459 during a period of Lancastrian dominance Hales was provided to Lichfield, the last Lancastrian appointment. In short, the composition and character of the late Lancastrian episcopate owed more to papal indifference than to papal interference or resolution, and it reflected the unstable and improvident government which appointed it. For this among other reasons, the prelates were scarcely likely to exert a notable, let alone a powerful, influence upon their political context which during the 1450s steadily deteriorated.

(iii) Church Liberties

The clergy in Henry VI's reign had remarkably few grievances about encroachments upon their liberties and franchises or simple oppression. The kind of crown oppressions which had once obsessed convocations had now either declined in response to changing conditions or royal concessions (as with royal patronage or purveyances) or were now an accepted part of clerical life (as with the definition of the lay fee to include, for example, vicarages). Royal taxation, by which the crown's weight was most acutely and widely felt among the clergy, became modest in comparison with earlier reigns. From 1437 to 1453 subsidies were no more frequently and no more generously granted than they had been in the minority. The Canterbury clergy almost invariably spread their tenths over two years, while York in the four years when it made a grant at all proffered half tenths to be collected usually by quarters in successive years. Nothing was provided between 1442 and 1449 from the southern province; indeed, as we have seen above, in 1444 a meeting of convocation was deliberately avoided lest it attract royal demands. Nor was anything forthcoming from York for eight years. After 1453, when two tenths were spread over four years, Canterbury made no further grants to Henry VI; York granted and paid nothing after that year. All of this took place while the crown plunged ever more deeply into debt – £372,000 in 1450, parliament claimed – and for much of the time costly expeditions were made to France; it took place, too, without any vociferous demands in parliament or from the laity outside for the confiscation of church wealth or estates; even though in 1450 an act of resumption was passed for the recovery of crown grants, there was no attempt to extend this to church lands. The aim of the whole community, lay and clerical, now was to make the king live off his own landed resources, not off the taxes of his subjects.

It was not the king but his subjects that caused the church concern, particularly with reference to two items: malicious accusations of felony against clerks (which has been discussed above), and the novel use of premunire writs against the ecclesiastical courts. The two statutes of *Praemunire*, of 1353 and 1393, applied only where the crown's regality or the realm's laws were prejudiced and then only as a result of action at Rome or outside the realm. Unfortunately for the church, the 1393 statute spoke of decisions at Rome 'or elsewhere', a formula which did not literally exclude causes and actions within England, and by 1434 Chichele was complaining that *Praemunire* writs were now being used against the church courts in England. In December 1439 both convocations repeated this complaint in a petition that the writ issued under the statute of 1393 be confined to cases in Rome or in other courts outside England. The immediate royal response was to order that no such writs should be issued without prior discussion and approval by the king's council until the next parliament, but when that met in 1442 it ignored the subject.[81] Five years later the clergy of England again protested to the king on this matter and sought a similar remedy.[82] On this occasion they coupled with *Praemunire* the statute of 1402 against various papal dispensations, which by the 1430s was being so widely interpreted as to cover, for example, a papal dispensation for a monk to hold a secular benefice (John Spencer of Muchelney abbey in 1438) and even a licence for a monk of Glastonbury abbey in 1449 to move to a stricter order.[83] Again no parliamentary action followed. *Praemunire* was next on the agenda of convocation in

1460, and eventually Edward IV conceded protection against it in his charter to the clergy in 1462, though his concession was specifically restricted to tithe cases.[84] The writ was certainly activated against English church courts in the later years of the century, not least by Henry VII himself, and was to become a formidable weapon of intimidation under Henry VIII.[85]

The 1393 statute of *Praemunire* had seemingly lain dormant and neglected until the 1430s, a lapse not entirely without parallel, for we have seen above how judges in Henry IV's reign could be surprisingly ignorant of quite recent and important legislation. Its neglect is almost less of a mystery than its discovery. W. T. Waugh speculated that Duke Humphrey's prosecution of Beaufort drew attention to this neglected item on the statute book, a surmise which is strengthened by the association of the 1393 statute with the 1402 measure both by Gloucester in 1431–2 and by the clergy in 1447. Nevertheless, there are still difficulties in linking the action by Gloucester with those who first employed the writ against the church courts in England: the charge against Beaufort did not concern the church courts of England or litigation at all, but the obtaining of an undesirable bull from the pope. What was particularly ironic was the early and apparently frequent use made of the writ by clergy themselves who thereby helped to forge a weapon which was to be used so brutally against them in the next century.

(iv) The Last Act

The murder of Suffolk brought no relief as the late Cardinal Beaufort's brothers and the queen pursued similar policies. Territorial losses gathered momentum and by 1453 English possessions in France scarcely extended beyond Calais; control of the Channel was lost and trade disrupted; alongside returning soldiers came the settlers displaced from Normandy. The hopes and dreams of 1422 were extinguished amidst bitterness and recrimination; the audacious claims of Edward III which had mesmerized English monarchs and the nation for over a century were now demonstrated to be a fantasy incapable of realization. Further political crisis could hardly be avoided in the circumstances, though its outcome was neither predictable nor secure.

Richard of York had returned from Ireland only to find his way to power barred by the Beaufort duke of Somerset. Frustrated to the point of raising troops, York was nevertheless compelled to yield and in 1452 was briefly imprisoned. The triumph of the court, however, was undermined when the king suffered a breakdown in August 1453 (although this was not publicly acknowledged for several months) and expulsion from France was completed in October that year. During the king's illness York was eventually, in March 1454, recognized as protector, a post which he held and exploited until he was dismissed by a recovered king a year later. While acting as protector Richard had incarcerated his enemies and promoted his friends, among these not only Bourgchier to Canterbury but also the Neville earl of Warwick to the captaincy of the vital garrison of Calais where he had at his command a standing army and a formidable stronghold. Meanwhile, a further threat to tranquillity and equilibrium had occurred in October 1453 when a son and heir was born to Henry and Margaret.

Soon after the end of the protectorate a skirmish took place in May 1455 at St Albans where York prevailed and Somerset died. In the wake of this and with the reluctant help, it would seem, of his friends, York became protector again from November 1455 to February 1456 during which time George Neville was appointed bishop of Exeter. When the court party, led by the queen, regrouped and dismissed York again, he returned to Ireland. In the course of the next three years, after vain efforts at reconciliation, the queen and her opponents manoeuvred for advantage, neither party being able to placate or effectively crush the other: Margaret was too tactlessly vigorous for her enemies, York too blatantly covetous of the crown for his friends who seem to have been intent rather on depriving the queen of power than the king of his throne.

Hostilities were openly resumed in 1459 and York, who had come back again from Ireland, was defeated but not captured at the battle of Ludford Bridge. The Lancastrian parliament which met at Coventry in November that year attainted Duke Richard, his son and a score of others, mostly in their absence. The Yorkist response came in the summer of 1460 from Calais with a force led by the earls of Warwick and Salisbury accompanied by York's son Edward, earl of March, and Francesco Coppini, bishop of Terni, cardinal and papal legate. They advanced on London where they addressed convocation and added eight bishops to their party before proceeding northwards to engage and defeat the Lancastrian army at Northampton in July. The victors returned to London with the king among their prisoners: Warwick took over the government, appointed his brother, the young bishop of Exeter, chancellor and Viscount Bourgchier treasurer, and called a parliament for October. In September Richard of York arrived in parliament to claim the crown; he made straight for the vacant throne and placed his hand on it as a sign of his claim, only to suffer a remarkable humiliation: no acclamation or assent was heard, and Archbishop Bourgchier asked him – somewhat pointedly – if he wished to see the king. Richard argued his case on the basis of Lancastrian usurpation, but all that the peers would grant was a promise of his and his heirs' succession after Henry's death – the king's own son thus being disinherited – and an annuity of 10,000 marks until then. The queen could be expected to have some objections to this, and Lancastrian forces in the west and north prepared to recapture the king and control of the government. To counter this, while Warwick kept London the duke of York went north to tackle the queen's host, and the earl of March westwards to engage other Lancastrian supporters in Wales. York, however, suffered a crushing defeat and lost his own life at Wakefield on 30 December; thereupon Margaret quickly led her victorious army south, defeated Warwick at St Albans on 18 February and freed her husband and king. It was then that she made a crucial mistake by deciding not to seize London. Edward, formerly earl of March and now duke of York, returned from a victory at Mortimer's Cross in early February, joined with the remnants of Warwick's force and took London, where, at the beginning of March, he had himself proclaimed king. Towards the end of the month the Lancastrian forces were slaughtered at Towton, after which Henry and Margaret proceeded towards Scotland in order to enlist wider support for their cause. Meanwhile they left Edward with the appearance of unchallenged success and apart from a few months of restoration in 1470–1 Henry's reign was at an end.

The role of the clergy in these developments was negligible and more ceremonial than determining. Bourgchier, despite his family connections, was uncommitted politically except perhaps to mediating, which was a task assigned to him early in 1455 when he was commissioned to reconcile York and Somerset. In the convocation of 1460, which had been called by the king, the archbishop showed himself more interested in amending the discipline of the clergy than in exploiting or ameliorating the political situation.[86] It was George Neville of Exeter and William Grey of Ely who went to meet the invading force from Calais and invite them to address the assembly. The fact that eight bishops then accompanied Warwick on his pursuit of the Lancastrians is no indication of Yorkist inclinations on their part: at convocation Warwick and March and Salisbury had sworn on the cross of Canterbury their loyalty to the king, and the bishops went from convocation to act as mediators. This role was abandoned in March 1461. On Sunday 1 March Bishop Neville addressed a large assembly of Yorkist supporters in St John's Field, enlarging upon the failures of Lancastrian kings and extolling York's title to the crown. Two days later a council which included Bourgchier, Neville and Beauchamp of Salisbury confirmed York's claims and on the next day he was formally recognized as king in the King's Bench and in Westminster Abbey. His coronation followed in June, but he was already effectively monarch. The clergy could not be left out of these affairs, any more than they could be omitted from the council, but apart perhaps from Neville, Edward commanded no more enthusiasm among the bishops than he did among the lay nobility. There is an air of understandable weariness and resignation about politics in 1460–1, disillusion with the regime of Henry and Margaret, certainly, but little confidence that Richard or Edward could bring stability, justice and peace to the realm. There was no one among the bishops with Arundel's sharp-eyed vigour and resolution, but then there was none with his particular grievance: bishops were no longer deposed or translated to match the changing kaleidoscope of government – Bourgchier retained his see after the end of the protectorate. Nor was there any longer the threat of lollardy or parliamentary anticlericalism to enhance the claims of a usurper.

The grievances which occupied the clergy in 1460–1 were by then longstanding and without solution from Henry's government, but they were of a different order from those of Richard II's time and there was no assurance that a Yorkist king would provide effective remedies. Not till 1462, and then in a charter not a statute, did Edward publicly acknowledge clerical grievances: such was the value which he put upon their support.

It might be thought that Edward derived more significant support from the papal legate.[87] Coppini, after all, is alleged to have raised the papal standard in the Yorkist camp before the battle of Northampton, granted plenary remission of sins for those fighting on the Yorkist side, and excommunicated followers of Henry VI. He denied this accusation when reproached by the pope, but what is undeniable is his presence with the Yorkists, although he had originally been sent to Henry in 1459 in order to pacify the realm and elicit support for a crusade against the Turks. There was little hope, of course, that even had he succeeded in peace-making he could have raised much response with regard to the Turks: Calixtus III's emissary had signally failed to do so immediately after the fall of Constantinople. England's record on this score was not encouraging. Early in 1460, therefore, Coppini was recruited by Warwick who promised him assistance, it was alleged, once the king was freed from the influence of his evil counsellors and queen. Coppini may have been duped by Warwick into giving the Yorkist cause a specious appearance of papal approval – Pius II did not formally recognize Edward IV until 1462 – but there is no persuasive evidence that his presence significantly enhanced Yorkist fortunes: papal agents – least of all foreigners, legates, cardinals and tenth-collectors – were more likely to prove an embarrassment than an asset to a political cause. Edward's succession was decided on the battlefield and by the flight of Henry and Margaret from London. The acquiescence of the estates in his coup has little if anything to do with Coppini and most probably stemmed from despair after five battles and bewildering fluctuations in a mere eighteen months: public fatigue and inertia were the key elements in York's success.

The Lancastrian dynasty which had seized the throne as the champion of orthodoxy against heresy and as the defender of ecclesiastical privileges and property, was divested of the throne without any clerical protest or alarm. This was not so much because more was expected from, still less promised by, the Yorkists, but because by 1461 the English church appeared to have weathered the storms which were gathering in 1399. Lollardy, whatever its dimensions really were, was now much less of a threat: socially restricted, intellectually deprived, menaced by statutes and so discredited that even a bishop who had devoted singular learning, daring originality and vast efforts to the conversion of lollards could be successfully humiliated. Moreover, the less heterodox claims to secularize all church income and wealth subsided as they were effectively snubbed by successive kings, partially met by the seizure of alien priories, and as the war expired and its attendant burdens of taxation diminished. The century opened with the papacy in schism, much to the advantage of the crown, but well before 1461 the schism had been resolved through general councils which in their turn were discredited and discarded; popes now concentrated upon independence by fighting for their state in Italy and keeping a low profile elsewhere in Europe. After Martin V and Eugenius IV, there was no conflict about the papal role in England, where influential agents and congenial circumstances had failed to realize the aims of these two resolute pontiffs: provisions were a trickle now and the question of Provisors was long dead by 1461. Equally quiescent as a matter for public and political consideration was the question of church reform: the early hopes of the century had proved extravagant beyond the capacity of councils and the will of kings; simply ending the schism had removed at least the disastrous effects of popes outbidding each other for support and income with reckless dispensations and indulgences.

With all these anxieties and uncertainties removed, what had the church to hope for from a new dynasty? Perhaps some slackening of taxation, though it was now already restrained, and such hopes – and promises – had proved false in 1399; perhaps some protection of the clergy from malicious accusation and harassment, which raised a question of political will and circumstances under a new king; perhaps some curtailment of the abuse of writs of *Praemunire*. A new dynasty might at least end the political uncertainty and consequent social unrest which had marked the last decade of Henry VI's reign, but no one who had heard of the last usurpation could be sanguine about this. At best one might expect the usurper to do nothing to disturb the existing equilibrium of the crown and church, even if he did nothing to protect further the church's liberties. By comparison with 1399 there was certainly a dearth of major ecclesiastical issues in jeopardy.

The Lancastrian dynasty had profited significantly by the existence of these problems. Henry IV's political credibility was partly founded upon his role as persecutor of lollards, and the liberties which he and his son took with clerical taxation – far beyond clerical expectations and sometimes to the limits of clerical capacity – were mitigated by the common knowledge that the king above all kept them safe from the lollard and wider demands for the confiscation of church property and income. The uncertainties arising from the schism provided the king with a guarantee of immunity from papal condemnation and considerable assurances of papal collaboration. Under Henry V the Council of Constance afforded an occasion for running with the conciliar hounds and then hunting with the papal hare, whereby Henry was able to satisfy his clerics and his conscience at the same time as he was elaborating his diplomatic preparations for renewed war with France. Even Henry VI's government kept at bay the ambitions of Martin V and Eugenius IV in the knowledge that the popes could not afford to alienate its support when the church was threatened in turn by heresy in Bohemia, by overweening councils, and latterly by the Turks. Furthermore, during Henry VI's reign the Council of Basle had provided invaluable cover for war and peace diplomacy, although this had been used more adroitly by England's enemies.

The Lancastrian dynasty did not owe either its rise or its fall solely, or predominantly, to ecclesiastical influence or issues. Certainly its establishment was significantly assisted by its posture in ecclesiastical affairs, but its fall was neither impeded nor accelerated by the clergy and their interests. Nevertheless, in ideas, manpower, money and occasional devices, the church had served the Lancastrians well – better perhaps than the kings had served the church.

Conclusions

The fall of the Lancastrians marked no significant change in the relations of church and realm. Edward IV only reluctantly responded to the clergy's grievances, and then with a charter which remained a dead letter. Taxation rose slightly. The pattern of Anglo–papal links remained as it had become under Henry VI. Even the effects of the Wars of the Roses upon the church were no greater than those which had resulted from the civil disturbances of Edward II's reign. Few, if any, notable consequences for the church followed from Edward's accession. Such remarkable transformations, however, had taken place before then that the circumstances of the church in 1461 were radically different from those which had obtained in 1272.

Between the accession of Edward I and that of Edward IV nowhere were these changes more dramatic than in the matter of taxation. When our period opened, the procedures and theory of mandatory taxation were far more developed by the papacy than by the crown; but even before the end of the fourteenth century papal levies from the clergy had become negligible while royal taxation of both the clergy and the laity had emerged as a normal incident of government.

Although papal taxation worked to the advantage of the first two Edwards, who exploited for their own profit the pope's mandatory taxes of the clergy – the crown derived more than £360,000 in this way between 1300 and 1336, three times the amount then raised by royal taxes of the clergy – this source of revenue dried up when the Hundred Years War began and a French pope, surrounded by French cardinals, sat enthroned at Avignon. Papal taxes became subject to the king's veto and were rarely allowed except – as in 1362 – for his profit. In 1388 a parliamentary statute which banned

347

the shipment of money abroad, ensured that henceforth only on rare occasions and to small effect could the pope tax the English clergy.

The popes still profited from annates and services, yet by the fifteenth century the legislation against provisions had effectively reduced the yield of annates to a trickle. Whereas John XXII had filled some forty English livings a year by provision, and Clement VI provided to nearly 1600 in a mere decade, after the death of Edward III and the outbreak of the schism such appointments were greatly reduced; at the end of our period Eugenius IV in a sixteen-year pontificate succeeded in making only eleven provisions (apart from appointments to bishoprics), and Pius II in six years provided to only four. Services, payable by bishops on provision to their sees, continued to produce substantial funds for the Curia, the more so as from 1344 all bishops were appointed by provision and particularly when translations occurred (as in the 1380s and 1390s), but the occasions were irregular and the amounts fixed. The king presumably thought services a reasonable concession in exchange for having prelates appointed who were either chosen by, or acceptable to, him.

The royal grip on papal revenues raised from England contrasted sharply with the abortive attempt by Boniface VIII to stop the king taxing the clergy without papal assent. Had the papacy successfully enforced and maintained the veto which Boniface claimed, the crown would have faced even graver financial problems than in fact it did. No king under the pressures of fourteenth-century warfare could have been content to rely on papal consent or favour. Nor indeed could Edward III and his successors have tolerated for long the conscientious restrictions on clerical subsidies to the crown which Winchelsey sought to impose. After Winchelsey archbishops of Canterbury had generally served their apprenticeship in royal service and were more notable for the resolution and ingenuity which they employed in extracting grants from the clergy on an almost annual basis and even on some occasions when the laity refused a subsidy. Consciously or not, they were all inhibited by royal service or royal priorities or by their sense of paternalist responsibility for the welfare of the kingdom: before everything else they were the king's chief officer responsible for his church and in particular for extracting subsidies from it. The significance of clerical subsidies for royal finances in this period can hardly be exaggerated, contributing as they did some £300,000 in the reign of Edward I, in excess of half a million pounds for Edward III, on average over £10,000 a year under Henry IV, and nearly £17,000 per annum to Henry V – in short, considerably more than a third of the sum accruing to each monarch from direct taxation.

One result of the king's demands for taxes and the clergy's insistence on their right to consent separately to them was the emergence of convocation as the normal assembly of the clergy in each province. Convocation, however, was increasingly devoured by the business of royal taxation, so much so that in the 1440s the clergy, when they could, deliberately avoided convening lest they should attract further tax demands from the crown.

From the mid-fourteenth century, largely as a consequence of collusion between pope and king over provisions, the episcopal bench, though never completely homogeneous, mostly reflected the tastes and policies of the king. By then, however, the king's dependence on clerical manpower extended far beyond bishops or potential bishops to fill the major offices of chancellor, treasurer (though he was often a layman), keeper of the privy seal, and (by Richard II's time) secretary. Until well into Edward I's reign judges in the common law courts were ecclesiastics; in later years clergy, trained in canon and civil law, continued to preside over such conciliar and prerogative courts as chancery and admiralty. Civil lawyers especially were required to conduct the complex international negotiations over territorial rights and limits which then abounded, notably in the reigns of Henry V and Henry VI. War finance and organization, as well as diplomacy, necessitated the recruitment of literate and trained minds then most readily available among the clergy, who increasingly during this period attended the expanding universities. The king and his servants acknowledged this by their own endowment of colleges and patronage of students. The university-trained secular cleric dominated ecclesiastical and royal government in our period, as the monk had done in Anglo–Norman times. Until well into Henry VI's reign the civil service was extensively and predominantly manned by secular clergy. Advantageous, however, as all this was for the crown, its effects were less salutary for the church.

Among the cathedral canons and the beneficed clergy the king's influence was pervasive, as both Pecham and Winchelsey discovered. After their time, in order to staff expanding royal administration, royal patronage so increased – from nearly 1500 presentations under Edward II to over 3000 in the first twenty-five years of Edward III – that the church was even more compromised by courtly values. In the early fourteenth century, particularly, the king's clerks preyed on benefices with a greedy ferocity which led frequently to violence or at the least to insecurity among the incumbents. Royal writs, corrupt juries, and unsympathetic lay judges were all exploited for the advance and intrusion of royal servants. Not even papal rivals were safe, nor were bishops – or archbishops such as Zouche in the 1340s – who dared to defy the king's writs and courts. Indeed, long before the famous statutes of Provisors and *Praemunire*, the king and his justices had made it clear that where the crown's interests were at stake no authority ran against the king: in 1304 Corbridge, a predecessor of Zouche at York, could testify to this. In the search for patronage successive kings extended their regalian rights in vacant sees to claim benefices retrospectively for their clerks, and even though Edward III eventually conceded some limits to this, it is a measure of royal power that he disregarded them when it pleased him to do so. Similarly the coercive act of arbitrarily seizing episcopal temporalities although renounced by Edward also continued at his pleasure.

Royal patronage was augmented by the seizure of alien priories and the lands of the Templars. These actions not only contributed to a net fall in the number of religious houses but, coupled with some of the implications of Mortmain, and chapter 41 of Westminster II (about the recovery of misused endowments), and combined with the exploitation of regalian rights, they also helped to encourage the notion of the king as patron paramount in a church coterminous with the realm – a notion made explicit in judgements in the king's courts and, most publicly, in the statute of Provisors in 1351.

This insularity was nourished by war-time sentiments which the church in no small degree had propagated. The crown, depending already so heavily on clerical taxes and clerical manpower, was still more indebted to the clergy for war-time propaganda. There was, after all, no other institution which reached into so many corners of the realm; the 9000 parish churches alone made ideal 'broadcasting stations' for national prayers imploring, or acknowledging, divine aid against the French. The unity of the realm and the vigour of its war efforts were marshalled and enlisted especially through the machinery of the church. If this later proved under Henry V to be a less than perfect vehicle, it was nonetheless unrivalled in its range and opportunities. The martial activities of the clergy themselves, however, with few exceptions – as at Neville's Cross in 1356 and at Paris in 1429 – mostly raised problems for the church without significantly helping to solve those of the crown and the realm; not least was this so with Despenser's crusade.

National sentiment was most obviously apparent in parliament, itself no insignificant vehicle of propaganda when its members dispersed to their constituencies and its peers to their estates. Through its statutes and records parliament also provided the realm with its collective memory. Upon the origins of this assembly and its early procedures the influence of the clergy remains almost as obscure as it must have been considerable. Throughout our period and beyond, the spiritual peers were undoubtedly a crucial element, as the stratagems of Richard II to secure their assent and oaths to his sentences and measures bear witness. The clerical proctors in the lower house, however, prove shadowy in the extreme after the 1320s when their assent to clerical taxes was assigned to convocation. They continued to be summoned and on some occasions were undeniably present, but their influence largely eludes detection. Possibly the proctors and bishops were at their most effective in the parliaments of the 1340s when they not only extracted from Edward III important, if ephemeral, concessions but also pressured him on the subject of papal provisions. Thereafter the clergy undoubtedly played a less effective role in the commons.

Parliament is more notable in the late fourteenth century for its persistent anticlericalism, provoked no doubt by the exigencies of taxation and the scandals of the Avignon and schismatic popes, but also encouraged by the absence or the separatism of the clergy. Benefit of clergy, sanctuary, probate fees, the commutation of penance into fines, and tithes of cut wood, were recurring subjects of parliamentary petitions and lay assaults after the mid-fourteenth century. Like the laity, the stipendiary clergy too had their wages regulated by parliament. Moreover, parliament was the receiver of, if not the arena for, plans for the disendowment of the church.

Yet despite complaints by the clergy and accusations by the laity, in practice the jurisdictional relations of church and realm were more often characterized – certainly after the early fourteenth century – by collaboration and mutual assistance than by abrasive conflict. Writs of prohibition were by no means always successful – nor indeed as frequent as is often implied – and lay judges and courts can be seen, for example in 1421, to have taken remarkable pains to act fairly in accordance with the law, even if at other times, as in 1409, they were surprisingly ill-informed about recent legislation. On matters such as sanctuary and benefit of clergy, practical abuses rather than principles were the object of attack; violation of sanctuary was sensational because it was exceptional – and on one occasion it was even defended by Archbishop Arundel himself. The ambivalence or expediency which Arundel displayed then characterized also those lesser clergy who in the fifteenth century first sought a wider interpretation of the 1393 statute of *Praemunire*; not till Henry VII did a king exploit this statute on his own initiative. As for excommunication, although Edward I firmly repudiated its application to his servants and ministers, it was in his reign that royal writs of *de excommunicato capiendo* to help enforce ecclesiastical censures proliferated. (That by Richard II's time these writs were most frequently employed to coerce the clergy into paying their taxes to the king is an eloquent commentary on intervening developments.) The general sentence of excommunication, employed by Pecham and Winchelsey to support Magna Carta against royal violations, was later deployed against those who threatened the king or his peace.

Before the end of the fourteenth century Wyclif and lollardy transformed the context of the English church. Pantin long ago pointed out that Wyclif's controversial ideas had their roots in the

academic controversies and polemical writings of the early fourteenth century and in commonly voiced sentiments already
evident in contemporary sermons. It is now clear that Wyclif drew
as well upon the royalist-proprietorial and insular notions implicit
and explicit not only in Edwardian legislation but especially in
royal writs of prohibition (and later of *praemunire*) and in
pronouncements by royal judges. Moreover, he gave voice, too, to
the anxieties of the survivors of the plague and to the aspirations of
the newly educated laity. Above all, he was the voice of reform in a
church headed first by a partial and then by a divided papacy and
increasingly exposed to royal exploitation. Thus he spoke for
many in the kingdom. Nevertheless, the popular movement which
embraced his sentiments was denounced as a social and political
threat, as well as a religious one, and Richard II and his
Lancastrian successors energetically repelled a movement which
had cast the king as reformer and master of the church. Numerous
petitions in parliament against alleged clerical abuses foundered
on the rock of royal defence. Yet ironically royal control of the
church did increase as government took upon itself responsibility
for protecting orthodoxy: from 1401 obdurate or recidivist
heretics were to be burnt by the lay power; from 1414 all lay
officers in the realm swore to seek out and prosecute lollards. The
king became defender of the faith, though not yet definer of it.

Lollardy shaded off into anticlericalism and lay proprietorship;
it was a reform movement which helped to discredit reformers and
to embarrass a king like Richard II whose reign was already
complicated and unstable enough. In such a reign the possibility of
heresy triumphing over orthodoxy might not have seemed at all
remote. Henry IV's usurpation, therefore, profited from hopes of
a stouter defence of orthodoxy, hopes which won acquiescence not
only in his seizure of power but even in his extravagant taxation of
the clergy. The legitimacy of Lancastrian rule in particular, but of
any medieval monarch in fact, depended upon the acquiescence
and support of the church or at least of its leading prelates. The
clergy did not overthrow Edward II or Richard II or Henry VI,
but only when they transferred their allegiance could the transfer
of power be effective: they played a vital ceremonial role in the
coronation but a no less significant part as advocates and

persuaders, by example and by words. Especially was this so in 1399 when the legitimacy of both the church and the king were at risk and mutually dependent. Then the church was led, and Henry IV abetted, by an archbishop of singularly extensive political and administrative experience, who had been embittered by the treatment which he received from Richard II. With Arundel's help, Henry succeeded in deposing a dynasty. With the king's assistance, Arundel squeezed heresy out of Oxford, thus cutting off its intellectual nourishment. For Henry V crushing heresy was not only insurance for the Lancastrian regime but also a further demonstration of his piety and of his vision of a united Christendom: by his defeat of Oldcastle's rebellion, Henry severed lollardy from the vital support of the knightly and gentry classes. Some time elapsed before the significance of these victories by Arundel and Henry V was fully appreciated: into the 1430s the alarm provoked by heresy was fanned by news from Bohemia and the eruption of Perkins's feeble rebellion; even in the 1450s a too daring combatant of heretics himself alarmed the authorities and incurred condemnation.

The atmosphere of earnest dissent, the prevalent criticism levelled at the clergy, and disillusion with a divided church probably account for the decline in clerical recruitment that marked the early fifteenth century in England. As a consequence partly of that and partly of the widening opportunities for lay education, a notable shift in the ranks of royal servants occurred. By the 1430s laymen were supplanting clerics in the lower echelons of governmental bureaucracy. While the king's ministers continued in the main to be ecclesiastics – the chancellor until 1529 – the clergy were migrating from the corridors of power and leaving them to laymen. This had two important effects: on the one hand it relieved the king's pressure on ecclesiastical patronage and released many cathedral, and some parochial, benefices to clergy who were no longer serving the crown before the church; on the other hand, it diminished the influence of clergy where decisions were taken and doubtless encouraged the emergence of secularist, and even Erastian, royal servants. Although under Henry VI, first because of a minority during which many leading nobles were campaigning in France, and then because of a king who confused

piety with political judgement, bishops occupied a more prominent role than ever, they were not wisely chosen by the new king
and lacked the political experience and acumen to exert a beneficial
or positive influence on the later events of the reign. They reflected
and accentuated the lack of governance which characterized these
years. By that time bastard feudalism was as much a fact of
ecclesiastical as of lay society, frustrating diocesan order and
clerical discipline just as it menaced the security and peace of
laymen. Yet no cleric seriously appraised the problem or its
solutions. That was left to the common lawyer, layman and judge,
Sir John Fortescue. It is true that the clergy offered the crown the
support of general sentences of excommunication against its
enemies and disturbers of the peace, an offer even sought by
parliament, but bishops – as the letters of Beckington witness –
were powerless against these violators, and ironically the church
itself had long needed the assistance of the secular arm to make its
sanctions effective. The clergy's best hope – as they had recognized even in the early fourteenth century – lay in themselves
giving and receiving fees and pensions, and bestowing and seeking
good lordship. This abdication, as Genet has called it, from the
effort to seek a general solution sprang no doubt from the problems
of lollardy which preoccupied ecclesiastical writers in fifteenth-
century England, inclined them to complacent satisfaction with
the crown, and undermined their confidence in an appeal to the
political nation at large.

In the light of all this there is a temptation to regard the
Henrician Reformation of the sixteenth century as a natural
evolution from medieval developments, as though it were just a
little further 'down the ringing grooves of change'. Several
distinguished medievalists have pointed to the virtual sovereignty
exercised by the later Plantagenets. Yet that is to view the
Reformation too narrowly in constitutional terms as well as to
exaggerate the powers and claims of medieval kings, who at the
very least relied upon popes to appoint royal nominees to
bishoprics or, like even Henry VII, sought papal dispensations for
political matches (as for his marriage to Elizabeth of York or for his
son, Henry, to marry Catherine of Aragon). It may be that some
features of the Henrician Reformation have medieval roots:

anticlericalism can certainly be paralleled earlier, not only in the furore about benefit of clergy but also in the criticism of non-residence and of probate fees, and not least in the confiscations of, and plans to confiscate, church property. Nor would the attendance of lay grandees – such as the third duke of Norfolk – at convocation have surprised fourteenth-century observers. What the Tudor church lacked – conspicuously so under Warham – was independent political, and perspicacious moral, leadership, and this undoubtedly was the result of medieval developments dating back to the time of Edward III. Above all, Henry VII and Henry VIII exploited the 1393 statute of *Praemunire* to the crown's advantage, although it was the clergy themselves who around the 1430s first seem to have called attention to the wide potential of this neglected statute and brought it into the consciousness of the realm. None of this, however, entitles us to regard the English church as sliding gently but inexorably and almost imperceptibly from 1461 down into the schism of 1534. It is clear that while heresy revived in the later fifteenth century, so too did the orthodox church itself in the vitality of its spiritual life, the vigour of its self-criticism and the recruitment of clergy. Moreover, on the very eve of the Reformation the pope still enjoyed wide popular support and extensive powers in England. The orthodox still sought in Rome, and in great numbers, licences and dispensations from the law of the church. Pilgrims still made their way to the Holy City and lodged in the English College there – over a thousand in the Holy Year of 1500, some 400 in April alone in the next Holy Year, 1525.

In spite of the limitations on the exercise of papal authority which the medieval government imposed, the pope still had a substantial 'presence' in England. This emerges nowhere more clearly than from the great Reformation statutes themselves. The Act in restraint of appeals (1533) reminds us that the pope stood at the apex of ecclesiastical jurisdiction in England and was, despite all the writs and statutes of medieval times, resorted to by English litigants in all manner of causes – matrimony, divorce, tithes, testaments, and so on. Not only do the extant calendars of papal letters bear out this steady flow of business from Englishmen to Rome, but the maintenance of legal representatives there confirms it too. Indeed, to the majority of Englishmen the papacy must have been most familiar as a legal dispenser. The Act forbidding papal dispensations and payment of Peter's Pence (1534) reminds us of a negligible and ancient hearth tax, Peter's Pence, that was still being paid annually to papal collectors; more significantly, it draws our attention to that vast traffic in dispensations sought by English folk who wanted to marry within the forbidden degrees of affinity, or to take holy orders though illegitimately born or physically defective, or to hold benefices in plurality, or even to have a private altar. Through litigation and dispensation a large number of private individuals were still on the very eve of the Reformation made aware of papal authority and its claims. As for the Act in absolute restraint of annates (1534), this finally extinguished the theory as well as the fact of papal participation in episcopal appointments, and such fees – actually services – which were once collected from newly elected bishops were now transferred to the king. Papal collectors, nuncios and pardoners came to England no more; English kings, bishops, litigants and aspirants no longer solicited grants and paid fees in Rome. A whole flood of people, letters and money was suddenly dammed and redirected to Lambeth or Westminster.

The break from Rome in the 1530s was not a matter of merely making the implications of previous legislation explicit, nor yet a matter of extending slightly the already considerable restraints upon papal jurisdiction in England. It was not a surreptitious, imperceptible adjustment of frontiers, but a public demolition of what remained of papal authority, followed by a deliberate campaign to root out papal sentiments and loyalties from English hearts. The progress from *Praemunire* to Protestantism was not one of evolution, but revolution, and we should not allow this fact to be blurred by failing to recognize the novelty of the Reformation statutes. Their practical provisions were quite as revolutionary in the experience of the English people as their theoretical pre-ambles. In terms of church and realm relations, 1461 was as far removed from 1534 as it was from 1272.

Glossary

ADVOWSON	The right to present to, or patronage of, a benefice.
ALIEN PRIORY	Monastic house or estate dependent upon and subordinate to a continental, usually a Norman, monastery.
ALIENATION	The sale or gift of land or rights from one owner to another.
ANNATES	First year's income paid to the papacy by the incumbent of a benefice to which he had been papally provided. (See also services.)
APPROPRIATION	The conversion of the right of presentation to a rectory into possession of that rectory, usually by a religious house or collegiate church.
BENEFICE	Normally referring to the income, endowments and rights (or the living) of a parish church, but generally used of any church with income. Derived from *beneficium*, the feudal land given in return for service.
BENEFIT OF CLERGY	The legal privilege of those who could prove they were clergy to be tried and sentenced for felonies in the church courts and punished by the church.
BULL	An authoritative papal letter, sealed with the lead seal, or *bulla*, of the pope.

CANON — A church law or decree incorporated into the body of church law.

CANON/SECULAR CANON — A prebendary of a cathedral or collegiate church.

CANON LAW — The law of the church.

CANON LAWYER — A student of, or graduate in, canon law and often a practitioner in the church courts.

CANON REGULAR — A clerk who was not a monk but who lived in a community governed by a rule and belonged to one of the religious orders of canon regulars.

CAPITULAR — Relating to a chapter.

CHANTRY/IES — Endowments of masses, or of chaplains to say masses, for the souls of deceased testators and their nominees.

CHAPTER — The governing body of an ecclesiastical corporation, whether monastic community or cathedral clergy.

CIRCUMSPECTE AGATIS — First words of a writ of 1286, later regarded as a statute, which defined some boundaries between ecclesiastical and secular jursidiction.

COLLATE/ COLLATION — The episcopal act of appointing to a benefice where the bishop was, or was acting as or for, the patron.

COLLEGE — An ecclesiastical corporation having its own legal identity; not applicable to monastic houses, but it does embrace academic – which were then ecclesiastical – communities.

COMPURGATION	The process of establishing innocence, or failing to, in an ecclesiastical court, whereby six or usually a dozen men swear to the truth of the accused's assertion of innocence.
CONGÉ D'ÉLIRE	The royal licence permitting a cathedral chapter to elect a bishop; monastic houses which claimed the king as their patron or held their land directly from him, in return for a now notional feudal service, were also obliged to seek this licence before they elected their superior.
CONSULTATION	A writ which quashed prohibitions and allowed the church court to resume hearing the case.
CONTUMACY	Defiance of, or failure (when summoned) to appear in, an ecclesiastical court.
CORRODY	In effect board and lodging sold or granted by a religious house to laymen and women.
COURTS CHRISTIAN	The church courts of all kinds.
CURATE	Priest who exercised the cure of souls in a parish or who held an office to which it was attached in a cathedral; in parishes the curate could thus be the rector or vicar or the senior chaplain acting for them in their absence.
CURE (OF SOULS)	Responsibility for the care of souls of others.

CURIA | Latin for a court – in both senses of that word, royal and legal; applied to the king's court as well as the papal, but usually in this period chiefly with reference to the papal court or household.

DEAN | Head of a collegiate or secular cathedral chapter. Rural deans were diocesan officers usually appointed from the local clergy.

DECRETAL | A judicial decision made by or on behalf of the pope with reference to a particular case, but often collected afterwards to provide or illuminate legal principles.

DE EXCOMMUNICATO CAPIENDO | Royal writ for the capture, arrest and imprisonment of an excommunicate who after forty days was still unreconciled and whose name had been sent to the chancery by the bishop. (See signification.)

DE HERETICO COMBURENDO | The statute of 1401 for the burning of heretics.

DISPENSATION | A papally granted licence to do what is not permitted by canon law, or at least by the human laws of the church; it cannot alter what is deemed to be divine law, e.g. the Ten Commandments.

EXCOMMUNICATION | A sentence (in various forms and different degrees), pronounced in a court or by a bishop, which excluded the offenders to whom it applied from the sacraments and church services, or in the case of greater excommunication from law and society, until absolution was granted.

EX OFFICIO *PROCEEDINGS*	In effect prosecution in the church courts by the authorities for some offence against church discipline; contrast instance causes.
FAMILIA	The members of the household of a prelate or of a king.
GRAVAMINA	Official collective complaints by the clergy about infringements of the church's liberties and rights.
HOLY ORDERS (OR MAJOR)	Subdeacon, deacon and priest, to whom marriage was forbidden.
HOST	The consecrated bread of the mass.
INCUMBENT	The rightful holder of a benefice.
INDULGENCE	A grant of remission of penance for sins, usually emanating from the pope, but also, on a lesser scale of remission, from bishops; always in return for some specifically required act and on the assumption of full contrition by the recipient.
INSTANCE CAUSES	Causes in which one person sues another in the church courts.
JUDGE DELEGATE	Appointed from the local clergy, usually prelates or dignitaries, to judge locally on behalf of the pope an appeal or case brought before the papal court.
LAY	Any person not a clerk; that is, not in any orders, minor or holy, and any non-ecclesiastical office or property.
LAY FEE	Land or associated rights which fell within the competence of the king's courts.

LEGATE — Normally refers to the legate *a latere*, who was a papal plenipotentiary sent to reform the local church and overriding archiepiscopal authority. The English archbishops had a courtesy title of legate *natus*.

LOLLARD — Term of abuse, literally meaning 'mumbler', commonly applied to those who espoused Wyclif's heretical ideas or ideas similar to his.

MENDICANTS — The orders of friars, especially but not only the Franciscans, who lived by begging and not upon landed endowments like the traditional monastic orders.

METROPOLITAN — An archbishop.

MINOR ORDERS — The first tonsure and the four grades of clerkship below subdeacon, committing recipients neither to a clerical career nor to celibacy.

MOIETY — Literally half, commonly with reference to half a tenth.

MORTMAIN — Literally 'dead hand'; a term which was applied to land granted in perpetuity to the church; also the title of the statute of 1279 which barred all such grants.

NE ADMITTAS — Writ prohibiting a bishop from admitting a candidate to a benefice which was the subject of litigation in the king's court.

OFFICIAL — Deputy of archdeacon or bishop, presiding over their courts.

OFFICIAL PRINCIPAL — The bishop's deputy who presides over the bishop's consistory court.

ORDERS

Referring either to the grades of clerkship (holy or minor orders) or to the different associations of religious.

ORDINARY

A bishop or other prelate who exercises the jurisdiction of a bishop over a diocese or an enclave in a diocese.

ORDINATION

The ceremony by which clergy are promoted through the various grades, or orders, of clerkship. Also refers to the legal instrument by which a vicarage is endowed and permanently established.

PARSON

The rector of a church.

PATRON

The founder of a church, or the founder's descendant or successor, in whom was vested the right to present to a parish living, or – in the case of a religious house – various rights including that of consenting to the election of the head of the house.

PLENARTY

The question of whether or not a benefice was filled.

PLENITUDE OF POWER

The *plenitudo potestatis* or the papal claim to sovereignty over the clergy and church property.

PLURALISM

The holding of two or more benefices simultaneously, either within the limits approved by the law of the church or without them (when it required a dispensation or was punishable).

PRAEMUNIRE

Name of the writ and of two statutes (of 1353 and 1393) which threatened severe penalties for those who sued in church courts on matters which were deemed to be subject to the king's authority.

PREBEND

The endowment and income of a cathedral or collegiate canonry; could be estates or parish churches and their estates or even a fixed cash sum. Hence often a synonym for canonry, and a canon was often referred to as a prebendary.

PREBENDARY

Holder of a prebend, therefore usually a secular canon.

PRELATE

Archbishop, bishop or head of a religious house.

PRESENTEE

Candidate nominated by the patron for appointment to a benefice.

PROCTORS

Sworn representatives empowered to commit their principal, as in law suits; also elected representatives of lesser clergy in parliament and in convocation.

PROHIBITIONS

Writs suspending cases in, and removing them from, ecclesiastical courts for consideration in the king's courts.

PROVIDE

Direct papal appointment to a benefice, dignity or bishopric, overriding local patrons and electors, and based on the theory of the papal plenitude of power.

PROVINCE

Usually referring to a group of bishoprics subordinate to a metropolitan or archbishop; some religious orders, particularly the friars, were also organized into provinces.

PROVISION

The resulting appointment when a pope exercised his right to provide.

PROVISORS

Title of the statutes of 1351, 1365 and 1390 which attempted to limit the exercise of papal provision in England.

QUARE IMPEDIT	Writ sent to a bishop who refused to admit a presentee because the benefice was already full.
QUARE NON ADMISIT	Writ penalizing a bishop who had ignored a royal mandate to admit a presentee to a benefice.
RECTOR	The holder of a rectory.
RECTORY	The full income, endowments and office attached to the benefice of a parish church. Contrast 'vicarage'.
REGALIAN RIGHT	The king's customary right to enjoy the estates, lay income and the patronage – particularly ecclesiastical patronage – pertaining to a bishopric while vacant.
REGULAR	A monk, friar, nun or canon belonging to an order and living by its rule, or *regula*.
RELIGIOUS	See regular.
RESERVATIONS	The papal act of ear-marking specific benefices for future provisions.
SACRAMENTS	Seven sacred acts which were deemed in medieval theology to confer grace; the most esteemed was the celebration of the mass, sometimes simply referred to as 'the sacrament'.
SANCTUARY (RIGHT)	Churches or areas in their jurisdiction which were recognized as offering fugitives from the king's justice a refuge for forty days after which they had to leave its safety and abjure the realm as outlaws.
SECULAR ARM	The jurisdiction and law officers of the crown.

SECULAR CLERGY	Any cleric who was not a regular, but lived under no role and outside communities, in the world or *in saeculo*. The term applied to nearly all the parish clergy, most collegiate clergy and the canons of the secular cathedrals.
SEDE VACANTE	Vacant see (or bishopric).
SEE	The seat of a bishop, i.e. his bishopric.
SERVICES	A fixed sum due to the papacy from a prelate who had been provided to his see or abbacy.
SIGNIFICATION	Letter from the bishop informing the chancery of the king that a person had been an unreconciled excommunicate for more than forty days and requesting the crown to issue the writ *de excommunicato capiendo* for his arrest and imprisonment.
SILVA CEDUA TITHES	Strictly this referred to coppice wood not mature timber, but its precise application was much disputed.
SIMONY	The sin of purchasing spiritual office or grace.
SPIRITUALIA/ SPIRITUALITIES	Income or rights arising directly from the exercise of spiritual, sacramental or pastoral authority and duties.
SUBSIDY	Taxation granted by the clergy or laity to the crown.
SUFFRAGAN BISHOP	Usually refers to the deputy who fulfilled the diocesan bishop's spiritual functions, such as ordination, consecration, confirmation etc. Also used to designate the diocesan bishops of a province who were subject to the archbishop.

TEMPORALIA/
TEMPORALITIES

Income or rights arising from the possession of estates or the exercise of jurisdiction over, or in virtue of, them.

TENANTS-IN-CHIEF

Landowners who held some or all of their land direct from the king; among these were most of the bishops and the heads of many early religious houses.

TENTH

The common rate of clerical taxation, usually granted in multiples or fractions (e.g. half or moiety) of tenths.

TITHES

Theoretically a tenth of a parishioner's annual income or profit, and due by canon law to the incumbent of the parish. Normally regarded as *spiritualia* but when the proportion in question affected significantly the value of the benefice and hence of the advowson, then they were deemed to be lay fee.

USES

Effectively a form of trust whereby land or income from land was held by a number of trustees for the use of another person.

VICAR

Substitute for a rector and holder of the vicarage.

VICARAGE

The portion of an appropriated rectory which was set aside to support the vicar.

VICAR-GENERAL

The chief administrative deputy for the bishop, usually when the latter was absent from his diocese.

Abbreviations

AHR	*American Historical Review*
BIHR	*Bulletin of the Institute of Historical Research*
BJRL	*Bulletin of the John Rylands Library*
Econ.HR	*Economic History Review*
EHD: III	*English Historical Documents*: Vol. III
EHD: IV	*English Historical Documents*: Vol. IV
EHR	*English Historical Review*
JEH	*Journal of Ecclesiastical History*
JMH	*Journal of Medieval History*
PPC	*Proceedings and Ordinances of the Privy Council*, ed. H. Nicolas
RP	*Rotuli Parliamentorum*
SCH	*Studies in Church History*
TRHS	*Transactions of the Royal Historical Society*

References

Except where otherwise indicated, Roman numerals refer to volumes, Arabic to pages. Where they are not given in these references, full details of titles and of dates and places of publication will be found in the Select Bibliography below.

INTRODUCTION

1. For the various texts of Magna Carta see in *EHD: III*; 316 *sqq.*
2. Compare also on what follows J. R. Maddicott, 'Magna Carta and the Local Community 1215–1259', *Past and Present*, no. 102, pp. 25–65.
3. Any attempt to assess the church's share of the landed wealth of the realm runs into complex problems of definition and source material: see the article by A. Ayton and V. Davis, 'Ecclesiastical Wealth in England in 1086' *SCH*, xxiv (1987), 47–60, and S. Raban, *Mortmain Legislation and the English Church*, 7.
4. For the decrees of the Fourth Lateran, see *EHD: III*, 643–76.

CHAPTER 1   EDWARD I

1. See M. Prestwich, 'The Piety of Edward I'.
2. *Statutes of the Realm*, i, 26.
3. *Ibid.*, i, 55.
4. *Ibid.*, i, 147–8.
5. D. L. Douie, *Archbishop Pecham*, 129–30.
6. For this and what follows see Douie, *op. cit.*, ch. iii and the references there. See also R. Helmholz, 'The Writ of Prohibition to Court Christian before 1500'.
7. Fully examined and discussed in M. Howell, *Regalian Right in Medieval England*. See also for the revenue

accruing to the crown M. Prestwich, *War, Politics and Finance*, 178.

8. See for a full account F. D. Logan, *Excommunication and the Secular Arm in Medieval England*.

9. *Foedera*, I.ii, 593.

10. W. R. Jones, 'Relations of the Two Jurisdictions', 147.

11. F. M. Powicke, *The Thirteenth Century*, 356, n.1, citing G. O. Sayles, *Select Cases in the Court of King's Bench*, vol. i.

12. *Foedera*, I.ii, 598.

13. See note 5 above.

14. Douie, *Archbishop Pecham*, 123–30; C. Roth, *A History of the Jews in England* (Oxford, 3rd edn 1964), 68–90.

15. For texts see *EHD: III*, 462–4.

16. Logan, *Excommunication and the Secular Arm*, 66–8.

17. *Provinciale*, 353–5.

18. P. C. Saunders, *Royal Ecclesiastical Patronage in England 1199–1350*, 251–2, 391–3.

19. *The Chronicle of Walter of Guisborough*, 358–9.

20. Saunders, *Royal Ecclesiastical Patronage*, 288; Howell, *Regalian Right*, 186–93.

21. See J. H. Tillotson, 'Pensions, Corrodies and Religious Houses'.

22. Reviewed in T. F. T. Plucknett's *Legislation of Edward I* (Oxford 1949) and *Edward I and Criminal Law* (Cambridge 1959). For texts extensively abstracted from *Statutes of the Realm* see *EHD: III*, 384–466.

23. For discussion of the English episcopal legislation see M. Gibbs and J. Lang, *Bishops and Reform 1215–1272* (Oxford 1934), and C. R. Cheney, *English Synodalia of the Thirteenth Century* (Oxford 1941); above all, for the texts as well, see *Councils and Synods with Other Documents Relating to the English Church, II 1205–1313*, ed. F. M. Powicke and C. R. Cheney (Oxford 1964).

24. *Select Cases in the Court of King's Bench*, vol. i, pp. lxiii; iv, p. xix; Maddicott, *Law and Lordship*, 17–18; and P. A. Brand, 'Courtroom and Schoolroom'.

25. See J. M. W. Bean, *The Decline of English Feudalism 1215–1540* (Manchester 1967), S. A. Standen, *The*

Administration of the Statute of Mortmain, and S. Raban, *Mortmain Legislation and the English Church*; and P. A. Brand, 'The Control of Mortmain Alienation', where a case is made for tracing the origin to a *cause célèbre* in 1279.

26. This did not apply, of course, to the lands of bishoprics which were held by barony and reverted to the crown during vacancies, as did the lands of monastic prelates holding by barony.

27. See E. B. Graves, 'Circumspecte Agatis', *EHR* (1928), 1–20. For text see *Documents Illustrative of Church History*, 83–5.

28. The best and fullest account of this is in D. W. Sutherland, *Quo Warranto Proceedings in the Reign of Edward I, 1278–94* (1963).

29. For what follows see Plucknett, *Legislation of Edward I*, 90–4, and K. L. Wood-Legh, *Studies in Church Life*, 8–9.

30. c.4.X.3.18. A notion originating with Justinian for whom the time was three years (Pollock and Maitland, *History of English Law*, i, 353). Plucknett, *Legislation of Edward I*, 90, found some English sources, principally in the distraint of chattels.

31. M. Prestwich, *War, Politics and Finance* and J. H. Denton, *Robert Winchelsey and the Crown* provide the fullest and most recent accounts of these troubled years.

32. For English text see *Documents Illustrative of Church History*, 87–9.

33. *EHD: III*, 211.

34. *Ibid.*, 481.

35. English text in *Documents Illustrative of Church History*, 92–5.

36. D. J. A. Matthew, *The Norman Monasteries and their English Possessions*, 81–6. For the somewhat mysterious Cistercian angle see L. A. Desmond, *The Statute Legislation of Edward I and its Effects upon the English Cistercians to 1399*, 228–42.

37. G. O. Sayles, *The King's Parliament of England* and R. G. Davies and J. H. Denton, *The English Parliament in the Middle Ages* provide fuller bibliographical guidance.

38. F. W. Maitland, *Selected Historical Essays*, 53.
39. E. B. Fryde and E. Miller, *Historical Studies of the English Parliament* (Cambridge 1970), i, 150–67.
40. H. G. Richardson, 'The English Coronation Oath', *Speculum*, xxiv (1949), 49–50.
41. W. E. Lunt, *Financial Relations of England and the Papacy to 1327*, 157–65.
42. J. R. Wright, *The Church and the English Crown 1305–1334*, 157–63.
43. F. Cheyette, 'Kings, Courts, Cures and Sinecures', 312.
44. E. L. G. Stones and G. G. Simpson, *Edward I and the Throne of Scotland 1290–1296*, 2 vols (Oxford 1978), especially vol. i, chapter vi.

CHAPTER 2   EDWARD II

1. *Reg. Simonis de Gandavo*, vol. i, 237.
2. *Reg. Ricardi de Swinfield*, 451–2.
3. *Reg. Henrici de Woodlock*, vol. i, 370–1.
4. *Chronica Monasterii S. Albani: Johannis de Trocklowe*, 77–8.
5. *Chronicles of the Reigns of Edward I and Edward II: Gesta Edwardi auctore canonico Bridlingtoniensis* [henceforth *Chron. Bridlington*], ii, 66–9.
6. *Reg. Ade de Orleton*, 206–8; *Reg. Roger Martival*, vol. ii(2), 372.
7. *Chron. Bridlington*, 70–2.
8. *Reg. Martival*, vol. ii(2), 375–8.
9. M. Buck, *Politics, Finance and the Church in the Reign of Edward II*, 138.
10. *Reg. Orleton*, 235–7; *Reg. John Halton*, vol. ii, 219.
11. All of this is now fully documented in N. Fryde, *The Tyranny and Fall of Edward II*.
12. For fuller narratives of the deposition and discussion of the complex sources see Fryde, *Tyranny and Fall*; Buck, *Politics, Finance and the Church*; and R. M. Haines, *The Church and Politics in Fourteenth-Century England*, especially 161–80.
13. The queen's party which Kathleen Edwards identified in

her article 'The Political Importance of the English Bishops during the Reign of Edward II', has been demolished by Haines, *Church and Politics*, 154–5.

14. See N. Fryde, 'John Stratford, Bishop of Winchester, and the Crown, 1323–30'.

15. Haines, *Church and Politics*, 144–7.

16. Edwards, 'The Political Importance of the English Bishops', 328.

17. *Adae Murimuth Continuatio Chronicarum*, 37–8.

18. *Chron. Bridlington*, 79–82.

19. *Reg. Swinfield*, 490–1.

20. See W. E. Lunt, 'Clerical Tenths Levied in England . . . during the Reign of Edward II'.

21. Cited by W. A. Pantin, *The English Church in the Fourteenth Century*, 72.

22. See Davies and Denton, *The English Parliament*, 88–108, and Denton, 'The Making of the Articuli Cleri of 1316'.

23. For what follows see especially J. R. Wright, *The Church and the English Crown*, 101–35.

24. *Ibid.*, 246–7.

25. *Ibid.*, 72–93.

26. *Ibid.*, 142–54.

27. *Ibid.*, 225–7.

28. For a full study of Stapledon see Buck, *Politics, Finance and the Church*.

29. A. M. Leys, 'The Forfeiture of the Lands of the Templars in England'.

30. The classic account of these developments is to be found in T. F. Tout's *Chapters in Medieval Administrative History*, but Fryde, Buck and Saunders have recently added significantly to the picture.

31. The figures which follow are cited by J. S. Roskell, 'A Consideration of Certain Aspects and Problems of the English *Modus Tenendi Parliamentum*', 425–30.

32. For these see J. H. Denton, *English Royal Free Chapels, 1100–1300* (Manchester 1970), and *Victoria County History of Staffordshire*, iii (1970), 298ff.

33. J. L. Grassi, 'Royal Clerks from the Archdiocese of York', 16.
34. For this paragraph see Saunders, *Royal Ecclesiastical Patronage*, 251–3, 269, 317, 391–3.
35. Howell, *Regalian Right*, 194.
36. Wright, *The Church and the English Crown*, 230.
37. *Ibid.*, 169.

CHAPTER 3   EDWARD III
1. *EHD: IV*, 497.
2. See particularly Wright, *The Church and the English Crown*, 348–60; J. Barnie, *War in Medieval Society*, *passim*; W. R. Jones, 'The English Church and Royal Propaganda during the Hundred Years War'; A. K. McHardy, 'Liturgy and Propaganda in the Diocese of Lincoln during the Hundred Years War'.
3. Cited by Jones, 'The English Church and Royal Propaganda', 27.
4. G. R. Owst, *Literature and Pulpit*, 75–6.
5. Jones, *op. cit.*, 26.
6. *Ibid.*, 27.
7. *Ibid.*, 28.
8. McHardy, 'Liturgy and Propaganda', 217.
9. Jones, *op. cit.*, 22.
10. J. Coleman, *English Literature in History 1350–1400*, 72–3.
11. *Ibid.*, 266–7.
12. Barnie, *War in Medieval Society*, 117.
13. J. R. L. Highfield, *Relations between the Church and the English Crown 1349–78*, 193.
14. *Ibid.*, 195.
15. For what follows see B. McNab, 'Obligations of the Church in English Society, 1369–1418'.
16. See Matthew, *The Norman Monasteries and their English Possessions*, 151–2; G. L. Harriss, *King, Parliament and Public Finance to 1369*, 148; and L. A. Desmond, *The Statute Legislation of Edward I*, 253–5.
17. *Cal. Patent Rolls, 1340–3*, 129.
18. Highfield, *Relations between the Church and the English Crown*, 451–2.

19. V. H. Galbraith, 'Articles laid before the Parliament of 1371', *EHR*, xxxiv (1919), 579–82.

20. On this and its ramifications see G. Holmes, *The Good Parliament*.

21. The clearest account of this complex crisis is now to be found in R. M. Haines, *Archbishop Stratford*, 278–327. For a less charitable view of Stratford see N. Fryde's articles, 'John Stratford, Bishop of Winchester' and 'Edward III's Removal of his Ministers'.

22. On the origins of chancery jurisdiction see B. Wilkinson, *The Chancery under Edward III* (Manchester 1929).

23. See below.

24. L. McFarlane, 'An English Account of the Election of Urban VI, 1378', *BIHR* (1953), 83–4, reporting the views and reactions of temporal lords in answer to a French cardinal's enquiry.

25. Saunders, *Royal Ecclesiastical Patronage*, 391–3, for these figures, and elsewhere in his thesis for what follows in this paragraph.

26. A. K. McHardy, 'The Alien Priories and the Expulsion of Aliens from England in 1378', where Dr McHardy notes that between 1369 and 1398 in that diocese 223 benefices formerly in the gift of alien priories or foreign houses were filled with crown presentees.

27. Saunders, *op. cit.*, 345–7.

28. Pantin, *The English Church in the Fourteenth Century*, 47–75.

29. Highfield, *Relations between the Church and the English Crown*, 406–9, and Wright, *The Church and the English Crown*, 5–14, 275.

30. Pantin, *op. cit.*, 49.

31. *Idem*.

32. E. F. Jacob, *Essays in the Conciliar Epoch*, chapter 12.

33. Pantin, *op. cit.*, 70.

34. *Ibid.*, 83.

35. W. E. Lunt, *Financial Relations of the Papacy with England 1327–1534*, chapters v–viii; Appendix ii, pp. 724–800, 825–31.

36. I am indebted to Dr J. J. N. Palmer for the details of this argument which are contained in his unpublished paper on the subject.
37. *Statutes of the Realm*, ii, 316–18.
38. F. Cheyette, 'Kings, Courts, Cures and Sinecures', 322, n.82; and Howell, *Regalian Right*, 186–93.
39. See the figures quoted in Wright, *The Church and the English Crown*, 275, and the discussion by Cheyette, *op. cit.*
40. E. B. Graves, 'The Legal Significance of the Statute of *Praemunire* of 1353', 60, n.17.
41. *Statutes of the Realm*, i, 329. Also *Documents Illustrative of Church History*, 103–4.
42. See J. J. N. Palmer, 'England, France, the Papacy and the Flemish Succession'.
43. For what follows see J. J. N. Palmer and A. P. Wells, 'Ecclesiastical Reform and the Politics of the Hundred Years War'.
44. Lunt, *Financial Relations . . . 1327–1534*, 66–73.
45. W. R. Jones, 'Bishops, Politics and the Two Laws', 227–34.
46. *Statutes of the Realm*, i, 324–6.
47. See Highfield, 'The English Hierarchy in the Reign of Edward III'.
48. Haines, 'An English Archbishop and the Cerberus of War', 165.
49. Highfield, *op. cit.*
50. For Bradwardine see *Dictionary of National Biography* and A. B. Emden, *Biographical Register of the University of Oxford*.
51. On Langham see *Dict. Nat. Biog.*
52. See R. G. Davies, 'The Anglo–Papal Concordat of Bruges 1375'.
53. *Dict. Nat. Biog.*
54. *Dict. Nat. Biog.*
55. See Holmes, *The Good Parliament*.
56. See above, p. 116.

CHAPTER 4   PLAGUE AND DISRUPTION

 1. The now extensive literature on this topic is succinctly

reviewed in J. Hatcher, *Plague, Population and the English Economy 1348–1530* (1977).

2. J. F. D. Shrewsbury, *The History of Bubonic Plague in England* (Cambridge 1973), reviewed by C. Morris, 'The Plague in Britain', *Historical Journal*, xiv (1971), 205–15.
3. Hatcher, *op. cit.*, 22–4.
4. D. Knowles, *Religious Orders in England*, vol. ii, 10–11.
5. A. H. Thompson, 'The Register of John Gynewell', 311.
6. See A. R. Bridbury, 'The Black Death' and 'Before the Black Death'; A. H. Thompson, 'The Register of John Gynewell' and 'Pestilences of the Fourteenth Century in Yorkshire'; A. Jessop, *The Coming of the Friars and Other Essays* (1889), 205.
7. For the Collingtons see *Reg. Johannis Trillek*, 174–6; for Winchester diocese see *Wykeham's Register*, vol. ii, 121–2.
8. See B. Putnam, 'Maximum Wage-Laws for Priests after the Black Death, 1348–81'.
9. *EHD: IV*, 728–9.
10. J. A. Raftis, 'Changes in an English Village after the Black Death', *Medieval Studies*, xxix (1967), 158–77.
11. R. H. Hilton, *The Decline of Serfdom in Medieval England* (1969), 54.
12. A. H. Thompson, *The English Clergy and their Organization*, 107–9.
13. R. L. Storey, *Diocesan Administration in the Fifteenth Century* (2nd edn), 14–15.
14. K. L. Wood-Legh, *Studies in Church Life*, 124–5.
15. A. H. Thompson, 'The Register of John Gynewell', 310; 'Pestilences of the Fourteenth Century in Yorkshire', 116.

CHAPTER 5   LEARNING AND LITERACY

1. See above, p. 99.
2. T. H. Aston, 'Oxford's Medieval Alumni' and 'The Medieval Alumni of the University of Cambridge'.
3. A. B. Cobban, *The King's Hall within the University of Cambridge* (Cambridge 1969).
4. See T. H. Aston, *op. cit.*, J. Dunabin, 'Careers and Vocations', and G. F. Lytle, *Oxford Students and English Society: c. 1300–c. 1510*.

5. *RP*, iii, 459.
6. On these see J. Coleman, *English Literature in History*, 31 (citing Tout's *Chapters*).
7. Pantin, *The English Church in the Fourteenth Century*, 128.
8. Convincingly resolved in Coleman, *op. cit.*
9. It was G. R. Owst, in *Literature and Pulpit*, who expressed it in this way.
10. Douie, *Archbishop Pecham*, 134–5, 138–42.
11. M. T. Clanchy, *From Memory to Written Record*.
12. Pantin, *op. cit.*, chapters ix–x.
13. N. Orme, *English Schools in the Middle Ages*, chapters 6 and 7; J. A. H. Moran, *The Growth of English Schooling 1340–1548*, chapters 4 and 5.
14. See H. G. Richardson, 'Business Training in Medieval Oxford'.
15. Dobson, 'The Late Middle Ages, 1215–1500', 67, 69–71.
16. Well documented by Coleman, *op. cit.*, 40, 51–2, 170–2.

CHAPTER 6   WYCLIF AND LOLLARDY
1. A. Gransden, *Historical Writing in England*, vol. ii, 131; *English Wycliffite Writings*, 33, 159.
2. W. Farr, *John Wyclif as Legal Reformer*, 26.
3. *EHD: IV*, 656–7.
4. Farr, *op. cit.*, 29.
5. *Ibid.*, 68–9, 85; *EHD: IV*, 656.
6. Farr, *op. cit.*, 43.
7. *Ibid.*, 153, n.90.
8. *Ibid.*, 37: 'Just as members of the body are not that body, so particular churches are not that holy church, but members of it.'
9. *EHD: IV*, 657.
10. M. Wilks, 'Royal Priesthood: the Origins of Lollardy', 63–70.
11. K. B. McFarlane, *Lancastrian Kings and Lollard Knights*, part II.
12. See below, p. 211.
13. G. O. Sayles, 'King Richard II of England: a Fresh Look', in his *Scripta Diversa* (1982), 282.

14. K. B. McFarlane, *Lancastrian Kings and Lollard Knights*, 196.
15. A. Hudson, 'Wyclif and the English Language'.
16. See H. Hargreaves, 'The Wycliffite Versions' in *Cambridge History of the Bible*, ii, ed. G. W. H. Lampe (Cambridge 1969), 387–415, and A. Hudson, 'Wyclif and the English Language'.
17. M. Aston, 'John Wycliffe's Reformation Reputation'.
18. For the familiarity see Owst, *Literature and Pulpit*, and Pantin, *The English Church in the Fourteenth Century*.
19. A point underlined by A. Hudson, 'Wycliffism in Oxford 1381–1411'.
20. For this paragraph I am principally indebted to Dr Kightly's York Ph.D. thesis, *The Early Lollards*.
21. See especially Hudson's introduction to her edition of *English Wycliffite Sermons*, vol. i, 187–202.
22. For this paragraph see H. G. Richardson, 'Heresy and the Lay Power under Richard II'.
23. See below, pp. 251–2.

CHAPTER 7 RICHARD II
1. E. B. Fryde's 'Introduction', pp. xi–xviii in C. Oman, *The Great Revolt of 1381* (1969 edn).
2. For the details which follow see *The Church in London 1375–1392*, pp. ix–xv; J. L. Kirby, 'Two Tax Accounts of the Diocese of Carlisle, 1379–80' and 'Clerical Poll Taxes in the Diocese of Salisbury, 1377–81'.
3. A. J. Prescott, *Judicial Records of the Rising of 1381*.
4. Further on Sudbury see W. L. Warren, 'A Re-appraisal of Simon Sudbury'.
5. R. H. Hilton, *Bond Men Made Free* (1973), 207–13; H. B. Workman, *John Wyclif* (Oxford 1926), ii, 225, n.3 for list of clerics.
6. Gransden, *Historical Writing in England*, ii, 133, 169.
7. F. R. H. Du Boulay, *The Lordship of Canterbury*, 189, 249.
8. See for the animus against lawyers and contemporary comments on this, J. R. Maddicott, *Law and Lordship*, 61–2.

9. For the details consult M. Aston, 'The Impeachment of Bishop Despenser'.

10. J. J. N. Palmer, *England, France and Christendom*, chapter 11.

11. For Courtenay's leadership in this period see J. Dahmus, *William Courtenay, Archbishop of Canterbury*. Details of the subsidies are to be found in the *Calendar of Fine Rolls*.

12. *Cal. Fine Rolls, 1383–91*, 125.

13. F. D. Logan, *Excommunication and the Secular Arm*, 55–7.

14. *RP*, iii, 250.

15. *Annales Ricardi Secundi et Henrici Quarti*, 212–13.

16. *Ibid.*, 210–13.

17. *RP*, iii, 348; see also R. G. Davies who offers a fuller and rather different account in 'Richard II and the Church in the Years of Tyranny', 337–41.

18. *RP*, iii, 351.

19. *Ibid.*, 356.

20. *Ibid.*, 372, 359, 381.

21. C. Barron, 'The Tyranny of Richard II', 15.

22. For this paragraph see *EHD: IV*, 167–9; *RP*, iii, 341, 434.

23. C. Given-Wilson, *The Royal Household and the King's Affinity* (Yale, 1986), 182.

24. *RP*, iii, 25–7.

25. *Ibid.*, 37, 50–1.

26. *Westminster Chronicle*, 311–13, 324–5.

27. *Ibid.*, 327.

28. *Select Cases in the Court of King's Bench*, vol. vii, 120–1.

29. *RP*, iii, 25.

30. *Ibid.*, 25, 43.

31. *Ibid.*, 27, 43, 65, 116, 201, 281, 295, 307, 318 for petitions in 1377, 1378, 1379, 1381, 1384, 1390, 1391, 1393 and 1394. See N. Adams, *EHR* (1937), 19–21.

32. *Ibid.*, 19, 29; S. A. Standen, *The Administration of the Statute of Mortmain*, 143–6.

33. *RP*, iii, 117.

34. *Ibid.*, 294, 319.

35. R. G. Davies, 'The Episcopate and the Political Crisis in England of 1386–88', has unravelled this complex affair.

36. *Statutes of the Realm*, ii, 60.

37. *RP*, iii, 266–7.

38. *Statutes of the Realm*, ii, 69–74.

39. *RP*, iii, 264.

40. *Foedera*, III, iv, 68.

41. *Cal. Papal Letters, 1362–1404*, 277; *RP*, iii, 201.

42. Fully discussed by W. T. Waugh, 'The Great Statute of *Praemunire*'.

43. *RP*, iii, 304.

44. See the references in W. Ullmann, ' "This Realm of England is an Empire" '.

45. *PPC*, i, 53–4.

46. *RP*, iii, 340–1.

47. *Ibid.*, 341.

48. *PPC*, i, 80–1.

49. For the text see E. Perroy, *L'Angleterre et le grand schisme*, 419–20. For correction of Perroy's interpretation of the schism in Anglo–papal relations see J. J. N. Palmer, 'England and the Great Western Schism'.

50. See note 23 above.

CHAPTER 8   HENRY IV

1. For much of what follows on Arundel see K. B. McFarlane, *Lancastrian Kings and Lollard Knights*, 50–3, and R. L. Storey, 'Episcopal King-Makers'.

2. On the problem of the evidence see J. J. N. Palmer, 'The Authorship, Date and Historical Value of French Chronicles of the Lancastrian Revolution', 417–19.

3. *Annales Ricardi Secundi et Henrici Quarti*, 252.

4. *Chron. Adae de Usk*, 181–3.

5. G. E. Caspary, 'Deposition of Richard II and Canon Law'.

6. W. Ullmann, 'Thomas Becket's Miraculous Oil'; T. A. Sandquist, 'The Holy Oil of St Thomas of Canterbury'; J. W. McKenna, 'The Coronation Oil of Yorkist Kings'.

7. R. L. Storey, 'Clergy and Common Law', 342.

8. *Chron. Adae de Usk*, 193.

9. See note 2 above.

10. For much of what follows see J. W. Dahmus, 'Thomas Arundel and the Baronial Party under Henry IV'.

11. J. L. Kirby, 'Councils and Councillors', *TRHS* (1964), 46.

12. Quoted by Kirby, *ibid.*, 41.

13. *RP*, iii, *passim*.

14. E. F. Jacob, 'The Canterbury Convocation of 1406', 348–50.

15. *Royal and Historical Letters of the Reign of Henry IV*, vol. i, 413–14.

16. *PPC*, ii, 100.

17. *Cal. Signet Letters*, no. 328.

18. A. Steel, *Receipt of the Exchequer*, 134–5.

19. *Cal. Signet Letters*, no. 939.

20. B. Wilkinson, *Constitutional History of England in the Fifteenth Century*, 306–7.

21. *Wykeham's Reg.*, ii, 500; *Reg. Repingdon*, i, 18–20, 47–8; *Reg. Mascall*, 6; *Reg. Bubwith*, i, 126.

22. See Glanmor Williams, *Owen Glendower*, for an excellent brief account.

23. Glanmor Williams, *The Welsh Church from Conquest to Reformation*, chapter VI.

24. *Cal. Close Rolls, 1399–1402*, 28; *Annales Henrici IV*, 314.

25. *Cal. Patent Rolls, 1399–1401*, 385.

26. *Cal. Close Rolls, 1399–1402*, 34. See for his trial *Select Cases in the Court of King's Bench*, vol. vii, 102–5.

27. *Ibid.*, 108, 167.

28. *Chron. Adae de Usk*, 204.

29. *Ibid.*, 231–6.

30. Wylie, *History of England under Henry IV*, i, 266.

31. For a full account see D. W. Whitfield, 'Conflicts of Personality and Principle', and for a different interpretation of some details, M. W. Sheehan, *Franciscan Poverty in England 1348–1538*, 202–19.

32. *Cal. Close Rolls, 1402–5*, 338–9.

33. But see Sheehan, *op. cit.*, 208.

34. J. H. Wylie, *History of England under Henry IV*, i, 420–8; J. L. Kirby, *Henry IV*, 172.

35. Kirby, *Henry IV*, 190; R. Griffiths, 'Some Secret Supporters of Owain Glyn Dŵr', *BIHR* (1964), 77–100.
36. P. McNiven, 'The Betrayal of Archbishop Scrope', and J. W. McKenna, 'Popular Canonization as Political Propaganda'.
37. *Historians of the Church of York*, iii, 294–304.
38. *Cal. Signet Letters*, nos 941, 944.
39. *Reg. Repingdon*, i, 135–40.
40. Wylie, *op. cit.*, iii, 153–8.
41. P. McNiven, 'The Problem of Henry IV's Health 1405–13', for the fullest and best analysis of this subject.
42. *EHD: IV*, 664–5.
43. *RP*, iii, 454.
44. For tax details see A. Rogers, 'Clerical Taxation under Henry IV', and E. F. Jacob, 'The Canterbury Convocation of 1406'.
45. See note 15 above.
46. *Reg. Mascall*, 201; *Cal. Signet Letters*, no. 410.
47. On resistance see *Cal. Patent Rolls, 1401–5*, 484; *Cal. Patent Rolls, 1405–8*, 408; *Cal. Patent Rolls, 1409–13*, 356–7.
48. *PPC*, i, 102–5.
49. *Ibid.*, i, 199–203.
50. *Cal. Signet Letters*, no. 208.
51. *PPC*, i, 270–1; *Cal. Signet Letters*, no. 939.
52. *PPC*, ii, 31–2.
53. *Statutes of the Realm*, ii, 132–3.
54. Storey, 'Clergy and Common Law', 344.
55. *Ibid.*, 352.
56. *RP*, iii, 494.
57. *Statutes of the Realm*, ii, 133.
58. *RP*, iii, 438.
59. *Ibid.*, ii, 507; *Statutes of the Realm*, ii, 139–40.
60. e.g. *RP*, iii, 438.
61. *Ibid.*, iii, 470.
62. *Wykeham's Reg.*, ii, 617–18.
63. Storey, 'Clergy and Common Law', 347–8.
64. *Ibid.*, 350–1.

65. *Cal. Signet Letters*, no. 945.
66. Wylie, *op. cit.*, i, 178.
67. *Cal. Close Rolls, 1399–1402*, 185.
68. Wylie, *op. cit.*, i, 181–6.
69. *RP*, iii, 466–7.
70. *Ibid.*, iii, 473–4; *Statutes of the Realm*, ii, 125–8.
71. *RP*, iii, 583–4.
72. *EHD: IV*, 855–7.
73. *Statutes of the Realm*, ii, 159.
74. *Cal. Signet Letters*, no. 745.
75. *Statutes of the Realm*, ii, 166.
76. G. Leff, *Paris and Oxford Universities in the Thirteenth and Fourteenth Centuries* (1968), 308.
77. *Loci e Libro Veritatum*, 181.
78. On Cheyne see J. S. Roskell, *The Commons and their Speakers in English Parliaments 1376–1523* (Manchester 1965), 26, 68–9; and K. B. McFarlane, *Lancastrian Kings and Lollard Knights*, 168–71.
79. *Annales Ricardi Secundi et Henrici Quarti*, 373–4.
80. *Ibid.*, 391. The spokesman for these men is said to be no other than Cheyne, the dismissed speaker of 1399; but Cheyne was no longer even an MP and there is clearly some confusion in the sources, so much so that some historians prefer to place this event in 1399. That, however, still raises problems about his role, and the proposal to seize the temporalities in 1404 chimes well with other measures then being forced upon the king for the resumption of all crown grants.
81. Many clergy were to suffer anyway under the Act of Resumption, for their annuities, like laymen's, fell under the ban too; see *Cal. Signet Letters*, no. 674.
82. *EHD: IV*, 668–70, where, however, the number of clerks is wrongly given as 1500 – not a figure from the texts; see also *English Wycliffite Writings*, 135–7, 203–7.
83. *St Albans Chronicle*, 56.
84. McFarlane, *Lancastrian Kings and Lollard Knights*, 191–2; Roskell, *The Commons and their Speakers*, 353–4.
85. *RP*, iii, 644.

86. *Reg. Langley*, i, 103–5; P. Heath, 'North Sea Fishing in the Fifteenth Century: the Scarborough Fleet', *Northern History*, iii (1968), 54–5.

87. *RP*, iii, 465.

88. *Royal and Historical Letters*, ii, 141–4.

89. *RP*, iii, 428–9.

90. *Ibid.*, iii, 458–9.

91. *Ibid.*, iii, 621.

92. *PPC*, i, 250; ii, 60; and *Royal and Historical Letters*, ii, 45.

93. *Royal and Historical Letters*, ii, 139–41; *Cal. Signet Letters*, no. 688.

94. *PPC*, i, 282; ii, 113.

95. Storey, 'Clergy and Common Law', 348.

96. *EHD: IV*, 666–7 and references there; Storey, 'Clergy and Common Law', 349.

97. *RP*, iii, 465, 470.

98. *Ibid.*, iii, 596.

99. Lunt, *Financial Relations . . . 1327–1534*, 404–5.

100. *RP*, iii, 468; *Statutes of the Realm*, ii, 121.

101. *RP*, iii, 465.

102. E. F. Jacob, 'A Note on the English Concordat of 1418', 357.

103. *RP*, iii, 505.

104. *Statutes of the Realm*, ii, 80, 136–7.

105. Jacob, 'A Note on the English Concordat', 357.

106. *Cal. Signet Letters*, no. 929.

107. *RP*, iii, 542.

108. E. F. Jacob, *Essays in Later Medieval History*, 68, n.3.

109. *RP*, iii, 557; *Statutes of the Realm*, ii, 148–9; Lunt, *Financial Relations . . . 1327–1534*, 298–9.

110. Lunt, *op. cit.*, 119–25.

111. *PPC*, i, 115–17.

112. *RP*, iii, 460.

113. On these events see R. G. Davies, 'After the Execution of Archbishop Scrope'.

114. *Cal. Signet Letters*, no. 943.

CHAPTER 9   HENRY V

1. *RP*, iii, 583–4, briefly extracted and translated in Wilkinson, *Constitutional History*, 391.
2. See *Four English Political Tracts of the Later Middle Ages*, 40–168.
3. G. L. Harriss has edited the Oxford defence, *Henry V: The Practice of Kingship*.
4. *Gesta Henrici Quinti*, pp. xxix–xxx.
5. *Ibid.*, Appendix II, 186–7; and also for the Celestines, *St Albans Chronicle*, 82.
6. *Gesta Henrici Quinti*, 155.
7. *Ibid.*, 145–7.
8. K. B. McFarlane, *John Wycliffe and the Beginnings of English Non-conformity*, 160–85, and Dr Catto, 'Religious Change under Henry V'. See the account of the rising in *Select Cases in the Court of King's Bench*, vii, 217–20.
9. J. Catto, 'Religious Change', 97–8.
10. *Gesta Henrici Quinti*, 5, citing I Cor. 10:13.
11. *Statutes of the Realm*, ii, 181–4.
12. *PPC*, ii, 167.
13. *Reg. Bubwith*, i, 244.
14. *Ibid.*, i, 283–90.
15. *St Albans Chronicle*, 88.
16. Hoccleve, quoted by Catto, 'The King's Servants', 80.
17. *Reg. Bubwith*, i, 245. Mandates for prayers abound in the bishops' registers of the time.
18. *Reg. Lacy*, 63–5.
19. *Reg. Repingdon*, iii, 289; *Reg. Lacy*, 81–3.
20. *Gesta Henrici Quinti*, 85–7, 89.
21. *Reg. Chichele*, iii, 8–10.
22. E. F. Jacob, *Henry Chichele*, 67.
23. *Reg. Repingdon*, iii, 95.
24. Fully described in *Gesta Henrici Quinti*, 101–13.
25. For details of the grants, conditions and collection see *Cal. Fine Rolls*.
26. See Steel, *Receipt of the Exchequer*.
27. See especially McNab, 'Obligations of the Church', 293–314.

28. *Reg. Bubwith*, i, 214–15; *Reg. Repingdon*, iii, 54–5, where the arithmetic poses problems; McNab, *op. cit.*, 308.
29. McNab, 312; *Reg. Lacy*, 32–4.
30. R. L. Storey, *Thomas Langley and the Bishopric of Durham*, 211.
31. Catto, 'The King's Servants', 87–8.
32. *Gesta Henrici Quinti*, 50, n.3.
33. E. F. Jacob, *Henry V and the Invasion of France*, 38.
34. *Statutes of the Realm*, ii, 176; see also Helmholz, 'The Writ of Prohibition to Court Christian'.
35. *RP*, iv, 153; compare Helmholz, *op. cit.*, and 'Writs of Prohibition and Ecclesiastical Sanctions in English Courts Christian'.
36. *PPC*, ii, 181–2.
37. *RP*, iv, 21.
38. *Ibid.*, iv, 8–9, 19, 84; *Statutes of the Realm*, ii, 195–6; *Chron. Adae de Usk*, 304.
39. *Statutes of the Realm*, ii, 188; *RP*, iv, 51–2, 121.
40. *Reg. Langley*, ii, 184–6; iii, 45.
41. *Handbook of British Chronology*, ed. E. B. Fryde *et al.* (3rd edn, 1986), 209–99.
42. See Emden, *Biographical Register of the University of Oxford* and *Biographical Register of the University of Cambridge*, and the *Dict. Nat. Biog.* for details and references.
43. On Courtenay see Catto, 'The King's Servants', 87.
44. Storey, *Thomas Langley*, 38–9, for this and what follows in this paragraph.
45. I have based what follows on C. M. D. Crowder, 'Henry V, the Emperor Sigismund and the Council of Constance'.
46. E. F. Jacob, 'A Note on the English Concordat'.
47. See K. B. McFarlane, 'Henry V, Bishop Beaufort and the Red Hat'.
48. Quoted by G. L. Harriss, *Henry V*, 46.
49. Catto, 'Religious Change', 115.

CHAPTER 10 HENRY VI

1. *Memorials of the Reign of Henry VI*, i, 155–7.

2. Cited in C. Head, 'Pope Pius II and the Wars of the Roses', 145.

3. *PPC*, iii, 330–8, 339–42; iv, 16. For a full account of this episode see G. A. Holmes, 'Cardinal Beaufort and the Crusade against the Hussites'.

4. *Ibid.*, iii, 323; iv, 100–1; *RP*, iv, 390–2.

5. *Letters and Papers Illustrative of the Wars . . . during the Reign of Henry VI*, ii, 443.

6. Fully explored in R. A. Griffiths, 'The Trial of Eleanor Cobham'.

7. For the Canterbury grants see *Reg. Chichele*, iii, 88–98, 101–3, 180–1, 183–215, 218–26, 230–6, 242–52. Summarized by A. K. McHardy, 'Clerical Taxation in Fifteenth-Century England', 183–6.

8. For York see McHardy, *op. cit.*, 179–82.

9. Steel, *Receipt of the Exchequer*, chapters III, IV, VII.

10. See for the financial details G. L. Harriss, 'Cardinal Beaufort, Patriot or Usurer?'

11. R. G. Davies, 'Martin V and the English Episcopate'.

12. Jacob, *Henry Chichele*, 42–8; *RP*, iv, 322.

13. Lunt, *Financial Relations . . 1327–1534*, 432–6.

14. *Ibid.*, chapters v–viii and Appendix ii, 724–800, 825–31.

15. *PPC*, iii, 210; see also Davies, 'Martin V and the English Episcopate'.

16. *PPC*, iii, 269.

17. *Ibid.*, iv, 285, 286.

18. *Cal. Papal Letters, 1427–47*, 230–1, 254.

19. R. B. Dobson, *Durham Priory*, 226–7.

20. Lunt, *op. cit.*, 125–31; *Memorials of the Reign of Henry VI*, i, 255–7.

21. Lunt, *ibid.*, 131–40; Jacob, *Essays in Later Medieval History*, 52–7.

22. For what follows and for further references see M. Aston, 'Lollardy and Sedition' and 'William White's Lollard Followers'; for northern action in 1428 see *Reg. Langley*, iii, 88–9.

23. *Reg. Chichele*, iii, 84–5.

24. E. F. Jacob, 'Reynold Pecock, Bishop of Chichester'.

25. *EHD: IV*, 490–1; but compare *EHD: V*, 563–8. See also E. W. Ives, 'The Common Lawyer in Pre-Reformation England', *TRHS* (1968), 145–73; and P. A. Brand, 'Courtroom and Schoolroom'.
26. R. L. Storey, 'Recruitment of the English Clergy in the Period of the Conciliar Movement'.
27. See particularly for this paragraph C. W. Smith, 'Some Trends in the English Royal Chancery'.
28. R. L. Storey, 'Gentlemen-Bureaucrats', 99–100.
29. *Ibid.*, 97–100, 110–21.
30. J. Otway-Ruthven, *The King's Secretary*, 126–31.
31. See R. A. Griffiths, 'Public and Private Bureaucracies in England and Wales'.
32. *RP*, iv, 305–6.
33. R. B. Dobson, 'The Late Middle Ages 1215–1500', 66, 73–4.
34. J-P. Genet, 'Ecclesiastics and Political Theory', especially 35–6.
35. *PPC*, iii, 66; v, 265.
36. *Ibid.*, iii, 311; v, 9; vi, 24–5, 52. On Kemp see now J. A. Nigota, *John Kempe*, 319–26.
37. *Ibid.*, iv, 69–71.
38. *Ibid.*, v, 341–2.
39. *Memorials of the Reign of Henry VI*, i, 38–41, 50; J. M. George, *The English Episcopate and the Crown 1437–1450*, 184; Nigota, *John Kempe*, 308–18.
40. M. S. Blust, *English Clerical Diplomats 1327–1461*, 29–52.
41. I am indebted to Dr Virginia Davis's unpublished thesis on Waynflete for calling my attention to this subject. The evidence is available in the commissions of the peace listed in the *Cal. Patent Rolls*.
42. *Reg. Spofford*, 289–91; *Reg. Lacy*, i, 253; iii, 54–5.
43. *Reg. Lacy*, i, 273–8.
44. *PPC*, v, 421–2.
45. See below, pp. 326–7.
46. On the nature of bastard feudalism the best guides are K. B. McFarlane, 'Bastard Feudalism'; G. Holmes, *The Estates of the Higher Nobility in the Fourteenth Century*

(Cambridge 1959); W. H. Dunham, Jnr, *Lord Hastings's Indentured Retainers* (Connecticut 1955); and – for some details of the disorder in Lancastrian England – R. L. Storey, *The End of the House of Lancaster* (1966).

47. K. B. McFarlane, 'The Wars of the Roses', *Proceedings of the British Academy* (1964), 109.

48. F. R. H. Du Boulay, *The Lordship of Canterbury*, 270.

49. *Ibid.*, 275–6.

50. *Statutes of the Realm*, ii, 74–5, 155, 240–1.

51. See E. D. Jones, 'The Church and Bastard Feudalism', for what follows.

52. See N. Ramsay, 'Retained Legal Counsel *c*.1275–*c*.1475', *TRHS* (1985), especially 96–103; and R. W. Dunning, 'Patronage and Promotion in the Late Medieval Church', 169.

53. *Letters of Queen Margaret of Anjou*, 103.

54. *Ibid.*, 119–20.

55. *RP*, iii, 489.

56. *Ibid.*, iv, 407–8, 506–7; v, 325–6.

57. *PPC*, v, 241.

58. *Ibid.*, v, 151–2.

59. *Ibid.*, v, 273–5, 309.

60. P. Heath, 'The Medieval Archdeaconry and Tudor Bishopric of Chester', 251.

61. *Memorials of the Reign of Henry VI*, ii, 340–2, corrected in *Reg. Bekynton*, ii, 550.

62. *Memorials of the Reign of Henry VI*, ii, 342–3.

63. *PPC*, v, 124–6.

64. See for these examples L. C. Gabel, *Benefit of Clergy in England in the Later Middle Ages* (Northampton, Mass. 1929).

65. *Reg. Chichele*, iii, 211, 284–5; Jacob, *Essays in Later Medieval History*, 52.

66. *RP*, v, 152–3; *Statutes of the Realm*, ii, 352.

67. *RP*, v, 151.

68. *Ibid.*, v, 333–4.

69. *Provinciale*, 353–5; *Reg. Chichele*, iii, 224–6, 253–8; *RP*, iv, 421; *John Mirk's Instructions for Parish Priests*, 105.

70. *Reg. Spofford*, 198–201; *Reg. Lacy*, ii, 8–10; *John Mirk's Instructions for Parish Priests*, 104–6.
71. *Reg. Lacy*, iii, 39–41, 56–8.
72. Dobson, *Durham Priory*, 197–202. Further on arbitration see E. Powell, 'Arbitration and the Law in England in the Later Middle Ages', *TRHS* (1983), 49–67.
73. *PPC*, v, 225.
74. See G. L. Harriss, 'Marmaduke Lumley and the Exchequer Crisis of 1446–9'.
75. George, *The English Episcopate and the Crown 1437–1450*, 201.
76. R. A. Griffiths, *The Reign of Henry VI*, 639–40; B. Wolffe, *Henry VI*, 17.
77. Griffiths, *Reign of Henry VI*, 640.
78. C. L. Kingsford, *Prejudice and Promise in Fifteenth-Century England*, 49.
79. George, *The English Episcopate*, 90–6, for clarification of this episode.
80. *Ibid.*, 76–90, where Lyhert's appointment is disentangled from myth.
81. *Reg. Chichele*, iii, 283–4. See for a full discussion W. T. Waugh, 'The Great Statute of *Praemunire*'.
82. *EHD: IV*, 684–5.
83. *PPC*, v, 84–5; vi, 66–7.
84. *EHD: IV*, 690–1; R. L. Storey, 'Episcopal King-Makers', 89, 92–3.
85. See for Henry VII's exploitation of it R. L. Storey, *Diocesan Administration* (2nd edn), 31.
86. On this convocation and the role of Bourgchier see Storey, 'Episcopal King-Makers', 86–7, 89–90, 92–3.
87. See note 2 above.

Select Bibliography

PRIMARY SOURCES

Accounts Rendered by Papal Collectors in England 1317–1378, ed. W. E. Lunt and E. B. Graves (American Philosophical Society), Philadelphia 1968.

Adae Murimuth Continuatio Chronicarum, ed. E. M. Thompson (Rolls Series), 1889.

Annales Ricardi Secundi et Henrici Quarti (Rolls Series), vol. iii (1866) of *Chron. S. Albani* below.

Calendar of Close Rolls, 1900–41.

Calendar of Fine Rolls, 1911–49.

Calendar of Patent Rolls, 1893–1910.

Calendar of Papal Letters, 1893–1955.

Calendar of Papal Petitions, 1896.

Calendar of Signet Letters of Henry IV and Henry V, 1399–1422, ed. J. L. Kirby, 1978.

Chronica Monasterii de Melsa, ed. E. A. Bond (Rolls Series), 3 vols, 1866–8.

Chronica Monasterii S. Albani, ed. H. T. Riley (Rolls Series), 12 vols, 1863–76.

The Chronicle of Walter of Guisborough, ed. H. Rothwell (Camden Third Series lxxxix), 1957.

Chronicles of the Reigns of Edward I and Edward II, ed. W. Stubbs (Rolls Series), 2 vols, 1882–3.

Chronicon Adae de Usk, ed. E. M. Thompson, 1904.

Chronicon Henrici Knighton . . . monachi Leycestrensis, ed. J. R. Lumby (Rolls Series), 2 vols, 1889–95.

The Church in London 1375–1392, ed. A. K. McHardy (London Record Society), 1977.

Concilia Magnae Brittaniae et Hiberniae, ed. D. Wilkins, 4 vols, 1737.

Councils and Synods, with Other Documents Relating to the English Church, II 1205–1313, ed. F. M. Powicke and C. R. Cheney, Oxford 1964.

Documents Illustrative of English Church History, ed. H. Gee and W. J. Hardy, 1896.

Early Registers of Writs, ed. E. de Hass and G. D. G. Hall (Seldon Soc. 87), 1970.

An English Chronicle of the Reigns of Richard II, Henry V and Henry VI, ed. J. S. Davies, London (Camden Soc. Old Series), 1856.

English Historical Documents, III: 1189–1327, ed. H. Rothwell, 1975.

English Historical Documents, IV: 1327–1485, ed. A. R. Myers, 1969.

English Wycliffite Sermons, vol. i, ed. A. Hudson, Oxford 1983.

English Wycliffite Writings, Selections from, ed. A. Hudson, Cambridge 1978.

Foedera, conventiones, literae et . . acta publica, ed. T. Rymer, 1816.

The Formulary of Thomas Hoccleve, 2 vols, ed. E. Bentley (Emory University Ph.D. thesis 1965, University Microfilms, Ann Arbor 1976).

Four English Political Tracts of the Later Middle Ages, ed. J-P. Genet (Camden Fourth Series 18), 1977.

Gesta Henrici Quinti, ed. F. Taylor and J. S. Roskell, Oxford 1975.

Historians of the Church of York, ed. J. Raine (Rolls Series), 3 vols, 1879–94.

John Mirk's Instructions for Parish Priests, ed. G. Kristensson, Lund 1974.

The Kirkstall Chronicle 1355–1400, ed. M. V. Clarke and N. Denholm-Young, *BJRL*, xv (1931), 100–37.

Letters and Papers Illustrative of the Wars of the English in France during the Reign of Henry VI, ed. J. Stevenson (Rolls Series), 1861–4.

Letters of Queen Margaret of Anjou and Bishop Beckington and Others, ed. C. Monro (Camden Soc. Old Series lxxxvi), 1863.

Literae Cantuarienses. The Letter Books of the Monastery of Christ Church, Canterbury, ed. J. B. Sheppard (Rolls Series), 3 vols, 1887–9.

Loci e Libro Veritatum, ed. J. E. T. Rogers, Oxford 1881.

Medieval Legal Records Edited in Memory of C. A. F. Meekings, ed. R. F. Hunnisett and J. B. Post, 1978.

Memorials of the Reign of Henry VI, ed. G. Williams (Rolls Series), 2 vols, 1872.

The Peasants Revolt of 1381, ed. R. B. Dobson, 2nd edn, 1983.

Proceedings and Ordinances of the Privy Council of England, ed. H. Nicolas, 7 vols, 1834–7.

Provinciale seu Constitutiones Angliae, W. Lyndwood, Oxford 1679.

The Register of Thomas Bekynton, bishop of Bath and Wells 1443–1465, ed. H. C. Maxwell Lyte and M. C. B. Dawes (Somerset Record Soc.), 2 vols, 1934–5.

Registrum Thomae Bourchier [Canterbury 1454–1486], ed. F. R. H. Du Boulay (Canterbury and York Soc.), 1957.

Register of Wolstan de Bransford [Worcester 1339–1349], Calendar of, ed. R. M. Haines (Worcestershire Historical Soc.), 1966.

The Register of Nicholas Bubwith [Bath and Wells, 1407–1424], ed. T. S. Holmes (Somerset Record Soc.), 2 vols, 1914.

The Register of Henry Chichele, archbishop of Canterbury 1413–1443, ed. E. F. Jacob (Canterbury and York Soc.), 4 vols, 1943–7.

Registrum Simonis de Gandavo [Salisbury 1297–1315], ed. C. T. Flower and M. C. B. Dawes (Canterbury and York Soc.), 2 vols, 1934.

The Register of John de Halton [Carlisle 1292–1324], ed. W. N. Thompson and T. F. Tout (Canterbury and York Soc.), 2 vols, 1913.

The Register of Edmund Lacy, bishop of Exeter 1420–1455, ed. G. R. Dunstan (Canterbury and York Soc.), 5 vols, 1963–72.

The Register of Thomas Langley, bishop of Durham 1406–1437, ed. R. L. Storey (Surtees Soc.), 6 vols, 1956–70.

The Registers of Roger Martival [Salisbury 1315–1330], ed. K. Edwards *et al.* (Canterbury and York Soc.), 1959–.

Registrum Ade de Orleton [Hereford 1317–1327], ed. A. T. Bannister (Canterbury and York Soc.), 1908.

Register of Adam de Orleton [Worcester 1327–1333], Calendar of, ed. R. M. Haines (Worcestershire Historical Soc.), 1979.

The Register of Bishop Philip Repingdon, 1405–1419, ed. M. Archer (Lincoln Record Soc.), 3 vols, 1963–82.

Registrum Thome Spofford [Hereford 1422–1448], ed. A. T. Bannister (Canterbury and York Soc.), 1919.

Registrum Ricardi de Swinfield [Hereford 1283–1317], ed. W. W. Capes (Canterbury and York Soc.), 1909.

Registrum Johannis de Trillek [Hereford 1344–1361], ed. J. H. Parry (Canterbury and York Soc.), 1912.

Registrum Henrici Woodlock [Winchester 1305–1316], ed. A. W. Goodman (Canterbury and York Soc.), 2 vols, 1940–1.

Rotuli Parliamentorum; ut et petitiones, et placita in parliamento, 6 vols, 1783.

Rotuli Parliamentorum Anglie Hactenus Inediti, ed. H. G. Richardson and G. O. Sayles (Camden Third Series, li), 1935.

Royal and Historical Letters during the Reign of Henry IV, ed. F. C. Hingeston (Rolls Series), 1860.

St Albans Chronicle 1406–1420, ed. V. H. Galbraith, Oxford 1937.

Select Cases in the Court of King's Bench, vol. VII, G. O. Sayles (Seldon Soc. 88), 1971.

The Sermons of Thomas Brinton, ed. M. A. Devlin (Camden Third Series lxxxv–vi), 2 vols, 1954.

Statutes of the Realm, vols i, ii (1810–16).

Vita Edwardi Secundi, ed. N. Denholm-Young, 1957.

The Westminster Chronicle 1381–1394, ed. L. C. Hector and B. F. Harvey, Oxford 1982.

William Thorne's Chronicle of St Augustine's Abbey, ed. A. H. Davis, Oxford 1934.

Wykeham's Register, ed. T. F. Kirby (Hampshire Record Soc.), 2 vols, 1896–9.

SECONDARY WORKS

Allmand, C.T. (editor), *War, Literature and Politics in the Late Middle Ages: Essays in Honour of G. W. Coupland* (Liverpool 1976).

Aston, M., 'Lollardy and Sedition', *Past and Present*, xvii (1960), 1–44.

——'The Impeachment of Bishop Despenser', *BIHR*, xxxviii (1965), 127–48.

——'John Wycliffe's Reformation Reputation', *Past and Present*, no. 30 (1965), 23–51.

——'Lollardy and Literacy', *History*, lxii (1977), 347–71.

——'William White's Lollard Followers', *Catholic Historical Review*, lxviii (1982), 469–97.

——' "Caim's Castles": Poverty, Politics and Disendowment', pp. 45–81 in R. B. Dobson, *Church, Politics and Patronage*.

Aston, T.H., 'Oxford's Medieval Alumni', *Past and Present*, no. 74 (1977), 3–40.

Aston, T.H., Duncan, G.D. and Evans, T.A.R., 'The Medieval Alumni of the University of Cambridge', *Past and Present*, no. 86 (1980), 9–86.

Barnie, J., *War in Medieval Society: Social Values and the Hundred Years War 1337–99* (1974).

Barron, C.M., 'The Tyranny of Richard II', *BIHR*, xli (1968), 1–18.

Betcherman, L.-R., 'The Making of Bishops in the Lancastrian Period', *Speculum*, xli (1966), 397–419.

Blust, M.S., *The English Clerical Diplomats, 1327–1461* (Loyola University of Chicago Ph.D. thesis 1977, University Microfilms, Ann Arbor 1979).

Brand, P.A., 'The Control of Mortmain Alienation in England 1200–1300', pp. 29–40 in *Legal Records and the Historian*, edited by J. H. Baker (1978).

——'Courtroom and Schoolroom: the Education of Lawyers in England prior to 1400', *BIHR*, lx (1987), 147–65.

Bridbury, A.R., 'The Black Death', *Econ.HR*, xxvi (1973), 577–92.

——'Before the Black Death', *Econ.HR*, xxx (1977), 393–410.

Brockwell, C.W. Jnr, *Bishop Reginald Pecock and the Crisis and Challenge of the Laity in the English Church in the Fifteenth Century* (Duke University Ph.D. thesis 1971, University Microfilms, Ann Arbor 1980).

Brown, A.L., 'The Privy Seal Clerks in the Early Fifteenth Century', pp. 260–81 in *The Study of Medieval Records*, edited by D. A. Bullough and R. L. Storey (Oxford 1971).

Bryson, W.H., 'Papal Releases from Royal Oaths', *JEH*, xxii (1971), 19–33.

Buck, M., *Politics, Finance and the Church in the Reign of Edward II: Walter Stapledon, Treasurer of England* (Cambridge 1983).

Burrows, R., *Community and Conflict: the English Church, 1350–1381* (Duke University Ph.D. thesis 1976, University Microfilms, Ann Arbor 1979).

Butler, L.H., 'Archbishop Melton, His Neighbours and Kinsmen 1317–40', *JEH*, ii (1951), 54–68.

Carson, T.E., *A Socio-Economic Study of East Anglian Clergy in the Time of Henry Despenser 1370–1406* (Michigan University Ph.D. thesis 1972, University Microfilms, Ann Arbor 1979).

Caspary, G.E., 'The Deposition of Richard II and Canon Law', *Proceedings of the Second International Congress of Medieval Canon Law* (Rome 1965), 189–202.

Catto, J.I. (editor), *A History of the University of Oxford, vol. I: The Early Schools* (Oxford 1984).

——'The King's Servants' in G. L. Harriss, *Henry V: The Practice of Kingship*, 75–95.

——'Religious Change under Henry V', *ibid.*, 97–115.

——'Wyclif and the Cult of the Eucharist', *SCH*, Subsidia 4 (1985), 269–86.

Cheney, C.R., 'Law and Letters in Fourteenth-Century Durham: a Study of Corpus Christi College, Cambridge, MS 450', *BJRL*, lv (1972–3), 60–85.

Cheyette, F., 'Kings, Courts, Cures and Sinecures: the Statute of Provisors and the Common Law', *Traditio*, xix (1963), 295–349.

Clanchy, M.T., *From Memory to Written Record: England 1066–1307* (1979).

Clarke, M.V., *Medieval Representation and Consent* (Oxford 1936).

——*Fourteenth-Century Studies*, edited by L. S. Sutherland and M. McKisack (Oxford 1937).

Clough, C.H. (editor), *Profession, Vocation and Culture in Later Medieval England* (Liverpool 1982).

Coleman, J., *English Literature in History 1350–1400: Medieval Readers and Writers* (1981).

Crowder, C.M.D., 'Henry V, the Emperor Sigismund and the Council of Constance', *Historical Studies, 5th Conference of Irish Historians*, iv (1963), 93–110.

Dahmus, J., *William Courtenay, Archbishop of Canterbury 1381–1396* (1966).

Dahmus, J.W., *Thomas Arundel, Archbishop of Canterbury 1396–1414: Churchman and Statesman* (Cornell University Ph.D. thesis 1970, University Microfilms, Ann Arbor 1986).

——'Thomas Arundel and the Baronial Party under Henry IV', *Albion*, xvi (1984), 131–49.

Davies, R.G., *The Episcopate in England and Wales, 1375–1443* (Manchester University Ph.D. thesis 1974).

——'Richard II and the Church in the Years of Tyranny', *JMH*, i (1975), 329–62.

——'The Episcopate and the Political Crisis in England of 1386–88', *Speculum*, li (1976), 659–93.

——'After the Execution of Archbishop Scrope', *BJRL*, lix (1976–7), 40–74.

——'Martin V and the English Episcopate, with Particular Reference to his Campaign for the Repeal of the Statute of Provisors', *EHR*, xcii (1977), 309–44.

——'The Anglo–Papal Concordat of Bruges, 1375. A Reconsideration', *Annuarium Historiae Pontificiae*, xix (1981), 97–146.

——'The Episcopate', pp. 51–89 in C.H Clough, *Profession, Vocation and Culture*.

——'The Attendance of the Episcopate in English Parliaments, 1376–1461', *Proceedings of the American Philosophical Society*, cxxix (1985), 30–81.

Davies, R.G. and Denton, J.H. (editors), *The English Parliament in the Middle Ages* (Manchester 1981).

Davis, V.G., *The Life and Career of William Waynflete, Bishop of Winchester* (Trinity College Dublin Ph.D. thesis 1985).

Deeley, A., 'Papal Provision and Royal Rights of Patronage in the Early Fourteenth Century', *EHR*, xliii (1928), 497–527.

Deighton, H.S., 'Clerical Taxation by Consent 1279–1301', *EHR*, lxviii (1953), 161–92.

Denton, J.H., *Robert Winchelsey and the Crown 1294–1313* (Cambridge 1980).

——'Pope Clement V's Early Career as a Royal Clerk', *EHR*, lxxxiii (1968), 303–14.

——'Canterbury Archiepiscopal Appointments: the Case of Walter Reynolds', *JMH*, i (1975), 317–27.

——'Walter Reynolds and Ecclesiastical Politics 1313–16: a Post-script to *Councils and Synods II*', pp. 247–74 in *Church and Government in the Middle Ages*, edited by C. N. L. Brooke, D. E. Luscombe, G. H. Martin and D. M. Owen (Cambridge 1976).

——'The *Communitas Cleri* in the Early Fourteenth Century', *BIHR*, li (1978), 72–8.

——'The Making of the *Articuli Cleri* of 1316', *EHR*, ci (1986), 564–95.

Desmond, L.A., *The Statute Legislation of Edward I and its Effects upon the English Cistercians to 1399* (Fordham University Ph.D. thesis 1967, University Microfilms, Ann Arbor 1986).

——'The Statute of Carlisle and the Cistercians, 1298–1369', pp. 138–62 in *Studies in Medieval Cistercian History, Presented to J. F. O'Sullivan* [Cistercian Studies Series, 13 (Shannon 1971)].

Dobson, R.B., *Durham Priory 1400–1450* (Cambridge 1973).

——'The Later Middle Ages, 1215–1500', pp. 44–109 in *A History of York Minster*, edited by G. E. Aylmer and R. Cant (Oxford 1977).

——'The Residentiary Canons of York in the Fifteenth Century', *JEH*, xxx (1979), 145–74.

——(editor), *The Church, Politics and Patronage in the Fifteenth Century* (Gloucester 1984).

Douie, D.L., *Archbishop Pecham* (Oxford 1952).

Du Boulay, F.R.H., *The Lordship of Canterbury* (1966).

——*An Age of Ambition* (1970).

——'The Fifteenth Century', pp. 195–242 in C. H. Lawrence, *The English Church and the Papacy* (1965).

Dunabin, J., 'Careers and Vocations', pp. 565–605 in J. I. Catto, *A History of the University of Oxford, vol. I*.

Dunning, R.W., 'Patronage and Promotion in the Late Medieval Church', pp. 167–80 in R. A. Griffiths (ed.), *Patronage, the Crown and the Provinces* (Gloucester 1981).

Edwards, K., *The English Secular Cathedrals in the Middle Ages* (2nd edn, Manchester 1967).

——'The Political Importance of the English Bishops during the Reign of Edward II', *EHR*, lix (1944), 311–47.

——'The Social Origins and Provenance of the English Bishops during the Reign of Edward II', *TRHS*, 5th series, ix (1959), 51–79.

Emden, A.B., *A Biographical Register of the University of Oxford to A.D. 1500*, 3 vols (Oxford 1957–9).

——*A Biographical Register of the University of Cambridge to 1500* (Cambridge 1963).

Farr, W., *John Wyclif as Legal Reformer* (Leiden 1974).

Ferguson, J., *English Diplomacy 1422–1461* (Oxford 1972).

Fitzgerald, R.B., *Community and Conflict: the English Church, 1350–1381* (Duke University Ph.D. thesis 1976, University Microfilms, Ann Arbor, 1979).

Flahiff, G.B., 'The Use of Prohibitions by Clerics against Ecclesiastical Courts in England', *Medieval Studies*, iii (1941), 101–16.

——'The Writ of Prohibition to Court Christian in the Thirteenth Century', *Medieval Studies*, vi (1944), 261–313; vii (1945), 229–90.

Fryde, N., *The Tyranny and Fall of Edward II* (Cambridge 1979).

——'John Stratford, Bishop of Winchester, and the Crown, 1323–30', *BIHR*, xliv (1971), 153–61.

——'Edward III's Removal of his Ministers and Judges, 1340–1', *BIHR*, xlviii (1975), 149–61.

Genet, J-P., 'Ecclesiastics and Political Theory in Late Medieval England: the End of a Monopoly', pp. 23–44 in

R. B. Dobson, *Church, Politics and Patronage*.

George, J.M. Jnr, *The English Episcopate and the Crown 1437–1450* (Columbia University Ph.D. thesis 1976, University Microfilms, Ann Arbor 1979).

Gradon, P., 'Langland and the Ideology of Dissent', *Proceedings of the British Academy*, lxvi (1980), 179–205.

Gransden, A., *Historical Writing in England, ii: c.1307 to the Early Sixteenth Century* (1982).

Grassi, J.L., 'Royal Clerks from the Archdiocese of York in the Fourteenth Century', *Northern History*, v (1970), 12–33.

Graves, E.B., 'The Legal Significance of the Statute of Premunire of 1353', pp. 57–80 in *Haskins Anniversary Essays in Medieval History*, edited by C. H. Taylor and J. L. La Monte (New York 1929).

Griffiths, R.A., *The Reign of King Henry VI* (1981).

——'The Trial of Eleanor Cobham: An Episode in the Fall of Duke Humphrey of Gloucester', *BJRL*, li (1968–9), 381–99.

——'Public and Private Bureaucracies in England and Wales in the Fifteenth Century', *TRHS*, 5th series, xxx (1980), 109–30.

Haines, R.M., 'Education in English Ecclesiastical Legislation of the Later Middle Ages', *SCH*, vii (1971), 161–75.

——'Church, Society and Politics in the Early Fifteenth Century as Viewed from an English Pulpit', *SCH*, xii (1975), 143–57.

——' "Our Master Mariner, Our Sovereign Lord": a Contemporary Preacher's View of Henry V', *Medieval Studies*, xxxviii (1976), 85–96.

——'An English Archbishop and the Cerberus of War', *SCH*, xx (1983), 153–70.

——*The Church and Politics in Fourteenth-Century England: the Career of Adam Orleton c.1275–1345* (Cambridge 1978).

——*Archbishop John Stratford* (Toronto 1986).

Harriss, G.L., 'Preference at the Medieval Exchequer', *BIHR*, xxx (1957), 17–40.

——'Aids, Loans and Benevolences', *The Historical Journal*, vi (1968), 1–19.

——'Cardinal Beaufort, Patriot or Usurer?', *TRHS*, 5th series, xx (1970), 129–48.

——*King, Parliament and Public Finance in Medieval England to 1369* (Oxford 1975).

——'Marmaduke Lumley and the Exchequer Crisis of 1446–9', pp. 143–78 in J. G. Rowe (ed.), *Aspects of Late Medieval Government and Society* (Toronto 1986).

——(editor), *Henry V: The Practice of Kingship* (Oxford 1985).

Harvey, M., *Solutions to the Schism: a Study of Some English Attitudes 1378–1409* (Kirchengeschichtliche Quellen und Studien, 12; St Ottilien 1983).

Hay, D., 'The Church of England in the Later Middle Ages', *History*, liii (1968), 35–50.

Head, C., 'Pope Pius II and the Wars of the Roses', *Archivum Historiae Pontificiae*, viii (1970), 139–78.

Heath, P., 'The Medieval Archdeaconry and Tudor Bishopric of Chester', *JEH*, xx (1969), 243–52.

Helmholz, R.H., *Canon Law and English Common Law* (1983).

——'Writs of Prohibition and Ecclesiastical Sanctions in English Courts Christian', *Minnesota Law Review*, lx (1976), 1011–33.

——'The Writ of Prohibition to Court Christian before 1500', *Medieval Studies*, xliii (1981), 297–314.

Hewitt, H.J., *The Organization of War under Edward III, 1338–62* (Manchester 1966).

Highfield, J.R.L., *Relations between the Church and the English Crown from the Death of Archbishop Stratford to the Opening of the Great Schism (1349–1378)* (Oxford University D.Phil. thesis 1952).

——'The English Hierarchy in the Reign of Edward III', *TRHS*, 5th series, vi (1956), 115–38.

Hilton, R.H. and Ashton, T.H. (editors), *The English Rising of 1381* (Cambridge 1984).

Holmes, G.[A.], *The Good Parliament* (Oxford 1975).

——'Cardinal Beaufort and the Crusade against the Hussites', *EHR*, lxxxviii (1973), 721–50.

Howell, M., *Regalian Right in Medieval England* (1962).

Hudson, A., 'Lollardy: the English Heresy?', *SCH*, xviii (1982), 261–83.

——'The Debate on Bible Translation, Oxford 1401', *EHR*, xc (1975), 1–18.

——'Wycliffism in Oxford 1381–1411' in A. Kenny, *Wyclif in His Times*, 67–84.

——'Wyclif and the English Language', *ibid.*, 85–103.

Hughes, D., *A Study of Social and Constitutional Tendencies in the Early Years of Edward III* (1915).

Jacob, E.F., *Essays in the Conciliar Epoch* (2nd edn, Manchester 1953).

——*The Fifteenth Century 1399–1485* (Oxford 1961).

——*Henry Chichele* (1967).

——*Essays in Later Medieval History* (Manchester 1968).

——'Reynold Pecock, Bishop of Chichester', *Proceedings of the British Academy*, xxxvii (1951), 121–53 [reprinted in *Essays in Later Medieval History*].

——'A Note on the English Concordat of 1418', pp. 349–58 in *Medieval Studies Presented to Aubrey Gwynn*, edited by J. A. Watt, J. B. Morrall and F. X. Martin (Dublin 1961).

——'The Canterbury Convocation of 1406', pp. 345–53 in *Essays in Medieval History Presented to Bertie Wilkinson*, edited by T. A. Sandquist and M. R. Powicke (Toronto 1969).

Jewell, H., 'The Cultural Interests and Achievements of the Secular Personnel of Local Administration', pp. 130–54 in C. H. Clough, *Profession, Vocation and Culture*.

Jones, E.D., 'The Crown, Three Benedictine Houses and the Statute of Mortmain 1279–1348', *Journal of British Studies*, xiv (1975), 1–28.

——'The Church and "Bastard-Feudalism": the Case of Crowland Abbey from the 1320s to the 1350s', *Journal of Religious History*, x (1978–9), 142–50.

Jones, W.R., 'Bishops, Politics and the Two Laws; the Gravamina of the English Clergy, 1237–1399', *Speculum*, xli (1966), 209–45.

——'Relations of the Two Jursidictions: Conflict and Cooperation in England during the Thirteenth and Fourteenth Centuries', *Studies in Medieval and Renaissance History*, vii (1970), 79–210.

——'The English Church and Royal Propaganda during the Hundred Years War', *Journal of British Studies*, xix (1979), 18–30.

Keen, M., 'Wyclif, the Bible, and Transubstantiation', pp. 1–16 in A. Kenny, *Wyclif in His Times*.

——'The Influence of Wyclif', pp. 127–45, *ibid.*

Kemp, E.W., *Counsel and Consent* (1961).

Kenny, A. (editor), *Wyclif in His Times* (Oxford 1986).

Kightly, C., *The Early Lollards. A Survey of Popular Lollard Activity in England, 1382–1428* (York University Ph.D. thesis 1975).

King, H.P., 'A Dispute between Henry IV and the Chapter at Lincoln', *Archives*, iv (1959–60), 81–3.

Kingsford, C.J., *Prejudice and Promise in Fifteenth-Century England* (Oxford 1925).

Kirby, J.L., *Henry IV of England* (1971).

——'Two Tax Accounts of the Diocese of Carlisle, 1379–80', *Transactions of Cumberland and Westmorland Antiquarian and Archaeological Society*, lii (1952), 70–84.

——'Clerical Poll Taxes in the Diocese of Salisbury, 1377–81', *Collectanea of the Wiltshire Archaeological and Natural History Society, Records Branch*, xlii (1956), 157–67.

Knowles, D.M., *Religious Orders in England*, vols i, ii (Cambridge 1948–57).

Lambrick, G., 'The Impeachment of the Abbot of Abingdon in 1368', *EHR*, lxxxii (1967), 250–76.

Lawrence, C.H. (editor), *The English Church and the Papacy in the Middle Ages* (1965).

——'The Thirteenth Century', pp. 117–56, *ibid.*

Leys, A.M., 'The Forfeiture of the Lands of the Templars in England', pp. 155–63 in *Oxford Essays in Medieval History Presented to H. E. Salter* (Oxford 1934).

Logan, F.D., *Excommunication and the Secular Arm in Medieval England* (Toronto 1968).

Lunt, W.E., *Financial Relations of the Papacy with England to 1327* (Cambridge, Mass. 1939).

——*Financial Relations of the Papacy with England 1327–1534* (Cambridge, Mass. 1962).

——'Clerical Tenths Levied in England by Papal Authority during the Reign of Edward II', pp. 157–82 in *Haskins Anniversary Essays*, edited by C. H. Taylor and J. L. La Monte (New York 1929).

Lytle, G.F., *Oxford Students and English Society:* c.*1300*–c.*1510* (University of Princeton Ph.D. thesis 1976, University Microfilms, Ann Arbor 1979).

McFarlane, K.B., *John Wycliffe and the Beginnings of English Non-conformity* (1952).

——*Lancastrian Kings and Lollard Knights* (Oxford 1972).

——'Bastard Feudalism', *BIHR*, xx (1945), 161–80.

——'Henry V, Bishop Beaufort and the Red Hat, 1417–21', *EHR*, lx (1945), 316–48.

——'At the Deathbed of Cardinal Beaufort', pp. 405–28 in *Studies in History Presented to F. M. Powicke*, edited by R. W. Hunt, W. A. Pantin and R. W. Southern (Oxford 1948).

McHardy, A.K., *The Crown and the Diocese of Lincoln during the Episcopate of John Buckingham, 1363–98* (Oxford University D.Phil. thesis 1972).

——'The Representation of the English Lower Clergy in Parliament during the Later Fourteenth Century', *SCH*, x (1973), 97–107.

——'The Alien Priories and the Expulsion of Aliens from England in 1378', *SCH*, xii (1975), 133–41.

——'Liturgy and Propaganda in the Diocese of Lincoln during the Hundred Years War', *SCH*, xviii (1982), 215–27.

——'The English Clergy and the Hundred Years War', *SCH*, xx (1983), 171–8.

——'Clerical Taxation in Fifteenth-Century England: the Clergy as Agents of the Crown', pp. 168–92 in R. B. Dobson, *Church, Politics and Patronage*.

McKenna, J.W., 'The Coronation Oil of Yorkist Kings', *EHR*, lxxxii (1967), 102–4.

——'Popular Canonization as Political Propaganda: the Cult of Archbishop Scrope', *Speculum*, xlv (1970), 608–23.

McKisack, M., *The Fourteenth Century* (Oxford 1959).

——'Edward III and the Historians', *History*, xlv (1960), 1–15.

McNab, B., 'Obligations of the Church in English Society:

Military Arrays of the Clergy, 1369–1418', pp. 293–314 in *Order and Innovation in the Middle Ages: Essays in Honor of Joseph R. Strayer*, edited by W. C. Jordan, B. McNab and T. F. Ruiz (New Jersey 1976).

McNiven, P., 'The Betrayal of Archbishop Scrope', *BJRL*, liv (1971–2), 173–213.

——'The Problem of Henry IV's Health 1405–13', *EHR*, c (1985), 747–72.

Maddicott, J.R., *Thomas of Lancaster 1307–1322* (Oxford 1970).

——*Law and Lordship: Royal Justices as Retainers in Thirteenth- and Fourteenth-Century England* [*Past and Present* Supplement no. 4 (1978)].

Maitland, F.W., *Selected Historical Essays*, edited by H. M. Cam (Boston, Mass. 1962).

Matthew, D., *The Norman Monasteries and their English Possessions* (Oxford 1962).

Miller, E., *War in the North* (Hull 1960).

——'War, Taxation and the English Economy in the Late Thirteenth and Early Fourteenth Centuries', pp. 11–31 in *War and Economic Development. Essays in Memory of David Joslin*, edited by J. M. Winter (Cambridge 1975).

Moran, J.A.H., *The Growth of English Schooling 1340–1548* (New Jersey 1985).

——'Clerical Recruitment in the Diocese of York, 1340–1530: Data and Commentary', *JEH*, xxxiv (1983), 19–54.

Morgan, M., 'The Suppression of the Alien Priories', *History*, xxvi (1941–2), 204–12.

Nigota, J.A., *John Kempe, a Political Prelate of the Fifteenth Century* (Emory University Ph.D. thesis 1973, University Microfilms, Ann Arbor 1979).

Oman, C., *The Great Revolt of 1381* (2nd edition, with introduction and notes by E. B. Fryde, Oxford 1969).

Orme, N., *English Schools in the Middle Ages* (1973).

——*Education in the West of England 1066–1548* (Exeter 1976).

Ormrod, W.M., 'Edward III and the Recovery of Royal Authority in England 1340–60', *History*, lxxii (1987), 4–19.

Otway-Ruthven, J., *The King's Secretary and the Signet Office in the XVth Century* (Cambridge 1939).

Owst, G.R., *Literature and Pulpit in Medieval England* (Cambridge 1933).

Palmer, J.J.N., *England, France and Christendom 1377–99* (1972).

——'England and the Great Western Schism', *EHR*, lxxxiii (1968), 516–22.

——'England, France, the Papacy and the Flemish Succession, 1361–69', *JMH*, ii (1976), 339–64.

——'The Authorship, Date and Historical Value of the French Chronicles of the Lancastrian Revolution', *BJRL*, lxi (1978–9), 145–81, 398–421.

Palmer, J.J.N. and Wells, A.P., 'Ecclesiastical Reform and the Politics of the Hundred Years War during the Pontificate of Urban V (1362–70)', pp. 169–89 in C. T. Allmand, *War, Literature and Politics in the Late Middle Ages*.

Pantin, W.A., *The English Church in the Fourteenth Century* (Cambridge 1955).

——'The Fourteenth Century', pp.157–94 in C. H. Lawrence, *The English Church and the Papacy*.

——'The Letters of John Mason: a Fourteenth-Century Formulary from St Augustine's Canterbury', pp. 192–219 in *Essays in Medieval History*, edited by T. A. Sandquist and M. R. Powicke (Toronto 1969).

Peel, J.V., *The Parliament of 1316* (Emory University Ph.D. thesis 1967, University Microfilms, Ann Arbor 1986).

Perroy, E., *L'Angleterre et le grand schisme d'Occident* (Paris 1933).

Phillips, J.S.R., *Aymer de Valence, Earl of Pembroke 1307–1324: Baronial Politics in the Reign of Edward II* (Oxford 1972).

Pollock, F. and Maitland, F.M., *The History of English Law before the Time of Edward I*, 2 vols (Cambridge 1895).

Postan, M.M., 'The Costs of the Hundred Years War', *Past and Present*, xxvii (1964), 34–53.

——'Some Social Consequences of the Hundred Years War', *Econ.HR*, xii (1942), 1–12.

Powicke, F.M., *King Henry III and the Lord Edward*, 2 vols (Oxford 1947).

——*The Thirteenth Century* (Oxford 1953).

Prescott, A.J., *Judicial Records of the Rising of 1381* (London University Ph.D. thesis 1984).

Prestwich, M., *War, Politics and Finance under Edward I* (1972).

——*The Three Edwards: War and State in England 1272–1377* (1980).

——'The Art of Kingship: Edward I, 1272–1307', *History Today* (May 1985), 34–40.

——'The Piety of Edward I', pp. 120–8 in *England in the Thirteenth Century*, edited by W. M. Ormrod (Woodbridge 1986).

Putnam, B., 'Maximum Wage-Laws for Priests after the Black Death, 1348–81', *AHR*, xxi (1916), 12–32.

Raban, S., *Mortmain Legislation and the English Church 1279–1500* (Cambridge 1982).

Richardson, H.G., 'Heresy and the Lay Power under Richard II', *EHR*, li (1936), 1–28.

——'Business Training in Medieval Oxford', *AHR*, xlvi (1940–1), 259–80.

Rogers, A., 'Clerical Taxation under Henry IV 1399–1413', *BIHR*, xliv (1973), 123–44.

Roskell, J.S., 'The Problem of Attendance of the Lords in Medieval Parliaments', *BIHR*, xxix (1956), 153–204.

——'A Consideration of Certain Aspects and Problems of the English *Modus Tenendi Parliamentum*', *BJRL*, 1 (1967–8), 411–42.

Rothwell, H., 'Confirmation of the Charters, 1297', *EHR*, lx (1945), 16–35, 177–91, 300–15.

——'Edward I and the Struggle for the Charters, 1297–1305', pp. 319–32 in *Studies in Medieval History Presented to F. M. Powicke*', edited by R. W. Hunt, W. A. Pantin and R. W. Southern (Oxford 1948).

Sandquist, T.A., 'The Holy Oil of St Thomas of Canterbury', pp. 330–44 in *Essays in Medieval History Presented to Bertie Wilkinson*, edited by T. A. Sandquist and M. R. Powicke (Toronto 1969).

Saunders, P.C., *Royal Ecclesiastical Patronage in England 1199–1350* (Oxford University D.Phil. thesis 1978).

Sayles, G.O., *The King's Parliament of England* (1975).

Schofield, A.N.E.D., 'England, the Pope and the Council of Basel, 1435–1449', *Church History*, xxxiii (1964), 248–78.

Sheehan, M.W., *Franciscan Poverty in England 1348–1538* (Oxford University D.Phil. thesis 1974).

Smalley, B., *Studies in Medieval Thought and Learning: from Abelard to Wyclif* (1981).

Smith, C.W., 'Some Trends in the English Royal Chancery: 1377–1483', *Medieval Prosopography*, vi (1985), 69–94.

Standen, S.A., *The Administration of the Statute of Mortmain* (Washington University Ph.D. thesis 1973, University Microfilms, Ann Arbor 1979).

Steel, A., *Receipt of the Exchequer* (Cambridge 1954).

Storey, R.L., *Thomas Langley and the Bishopric of Durham 1406–1437* (1961).

——*Diocesan Administration in the Fifteenth Century* (2nd edition, York 1972).

——'Recruitment of the English Clergy in the Period of the Conciliar Movement', *Annuarium Historiae Conciliorum*, vii (1975), 290–313.

——'Clergy and Common Law in the Reign of Henry IV', pp. 342–408 in *Medieval Legal Records*, edited by R. F. Hunnisett and J. B. Post (1978).

——'Gentlemen-Bureaucrats', pp. 90–129 in C. H. Clough, *Profession, Vocation and Culture*.

——'Episcopal King-Makers in the Fifteenth Century', pp. 82–98 in R. B. Dobson, *Church, Politics and Patronage*.

Swanson, R.N., *Universities, Academics and the Great Schism* (Cambridge 1979).

Tatnall, E.C., 'John Wyclif and the *Ecclesia Anglicana*', *JEH*, xx (1969), 19–43.

Thompson, A.H., *The English Clergy and their Organization in the Later Middle Ages* (Oxford 1947).

——'Register of John Gynewell, Bishop of Lincoln 1347–50', *Archaeological Journal*, lxviii (1911), 301–60.

——'The Pestilences of the Fourteenth Century in the Diocese of York', *Archaeological Journal*, lxxi (1914), 97–154.

Thomson, J.A.F., *The Later Lollards 1414–1520* (Oxford 1965).

——' "The Well of Grace": Englishmen and Rome in the Fifteenth Century', pp. 99–114 in R. B. Dobson, *Church, Politics and Patronage*.

Tillotson, J.H., 'Pensions, Corrodies and Religious Houses: an Aspect of the Relations of Crown and Church in Early Fourteenth-Century England', *Journal of Religious History*, viii (1974–5), 127–43.

Tout, T.F., *Chapters in the Administrative History of Medieval England*, 6 vols (Manchester 1920–33).

Tuck, J.A., *Richard II and the English Nobility* (1973).

——'The Cambridge Parliament, 1388', *EHR*, lxxiv (1969), 225–43.

Ullmann, W., 'Thomas Becket's Miraculous Oil', *Journal of Theological Studies*, viii (1957), 129–33.

——'Eugenius IV, Cardinal Kemp, and Archbishop Chichele', pp. 359–83 in *Medieval Studies Presented to Aubrey Gwynn*, edited by J. A. Watt, J. B. Morrall and F. X. Martin (Dublin 1961).

——' "This Realm of England is an Empire" ', *JEH*, xxx (1979), 175–203.

Vernon Harcourt, L.W., *His Grace the Steward and the Trial of Peers* (1907).

Warren, W.L., 'A Re-appraisal of Simon Sudbury', *JEH*, x (1959), 139–52.

Waugh, W.T., 'The Great Statute of *Praemunire*', *EHR*, xxvii (1922), 173–205.

Weske, D.B., *Convocation of the Clergy* (1937).

Whitfield, D.W., 'Conflicts of Personality and Principle. The Political and Religious Crisis in the English Franciscan Province 1400–1409', *Franciscan Studies*, xvii (1957), 321–62.

Wilkinson, B., *Constitutional History of Medieval England 1216–1399*, 3 vols (1948–58).

——*Constitutional History of England in the Fifteenth Century 1399–1485* (1964).

Wilks, M., '*Reformatio Regni*: Wyclif and Hus as Leaders of

Religious Protest Movements', *SCH*, ix (1972), 109–30.
——'Misleading Manuscripts: Wyclif and the Non-Wycliffite Bible', *SCH*, xi (1975), 147–61.
——'Royal Priesthood: the Origins of Lollardy', pp. 63–70 in *The Church in a Changing Society* [CIHEC] (Uppsala 1978).
Williams, Glanmor, *The Welsh Church from Conquest to Reformation* (Cardiff 1962).
——*Owen Glendower* (Oxford 1966).
Wolffe, B., *Henry VI* (1981).
Wood-Legh, K.L., *Studies in Church Life in England under Edward III* (Cambridge 1934).
——*Perpetual Chantries in Britain* (Cambridge 1965).
Wright, J.R., *The Church and the English Crown 1305–1334* (Toronto 1980).
Wylie, J.H., *History of England under Henry IV*, 4 vols (1884–98).
Wylie, J.H. and Waugh, W.T., *The Reign of Henry V*, 3 vols (Cambridge 1914–29).

Since this book was written the following relevant works have appeared:

Denton, J.H. and Dooley, J.P., *Representation of the Lower Clergy in Parliament, 1295–1340*.
McNiven, P., *Heresy and Politics in the Reign of Henry IV*.

Index

(Items which figure in the Glossary are asterisked)

Aberystwyth castle, 232
Abingdon (Berks.), 310
Acton Burnell, statute of (1283), 34
Adam of Usk, 228, 236
Admittatis, writ of, 124
*advowson, *see* lay fee
Agincourt, battle of, 272, 281
Aiscough, William (bishop of Salisbury 1438–50), 301, 305, 310, 333, 334
Alderton (Suffolk), 334
Alexander V, Pope (1409–10), 259, 263
Alfonso X, king of Castile, 34
*alien priories, 53, 54, 112, 113, 128, 147, 259–60, 273, 286
aliens, 262; clergy, 90
All Souls College, Oxford, 255
Alnwick, William (bishop of Norwich 1426–36), 317
Anglesey, 237
*annates, 128, 265, 306, 348; *see also* services
anticlericalism: 315, 321, 329–30; roots of, 39, 56–7, 61–2, 63, 121–3, 147–8, 165–6, 356; in parliament, 56–7, 63, 138, 142, 210, 212–13, 231, 246, 257, 258–9, 329–30; Black Death and, 152; John of Gaunt and, 142–3; resisted by Richard II, 210–13, 221, by Henry IV, 259, by Henry V, 285–8; *see also* antipapalism, literacy, lollardy, *Praemunire*, Provisors, Wyclif
antipapalism: roots, 52–3, 56–7, 60–1, 62, 63, 123–4; John of Gaunt and, 143; *see also* Praemunire, Provisors, statutes, Wyclif
appeals, to Rome, barred, 31, 59, 192; *see Praemunire*, prohibitions, privilege of England
Appellants, the, 185, 186, 203–4, 213–14
Appleby, Thomas (bishop of Carlisle 1363–95), 191
*appropriations: dispensations and statutes, 264–5, 294
Aquitaine, 231
archdeacons, *see* chapters
Arras, Congress of, 301
array of clergy, 46, 110–12, 284–5
Arteveldt, James van, 105

Articles upon the Charters/*Articuli super Cartas* (1300), 60, 63, 67
Articuli Cleri, 1316 (also known as *Pro Clero*), 86, 101, 227
Arundel, Richard, earl of (d. 1376), 115; Richard, earl of (d. 1397), 201, 204
Arundel, John (bishop of Chichester 1459–77), 311
Arundel, Thomas (bishop of Ely 1373–88, archbishop of York 1388–96, archbishop of Canterbury 1396–1414): appointment to Ely, 186, 202; appointment to York, 214; appointment to Canterbury, 204, 219; character, 211, 225, 228, 242; and anticlericalism, 256–9; and Appellants, 186, 202; and convocation, 230–1; and English Bible, 255–6; and Haxey, 209; and Henry IV, 230–2, 236; and lollardy, 183, 186, 254–5; and Scrope's murder, 242; and sanctuary, 211; and Schism, 261; and usurpation, 225–30; on Wyclif, 167; trial and exile, 204–8
Aston, John, 176
Austin friars, 116, 142, 162
Avignon papacy (1305–1418), 123, 130, 174, 195, 233; *see* cardinals, papacy
Ayermine, William (bishop of Norwich 1325–36), 75, 79, 82, 99

Badby, John, 252
Badlesmere, Lord, 78; estates of, 100
Baldock, Master Robert, 71, 78, 79; thwarted of bishopric, 93
Ball, John, 181, 194
Balliol, Edward, 105
Balliol College, Oxford, 167
Bampton (Oxon.), 234
Bangor diocese, clergy of, and poll tax, 191
Bangor, bishop of, rebel (1408), 243
Bannockburn, battle of, 70, 103
Bardolf, Lord, 240, 241
Barking (Essex), abbess of, 325, 334
Basle, Council of (1431–49), 300, 306
bastard feudalism, 322–28
Bath and Wells diocese, array of clergy, 284

Battle (Sussex), abbot of, 111

Beaubec, alien priory, 259

Beauchamp, Guy, earl of Warwick (d. 1315), 68, 70

Beauchamp, Richard (bishop of Hereford 1448–50, bishop of Salisbury 1450–81), 335, 342

Beauchamp, Richard, earl of Warwick (d. 1439), 293

Beauchamp, William, earl of Warwick (d. 1398), 201, 204

Beaufort, Henry (bishop of Lincoln 1398–1404, bishop of Winchester 1404–47): 229, 243, 266, 291, 299, 302; cardinalate, 294–5, 299–300; chancellor, 243, 287, 292; diplomacy, 294, 301, 317–18; legateship, 294–5, 299–300; loans to crown, 231, 283–4, 300, 302–5; martial activity, 300, 308; rivalry with Gloucester, 299–302, 339

Beaufort, Edmund, duke of Somerset (d. 1455), 340

Beaufort, Henry, duke of Somerset (d. 1464), 327

Beaufort, John, duke of Somerset (d. 1444), 326–7

Beaufort, Roger, brother of Gregory XI, 117

Beaumaris castle, 232

Beaumont, Viscount, 311

Beccles (Suffolk), 309

Becket, St Thomas: comparisons, 96, 120, 242; miraculous oil of, 226

Beckford (Glos.), 259

Beckington (Somerset), 327

Beckington, Thomas (bishop of Bath and Wells 1443–65), 317, 326–7

Bedford, John, duke of, 286–7, 292

Bedfordshire, lollards, 183

Beeleigh (Essex), abbot of, 239

Bek, Antony (bishop of Durham 1284–1311), 28

Benedict XII, Pope (1334–42), 123, 126

Benedictine monks, and Oxford University, 94, 274

*benefices, exchanges of, 153

*benefit of clergy, 137, 248, 328–30

Berners, Lord, brother of Abp. Bourgchier, 336

Berwick, 71, 81, 82, 108

Beverley (Yorks.), 82, 193; minster, 193; *see also* St John

Bible, in English, 170, 180, 255–6

Bicester (Oxon.), 192

Bicknor, Alexander de (archbishop of Dublin 1317–49), 75, 79

Bigod, earl, 49

Bintworth, Richard (bishop of London 1338–9), 118

bishops: 349–50, 354–5; under Edward I, character of, 46, 59; under Edward II, character of, 101, political role, 66, 67, 69, 70–1, 72, 73, 75, 76–80; under Edward III, character, 138–42; under Richard II, character of, 217, 219–22, political role of, 203, 205–8, 214, 216, royalism, 215–17; under Henry IV, character of, 267–8, political role of, 228–30, 247; under Henry V, character of, 290, 291, administrative and political role, 285, 287, 290, 292–3; under Henry VI, character of, 320, 335–6, political role of, 300–5, 310–11, 317, 342–3; diplomats, 139–40; graduates among, 139, 158; lawyers among, 139, 290; nobles, 141; diocesan management, 78–9, 96, 292–3; martial activity, 82, 110–11, 195–6, 300; promoting education, 159, 162–3, 309, 313; trials of, 205–8, 234–5; *see also* episcopal appointments, temporalities, loans

Black Death, 149–50, 151, 152, 153, 155; and provisions, 130; and Wyclif's ideas, 154–5

Blackhowe Moor (Yorks.), battle of, 82

Black Prince, 106, 107, 115, 127, 129–30

Blanquefort castle, 67

Blount, Sir Thomas, 234

Blust, M.S., 319

Boethius, translation into English, 165

Bohemia, 277, 309, 354; *see also under* crusades

Bohun, earl, 49

Bonaventura, St, works of, 313

Boniface of Savoy (archbishop of Canterbury 1243–70), 35

Boniface VIII, Pope (1294–1303), 35, 47–8, 52, 57–8, 60, 62, 158

Boniface IX, Pope (1389–1404), 215, 217–18, 264–5

Booth, William (bishop of Lichfield 1447–52, archbishop of York 1452–64), 310, 326, 333, 334, 335

Bordeaux, archbishop of, *see* Clement V

Bordesley (Worcs.), abbot of, 322

Boroughbridge, battle of, 72

Bossall (Yorks.), 262

Boulers, Reginald (bishop of Hereford 1450–53, bishop of Lichfield 1453–59), 333, 334

Bourgchier, Thomas (bishop of Worcester 1433–43, bishop of Ely 1443–54, archbishop of Canterbury 1454–86), 307, 336. 341–2

Bourgchier, Viscount, brother of Abp., 336, 341

Bowet, Henry (bishop of Bath and Wells 1401–7), 266

Boxley (Kent), parish church, 265

Brabant, duke of, 105
Bracton, Henry, 35
Bradwardine, Thomas (archbishop of
    Canterbury 1349), 109, 139–40, 154, 161
Bramham Moor, battle of, 240, 243
Brantingham, Thomas (bishop of Exeter
    1370–94), 142, 194, 203, 204, 205
Braybrooke (Northants.), 178–9
Brembre, Nicholas, 201, 203
Brest, siege of, 107
Brétigny, treaty of, 106, 123, 133
Bridbury, A.R., 150
Bridgetine Order, 273
Bridlington Priory, 82, 83, 259
Brinton, Thomas (bishop of Rochester 1373–
    89), 109, 162, 177
Bristol, lollards, 176, 182, 183; library, 313
Brittany, 106, 107, 232
Brome, Adam de, 159
Bromyard, John, O.P., 181
Brouns, Thomas (bishop of Worcester 1433–
    35, bishop of Rochester 1435–36, bishop of
    Norwich 1436–45), royal letter to, 307
Bruce, Robert, 81, 82, 84
Bruges: negotiations at, 107, 117, 142–3, 161;
    seized by Burgundy, 195
Bubwith, Nicholas (bishop of London
    1406–7, bishop of Salisbury 1407, bishop
    of Bath and Wells 1407–24), 267, 283, 292,
    293
Buckingham, John (bishop of Lincoln 1363–
    98), 178
Buckinghamshire, lollards, 183
*bulls, papal, annulling excommunication of
    Gaveston, 66, 67; in defence of
    Despensers, 72–3; restrictions placed
    upon, 134, 214, 262–5; impounded by
    Henry V, 295; see Clericis Laicos,
    Consueta, Cum ex eo, Etsi de statu, Ex
    debito, Execrabilis, Horribilis, and also
    Praemunire, prohibitions, Provisors
bureaucracy, royal, 16, 31, 98, 157–8, 314–
    16; records kept by, 98; see Chancery,
    Privy Seal Office, Signet Office
Burghersh, Henry (bishop of Lincoln 1320–
    40), 75, 78, 118
Burghill, John (bishop of Llandaff 1396–98,
    bishop of Lichfield 1398–1414), 217, 247
Burgundy, 196, 270–2, 299, 301
Burley, Simon, 201, 203
Burnell, Robert (bishop of Bath and Wells
    1275–92), 23; thwarted of bishoprics, 59
Burstwick (Yorks.), 82
Burton beside Lincoln, rector of, 324
Bury, Richard de (bishop of Durham 1333–
    45), 104, 118

Bury St Edmunds Abbey (Suffolk), 33, 193,
    239–40, 327–8
Byland Abbey (Yorks.), 82

cadaver tombs, 153
Cade rebellion, 334
Caen, siege of, 108
Caernarvon castle, 232
Caistor, Richard, hymn by, 165
Calais: captured, 106; truce of, 123; peace
    conference near, 301, 318; garrison of, 317,
    340; Staple at, 195
Calixtus III, Pope (1455–8), 343
Cam, Helen, 56
Cambridge, earl of; plot by, 277
Cambridge, Dominican friars, 237;
    Franciscan friars, 238
Cambridge, parliament at (1388), 203–4
Cambridge University: colleges, 158–9, 255;
    graduates/students, 160; and papal
    provisions, 127; absence of lollards, 183
*canon law: and popes, 34–5, 173; Wyclif's
    view of, 170; and Richard II's deposition,
    225
*canon lawyers, 160; and Richard II's
    deposition, 225, 325
Canterbury: province, 18; see of, 62;
    archbishop's servants and retainers, 323;
    Christchurch Priory, 150, 291; St
    Augustine's Abbey, monk of, 262
Canterbury, treaty of, 293
Canterbury College, Oxford, 167
cardinals: alien, 16, 84, 89–90, 126, 128, 341,
    343; English, 23–4, 89–90, 140, 318
Carlisle: city, 81; diocese, poll tax, 191, 192;
    bishop, 81–2; cathedral, 81; statute of
    (1307), 53–4, 56, 130
Carlisle, earl of, see Harclay
Carmarthen castle, 232
Carmelite friars, see Kenningham, Netter,
    Patrington
Carpenter, John (bishop of Worcester 1443–
    76), 313, 317, 335
Carthusian Order, 273
Catterick, John (bishop of St Davids 1414–
    15; bishop of Lichfield 1415–19, bishop of
    Exeter 1419), 292, 293
Celestine monks, 273
Cely family, correspondence, 313
Chancellor of realm, laymen as, 122–3, 142–3
Chancery clerks, 314
*chantries, 153
chapel royal, 274, 291
chaplains: taxation of, 191–2, 231, 245, 282,
    303; stipends of, 151, regulated by statute,
    288–9

*chapters of cathedrals: absentees, 98–9, 315–16; elections by, 307–8; graduates in, 158

Charles III, king of France, 74

Charles IV, king of France, 91

Charles V, king of France, 106

Chaucer, Geoffrey, 165

Chaundler, John (bishop of Salisbury 1417–26), 291

Chedworth, John (bishop of Lincoln 1451–71), 335

Chelmsford (Essex), lollards at, 309

Chepstow (Mon.), 75

Cheshire, maintenance in, 326

Chester, 224, 225

Cheyne, Sir John, 256, 259, 262, 311

Cheyne, Sir Thomas, 311

Chichele, Henry (bishop of St Davids 1408–14, archbishop of Canterbury 1414–43): career and character, 291–2; appeals to parliament on provisions, 306; diplomatic missions, 256, 262; loans to crown, 283, 304; lollards and, 278; member of council, 287; opposition to Beaufort, 295, 306; paternalism, 331

Chipping Warden (Northants.), 178

church: of England, structure of, 17–18; land and wealth, 17, coveted, 63, attacks on, 116; see also anticlericalism, confiscation, Mortmain, resumption, taxation

Circumspecte agatis, writ and statute, 30, 34, 39–41, 227

Cirencester (Glos.), 234

Cistercian monks, and statute of Carlisle, 53; apostates, 326

Citeaux, 53; cell of, 259

civil law, see Roman law

Clanvow, Sir John, 178

Claydon, John, 184

Clement V, Pope (1305–14): and Edward I, 52, 57, 60, 61; and Edward II, 91, 93–4; and Winchelsey, 52, 60, 66, 80, 93; and Gaveston, 66–7, 69, 90; and papal taxes, 52, 60; and provisions, 126; and canon law, 35; Curia of, 89

Clement VI, Pope (1342–52), chancellor to French king, 130; provisions by, 126–8; rebuke to Edward III, 113

clergy: and arbitration, 332; and Edward II's deposition, 76–7; and service of Edward III, 118, 122; and Peasants Revolt, 193–4; and Appellants, 204–5; and tyranny of Richard II, 206–9; and usurpation of Henry IV, 225–7, 233; and Yorkist usurpation, 343–5; poverty of, 83, 245, 303; recruitment declining, 313, 354, 356;

see also array of clergy, benefit of clergy, bishops, chapters, graduates, non-residence, pluralism, political theorizing, religious, taxation

Clericis Laicos, papal bull (1396), 47–8, 51–2, 60, 86

Clifford, Richard (bishop of Worcester 1401–7, bishop of London 1407–21), 266

Cobham, Eleanor, wife of Humphrey, duke of Gloucester, 301–2

Cobham, Lord, see Oldcastle, Sir John

Cobham, Thomas (bishop of Worcester 1317–27), 72, 93–4

Colchester (Essex), abbot of, 239; lollards at, 309

*collegiate churches, 99, 100

Collington, Great and Little, 150

common lawyers, 36, 122, 312–13, 324–5; see also Bracton, Fortescue, Glendower, Hengham, Inns of Court

Commons, see Parliament

Concordat, Anglo-papal: (1375–77), 117, 143; (1398), 217–18; (1418), 294

confession, 154–5

Confirmation of the Charters (1297), 49–50, 52, 60, 63

confiscation of temporalities, 62, 173; proposed, 231, 257, 258; see also resumption

Congé d'élire, writ of, 140, 308

Constance, Council of (1414–18), 261, 293–4, 309

Consueta, papal bull (1365), 134

Consultation: statute of, 30; writs of, 249

Contrariants, 73; lands, 98, 100; see also Mortimer, Roger

convocation: Canterbury Convocation, early history, 50–2, 72, 86–88; royal agents at, 46, 48, 72, 86, 115–16, 303, 356; taxation and, 88–9, 116, 197, 244–6, 308; dates of, 198; and appropriation, 264; and recall of Despensers, 72; significance of, 88–9, 116, 349; trying lollards, 309; on *Praemunire*, 338; on provisions, 129, 131; *gravamina* from, 138; and usurpation (1399), 226–7, (1461), 342–3; archbishops and, see Islip, Sudbury, Arundel; York Convocation, and taxation, 199–200, 244–6

Conway castle, 232; oath at, 224

Coppini, Cardinal, 341, 343

Corbridge, Thomas (archbishop of York 1299–1304), 31–2, 59, 146

Cornforth, John, 164

Cornwall, earl of, see Gaveston

coronation: oath of Edward I, 58, 135; oath of Edward II, 67; oath of Edward III, 130–1; miraculous oil, 226

*corrodies, 33, 100

councils: king's council, 103, 186, 189, 287, 298; general ecclesiastical councils, *see* Basle, Constance, Lateran, Lyons, Pisa; provincial ecclesiastical councils, 77; *and see* Lambeth, Reading, Convocation

Courtenay, Sir Philip de, 326

Courtenay, Richard (chancellor of Oxford University, bishop of Norwich 1413–15), 254, 285, 291–2

Courtenay, William (bishop of Hereford 1370–5, bishop of London 1375–81, archbishop of Canterbury 1381–96): career, 140; character, 115, 141, 194–5, 197–8, 218–19; decree against exchanges, 153; opposing Peasants Revolt, 194–5; opposing taxation, 115, 141, 197–8; opposing king, 201, 203; opposing Wyclif, 168–9; on *Praemunire* and Provisors, 215–17

Coventry, 183, 237, 310; parliament at (1404), 257, (1459), 340

Cranmer, Thomas (archbishop of Canterbury 1533–55), 144

Crécy, battle of, 106, 108, 109, 111

Creton, Jean, 228

criminous clergy, *see* benefit of clergy

Crowland (Lincs.), abbot of, 324

crown debts: Edward I, 45; Edward II, 85; Edward III, 105, 119; Henry VI, 303, 338

crusades: Edward I, 45–6, 58–9; Edward II, 73, 84, 85, 102; Edward III, 123; Richard II, 196–7; Henry V, 271; Bishop Despenser, 195–6; Bishop Beaufort, 299–300; levy for, 343; and Sir John Norbury, 258; indifference to, 308

Cumberland, Scottish raids in, 204

Cum ex eo, papal bull (1298), 158, 159

Dance of Death, 153–4

David II, king of Scotland, 104, 105, 106

*deans of cathedrals, *see* chapters

debts, *see* crown debts

De donis conditionalibus, *see* Westminster II, statute of

De excommunicato capiendo, writ of, 27, 30, 200, 352

De heretico comburendo, statute, 251, 252–3

Denton, J.H., 52, 379 n.22

Derby, Henry, earl of, *see* Henry IV

Derbyshire, lollards, 183

Dereham, Dr Richard, 262, 267

Despenser, Henry (bishop of Norwich 1370–1406): martial activity, 111, 195–6, 201; trial, 205–6; accused of rebellion, 229, 235

Despenser, Hugh the Elder, 65, 71–5 *passim*, 96

Despenser, Hugh the Younger, 65, 71–5 *passim*, 82, 96

Despenser, Lord, 235

De viris religiosis, statute of, *see* Mortmain

Devotio Moderna, 178

Dickinson, J.C., 13

diplomacy: and Edward III's legislation, 129–30, 133–4, 135; Henry V's preparations for war, 270–1, 290; John of Gaunt and the papacy, 142–3; peace endeavours of Beaufort and Suffolk, 300–2; *see also* diplomats, papacy

diplomats: bishops as, 78, 93, 139–40, 290, 292, 317–20; need of clerics for, 158; papal envoys, 16, 68–9, 75, 84, 91, 123, 133–4, 341, 343; *see also* Beaufort (Bp. Henry), Chichele, Courtenay (Richard), Langley, Moleyns, Stratford (John)

Ditchingham (Norfolk), 309

Dobson, R.B., 307–8

Donation of Constantine, 169, 170, 171

Doncaster (Yorks.): 'parliament' at, 81; Henry of Lancaster at, 228

Dominican friars, 23; as cardinals, 90

Dordrecht, 75

Dorset, lollards, 182

Duns Scotus, 165

Durham: archdeaconry of, 289; bishop of, 271; chapter of, 307–8; lollards in, 182; prior of, 332

East Anglia, 193, 309

East Hendred (Berks.), 310

Easton, Adam, 90

Edington (Wiltshire), 333

Edmund, earl of Lancaster, 45

education, *see* graduates, literacy, schools, universities, vernacular

Edward I: character and assessment, 21–3; crusader, 21, 29, 58, 59; piety, 22–3; policy towards church and clergy, 22–3, 61; political skill, 29–30, 38–9, 47, 49, 52, 57; *see also* episcopal appointments, regalian right, statutes, taxation

Edward II: character and circumstances, 65–66; policy, 65, 73; crusader, 73, 85; deposition, 76–7; relations with papacy, 90, 91–2; and Cambridge University, 159; and Contrariants, 73; and Scotland, 67, 70, 71, 74; and Gascony, 74, 80, 82

Edward III: as Prince of Wales, 74, 75; accession and seizure of power, 103–4; claim on French crown, 105; grip on church, 124, 140, 147; military strategy, 105–7, 118; political finesse and force, 105, 119–21, 125; disregard of parliament, 128–32, 147; disregard of laws, 136–8;

decline, 107; in English propaganda, 108, 109; *see also* Provisors, temporalities

Edward IV, 340

Eleanor, wife of Humphrey duke of Gloucester, *see* Cobham

English vernacular, 165, 313; *see also* Bible

episcopal appointments: under Edward I, 59; under Edward II, 92–3; under Edward III, 139–41; under Richard II, 213–14, 217, 221; under Henry IV, 250–1, 265–8; under Henry V, 290; under Henry VI, 307–8, 336; and papal provisions, 92–3, 140–1, 144, 146, 307; *see also* Baldock, Brouns, Burnell, Kemp, Lyhert, Merks, Orleton, Stratford (John), Tottington

Erghum, Ralph (bishop of Salisbury 1375–88, bishop of Bath and Wells 1388–1400), 140–1, 214

Espléchin, truce of, 105, 118

Essex, archdeaconry of, 191, 192; archdeacon of, 43; lollards in, 182; Peasants Revolt in, 192, 193

Eton, foundation of, 335

Etsi de statu, papal bull (1296), 173

Eugenius IV, Pope (1431–47), 306, 336–7

Evesham (Worcs.), abbot of, 322

exchanges, *see* benefices

*excommunication: general sentences, 30–1, 352; of felons and traitors, 330–2; of Gaveston and friends, 66, 68; of Henry IV, 242; of king's clerks, 25, 27–8, 49; of tax defaulters, 30, 50, 61, 200; of violators of Magna Carta, 60; of violators of Ordinances, 68; *see also De excommunicato capiendo*

Ex debito, papal bull (c. 1316), 126

Execrabilis, papal bull (1317), 92

exemptions, ecclesiastical, statute concerning (1402), 300, 338

Exeter, bishop of, 321; cathedral, 99; cathedral chancellors, *see* Bracton, Hengham

Exeter College, Oxford, 159

Farndon (Northants.), 234

FitzHugh, Lord, 293

FitzRalph, Richard (archbishop of Armagh 1346–60), 165

Flanders: Edward I and, 43, 48, 49; Edward III and, 105, 118, 129, 135; match with countess, 133–4; Despenser's crusade, 195–6; Henry VI and, 299; vital markets, 271

Fleming, Richard (bishop of Lincoln 1419–31), 292, 307, 309

Flint, 224

Floretum, 179

Folville, Gustave de, 324

Fordham, John (bishop of Durham 1382–88, bishop of Ely 1388–1425), 202, 214

Forest, Charter of, 16; confirmation (1297), 48, 49, 52; ordinance of (1306), 22

Fortescue, Sir John, 312, 355

Fountains Abbey (Yorks.), 17, 81, 326

France, hostilities with: Edward I, 43; Edward II, 74–5; Edward III, 105–7, 111, 117, 118, 142; Richard II, 189–91; Henry IV, 231–3, 239, 244; Henry V, 270–2; Henry VI, 300–2, 333, 339, 340

Franceys, John, 263

Franciscan friars, 237–9

friars, *see* Austin friars, Carmelite, Dominican, Franciscan

Frederick II, Emperor, deposition of and Richard II, 225

French, depictions in sermon propaganda, 108, 109

Frisby, Dr, O.F.M., 237–9

Frome (Somerset), 310

Fryde, E.B., 191

Gainsborough, William (bishop of Winchester 1303–7), 59

Gascoigne, Thomas, 255

Gascony, 43, 48, 74, 75, 80, 82, 105, 106

Gaunt, *see* John of Gaunt, duke of Lancaster

Gaveston, Piers, earl of Cornwall, 65, 66, 67, 68, 69

Gesta Henrici Quarti, 271, 274, 281, 282

Ghent, 105, 196

Ghent, Simon of (bishop of Salisbury 1297–1315), 67

Giffard, John, 211

Gilbert, John (bishop of Bangor 1372–5, bishop of Hereford 1375–89, bishop of St Davids 1389–97), 140, 202, 204, 214

Gilbert, Robert, 285, 289

Giles of Rome, 165, 172

Glastonbury Abbey (Somerset), 226, 339; loan to king, 247, 284

Glendower, Owen, rebellion of, *see under* Wales

Gloucester, 75; statute of (1278), 34

Gloucester, dukes of, *see* Humphrey, Thomas (of Woodstock)

Gloucestershire, lollards in, 183

The Golden Legend, 312

good lordship, 325

Good Parliament, the, 1376, 117, 143

Gower, John, 109, 165

Goxhill (Lincs.), 83

graduates, 133, 158, 160, 161; bishops, 139, 141; and provisions, 249

Grandisson, John (bishop of Exeter 1327–69), 127, 159

Grassi, Dr J.L., 99

gravamina, (1316), 86; under Edward III, 135–8; under Richard II, 209; and parliamentary petitions, 56

Graves, E.B., 132

Gravesend, Stephen (bishop of London 1280–1303), 79

Gray, William (bishop of London 1425–31, bishop of Lincoln 1431–6), 317

Greenfield, William (archbishop of York 1304–15), convening parliaments, 81

Gregory IX, Pope (1227–41), 92

Gregory X, Pope (1272–6), 35, 45, 57

Gregory XI, Pope (1371–8), 117, 123

Gregory XII, Pope (1406–9/14), 260, 265

Grey, Sir Thomas, 277

Grey, William (bishop of Ely 1454–78), 255

Guelders, count of, 105

Guisborough (Yorks.), prior of, 332

Guyenne, 244, 247, 317

Gynewell, John (bishop of Lincoln 1347–62), 111

Hainault: 249, 299; count of, 105; match with princess of, 129–30; *see also* Humphrey, duke of Gloucester.

Hales, John (bishop of Exeter 1455–6, bishop of Lichfield 1459–90), 335, 336, 337

Halesowen (Warwicks.), abbot of, 243, 322

Hallum, Robert (bishop of Salisbury 1407–17), 267, 292, 293

Harclay, Andrew, earl of Carlisle, 74

Harfleur, relief of, 274

Harlech castle, 232

Hartburn (Co. Durham), vicarage of, 100

Haseley, Thomas, 314

Hatfield, Thomas (bishop of Durham 1345–81), 111

Haulay, Robert, 209–10

Haxey, Thomas, petition of, 208–9, 219–20

Hengham, Ralph, 28, 35

Henry IV: character and experience, 203, 204, 223, 243; intention to usurp, 227–8; assistance from clergy, 225–8; assistance from Arundel, 228, 229–30; promises to convocation, 227, 244; execution of Scrope, 241–2; health, 243; policy on Schism, 260–1, 345; *see also* episcopal appointments, loans, patronage, taxation

Henry V: as Prince of Wales, 230, 243, 246, 253, 254, 258; character and achievements, 269, 270, 273–4, 293–4, 295–6; conception of kingship, 269; policy towards clergy, 285, 288–9, and Beaufort, 291, 295; policy towards Council of Constance, 293–4, 345;

reform of monasteries, 273–4; war aims, 270–1; *see also* episcopal appointments, loans, patronage, taxation

Henry VI: character and reign, 297–8, 301; and Cambridge University, 255; and papacy, 345; household bishops of, 335–6; marriage, 334

Henry VII, 340

Henry VIII, 340

Hereford, 182

Hereford, Nicholas, 176, 178, 180

Hereford diocese, 176, 284; impoverished benefices, 245; cathedral, canon of, *see* Hengham

Herefordshire, lollards, 183

heresy, statues concerning, (1407 and 1414), 253–4, 277–8; *see also* De heretico comburendo, lollards

Heron, William, 332

Hertfordshire, lollards, 183

Hethe, Hamo (bishop of Rochester 1317–52), 76, 79

Hexham Priory (Northumberland), 245; prebend in, 250–1

Heyworth, William (bishop of Lichfield 1420–47), 291

Hickling Priory (Norfolk), 150

Highfield, J.R.L., 14

Hilton, Walter, 313

Hoccleve, Thomas, 281

Holme Cultram Abbey (Cumberland), 81

Hook, Robert, 178

Horncastle (Lincs.), church of, 82

Horribilis, papal bull (1363), 133

Hospitallers of St John of Jerusalem, Order of, 96, 97

Hotham, John (bishop of Ely 1316–37), 75, 79, 82, 159

Hotspur, Henry Percy (d. 1403), 240

Hovingham, Dr John, 293

Hudson, Anne, 184

Humanism, 255, 319

Humphrey, duke of Gloucester, 255, 298–302, 306

Hungerford, Sir Walter, 293

Hunsley (Yorks.), 82

Huntingdon, prior of, 239–40

Huntingdonshire, lollards, 183

Ignorantia Sacerdotum, decree by Abp. Pecham, 162–3

Innocent III, Pope (1198–1216), 15, 18, 58

Innocent IV, Pope (1243–54), deposition of emperor, 225

Innocent VII, Pope (1404–6), 260

inns of court and of chancery, 160, 312–13; *see also* 36, 232

Invective against France, 109
Ireland, 224
Isabella, queen of Edward II, 21, 74–5, 103–4
Islip, Simon (archbishop of Canterbury 1349–66), 115, 138, 151, 324
Italian bankers, 43, 303–4
Ixworth (Suffolk), prior of, 239–40
Ixworth, Dr John, 262

Jessop, A., 150
Jewry, statute of (1275), 22
Jews, expulsion of, 29–30
John, duke of Bedford, 298
John of Gaunt, duke of Lancaster: 107, 189, 194, 201, 202; and Castile, 195, 202, 204; and convocation, 115; and crusade, 195; and papacy, 142–3; and papal provisions, 127; and sanctuary, 210; and Wykeham, 142, 143; and Wyclif and lollardy, 116, 117, 142, 168, 177
John, king of England, 15, 18, 21, 29, 144
John II, king of France, captured, 106; ransomed, 117
John XXII, Pope (1316–34): and Anglo-Scottish war, 84; and appointment of bishops, 91, 93, 101; and deposition of Edward II, 91; and Despensers, 72–3, 75; and pluralism, 92; and provisions, 126, 127; Curia, 89; policy towards England, 89–90, 91, 135, 293; verdict on plight of English church, 101
John XXIII, Pope (1410–15/19), 265, 293
judges, royal: clergy as, 17, 35–6, 349–50; laymen as, 36, 122, 352; itinerant justices and clergy, 39–40; answers to Richard II's questions, 203, 211; ignorance of recent statutes, 248; relations with clergy under Henry IV, 248; *see also* Hengham, Tresilian
Juliers, marquis of, 105
jurisdiction: boundaries between church and crown courts, 39–41, 136, 352; *see also gravamina*, lay fee, *Praemunire*, prohibitions, sanctuary
Justices of the Peace, 278, 289, 320–1

Keeper of the privy seal, 142
Kemp, John (bishop of Rochester 1419–21, bishop of Chichester 1421, bishop of London 1421–5, archbishop of York 1425–52, archbishop of Canterbury 1452–4), 285, 290, 301, 304, 306, 317
Kemp, Thomas (bishop of London 1448–89), 336
Kempe, Margery, 313
Kenningham, John, O. Carm., 167
Kent, 182, 192, 193
Kent, earl of, 103

Kilham (Yorks.), 83
Kilmore, see of, 203, 205, 214
Kilsby, William, 118, 121–2, 141
Kilwardby, Robert (archbishop of Canterbury 1272–8), 23–4, 59
king's clerks: 349–50; conflict with archbishop, 31, 33–4, 121–2; numbers increasing, 98, 138; recruitment, 99; laymen, 314–16, 354–5; and benefices, 98–9, 101, 125; and parliament, 55; and reform, 28; *see also* bishops, excommunication
King's College, Cambridge, 255, 335
King's Hall, Cambridge, 159
kingship: Pecham on, 24, 29; Edward I's ideal, 21–3; Wyclif on, 168, 173; Richard II's judges on, 203; Richard II's bishops on, 168, 173, 216–17; Henry V's conception of, 269
King's Lynn (Norfolk), 313
Kirkby, John (bishop of Carlisle 1332–52), 111
knighthood, *see under* oaths
Knighton, Henry, 167, 178
knights, *see under* lollards

Lacy, Edmund (bishop of Hereford 1417–20, bishop of Exeter 1420–55), 280, 291, 304, 332
Lacy, Peter, 142
laity, literate and articulate, 14th century, 161, 165–6; 15th century, 312–13, 328; *see also* Bible, education
Lambeth, council at (1281), 28–9, 39
Lancaster, Henry, earl of, 103
Lancaster, John, duke of, *see* John of Gaunt
Lancaster, Thomas, earl of, 69, 70, 72, 81, 96; estates of, 100
Langdon, John (bishop of Rochester 1422–34), 291
Langham, Simon, O.S.B. (bishop of Ely 1362–6, archbishop of Canterbury 1366–8), 90, 139, 140; and criminous clergy, 248
Langland, William, 110, 116, 162, 165, 181
Langley, Edmund, earl of Cambridge and duke of York (d. 1402), 133
Langley, Thomas (bishop of Durham 1406–37), 182, 259–60, 266–7, 271, 292, 335
Langton, Stephen (archbishop of Canterbury 1207–28), 35
Langton, Walter (bishop of Lichfield 1296–1321), 67, 94
La Rochelle, naval battle, 107
Lansell, Roger, 287
Lantern of Light, The, 184
Lateran Council, Third (1179), 50

Lateran Council, Fourth (1215), 18–19, 24, 50, 168
Latimer, Lord, 116
Latimer, Sir Thomas, 178–9, 184
Launde Priory (Leics.), 237
Lavendon (Bucks.), abbot of, 239–40
Laws and Customs of England, The, 35
lawyers, *see* canon, common, Roman
*lay fee, definition of, 32, 96, 100, 101, 337; *see also* patronage, regalian right
Lay Folks Catechism, The, 179
laymen at convocation, 46–7, 72, 86, 115–16, 303, 356
lay ministers, *see* chancellors, bureaucracy
lay rectors, 259
Leake, treaty of, 71
Leff, Gordon, 255
Leicester: abbot of, 176; lollards at, 177, 183; Franciscans' conspiracy, 237, 239
Leicester, earl of (1326), 75
Leicestershire, lollards, 183
legislation, episcopal, 35; *see also* Pecham, Stratford (John), Arundel (Thomas)
legislation, papal, 34–5, *see also* bulls
legislation, royal: 17; influences upon, 34–5, 40, 129–30, 133–5, influences of, 42, 132, 145; king's independence in, 120, 121, 129, 130, 131, 132, 136–7, 147 *and see Praemunire*, Provisors, statutes, Wyclif
Lewis of Bavaria, emperor, 105, 123
libraries, 'public', 313
Lichfield diocese, poll tax, 192; cathedral clergy, 99; prebends in, 250
Limburg, *see* Brabant
Lincoln diocese, 150, 183, 284
Lincoln Cathedral, 99, 242
Lincoln College, Oxford, 309
Linkinhorne (Cornwall), vicarage of, 264
Liskeard (Cornwall), vicarage of, 264
literacy, *see under* laity
livery, grants of, statutes of, and clergy, 323–5
Llanfaes Friary (Anglesey), O.F.M., 237, 238
Llewellyn, Lord of Snowdonia, 23
loans: from Winchelsey to Edward I, 50; from clergy to Edward II, 83; to Richard II, 304; to Henry IV, 231, 246–7; to Henry V, 283–4; to Henry VI, 304–5; *see also* Beaufort (Henry), Italian bankers
Lochmaben castle, 201
Loddon (Norfolk), 309
Logan, F.D., 30
lollard Bible, *see* Bible, English, 180
lollard knights, 175–6, 177–9
lollards, 182–7, 309–10; and politics of Richard II's reign, 185–6
*lollardy, 194–5, 251–6, 274–9, 309–10, 352–5; *see also* Heresy

London, 75, 96, 164, 183, 192, 310, 313
Cheapside, 75
Guildhall, assemblies at (1326–7), 76
St Giles Fields, 275, 277
St Mary Graces on Tower Hill, 334
St Mary Somerset, 211
St Paul's Cathedral, 99; canon of, *see* Hengham; dean of, dies, 46; churchyard, Ordinances published in, 67, Abp. Stratford preaching in, 108
Tower of London, 224; captured by citizens, 75
Stapledon, guardian of, 96
Longport (i.e. Lamport, Somerset), 326–7
Lords, *see* Parliament
Louis de Luxemburg (archbishop of Rouen, bishop of Ely 1437–43), 307, 336
Love, Nicholas, O. Carthus., 309
Ludford Bridge, battle of, 340
Lumley, Marmaduke (bishop of Carlisle 1430–50, bishop of Lincoln 1450), 310, 336
Lyndwood, William (bishop of St Davids 1442–6), 317
Lyons, Council of (1274), 23, 24, 45, 58
Lyhert, Walter (bishop of Norwich 1446–72), 310, 333, 334, 336–7

Macworth, John, 263
Magdalen College, Oxford, 255
Magna Carta: 15–17, 38, 227; published by Pecham and Winchelsey, 25, 27, 50; invoked by Stratford, 120; invoked by Richard II, 220; invoked by a knight (1404), 257; *see also* Confirmation of the Charters, excommunication
Maine, cession of, 302, 333, 334
maintenance, 325–8
Malestroit, truce of, 106, 123
Malton (Yorks.), 83
Manners, John, 332
March, earl of, *see* Mortimer (Edmund) and York (Edward duke of)
Margaret of Anjou, queen of Henry VI, 298, 302, 325, 334, 335, 340
Martham (Norfolk), 309
Martin V, Pope (1417–31), 290, 294–5, 299, 305–6, 307, 309
Martival, Roger (bishop of Salisbury 1315–30), 127
Mascall, Robert (bishop of Hereford 1404–16), 266
McFarlane, K.B., 270
McHardy, A.K., 192
McNiven, P., 240
Meaux Abbey, O. Cist. (Yorks.), 150
Meaux (Normandy), siege of, 272

Melton, William (archbishop of York 1317–40), 76, 79, 82, 99, 158

Merchants, statute of (1285), 34

Merciless Parliament, the (1388), 189, 203

Merks, Thomas (bishop of Carlisle 1397–99), 229, 233–5, 265–6

Merton College, Oxford, 167

Michaelhouse, Cambridge, 159

'Middle Party', the, 70

Milton Abbas (Dorset), abbot's loan to king, 247

ministers, king's, *see* Bureaucracy, Chancellor

Mirk, John, writings of, 312, 331

Mirror of the Blessed Life of Christ, 309

Mitford, Richard (bishop of Chichester 1390–5, bishop of Salisbury 1395–1407), 214, 247

Moleyns, Adam (bishop of Chichester 1445–50), 301, 310, 317, 333–4

monasteries: declining benefactions to, 37; lands secularized, 112–13; number of houses, 17, 37–8; war propaganda composed in, 109

monastic chronicles, 225

Mone, Guy (bishop of St Davids 1397–1407), 217

money, export of barred, 53, 214; *see also* ports

Montagu, Sir John, 178

Montague, William, 103–4

Montfort, John, 262

Moran, J.H., 163

Morgan, Philip (bishop of Worcester 1419–26, bishop of Ely 1426–35), 292, 317

Mortimer, Edmund, earl of March, 223, 277

Mortimer, Roger, 74, 103–4

*Mortmain, statute of (1279), 36–9, 132, 173; (1391), 213; English and foreign precedents, 38

Mowbray, Thomas, Earl Marshall (d. 1405), 240, 241

Mowbray, Thomas, earl of Nottingham, duke of Norfolk (d. 1399), 203, 204, 275

Muchelney Abbey (Somerset), monk of, 339

Multon (Suffolk), 334

Myton on Swale (Yorks.), battle of, 82

Najera, battle of, 108, 210

national church, 174, 386 (cap. 6, n. 8)

nationalism and church, 108–9, 190, 231, 279–80, 350–1

Neath (Glamorgan), 75

Netter, Thomas, O. Carm., 309

Nevill, Sir William, 178

Neville, Alexander (archbishop of York 1374–88), 141, 203, 205–6

Neville, George (bishop of Exeter 1456–65, archbishop of York 1465–76), 336, 337, 341, 342–3

Neville, Sir John, 326

Neville, Ralph, earl of Westmorland (d. 1425), 232

Neville, Richard, earl of Warwick (d. 1471), 336, 340, 341

Neville, Robert (bishop of Salisbury 1427–38, bishop of Durham 1438–57), 307

Neville's Cross, battle of, 106, 109, 111

New College, Oxford, 159

Newark (Notts.), 150, 242

Newcastle upon Tyne, 182

Newent (Glos.), alien priory, 259

Newnham (Beds.), prior of, 239–40

Newsham Abbey (Devon), 326

Nicholas III, Pope (1277–80), 23

Nicholas V, Pope (1447–55), 297–8, 336

Nicholls, Benedict (bishop of Bangor 1408–18, bishop of St Davids 1418–33), 285, 292

Nicopolis, battle of, 197

non-residence of clergy, 98–9, 315–16

Norbury, Sir John, 258

Norfolk, lollards, 182–3

Normandy, 106, 271–2, 285, 292, 300, 333, 339, 340; church of, 290, 300

Northampton: battle of, 343; council of clergy and laity at (1283), 51, 55; Franciscan rebels, 237; lollards, 179–84, 310; treaty of, 103

Northamptonshire, lollards, 183

Northburgh, Roger (bishop of Lichfield 1321–58), 99, 159

Northleach (Glos.), 313

Northumberland, county of, 182

Northumberland, earls of, *see* Percy

Norwich: city, 325; diocese, 150; bishop of, 271, 325; Franciscans of, 238

Nottingham: castle, 104; Franciscan rebels of, 238; lollards, 176, 182

Nottingham, earl of, *see* Mowbray

oaths: bishops' oaths of fealty, 59; of Abp. Arundel at Conway, 224; of clergy for liberties of London and Isabella, 76–7; of knights, 327; of peers and clergy to Richard II, 208; papal absolution of Edward I from oaths, 52, 60; papal release from oaths against Despensers, 72; *see also under* coronation

Ockham, William of, brief for Edward III, 161

Offord, John (archbishop-elect of Canterbury 1348–9), 122, 140

Oldcastle, Sir John, (Lord Cobham), 179, 184, 258, 274–6

Ordainers, the, 67–8, 69
Ordinances, the (1311), 67–8, 69; published by bishop of Salisbury, 67
Oriel College, Oxford, 159
Orleton, Adam (bishop of Hereford 1317–27, bishop of Worcester 1327–33, bishop of Winchester 1333–45): and deposition of Edward II, 75, 76, 78; papal promotion of, 93; royal diplomat, 93; to Flanders with Edward III, 118
Orléans, duke of, 239
Orme, N., 163
Otterburn, battle of, 204
Otto, cardinal legate, 35
Ottobuono, cardinal legate, 16, 35
Oxford, business school at, 164
Oxford Common, 237
Oxford University: academics and conciliar reforms, 294; and papal provisions, 127; colleges, 94, 158–9, 167, 255, 309; graduates/students, 43, 160; Franciscan rebels, 238; humanism and scholasticism, 255; liberties defended, 254–5, 291; lollardy, 176–7, 179, 182–3, 186, 254–5, 310; and vernacular Bible, 180; Wyclif expelled from, 168–9, writings suppressed and burnt, 179

Pantin, W.A., 13, 14, 163
papacy: Curia, Englishmen at, 89–90; King John, Henry III and, 15–16; Edward I and, 57–8; Edward II and, 69–70, letters to, 90; Edward III, secret letter to, 103–4; Gaunt and, 142–3; Richard II's tyranny and, 208, 220; Henry VI and, 343; Schism (1378–1418), 190, 260–1, 293, 352; Wyclif's views on, 167, 168, 169–70; *see also* annates, bulls, councils, crusades, Gaveston, Despenser, pluralism, provisions, Provisors, services, taxation
papal diplomacy and England, 65, 68–9, 75, 84, 123
papal tribute, 15, 58–9, 134–5
Paris, 40, 74, 224, 271, 272, 300; university, 43, 255
parish clergy, 125, 255; *see also* non-residence, education, patronage
parishes, 18
parliament: 350–2; origins of, 54–5; commons, 57, 87, 210; lords, 54, 210; lords spiritual, 54, 89, 109, 206–8, 351; proctor of spiritual peers, 206–8; peerage rights and Abp. Stratford, 120; clergy's role and influence, 55–6, 89; influence on anticlericalism, 56–7, 138; liberties of commons, 208–9; papal confirmation of acts, 208, 220; and doctrine, 253; and trial

of lollards, 253; king's independence of, 147; anticlericalism in, 246; *see also under* anticlericalism, *Praemunire*, Provisors, statutes, *and* Cambridge, Coventry, Good, Merciless, Westminster/Shrewsbury, Wonderful, Greenfield
Paston family, correspondence of, 313
pastoral role of church, impact of crown upon, 125, 141, 147–8
paternalism of archbishops, 29, 43, 46, 48, 66, 331
Patrington, Stephen, O. Carm., (bishop of St Davids 1415–17, bishop of Chichester 1417), 290–1
patronage, king's ecclesiastical: 350, 354; Edward I, 26, 31–2, 33–4, 59; Edward II, 100; Edward III, 124–5, 137; Henry IV, 250–1, 261–3; Henry V, 289; *see also* king's clerks, lay fee, prohibitions, regalian right
patron paramount, 97, 131–2; *see also* Statute of Carlisle
Peasants Revolt, 168, 175, 192–5
Pecham, John (archbishop of Canterbury 1279–92), 24, 29, 30, 35, 38–9, 59, 121, 331; decrees of, 25, 29, 162–3
Pecock, Reginald (bishop of Chichester 1450–7), 310–12
peers spiritual, *see* Parliament
Pembroke, earl of, *see* Valence
penances, commons petition on (1377), 212
pensions, 32–3, 100, *see also* corrodies
Percy, Henry, earl of Northumberland (d. 1408), 224, 232, 240
Percy, Henry, earl of Northumberland (d. 1455), 326
Percy, Henry, 'Hotspur', 240
Percy, Sir Thomas, 206–8
Percy, family, 240; and Scrope rebellion, 240–1
Perkins, William, rebellion (1431), 309–10
Perrers, Alice, 107
Pershore (Worcs.), abbot of, 322
Peterhouse, Cambridge, 158
Philip VI, king of France, 105
Philip, duke of Burgundy, 196
Phillips, J.S.R., 70
Piers Plowman, *see* Langland
Pilton, William, 250–1
Pisa, Council of (1409), 235, 260–1
Pius II, Pope (1458–64): verdict on Henry VI, 298; provisions by, 306; and Edward IV, 343; *see also* Coppini
*pluralism, 24–5, 28, 92, 99, 133–4, 294
Poitiers, battle of, 106, 108
Pole, Michael de la, earl of Suffolk (d. 1389), 189, 201, 202, 203

Pole, William de la, earl and duke of Suffolk (d. 1450), 327, 333–4
political theorizing by clergy, 316,355; *see also* Two Swords, Wyclif
poll tax: (1377–81), 190–2; on aliens (1439–40), 321
Polton, Thomas (bishop of Hereford 1420–1, bishop of Chichester 1422–26, bishop of Worcester 1426–33), 292
Pontefract (Yorks.), 81
ports, closed to papal bulls and money, 134, 214
*Praemunire: statutes, (1353), 132–3, 134, 144–5, 249; (1365), 134; (1393), 215–17, 300, 311, 338–9, 352, 353, 356, 357; writs of, 133, 249, 287
Praty, Richard (bishop of Chichester 1438–45), 317
prayers and processions, for war efforts and/or realm: under Edward I, 107; under Edward III, 107–10; under Henry IV, 231; under Henry V, 279–80, 284
Prestwich, M., 44
prises, *see* purveyances
privilege of England, 92
privy seal office, 315
probate fees, 212, 288
Pro Clero: letters patent (1316), *see Articuli Cleri*; statute of (1352), 136, 137, 248
processions, *see* prayers
proctor, for spiritual peers 1397–99, 206–8
*prohibitions, writs of: to ecclesiastical courts, 25–6, 32, 92, 132; to ecclesiastical councils, (1281) 28–9, (1341) 120; care over issue of, 286–7; disquiet about, 248–9; restrictions on, 40; statute concerning (1414), 286; *see also Circumspecte Agatis*, Consultation, ordinances
propaganda, *see* prayers, sermons
Prophet, John, 256, 267
*provisions, papal: 294, 348, 349, 350; origins, 125–6; numbers, 126, 262, 263, 306; occasions, 25, 31; resistance and opposition, 125, 127, 129, 213; bishops provided, 92–3, 140–2, 144, 146, 221, 265–8, 307–8; papal income from, 128–9; king's response, 58, 125, 129–30; bishops' objections, 127; commons and, 129, 213; nobles' response, 127; Black Death and, 130; universities and, 127, 241, 249; *see also* annates, services
*Provisors: statutes, (1351) 56, 128–32, 142, 143–4, (1365) 134, (1388) 213–4, (1390), 214–5, 217–8; attitude of commons towards, 261–2, of Henry IV, 261–3; papal response to, 130; papal efforts for repeal of, 214–18, 294–5, 305–6; *see also* Concordat

Purvey, John, 176, 180
purveyances, 16, 44, 46, 49–50, 113, 337

*Quare impedit, writ of, 124
*Quare non admisit, writ of, 124, 137, 316
Queen's College, Oxford, 167
Quia emptores, statute of, 34
Quo warranto, statute of, 34
Quarr Abbey (Isle of Wight), 111

Radcot Bridge, battle of, 203
Raftis, J.A., 152
Ramsey (Hunts.), abbot of, 286
Reading (Berks.): lollards at, 183; provincial council of (1279), 24, 25
Real Presence, Wyclif's interpretation, 168, 170–1
*rectors, see lay rectors
Reformation, Henrician statutes, 356–7
*regalian right: under Edward I, 26–7, 32; Edward II, 97, 100; Edward III, 124, 136; Henry IV, 250; *see also* patronage, lay fee
religious: loans to crown by, 247; and bulls of exemption for, 263; as bishops, 139; *see also* Austin friars, Benedictine, Bridgetines, Carmelite, Carthusian, Celestine, Cistercian, Citeaux, Dominican, Franciscan
Repingdon (*alias* Repton), Philip (bishop of Lincoln 1404–19): bishop, 266, 280; confessor of Henry IV, 236–7; loan to king, 283; lollard, 176–7, 181–2
resumption: of ecclesiastical endowments, 41, 173; Act of (1404), 257, 390 n.81; *see also* confiscation
retainers, and clergy, 322–3
Reynolds, Walter (bishop of Worcester 1308–13, archbishop of Canterbury 1313–27): character and leadership, 94–5; and Despensers, 70, 72; and deposition of Edward II, 75–80, 95; and taxation, 86, 87, 88; and Templars, 96
Richard II: character and policy, 190, 201–2, 204–9; autocracy, 201, 206–9; defender of church, 210–13, 221; household bishops, 208–9, 217, 219–20; abdication and capture, 224; death, 235–6; rumours of survival, 237; reburial (1413), 277
Richmondshire, Scottish raids, 81
Rievaulx Abbey (Yorks.), 82
Ripon (Yorks.), 81, 82
Rochester diocese: chaplains of, 284; priory, 265
Rochford, Sir Ralph, 293
Rolle, Richard, 165, 313
Roman law, 34, 35, 122, 159, 173

Roman lawyers, 349; *see* Chichele, Stapledon
Rome, pilgrims to, 356
Romeyn, John le (archbishop of York 1286–96), 28
Ross, John (bishop of Carlisle 1325–32), 79
Rouen, captured (1419), 280; archbishop of, *see* Louis de Luxemburg
royal clerks, *see* king's clerks
Royal Free Chapels, *see* collegiate churches
royal judges, *see* judges
Rudston (Yorks.), 83
Rushook, Thomas, O.P., (bishop of Llandaff 1388–5, bishop of Chichester 1385–8), 201, 203, 205–6, 214
Ryecroft, Nicholas, 287

saints, 280–1
St Albans Abbey (Herts.), 150, 193, 291, 295, 334
St Andrews, see of, 203, 204, 205, 214
St Barthe, alien priory of, 259
St Bridget, 313
St Chad, 281
St David, 281
St David's diocese, poll tax in, 191
St George, feast of, 281
St John of Beverley, feast and tomb, 281
St Osyth's Abbey (Essex), 239
St Pol, count of, 239
St Winifred, feast of, 281
Salisbury diocese: poll tax in, 192; cathedral chapter, 51, 99, 310; diocesan clergy oaths, 208; lollards, 310
Salisbury, earl of, 271
Salmon, John (bishop of Norwich 1299–1325), 59
*sanctuary, 168, 209–12
Sandiacre prebend (Lichfield cathedral), 250
Sawtry, William, 251
Sayles, G.O., 56
Scarborough (Yorks.), 193, 259
Shirley, John, 313
Schism, papal (1378–1418), *see under* papacy
scholars, and politics, 161
scholasticism, 255
schools, 163–5, 313; *see also* education
Scotland: and Edward I, 43, 44, 47, 48, 52, 60; and Edward II, 67, 70, 71, 74, 80–5, 91; and Edward III, 103, 104–5, 106, 109, 111; and Richard II, 191, 204; and Henry IV, 231, 233, 244, 245; and Henry VI, 343; and the English church, 81; and the papacy, 58, 60
Scrope, Henry (d. 1415), 277
Scrope, Lord, 332
Scrope, Richard le (bishop of Lichfield 1386–98, archbishop of York 1398–1405): and

deposition of Richard II, 226, 229; and royal taxation of clergy, 249; rebellion, 240–2; execution and reactions, 242–3, 249, 273
Scrope, William, earl of Wiltshire (d. 1399), 208
secularization, *see* alien priories, Templars, confiscation, resumption, lollards, Wyclif
Selby (Yorks.), abbot of, 82
Seley, Sir Benedict, 234
sermons: on war etc., under Edward I, 107, under Edward III, 108, 109; at deposition of Edward II, 76–7; at deposition of Richard II, 226; by Wyclif, 162, 177; by Brinton, 112, 162, 177; by Wimbledon, 162; mediating scholarship to public, 162; restrictions imposed by Arundel, 251, 255
*services paid to pope, 128, 265, 307, 348
Shaftesbury (Dorset), abbess of, loan to king, 247
Shakel, John, 209–10
Sheen Charterhouse (Surrey), 273–4
Shenley (Herts.), 178
Sherborne (Dorset), 326–7
Shipton Moor, battle of, 240
Shrewsbury, lollards at, 182
Shrewsbury, J.F.D., 149
Sigismund, Emperor, 293
signet office, laymen in, 315; *see also* bureaucracy
silva cedua, tithes of, 137, 212–13, 249, 287–8
Simeon, Simon, 324
Skirlaw, Walter (bishop of Lichfield 1386, bishop of Bath and Wells 1386–8, bishop of Durham 1388–1406), 214, 247
Sluys, naval battle of, 105, 198
Smith, William, 177
Somerset, dukes of, *see* Beaufort
Somersham (Hunts.), parson of, 286
Southwark (Surrey), mayor and bailiffs of, 249
Spencer, John, 338
Sprever, Dr William, 317
Squyer, John, 334
Stafford, John (bishop of Bath and Wells 1424–43, archbishop of Canterbury 1443–52), 247, 305, 317, 335
Stafford, earl of (d. 1372), 115
Stafford, Sir Humphrey, 322
Stamford (Lincs.), Franciscan rebels from, 238
Stanbury, John (bishop of Bangor 1448–53, bishop of Hereford 1453–74), 335, 337
Stapledon, Walter (bishop of Exeter 1308–26), 72, 75, 95–6, 159
Stapledon Hall, Oxford, 159

statutes: 34, 120–1; on regalian right, 136, 137–8; on stipends, 288–9; *see also* legislation, appropriations; Carlisle, *Circumspecte agatis*, Consultation, *De heretico comburendo*, exemptions, heresy, Jewry, livery, Mortmain, *Praemunire*, Provisors, *Quia emptores*, *Quo warranto*, Reformation, resumption, Templars, vicarages, Westminster

Staunton, Harvey de, 159

Stenton, Lady Dorothy, 35

stipends, *see* chaplains

Stirling Bridge, battle of, 49

Stokes, Dr John, 317 *bis*

Storey, R.L., 313

Stratford, John (bishop of Winchester 1323–33, archbishop of Canterbury 1333–48): character and assessment, 120–1; and Edward II, 75–8; and Edward III, 118–20, 139; and war, 108, 109, 121; on alien priories, 113; on diplomatic missions, 78, 93, 139; provincial constitutions, 116, 331

Stratford, Robert (bishop of Chichester 1337–62), 119, 122

Strickland, William (bishop of Carlisle 1399–1419), 250, 265–6

Studley (Warws.), prior of, 322

Sudbury, Simon (bishop of London 1362–75, archbishop of Canterbury 1375–81): career, character and death, 117, 140, 193–4; condemnation of clerical greed, 151; management of convocation, 115, 146

Suffolk, earl/duke of, *see* Pole

Sussex, lollards in, 182

Swaledale, Scottish raids in, 81

Swan, William, 317

Swinderby, William, 177

Swinfield, Richard (bishop of Hereford 1283–1317), 83

Syon Abbey (Mx.), 273–4

Talland (Cornwall), 264

Talleyrand, Cardinal, 125

Tavistock (Devon), abbot of, loan to king, 247

taxation, papal: 347–8; for advantage of Edward I, 45–6, 52–3, 61, 62–3; for Edward III, 85–6, 116–17; for Edward III, 145; allowed by Gaunt, 143; resisted by Henry IV, 265, 295, 308; under Henry V and Henry VI, 308

taxation, royal, of clergy: 348–9; under Henry III, 50–1; under Edward I, 45–52, 62–3; under Edward II, 83, 86; under Edward III, 113–16, 118–19, 137, 146–7; under Richard II, 191–2 (Poll Taxes), 197–200, 221; under Henry IV, 230–1,

244–6, 256–7; under Henry V, 281–3; under Henry VI, 303, 337–8; collected by clergy, 50; collected by laity, 241, 249; resisted, 115; defaulters excommunicated, *see: De excommunicato capiendo*

taxation, royal, of laity: 16, 44–5, 83, 118–19, 190–2

Templars, suppression of, 66, 96–7, 100; statute concerning lands of, 96–7; protest by Reynolds, 94, 96

*temporalities of bishops: 18, 59; seized by crown, 78–9, 100, 115, 124–5, 138, 140; seizure threatened by crown, 28–9; Wyclif on, 173; *see also* confiscation

Tendring (Essex), parson of, 239

Tenterden (Kent), lollards at, 183, 309

Teramo, Simon da, 295

Thetford (Norfolk), prior of, 239–40

Thirnyng, Chief Justice, 244

Thomas of Woodstock, duke of Gloucester, 201, 202, 203, 204

Thompson, A.H., 13, 150

Thoresby, John (bishop of St Davids 1347–9, bishop of Worcester 1349–52, archbishop of York 1352–73), 138, 141, 154, 165

Thorney Abbey (Cambs.), 311

Thorpe, William, 182

Tideman [of Winchcomb], (bishop of Llandaff 1393–5, bishop of Worcester 1395–1401), 217

*tithes, *see* Silva cedua

Torre Abbey (Devon), loan to king, 247

Tottington, Alexander (bishop of Norwich 1406–13), 250, 267

treasurer of realm, layman as, 142–3

Trefnant, John (bishop of Hereford 1389–1404), 226, 266

Trevisa, Nicholas, translator, 165

Tresilian, Robert, Chief Justice, 203, 210–11

Trevor, John II (bishop of St Asaph 1394–c.1410), 226

tribute, *see* papal tribute

Trillek, John (bishop Hereford 1344–60), 144

Troyes, treaty of (1420), 272, 297, 301, 302–3

Trussell, Sir William, 77

Turks, threat of, 271, 306, 308, 343

Two Swords, doctrine of, cited by Beckington, 327

Tynemouth (Northumberland), prior of, 113, 332

universities: 160–2; and papal provisions, 127, 141, 241; *see also* Cambridge, Oxford

Urban V, Pope (1362–70), 133

Urban VI, Pope (1378–89), 195

Usk, Adam of, *see under* Adam

Valence, Aymer de, earl of Pembroke, 96
Vale Royal Abbey (Cheshire), 22
Vere, Maud de, 239
Vere, Aubrey de, earl of Oxford etc., 189, 201, 202, 203
vernacular, *see* English vernacular
*vicarages: lay fee, 32; statutes concerning (1391 and 1402), 264

wages, clerical, *see* stipends
Wakefield, Henry (bishop of Worcester 1375–95), 141, 143, 194
Wakeryng, John (bishop of Norwich 1416–25), 287, 290
Walden, Roger (archbishop of Canterbury 1397–9, bishop of London 1404–6), 217, 219, 228–9, 267
Wales: conquest, 23, 29; church of, 18, 29, 139, 233; friars and rebellion, 233; Glendower rebellion, 232–3, 237, 238, 239, 240, 244, 245, 247; poll tax in, 192; Richard II in, 224; statute of (1284), 22, 34
Walsingham (Norfolk), Franciscans of, 238
Walsingham, Thomas, 110, 167
Walter, Hubert (archbishop of Canterbury 1193–1205), 94
Waltham (Essex), abbot of, 203
Waltham, John (bishop of Salisbury 1388–95), 214
Wantage (Berks.), 234
Warden (Beds.), abbot of, 239–40
Ware, Henry (bishop of Chichester 1418–20), 290
Ware (Herts.), Franciscans of, 238
Wars of the Roses, 347
Warwick, earls of, *see* Beauchamp, Neville
Warwickshire, lollards, 183
Waugh, W.T., 340
Waytestaythe, Nicholas, 177
wealth of church: 17; *see also* confiscation, taxation, Wyclif
Wells Cathedral, clergy of, 99
Welsh Marches: and Despensers, 71, 72; and lollards of, 183, 184
Westminster Abbey: abbot, 293; sanctuary, 209–11, 274; *see also* Merks
Westminster, statutes of, I (1275), 22, 34; II (1285), 34, 41–2, 173
Westminster/Shrewsbury, parliament at (1397–8), 206–8
Westmorland, raided by Scots, 204
Westmorland, earl of, *see* Neville (Ralph)
Whelpdale, Roger (bishop of Carlisle 1419–23), 291
White, William, 309

Whittlesey, William (bishop of Rochester 1360–4, bishop of Worcester 1364–8, archbishop of Canterbury 1368–74), 115, 193
Wilks, M., 176
Wiltshire, earl of, *see* Scrope (William)
Wimbledon, Thomas, 162
Winchelsea (Sussex), 111, 237, 274
Winchelsey, Robert (archbishop of Canterbury 1294–1313): character and ideals, 42–3, 121; crisis of 1297, 47–52; and Gaveston and Ordainers, 66–9; relations with Edward I, 30, 46, 48, 52, 59; suspended, 52; recalled, 66; and Clement V, 60, 93
Winchester: diocese, 151; bishop of, 249; school, 159; statute of (1285), 34
Windsor, 234, 291
witchcraft, political aspect of, 301–2
Woburn (Beds.), abbot of, 239–40
Wodehouse, Robert, 118
Wonderful Parliament, the (1386), 202
Wood-Legh, K.L., 153
Woodlock, Henry (bishop of Winchester, 1305–16), 67
wool: customs, 46; prise, 16, 49; trade, 16, 271
Worcester: diocese, bishop of, 322; library in, 313; lollards in, 176; priory of, 100; prior of, 293, 322
Wrawe, William 194
writs, 124, 137, 138; ordering prayers, etc., 107; *see also: Admittatis, Congé d'élire, De excommunicato capiendo, Praemunire,* prohibitions, *Quare impedit, Quare non admisit*
Wyclif, John: life and writings, 167–9; ideas and teaching, 169–74; on confiscation and defence, 173; on national churches, 384 (cap. 6, n.8); and Black Death, 154; and Edwardian legislation, 42; and John of Gaunt, 116, 117, 161, 168; and Peasants Revolt, 194–5; and sanctuary, 210; opposition from archbishop and pope, 168; writings burnt, 179; condemned at Constance, 309; significance of, 352–3
Wykeham, William of (bishop of Winchester 1366–1404): and education, 158, 159–60; and Gaunt, 116, 142, 143; loans to crown, 247; influence, 193, 203–5, 229; death, 266

York city: mayor of, 82; minster, 99, 242, 314–15; parliament at (1322), 72, 81, 82; royal court at, 80, 82, 99; St Mary's Abbey, 293, 332, abbot of, 82; schools in, 164

York province: 18; clergy of, 284; convocation, 282–3; archbishops, 326; council of clergy and laity at (1283), 51; diocese, Black Death in, 150; lollards in, 182

York: Edward, duke of, 341–2; Richard, duke of, 302, 333, 336, 340–1

Zouche, John, O.F.M., 239
Zouche, William (archbishop of York 1342–52), 111, 125, 129, 141, 146, 154